THE WORLD OF GAMES

Jack Botermans • Tony Burrett •

Pieter van Delft • Carla van Splunteren •

THE • WORLD • OF
G·A·M·E·S

Their Origins and History, How to Play Them, and How to Make Them

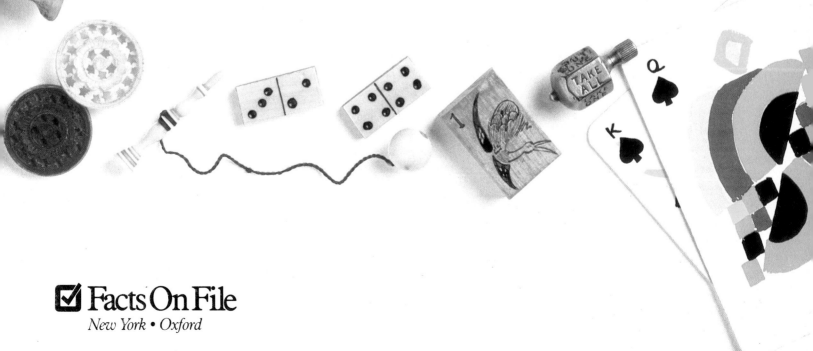

■ Facts On File
New York • Oxford

Right: A group of Chinese children in Shanghai play table hockey. The "players" in one team are all Mickey Mouse models, those in the other are Minnie Mouse.

THE WORLD OF GAMES
Their Origins and History, How to Play Them, and How to Make Them

Facts on File, Inc.   Facts On File Limited
460 Park Avenue South   or   Collins Street
New York NY 10016   Oxford OX4 1XJ
USA   United Kingdom

Library of Congress Cataloging-in-Publication Data

Wereld vol spelletjes. English.
    The World of games : their origins and history, how to play them,
and how to make them./ Jack Botermans ... [et al.].
       p.   cm.
    Translation of: Een Wereld vol spelletjes.
    Bibliography: p.
    ISBN 0-8160-2184-8 (alk. paper)
    1. Games--History.   I. Botermans, Jack.   II. Title.
GV1200.W4713   1989
796'.09--dc19   89-31359
                                             CIP

British CIP data available on request.

Facts On File books are available at special discounts when purchased in bulk quantities for businesses, associations, institutions or
sales promotion. Please contact the Special Sales Department of our
New York office at 212/683-2244 (dial 800/322-8755 except in NY,
AK or HI).

Originated by:	Jack Botermans and Pieter van Delft
Created by:	ADM International b.v., Amsterdam, the Netherlands
Edited by:	Carla van Splunteren
Text by:	Tony Burrett and Carla van Splunteren
Research by:	ADM International b.v.
Design by:	Jack Botermans and Pieter van Delft
Photographs by:	ADM International b.v., Beeldbank and Uitgeefprojecten b.v., Tim and Marko Hamoen, and others (see page 240)
Illustrations by:	Ellen Akkerman, Anne-Claire Alta, Utte Middelhoek, Joke Prins
Game models by:	George Nijs
Lithography by:	Nefli b.v., Haarlem, the Netherlands

Printed in Spain by Egedsa D.L. B-29.813-89

10 9 8 7 6 5 4 3 2 1

This book is printed on acid-free paper.

Contents

Below: A collection of marbles from many different countries. Some have strange and traditional names— taws, kabolas, pee- wees, pink pan- thers, Chinese bombers, milkies, steelies—among them.

Below: *Children have played with spinning tops since at least Roman times. In some countries of the Pacific tops are spun to ensure the well-being of newly planted crops. Tops shown here include models from Britain, Germany and China. The two brightly painted tops in the center are from Japan, a country where top making has been a traditional skill for centuries.*

Introduction

In his introduction to *Libro de Juegos* (Book of Games), Alfonso X, King of León and Castile, who was known as *El Sabio* (The Learned), declared that "God has intended men to enjoy themselves with many games." The book was compiled between 1251 and 1282 under the personal supervision of the king and published in 1283. It formed one of a series that included history, law, religion, astronomy and magic, subjects that were considered to be the most important of the day. Although *Libro de Juegos* concerns itself mainly with board games such as chess, backgammon and alquerque, the fact that games play was included at all in such a series speaks volumes for its importance in medieval life. And games continued to play an important role throughout history. Centuries after the *Book of Games*, the historian Johan Huizinga, in his treatise *Homo Ludens* (Man the Games Player), first published in 1938, was to write that "genuine, pure play is one of the main bases of civilization."

And indeed, the playing of games is one of the few of our regular activities that has managed to transcend the enormous social, cultural, political, linguistic and geographical barriers between people in this world of ours. At every moment of every day games are being played in all the four corners of the globe; games which reflect the history, folklore and traditions of peoples as diverse as the Icelandic fisherman and the Mali herdsman, the Peruvian copper miner and the Nepali hill farmer, the European factory worker and the Aboriginal tracker.

These people are from widely differing cultures, yet there are surprising similarities between the games they play. Consider, for example, that the making of cat's cradles–string figures woven between the fingers–is a favorite game among the Inuit of northern Canada and Greenland, the Maoris of New Zealand, the North American Indians and the indigenous peoples of New Guinea. Or that hopscotch is not only played by children in the back streets of Western cities, but also in the marketplaces of Nepal and northern India, and in the villages of Burma, China and Russia. Games play knows no geographical bounds.

Although we have no records dating back further than about 4000 B.C., we can safely assume that games of one sort or another have been played since the dawn of civilization. Evidence in the form of gaming boards and dice has been found in Crete, in Mesopotamia, in Greece and throughout the old Roman Empire. Several sets of hollows intended for a Mancala game were cut into roofing slabs of a temple built on the west bank of the Nile in about 1400 B.C. Today Mancala games are still played throughout Africa, in Sri Lanka and in parts of the West Indies and Guyana. An early form of backgammon was played by the Romans while that perennial favorite, chess, originated in India more than a thousand years ago.

As was mentioned earlier, games from different cultures show surprising similarities. But perhaps this is not quite so surprising as it appears at first. Many games, for instance, are relics of ancient religious rituals and these rituals themselves often show profound similarities. We see that hopscotch, for example, is related to ancient myths of labyrinths and mazes, and was later adapted to represent the soul's journey from earth to heaven. There is an Egyptian wall painting showing Ramses III, a pharaoh of the Twentieth Dynasty, engaged in a board game with Isis, wife of Osiris, Lord of the Dead. Even children's

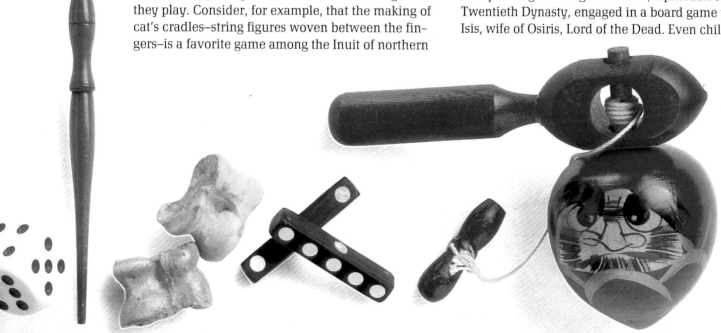

Above top: *A carved wooden mancala board, probably from Indonesia, consisting of two rows of seven cups and two stores.*

Above: *Deep in concentration, these young Indonesian children are oblivious to the photographer. They are playing* mancala, *a game that probably originated in Egypt and that spread throughout Africa and countries of the Middle and Far East.*

Above right: The Card Players, *by Theo van Doesburg, (1883-1931), a Dutch painter of* De Stijl, *to which group the well-known artist Mondrian also belonged.*

party games such as drop handkerchief were originally kissing games whose origins almost certainly lay in ancient fertility rites.

Card games and dice games are directly descended from the age-old practice of consulting the fates to determine the propitiousness of a contemplated action. Many ancient writers mention divination by the throwing of arrows or sticks, sometimes referred to as "the casting of lots." Over a period of time these primitive fortune-telling devices began to be used for games playing and their mystical significance was lost. The throws determined the winning score and decided the outcome of wagers. What had once been a liturgical rite became a game of chance.

Many of our modern gaming implements-dice, cards, dominoes, even chess pieces-can be traced back to the ancient practice of divination by arrows or sticks. As the arrows began to be used in gambling, three general types of game evolved: games of chance, games of skill and pure guessing games. In guessing games the arrow shaft became a gambling stick, marked to denote rank. In Korea this later evolved into strips of oiled paper. The Chinese had similar strips, known as *stick cards*, which bore figures remarkably similar to those on our present-day court cards. Nowadays, of course, playing cards are often used for the same purpose as the ancient divination arrows from

which they are descended–that of fortune-telling. In games of chance the arrow evolved first into the astragalus-a bone from the foot of a dog or sheep–and then into the die with which we are all familiar. There is strong evidence, indeed, that dice games were among the first, if not actually *the* first, games to be played by man. Dice of one sort or another have been found in the tombs of ancient Egypt and the Far East, and in prehistoric burial sites in both North and South America. In many early games the throw of the die controlled the moves of counters upon a marked playing surface, just as it does in many modern games. Later, when the die and thus the element of chance was omitted, games of pure skill, such as chess, checkers and go, were developed.

Other kinds of games undoubtedly originated as a means of training the young in the various hunting and fighting skills that were, and in many cases still are, of paramount importance to survival. An example of this type of game is ajaqaq, an Eskimo form of bilbouquet (cup and ball), which is intended to promote the hand-eye coordination so essential in hunting. American Indian youths developed similar skills by throwing darts through a rolling hoop. Virtually every game demanding strength or dexterity has its origins in one form of training or another. Other games were intended to sharpen mental rather than physical skills. An excellent example of this is chess, a game

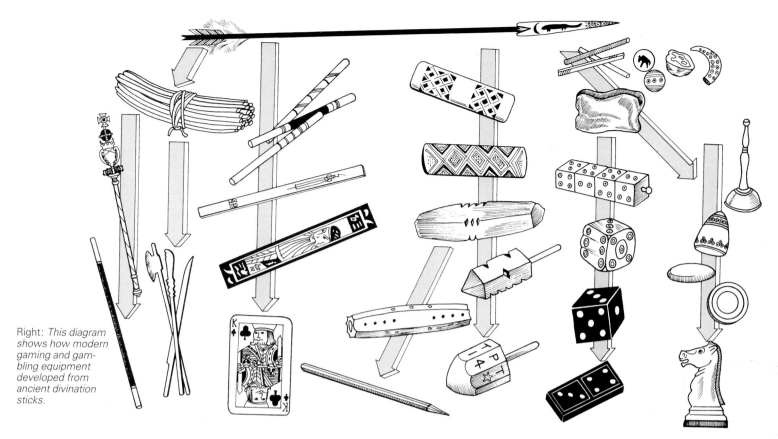

that is played all over the world. Chess is an imaginative reconstruction of a battlefield, and the strategy and foresight necessary to play provide excellent intellectual training.

Games of various kinds have been played in all parts of the world since the times of our earliest ancestors, for the instinct to play is buried deep inside us. There is a difference, however, between *playing* and *playing games*. Playing in itself is a spontaneous, informal activity with few rules and no fixed procedures. A game, on the other hand, is subject to definite rules and procedures and infringement of these is usually penalized. The action of a game proceeds along some prescribed route that generally results in a victory for one player or one side over the other. These parameters apply to games as different as chess and croquet, or lacrosse and liar dice.

It is rather more difficult, however, to make a meaningful distinction between a *game* and a *sport*. It would simplify matters if we could differentiate between games and sports on the grounds of professionalism, but that is not possible. Most of those who participate in sports are amateurs, while the best darts, chess and snooker players can earn vast sums of money. Nor can we make any distinction between the two on the grounds of the time, skill and sheer dedication involved. The will to win and the high degree of skill required to achieve this end are just as necessary in most competitive games as they are in sports. There is, in fact, a gray area, particularly where team games are concerned, in which one man's sport is another man's game.

To include every game ever invented in a book such as this would be impossible, of course. The authors have, however, been painstaking in their efforts to include a wide selection of those games that are of historical, geographical or social importance. Modern board games such as Monopoly are omitted simply because they are so widely known and in addition have little historical relevance. Pure gambling games are also omitted. A few games, such as bridge, are left out because they are highly specialized and complex enough to warrant their own body of literature. (Chess, on the other hand, *is* included because it is not only universally popular but also of historical importance.) And a few, in the Activity Games section,

Right: *This medieval painting illustrates the story of soldiers dicing for the robes of Christ at his crucifixion.*

Below: *A detail from a painting by the Flemish artist Jan Provoost (1465-1529), which depicts the same scene.*

are omitted because they fall into that gray area between games and sports already mentioned. What, then, are we left with? A great deal of thought went into the subdivision of the games included in this book. In the end it was decided that most games fall into one of five categories–board games, dice games, card games, domino games, and activity games–and these chapters form the substance of the book. In addition, the authors have included a "miscellaneous section" on subjects as diverse as puzzles, children's games, Indian games, and kite flying.

Most chapters are further divided into subsections. As far as board games are concerned, the authors are indebted to H.J.R. Murray's classic and definitive *A History of Board Games,* and have no hesitation in following the subdivision Murray used–namely, games of alignment and configuration, war games, hunt games, race games and Mancala games. Dice games are divided into sections according to what particular dice–numbered dice, poker dice, etc.–are used. Card games are similarly divided–many games that are popular in mainland Europe use 32-card

decks, in which cards below seven are not used; while other games use a basic pack with extra cards.

In his introduction to *Victorian Parlour Games for Today,* Patrick Beaver observed that "all games are imitations of real life situations." This being so, we could no more expect every game to fall neatly into a particular pigeonhole than we could expect every real-life situation to do so. Several of the games included here, therefore, could just as easily appear in a different section than the one chosen.

Finally we come to one of the most important features of this book–the *How to Make* projects. More than 40 craft projects are included, each listing the materials and tools required and giving clear and simple step-by-step instructions for making them, often accompanied by photographs. A wide variety of materials is suggested, including wood, cloth, plastic and clay, and the projects range from the comparatively simple to those requiring a high degree of craftsmanship. The authors sincerely hope that you, the reader, will derive much pleasure from making the games described and, of course, from playing them.

Below right: *Young girls, dressed in traditional costume, playing* hopscotch *on the Dutch island of Marken. This costume is still worn by some older people, and by many islanders on Sundays. Marken is joined to the mainland by a causeway and attracts thousands of tourists every year.*

Below: *A few examples of a well-known Dutch variety of* ludo, *a popular board game, which itself was derived from the old Indian game of* pachisi.

NOTE: The reader may observe that conversions from the metric system of measurement to the imperial system are not entirely consistent. Imperial measurements have sometimes been "rounded up" (or down) in order to simplify measuring and cutting of materials. Certain games boards are therefore of slightly different size (and/or shape) depending on which system is used.

13

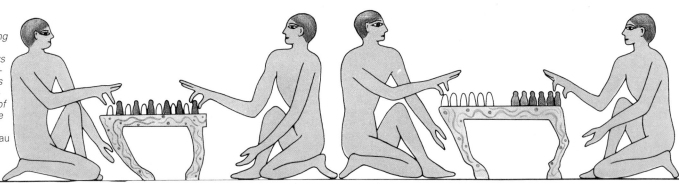

Right: *This painting from a tomb at Benihassan shows two games in progress. The players on the left are engaged in a game of senat, while those on the right are probably playing tau (robbers).*

Above: *Three typical senat playing pieces from the collection of the British Museum in London. Similar playing pieces have been found in burial chambers in many parts of Egypt.*

Right: *This illustration from a 3,000-year-old papyrus shows a man playing senat against an invisible opponent as his wife watches over his shoulder. Senat had a religious significance and the moves represented the journey of the soul to the underworld.*

Ancient Board Games

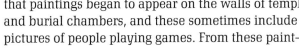

We know that board games have been played for more than 4,000 years, although the evidence relating to the first half of this period is very scanty. A few profile drawings of games in progress have been found in tombs and temples in ancient Egypt; early writings sometimes contain references to games play and some games materials have survived to modern times.

Since boards and pieces are usually made out of materials that decay and decompose relatively quickly, satisfactory and datable evidence of the playing of board games is generally restricted to those lands where it was customary to bury a man's possessions with him so that he could use them in his life after death. Games materials have been discovered in burial sites in Egypt, Mesopotamia, Assyria, Crete and Cyprus. Although the surviving drawings and materials are of great interest, they do not throw much light on the methods of play or the rules of these ancient games. Modern scholarship, however, has enabled feasible rules to be constructed for many of these ancient board games, and it is these that are given in this chapter.

It is now generally thought that the first board games had a religious rather than a secular use. The earliest known example of a gaming board dates from between 4000 and 3500 B.C., which means it is probably 1,000 years older than the next known example. This board, together with 11 conical pieces, was discovered in the early 1900s in a pre-dynastic burial ground at El-Mahasna, in Upper Egypt, and now resides in the Musée du Cinquantenaire, in Brussels. The archaeologists who found the tomb surmised from other objects that it might have been the grave of a medicine man or magician. Therefore, it cannot be said for certain that this board was used for a game; it may well have been used for divination or fortune-telling. It is, however, similar to boards found in later tombs in that it has three rows of six cells and was found together with conical pieces. This shows that the notion of moving men on a pattern of cells, an idea that is fundamental to all board games, had already been acquired by that time.

It was not until the Third Dynasty (2700-2600 B.C.) that paintings began to appear on the walls of temples and burial chambers, and these sometimes include pictures of people playing games. From these paint-

ings it is apparent that the Egyptians played at least three board games: sen't or *senat*, which was a race game, *tau* (robbers), which was a war game, and *han*, about which little is known. Another game, known as hounds and jackals, appeared later. This was a race game and it must have been very popular as boards have been found in Ur, Assyria and Palestine.

The Royal Game of Ur is another early race game. Several boards were found by Sir Leonard Woolley in 1926-7 in the royal burial chambers of the First Dynasty of Ur (in present-day Iraq). These boards are very similar to boards discovered in Egypt, and like them, have a drawer to hold the pieces and the lots. The Royal Game of Ur is very similar to senat–Murray, in fact, suggests that it is the same game–and in some ways it is like backgammon. Men are moved along a path and are then borne off according to the throws of the lots.

There is much written and material evidence that proves board games were popular among the Romans, but there is rather less evidence from ancient Greece. Many scholars believe that Roman and Greek games were derived from the older games of Egypt, Ur and Palestine, and that they reached Europe by way of the Mediterranean islands. Board games akin to Nine Men's Morris, checkers and backgammon were carried by the legions to the four corners of the Roman Empire.

Although board games of various kinds have been played for thousands of years in Egypt and the countries of what we now know as the Middle East, they seem to have appeared rather later in India and the Far East. *Ashtapada* and *desapada*, both of which are race games, were not played until about the fifth century B.C. Chess also originated in India, but this was not much more than 1,200 years ago. It was probably introduced into China via the ancient trading route through Kashmir. The Chinese had been playing games of alignment since the fifth century B.C., but their best native game, *wei-ch'i*, can be considered comparatively modern–according to Murray, it dates from about A.D. 1000.

In the following pages you will find the rules and methods of play of some of these ancient games, together with instructions on how to make the boards and pieces necessary to play them.

Senat

A wall painting in the tomb of Hesy of the Third Dynasty (c.2686–2613 B.C.) is the earliest record of *senat*, the Egyptian forerunner of the backgammon family of race games, although many similar paintings from later dynasties have been found. Several boards, some of them in a remarkable state of preservation, have also been discovered, together with casting sticks and playing pieces. Although the game was very popular and appears to have been played at all levels of society, none of the surviving papyrus texts tells us exactly how it was played. Nor do the many wall paintings shed much light on the subject, as the

artistic convention in ancient Egypt was to draw the human figure only in profile. The difficulties of making an accurate reconstruction of the rules and method of play can readily be seen if one imagines some future scholar attempting to reconstruct the modern game of backgammon from similar evidence. Nonetheless, a number of attempts to reconstruct the rules of senat have been made–although, it must be said, with varying degrees of success. The two we have chosen, although very different in their methods of play, are both played on the same board, with the same pieces and the same casting sticks.

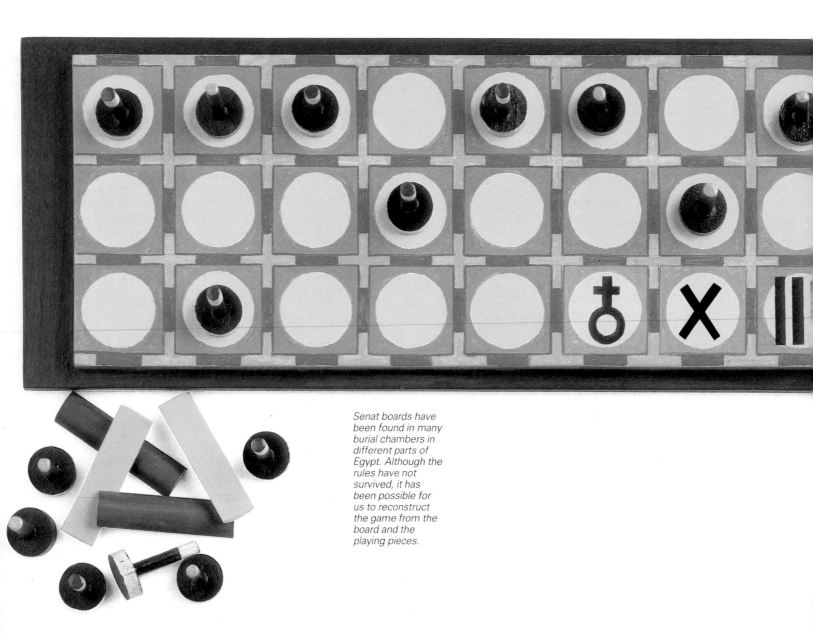

Senat boards have been found in many burial chambers in different parts of Egypt. Although the rules have not survived, it has been possible for us to reconstruct the game from the board and the playing pieces.

How to Play Senat *Version I*

The Swiss archaeologist Gustave Jéquier devised the rules for this first version. After conducting exhaustive research, the German Egyptologist Edgar B. Pusch confirmed the main points of Jéquier's method.

Equipment
Four half-round casting sticks or coins, five yellow-topped and five green-topped pieces.

The pieces are placed on squares 1 to 10 as shown in the diagram top right. The object of the game is to move the pieces along the first row, back down the second row and along the third, or "exit", row to square 30, from where they are borne off the board. Movement of the pieces is determined by throwing four half-round casting sticks or coins. The sticks score as follows:

One flat side (head) up	1 point
Two flat sides (heads) up	2 points
Three flat sides (heads) up	3 points
Four flat sides (heads) up	4 points
Four curved sides (tails) up	6 points

1. The players throw the sticks alternately until a 1 is thrown. The player who has thrown the 1 adopts the green pieces and moves the pieces on square 10 to square 11.

2. After the first move the same player continues to throw. If he throws 1, 4 or 6, he moves any piece the indicated number of squares along the track and throws again. If he throws 2 or 3, he moves a piece and the turn passes to his opponent. Pieces are allowed to jump over other pieces, whatever their color.

3. The second player makes his first move from square 9; he may move any piece on subsequent throws of the dice. Any turn ends with a throw of 2 or 3.

4. If a piece lands on a square that is occupied by an opposing piece, the opposing piece is attacked and must move back to the square just vacated by the attacker.

5. Two pieces of the same color may not occupy one square, but two pieces that occupy adjacent squares protect each other from attack by opposing pieces. Three pieces on adjacent squares form a block and cannot be

attacked or passed by opposing pieces. They do not, however, block the progress of pieces of the same color.

6. Any throw that cannot be used to make a forward move must be used for a move in the reserve direction. A piece may not be moved backward, however, to a square occupied by any other piece. If no move is possible, the turn passes to the other player.

7. A piece landing on square 27, marked "X", must return to square 1 (if that is occupied, to the first vacant square) and begin again.

8. Squares 26, 28, 29 and 30, marked ☥, III, II and I, are safe squares on which pieces are immune to attack.

9. When a player has moved all his pieces into the last row he may begin to bear them off the board by landing them exactly on square 30. If any pieces on the "exit" row are attacked and returned to the first or second rows, pieces of the same color remaining on the board may not be removed until those pieces return to the exit row.

10. The player who is the first to bear all his pieces off the board is the winner. In a series of games, score may be kept by awarding the winning player of each game 1 point for each opposing piece remaining in the exit row (unless they are in the safe squares), 2 points for pieces in the second row and 3 points for pieces in the first row.

How to Play Senat *Version II*

This version of the game was devised by R.C. Bell and its object is to be the first to marshall all one's pieces in position on the board. Each player begins with 10 men, green or yellow, and the casting sticks score in the same way as for the first game, except that four curved sides (or tails) up score 5 instead of 6 points. At the start of the game all the pieces are off the board.

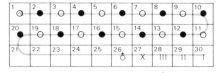

1. The players throw the sticks alternately, and enter their pieces onto the squares marked I, II, III, X and ☥, according to their scoring (X being 4 and ☥ being 5). The entry squares are marked A in the diagram at the foot of the last column on page 17.
Only one piece can occupy any one of these squares at one time. If the square corresponding to the number thrown is occupied, the turn passes to the other player.

2. A player may introduce another piece onto the board with any throw (if there is an available marked square), or he may advance a piece forward from a marked square. Pieces are moved along the first row, back along the second and along the third, as "the ox plows."

3. Pieces on marked squares are safe from attack by opposing pieces.

4. Only one piece may occupy a square at a time. After passing the fifth square, marked ☥ (the sign of the "door" or "gateway"), any piece which is "hit" by an opposing piece landing on the square it occupies is removed from the board and must be reentered on a marked square.

5. The first piece to land on square 1 wins a bonus score of five points and sets the pattern of subsequent play. This player must now land his remaining pieces on the even squares, while his opponent must land his pieces on the odd squares. The game ends when the pieces of both players are distributed alternately along the lower and middle rows.

6. When a piece is on its final square it is immune from attack.

7. The first player to marshal his pieces on his own squares wins the game and receives 10 points. An additional point is scored for each extra throw required by his opponent to complete his final formation.

How to Make the Game of Senat

Materials
a) For the board: a plywood sheet 12 cm x 40 cm x 8 mm (4⅞ in x 16¼ in x ⁵⁄₁₆ in), a plywood sheet 16 cm x 44 cm x 8 mm (6½ in x 17⅞ in x ⁵⁄₁₆ in, wood glue, primer, dark blue, light blue and yellow acrylic paint, varnish;

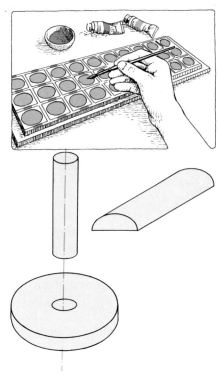

b) for the playing pieces: 85 cm (34 in) of 8 mm (⁵⁄₁₆ in) dowel, 12 cm (4½ in) of 28 mm (1⅛ in) dowel;
c) for the casting sticks: 20 cm (8 in) of 12 mm (½ in) half-round dowel.

Tools
Tenon saw, 8 mm (⁵⁄₁₆ in) drill, steel ruler, pencil, compasses, sandpaper and paintbrushes.

Method
a) To make the board:
Sand the smaller plywood and seal it with primer. Divide into 3 x 10 squares of 4 cm x 4 cm (1⅝ in x 1⅝ in), using a steel ruler and pencil. Mark lines ½ cm (³⁄₁₆ in) from both sides of each existing line and ½ cm (³⁄₁₆ in) from each edge. Find the center of each square by lightly marking the diagonals, and from these draw circles using compasses set to a radius of 1.2 cm (½ in). Seal the board with primer and then paint the edges green (green is made by mixing light blue and yellow).

Sand the large plywood sheet and seal with primer. Paint in dark blue acrylic. Mark lines 2 cm (¹³⁄₁₆ in) from each edge of the sheet. Within these lines glue the sheets together.

Paint the board following the basic color scheme shown in the model on the previous pages. Mark the symbols I, II, III, X and ☥ in the squares starting bottom right and working to the left. When the paint has dried thoroughly, give the board a coat of clear varnish.

b) To make the playing pieces:
Using a tenon saw and vise, cut 20 4 cm (1⅝ in) lengths from the same 8 mm (⁵⁄₁₆ in) dowel. In the same way cut 20 5 mm (³⁄₁₆ in) discs from the 28 mm (1⅛ in) dowel. Drill holes in the centers of these using an 8 mm (⁵⁄₁₆ in) drill. Apply a little glue to the ends of the 4 cm (1⅝ in) lengths and tap them into the holes in the discs. Seal each piece with primer. Paint the pieces black. Give 10 of them a yellow top and 10 a green top. Finish with a coat of varnish.

c) To make the casting sticks:
Cut the 20 cm (8 in) length of half-round dowel into 4 lengths of 5 cm (2 in). Seal with primer and paint all the flat sides one color and all the curved sides another. Finish them with a coat of varnish.

A similar effect can be achieved by using colored plastic adhesive tape, in widths of ½ cm (³⁄₁₆ in) and 1 cm (³⁄₈ in), and circles cut from the same material to make the board. If this method is preferred, a sharp hobby knife will be needed in addition to the tools listed above.

Below: The diagram below shows the basic pattern of the playing surface that must be drawn on the smaller plywood sheet.

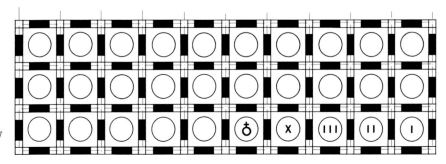

Hounds and Jackals

Nobody knows what the Egyptians called this game, but after a board was found at Thebes with ten carved ivory pins, five with the heads of dogs and five with the heads of jackals, it acquired the name *hounds and jackals*. The game first appears in tombs from the period between the Ninth and the Twelfth Dynasties and judging by the number of boards and fragments which have been found it must have been very popular for a time–not only in Egypt, but also in Palestine, Mesopotamia and Assyria.

Hounds and jackals is clearly a race game intended for two players and it is reasonable to assume that moves were decided by the throwing of casting sticks. The board is roughly rectangular but one end of the Egyptian boards is curved. The points of the track are holes which are intended for pegging pieces–rather like a modern cribbage board. Several points are distinguished by marks, inlays or circles, and some are connected by lines that may have served the same purpose as the ladders in the modern game of snakes and ladders; a man reaching point 6, for example, can move immediately to point 20.

As is the case with so many ancient games, none of the rules or methods of play have survived. With the help of the existing evidence, however, we have reconstructed what is probably a close approximation to the original game that used to be played so many centuries ago.

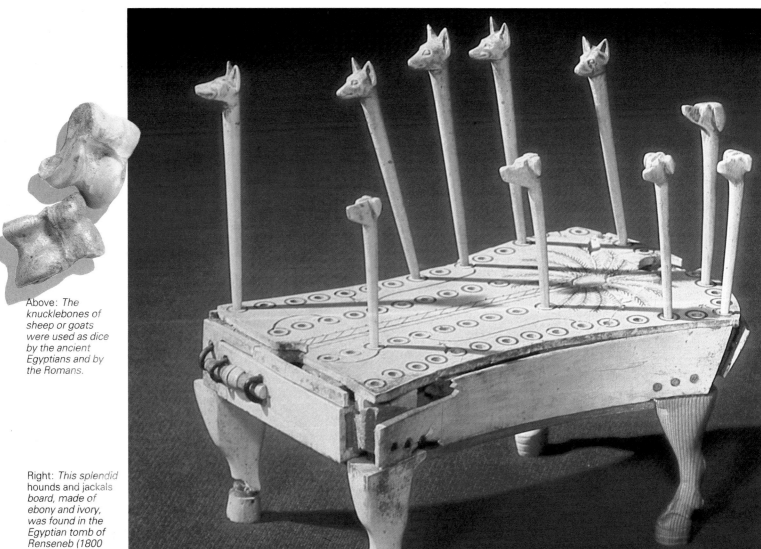

Above: *The knucklebones of sheep or goats were used as dice by the ancient Egyptians and by the Romans.*

Right: *This splendid* hounds and jackals *board, made of ebony and ivory, was found in the Egyptian tomb of Renseneb (1800 B.C.).*

How to Play Hounds and Jackals

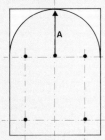

Below: This diagram shows the position of point A from which the arc must be drawn. The four dots at the

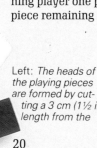

corners of the square show the positions of the feet on the underside of the board.

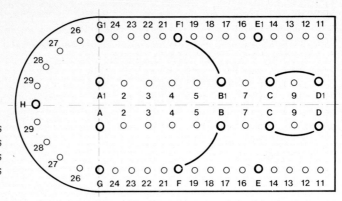

Left: This diagram shows the positions of the holes that must be drilled out. The heavier circles (marked A, A1, etc.) indicate the holes that must be circled with a differently colored paint.

Equipment

Four half-round casting sticks or coins, five "hounds" and five "jackals."

The casting sticks score as follows:

One flat side up	1 point
Two flat sides up	2 points
Three flat sides up	3 points
Four flat sides up	4 points
Four curved sides up	5 points

1. Players throw the sticks alternately until a 1 is thrown. This player then enters a piece at point A, and rethrows the sticks, moving the entered piece along the track according to the score achieved. The turn then passes to the other player.

2. Players throw alternately unless a 1 is thrown and a piece entered, in which case the player throws again.

3. The first player must enter all his pieces at A and move them along the track to H, from where the pieces may be borne off the board by throwing a 5. No piece can be borne off the board until all five pieces are in play. The second player moves his pieces along the track from A1 to H.

4. Players may move any piece they wish as long the move is in accordance with Rule 5.

5. Pieces stationed at D, E, F or G (and D1, E1, etc.) are deemed to be blocks and may not be jumped by other pieces. Pieces in other positions may be jumped.

6. Pieces landing on B or B1 can move directly to F or F1. Pieces landing on C or C1 move directly to D or D1. If F, F1, D, or D1 are occupied, the piece cannot be moved directly but must wait until the point is vacant. A throw of 1 is then necessary to complete the move.

7. The winner is the first player to bear off all five pieces. In a series of games score can be kept by awarding the winning player one point for each opposing piece remaining on the board.

How to Make Hounds and Jackals

Materials

a) For the board: a plywood sheet 20 cm x 30 cm x 12 mm (8 x 12 x ½ in), 4 furniture-leg studs 2 cm (1 in) in diameter, panel pins, glue, a roll of 3 mm (⅛ in) colored adhesive tape, acrylic paint, varnish;

b) For the playing pieces: 2.5 m (8 ft) of 1 cm x 1 cm (⅜ in x ⅜ in) wood, plastic-headed panel pins, acrylic paint, varnish.

Tools

Scroll saw, rasp, sandpaper, hobby knife, 4 mm (⅛ in) drill, hammer, compasses, ruler, pencil and paintbrushes.

Below: The key holes and joining lines of this model have been decorated with black adhesive tape, silver stickers and dark green paint.

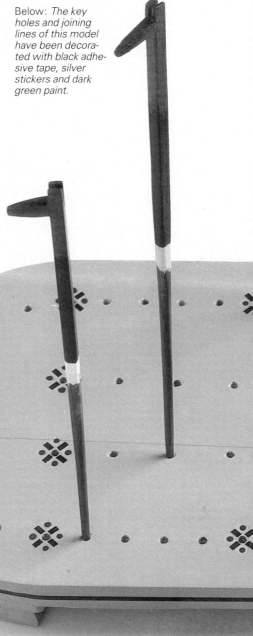

Left: The heads of the playing pieces are formed by cutting a 3 cm (1½ in) length from the end of each shaft and glueing and pinning in the V-shaped notch.

Method

a) To make the board:

Mark a point along the center line of the plywood sheet 10 cm (4 in) -(A)- from one end. Set the compasses to a radius of 10 cm (4 in). With this point as center, draw an arc as shown in the diagram (left margin). Cut along this arc with the scroll saw. Smooth the edge with the rasp. Mark the position of the holes as indicated in the diagram (page 20 top) and drill them out, using a 4 mm (1/8 in) drill.

Seal the board with primer and then paint it in acrylic paint. Circle the holes indicated in the diagram with a differently colored paint. Join the holes indicated using the colored adhesive tape.

Hammer the furniture leg studs into the underside of the board in the positions indicated in the diagram (left margin).

b) To make the playing pieces:

Cut the 2.5 m (8 ft) length of wood into 10 lengths of 25 cm (9½ in). Mark each length as shown in the diagram (left margin). Clamp them into a vise and cut the V-shaped notches. Taper each length to a point using the rasp. Cut a length of 3 cm (1¼ in) from the end. Glue this piece into the V-shaped notch to form the head, using plastic-headed panel pins to hold it in position. Paint five of the playing pieces one color and five another. Decorate them in any way you choose. Finish with a coat of clear varnish.

The casting sticks are identical to those used in the game of senat. The instructions are found on page 18.

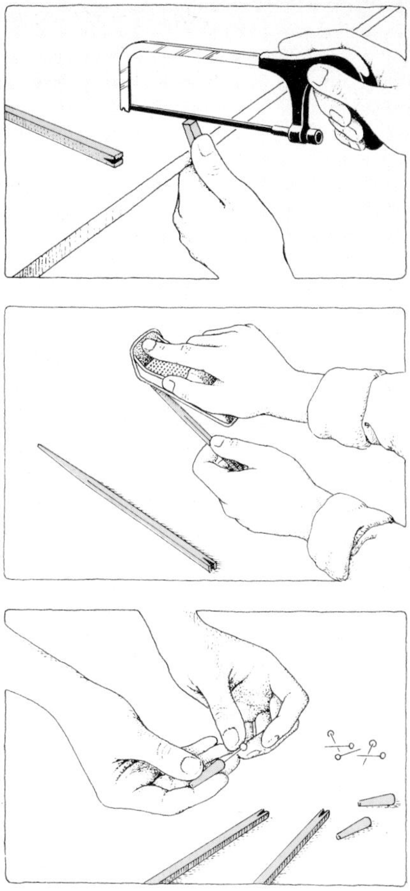

Right: *The steps to follow in making the playing pieces. (1) Cut the V-shaped notch with a hand saw. (2) Shave one end of each piece to a point using a rasp. (3) Cut off 3 cm (1½ in) from the pointed end and fix this in the notch with glue and a pin.*

The Royal Game of Ur

The greatest hoard of ancient art ever found in Mesopotamia (present-day Iraq and eastern Syria) was discovered in the mid-1920s by an expedition led by Sir Leonard Woolley, in which both the British Museum and the University of Pennsylvania participated. Sir Leonard excavated a number of royal tombs at Ur and among the many treasures he found were several remarkable gaming boards. This was a most exciting find, for they proved to be more than 4,500 years old, making them by far the oldest gaming boards ever discovered. The game seems to have been extremely popular among the Sumerian ruling classes and it was customary to place boards in the tomb of dead persons to help them to pass the time pleasantly during the journey to the next world.

Some of the boards are richly decorated; one of them is covered with an incrustation of shell plaques inlaid with lapis lazuli and red limestone. In other examples the plaques have engravings of animals. Two sets of seven counters were found with the boards. One side of these counters was white with five dark dots, the other side was black with five lighter dots. Six curious tetrahedron (pyramid-shaped) dice, each having two of the four points dotted with inlay, were also found. Three of the dice are white and three lapis lazuli, which suggests that they formed two sets, probably one for each player.

The game has become known as the Royal Game of Ur and it appears to be one of the original ancestors of the backgammon group of race games, preceding the Egyptian game of senat by perhaps two of three hundred years. It is yet another example of a game for which no written rules have survived. Luckily, however, it is possible to reconstruct possible methods of play from the boards and other available evidence. The version offered here is based on two earlier versions–one offered by R.C. Bell in his *Board and Table Games* (OUP, 1969) and another which is mentioned in *Games of the World* (Frederic V. Grunveld, ed., Holt, Reinhart and Winston, New York, 1975).

Below: This diagram shows the direction of play. The squares marked with rosettes (in the model they are filled with macaroni!) are safe squares where pieces of either color are immune from attack.

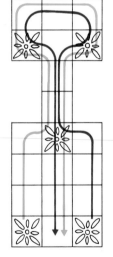

How to Play the Royal Game of Ur

Equipment
Six pyramid dice, three white and three blue, each marked in red at two corners, seven pieces with holes and seven without.

The Royal Game of Ur is a race game in which the object is to enter seven men onto the board, move them along a prescribed route of 20 squares and bear them off. Scoring is as follows:

Three marked tips uppermost scores 5 points and a free throw.
Three unmarked tips uppermost scores 4 points and a free throw.
Two unmarked tips uppermost scores 0 and the turn passes to the opponent.
One unmarked tip uppermost scores 1 point and the turn passes tot the opponent.

1. A coin is tossed to decide which player throws first.

2. At start of play all pieces are off the board and must be entered onto the first square by throwing a 4 or 5. They are then moved forward according to the scores obtained on subsequent throws.

3. Unless it is on a safe square (see rule 5), and after it has entered the central file, a piece is vulnerable to attack by opposing forces moving *in the same direction*. Should a piece land on a square occupied by an opposing piece, the opposing piece is sent off the board and must be reentered onto the first square by throwing a 4 or 5.

4. A player may have any number of pieces on the board at the same time but only one piece is allowed on any one square at the same time.
The squares marked with rosettes in the diagram in the margin and the exit square are exceptions to this rule (see rule 5).

5. The squares marked with rosettes and the exit square are safe squares where any number of pieces of either color may remain without danger of attack.

Right: This board was discovered in the royal tombs of Ur and is now on display in the Sumerian section of the British Museum in London.

6. Each piece must land exactly on the exit square from which it can be borne off the board by throwing a 4 or 5.

7. The winner is the first player to successfully bear off all seven pieces.

How to make the Royal Game of Ur

Materials
a) For the board: 2.1 m (approx. 7 ft) of 4.5 cm x 18 mm (1¹³/₁₆ in x ³/₄ in) planed softwood, 1.65 m (approx. 5½ ft) of 5.5 cm x 18 mm (2³/₁₆ in x ³/₄ in) planed softwood, a piece of hardboard measuring 21 cm x 55 cm (8³/₈ in x 22 in), a thin sheet of acrylic measuring 19.2 cm x 54.8 cm (approx. 8 in x 22 in), glue, panel pins, paint or varnish;
b) For the playing pieces: 50 cm (20 in) of 3.5 cm x 5 mm (³/₈ in x ³/₁₆ in) planed softwood;
c) For the dice: a sheet of thick card measuring 10 cm x 30 cm (4 in x 12 in), hobby clay, glue.

Tools
Tenon saw, an electric circular saw, two clamps with jaws of at least 25 cm (10 in), paintbrushes, hobby knife, ruler and pencil.

Method
a) To make the board:
From the 4.5 cm x 18 mm (1¹³/₁₆ in x ³/₄ in) softwood cut 19 pieces each 5 cm (2 in) in length and 2 pieces each 52.6 cm (21 in) in length. From the 5.5 cm x 18 mm (2 in x ³/₄ in) softwood cut 2 pieces each 52.6 cm (21 in) and 2 pieces each 22.2 cm (approx. 9 in) in length.
Note: It is possible that the exact thickness of planed softwood might vary fractionally from shop to shop. Check the thickness of your wood before cutting. The precise length of the longer pieces should be 40 cm (16 in) plus seven times the thickness. The precise length of the shorter pieces should be 15 cm (6 in) plus four times the thickness. It is essential to cut the 5 cm (2 in) lengths accurately to ensure that the resulting boxes are exactly square.

Both of the longer and one of the shorter 5.5 cm x 18 mm (2 in x ³/₄ in) lengths must now be grooved. Set your circular saw so that the blade projects 4 mm (⅛ in) below the base plate and its outside face is exactly 1 cm (³/₈ in) from the guide. When the saw is set accurately, clamp the pieces in a vise

Above: *The pyramidal dice, three white and three blue, which are used to play the Royal Game of Ur. Note that each die has two of its tips colored red.*

Right: *The boxes in this model have been filled with a variety of nuts, dried beans, macaroni, pebbles and coins. The oblong boxes are used to store the pieces.*

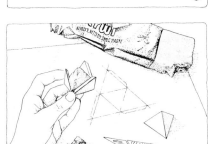

and cut the grooves. The second of the shorter lengths must be cut in two along its length, again with the blade set exactly 1 cm (³⁄₈ in) from the guide.

Note: If you do not have an electric saw suitable for this, your hobby shop will do it for you when you buy the wood.

Set out the pieces as shown in the illustration. The boxes formed are all 5 cm x 5 cm (2 in x 2 in) and the two end pieces are used to align the side and center lengths. Apply wood glue to the end of all the 5 cm (2 in) pieces,

clamp the whole frame together and allow the glue to dry. The grooved end and the wider remnant of the cut end are now glued and clamped. If you have no long clamps, then long thin panel pins can be used instead.

Center the hardboard base and fix it in place with glue and panel pins. Glue the thin strip to one end of the acrylic. This forms the lid and should slide easily into the groove.

The complete board should be sanded and painted or varnished to finish.

b) To make the playing pieces:
From the length of 3.5 cm x 5 mm (1³⁄₈ in x ³⁄₁₆ in) soft wood cut 14 pieces each measuring 3.5 cm (1³⁄₈ in) in length. Sand all the edges smooth. Use the 8 mm (⁵⁄₁₆ in) drill to drill holes in the centers of seven of the pieces. Paint or varnish to finish.

c) To make the dice:
Using a base unit of 2.8 cm (1 ¹⁄₈ in), draw six nets following the template shown on this page. Leave flaps as shown for glueing. Score the fold lines gently with a hobby knife. Mold pieces of hobby clay into rough pyramid shapes and put one into each die to weight it. Fold and glue to make tetrahedrons. Paint three dice white and three blue. Two tips on each die should be painted red.

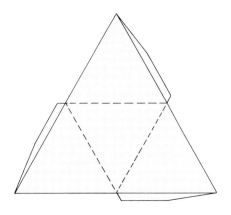

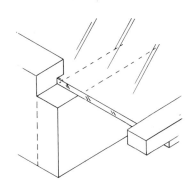

Above, top: *The template for making the dice. The base unit in the diagram is 2.8 cm (1¹⁄₈ in), but any unit between 2.5 cm (1 in) and 3 cm (1³⁄₁₆ in) can be used. Make*

sure the flaps are big enough to allow a good join.

Above, bottom: *This diagram shows how the end and lid should be constructed.*

Three Mysterious Games

A reconstruction of the rules and playing methods of the three board games so far described has been made relatively simple by the quantity and quality of existing archaeological evidence in the form of readily identifiable gaming boards, playing pieces and casting lots of various kinds. Unfortunately, it is not always quite so easy, for sometimes the evidence is insufficient or too inconclusive to allow an accurate reconstruction.

A good example of this can be seen in the case of a plaque found at Gezer, in Palestine. This plaque has a series of holes around the side edges and up the middle that would be identical with those of the Egyptian game of hounds and jackals–*if* the number of holes in the "head" were reduced to one! Professor Macalister, who discovered the plaque, thought that

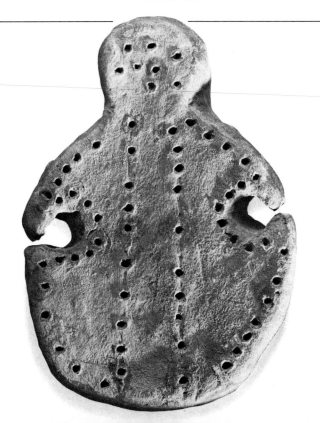

the holes were too small and shallow to hold a pegged piece. On the other hand, another scholar, J. Gadd, pointed out that a number of the holes were surrounded by a small circular spot of a darker color, just as they are in hounds and jackals boards. Was the Gezer plaque used to play a Palestinian version of the ancient Egyptian game? It might well have been, but no one knows for certain.

A very elaborate board, found in the Minoan palace at Knossos and dating from about 2000 B.C., presents another mystery. Although no pieces were found with it, it was assumed to be a gaming board. Some author- ities even suggested that it was a chessboard. The Knossos board is quite different from any other known gaming board and has only ten cells grouped at one end of it. One expert on board games and their ori- gins, Murray, doubts whether the board was intended for a game at all! Another tantalizing mystery that will not be resolved unless further evidence is uncovered at some future date.

Yet another mystery, although of a different sort, is posed by the ancient Welsh game of *gwyddbwyll,* (in Ireland known as fidchell). In the games mentioned so far there is physical evidence but no written material, but in this case the problem is quite the re- verse. No physical evidence whatsoever has been dis- covered and our limited knowledge of the game is derived completely from the writings of the time.

The game is mentioned several times in *Mabinogion* (Red Book of Hergest) but most entries simply record that two people are playing with men of gold on a sil- ver board. In the story of Peredur, he comes across a magic board on which the pieces are playing by themselves. Fidchell is also mentioned in *Cormac's Glossary* (c. A.D. 900) where we learn that "fidchell is four-cornered, its squares are right-angled and black and white men are on it...". This scanty evidence sug- gests that gwyddbwyll was a war game, played by two players with identical pieces. One possibility, suggest- ed by Murray, is that it is the same game as latrunculi, introduced into Britain by the Romans. He may well be right, but in the absence of physical evidence it is impossible to say with any degree of certainty, and how gwyddbwyll was played must remain yet an- other tantalizing mystery.

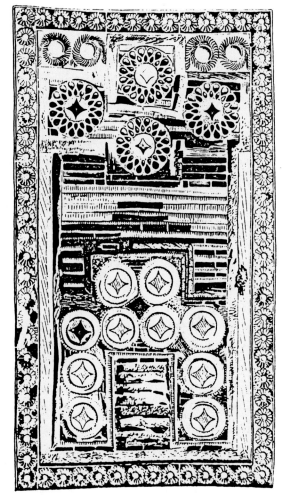

Latrunculi

The Roman game of *latrunculi,* or "soldiers", was carried by the legions to the very frontiers of the Empire, as is shown by the boards that have been discovered in mile-castles along Hadrian's Wall in northern England. Latrunculi was a war game played by two people on a latticed board, similar to our modern chessboard. The exact dimensions are not known, for the boards that were found had varying numbers of squares. Nor do we know for certain how many pieces each player had, although the term *mandra,* used by Juvenal–a Roman satirist and writer, who lived in the first century A.D.–to mean a drove of cattle, implies that the number must have been considerable. It is known, however, that each piece had the same powers of move and capture, and from this evidence it is possible to make a reasonable guess as to how the game was played. On reconstruction it appears that *latrunculi* bears a remarkable resemblance to a version of the modern Japanese game of hasami shogi, though it does differ in some important aspects. The rules and method of play described here have been put together from a number of different sources.

Right: *This diagram shows the methods of capture in* latrunculi. *The top two situations show capture by interception. A piece which is trapped in a corner is also forfeit.*

How to Play Latrunculi

As the exact size of the board and the number of pieces seem to be relatively unimportant, let us assume a board of 64 squares and 16 pieces for each player. The game can then be played on an ordinary chess board with 16 white and 16 black checkers pieces. Each player sets his pieces so that they fill the first two rows on his side of the board. A coin is tossed to determine which player moves first and subsequent moves are alternate. Moves are identical to the rook's move in chess; that is, any number of squares in an orthogonal direction–forwards or backwards, to the left or right. An opposing piece is captured by interception: that is, by enclosing it vertically or horizontally between two of your own pieces. Any piece trapped in a corner is also taken from the board. A player may, however, deliberately place a piece between two opposing pieces without capture. The first player to capture all his opponent's pieces is the winner. In the event of a stalemate the player who has captured the highest number of pieces is the winner.

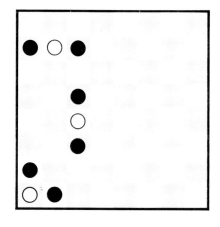

Right: *The first of two wall paintings discovered in a tavern during the excavation of Pompeii. The two men are playing* duodecim scripta *and one is accusing the other of cheating.*

Duodecim Scripta

What must have been an unimaginable catastrophe for the citizens of Pompeii turned out to be an unprecedented stroke of luck for later historians. In A.D. 79, when an eruption of Vesuvius buried the town under a thick layer of lava and ash, its everyday life was frozen in a time capsule that was not to be opened for almost 1,800 years. Among the thousands of important discoveries made during the early excavations were two paintings found in a tavern. In one painting, two men are sitting opposite each other with a gaming board between them. The player on the left is holding a dice cup and saying *"Exsi!"* (I am out!). The other player is pointing to the dice and saying *"Non tria, dvas est!"* (Not three, it's two!). In the second painting, the two players have jumped to their feet to trade both insults and blows and the innkeeper is pushing them out into the street, saying *"Itis foras rixsatis!"* (Go outside if you want to fight!).

The men in the paintings are squabbling over a game called *duodecim scripta*, or "twelve lines," a gambling game that was very popular at that time. There are frequent references to this forerunner of backgammon in Roman literature and a large number of boards has been found, most of them with 36 squares, known as points. These points are marked by symbols or letters forming a sentence that was usually funny or derogatory. The players threw three cubic dice, marked from one to six, to determine how a number of pieces would be entered on the board, moved along a prescribed route and taken off. The dice were often thrown into a *fritillus* or *pyrgus*, a wooden tower with a spiral staircase inside it, this to prevent cheating.

In the latter days of Rome, gambling became a mania and huge sums of money were wagered. It is said that the emperor Nero played for stakes as high as 400,000 sesterces a point (about $ 10,000!), and that another emperor, Commodus, turned the imperial palace into a casino!

Although the game enjoyed enormous popularity for a long time, it fell out of fashion during the first century A.D., being superseded by Tabula, a variation with only two rows of points. As is the case with so many ancient games, no written rules have survived. Authorities such as Murray and Bell have attempted to reconstruct *duodecim scripta*, and the version offered here is adapted from these reconstructions.

Right: *This handsome* duodecim scripta *board is not difficult to make. The ruder the six-word message the better. Remember each word must contain six letters.*

LEVATE ∘ DALOCV

LVDERE ∘ NESCIS

IDIOTA ∘ RECEDE

Right: *Pieces are
entered on points
A, each player ente-
ring in the points on
his right and mov-
ing counterclock-
wise through B, C,
D to E from where
the pieces are
taken off.*

Below: *Shaped
wooden spatulas
are useful tools for
molding and trim-
ming clay.*

How to Play Duodecim Scripta

Equipment

A playing board, three cubic dice, 15 black and 15 white pieces.

1. The pieces are off the board at the start of play. They are entered onto their own set of six "A" points according to the throws of the dice.

2. Any number of pieces may occupy the same point. When all a player's pieces have been entered they begin to move counterclockwise round the board in the direction A–B–C–D to E. When all 15 pieces are assembled in E they may be taken off the board.

3. Players throw alternately and the numbers scored can be used singly or in combination. EXAMPLE: A throw of 2, 3 and 6 can be used either to move three pieces 2, 3 and 6 places respectively; one piece 2 and one piece 9 places; one piece 3 and one piece 8 places; one piece 5 and one piece 6 places; or a single piece 11 places–providing that rest points and destination points are available for occupation (see rule 6).

4. Double or triple throws do not give an additional turn.

5. Once the pieces have left the A points they are vulnerable to attack by the opposition. Single pieces are known as *vagi* (wanderers) and are sent off the board when hit by an opposing piece. They must then be reentered on the next throw.

6. A player can pile any number of pieces on one point. These are known as *ordinarii* and are immune from attack. They hold the point against opposing pieces which are not allowed to rest or to land there.

7. Pieces that are blocked and cannot be moved on any number or combination of numbers thrown are known as *inciti* (immovables).

8. Every throw of the dice must be used if possible, however unfavorable or disadvantageous this may be.

9. The first player to bear off all his pieces is the winner.

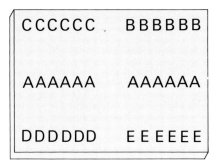

```
CCCCC    BBBBB

AAAAAA   AAAAAA

DDDDD    EEEEE
```

How to Make a Duodecim Scripta Board

Materials

a) For a board which does not need to be fired: ½ kg (1 lb) of hobby clay, a chipboard sheet 30 cm x 40 cm (1 ft x 1 ft 4 in), black and red acrylic paint, varnish;

b) For a board which must be fired: ½ kg (1 lb) modelmakers' clay, red and black clay glazing powder.

Tools

Rolling pin, hobby knife, spatula, 5 cm (2 in) boar's-bristle paintbrush, sponge.

Method

First soften the clay by kneading with your hands for a few minutes. Place it on the chipboard base and roll it out using the rolling pin. The finished board should cover the base and will be about 1½ cm (⅝ in) thick. Round off the edges by molding them with wet fingers.

Note: If modelmakers' clay is being used it is particularly important to knead well to remove air bubbles, which can cause the clay to explode during the firing process. The board is also rolled out on a flat surface and not on the chipboard.

The letters are incised to a depth of about 4 mm (³⁄₁₆ in) using a spatula. The original Roman boards often had derisory or ribald sentences incised on them. The original of the one shown on page 27 was found in Rome itself and first appeared in Austin's *Roman Board*

Games. A rough translation of the inscription is:

JUMP UP ● PUSH OFF
THE GAME ● IS LOST
GET OUT ● YOU FOOL

There is no obligation to copy this Latin inscription–you can make up your own suitable phrase. The only criterion is that each word must be of six letters to provide the right number of playing points.

When the letters have been inscribed the excess clay around their edges must be smoothed out. The board is then left to dry out in a warm, airy place for two or three days.

When the clay has dried the board is ready for painting. Use a fine paintbrush to fill in the letters with red acrylic paint. Leave to dry. The black paint is applied with a sponge or a soft cloth. This must be done carefully to ensure no black paint gets into the red letters. When paint is dry, finish the board with a coat of clear varnish. Note: If modelmakers' clay is used, the board must be fired in a kiln (*not* a domestic oven!) before it is glazed. The red glaze is brushed into the letters. The black glaze is brushed over the board with a medium (5 cm [2 in]) boar's-bristle brush. When the glaze has been applied, the board must be refired.

Below: *The letters are incised with a spatula and painted red. When the paint is dry, black paint is applied using a soft cloth or sponge. A coat of varnish adds* *the final touch. NOTE: If modelmakers' clay is used, the red and black glazes are applied before the second firing.*

Tabula

Tabula, a modified version of *duodecim scripta*, became popular in fashionable circles during the first century A.D. The Roman historian Suetonius recorded that the Emperor Claudius (41–54 A.D.) was so enamored of it that he wrote a book about the game and had a board fitted into his carriage so that he could play while he was traveling. Tabula retained its popularity for hundreds of years and spread to many countries. In Greece it was called *tablé*, in other countries it was known by its alternative name of *alea*. Because it was a gambling game, tabula attracted the attention of the Church. In Spain, Canon 9 of the Synod of Elvira (c. A.D. 305) condemned the playing of tabula for money while in Justinian's Code (c. A.D. 730) the clergy were forbidden to play at all. In later years, the Russian Church extended the ban on tabula to the laity, laying down that "no clergy or layman shall play at *zerniyu* (hazard), *shakhmate* (chess) or *tablei'* (tabula)." In 1561, Tsar Ivan IV went even further and made the game illegal under the civil code.

The basic difference between duodecim scripta and tabula was that the third row of points in the earlier game was omitted, thus shortening the track. The method of play was otherwise much the same except that both players entered their pieces into the same quarter of the board, a development that brought the game very close to the more modern game of backgammon. Tabula differed in that the pieces were entered onto the board, rather than being started from fixed positions; both sets of pieces traveled in the same instead of the opposite direction; and three dice were used instead of two. In addition, it is not entirely clear from the classical literature whether a piece could be taken off the board before all the pieces had entered the last quarter.

Over the centuries, there have been many versions of tabula (which later became known as "tables"), as it slowly developed into backgammon. Part three of the superb 13th-century manuscript compiled at the command of the Spanish king Alfonso X, for example, contains descriptions of 15 different tables games. In remote parts of Iceland, boards that are very similar to those of the late Roman period are still used today to play a game called *Ad Elta Stelpur*, or Chasing the Wenches. Since Iceland was originally populated by the Vikings, one can suppose that the original form of this game was played in Scandinavia more than 1,000 years ago.

Right: *Achilles and Ajax playing* tablé, *a Greek form of* tabula, *between skirmishes in the Trojan War. This lovely Etruscan vase can be seen in the Vatican Museum, Rome.*

Zeno's Losing Game

This game of *ta-bula,* played by the Emperor Zeno and described in epi-grammatic form by Agathias of Myrine, enabled scholars to determine exactly how the game was

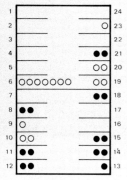

played. Zeno's game shows that white entered in 1-6, moved counter-clockwise and exit-ed in 19-24. Al-though it tells us nothing about black, it seems reasonable to assume that both sets of pieces entered, moved and exited in the same way, as they did in duodecim scripta. In the position shown in the illu-stration, the empe-ror, playing with the white pieces, threw 2, 5 and 6. A mo-ment's thought will show that for this throw the *ordinarii* on point 6 and the *vagus* on point 9 are *inciti* (immovables) and that the *vagus* on point 23 cannot be covered. Be-cause of the rule that all throws must be used if possible, however unfavor-able that may be to the player, Zeno was obliged to unpile his *ordinarii* on points 10, 19 and 20. This unfor-tunate throw left him with no fewer than eight *vagi* and a completely ruined position. The well-known phrase ''I Zeno solution to the problem'' is thought to have derived from this unhappy event.

How to Play Tabula

Equipment
A playing board, three cubic dice, 15 black and 15 white pieces.

1. The game is played on a board of 24 points by two players. All the pieces are off the board at the start of play.

2. Pieces are entered onto any of the first six points according to the throws of the dice. When all a player's pieces have been entered they are moved counterclockwise around the board until they are all assembled in the last quarter (points 19–24), from where they may then be taken off the board.

3. The numbers thrown can be used singly or in combination, provided that no rest point or destination point is occupied by more than one opposing piece.

For example: a throw of 1, 3 and 4 could be used to move three pieces 1, 3 and 4 points respectively; one piece 1 and one piece 3 + 4 or 4 + 3 points; one piece 3 and one piece 1 + 4 or 4 + 1 points; one piece 4 and one piece 1 + 3 or 3 + 1 points; or one piece 8 points—1 + 3 +4, or any reorientation of these numbers (e.g., 3 + 1 + 4 etc.), always with the provision that each rest point and destination point is free to land on.

4. If a player has two or more pieces on a point, that point is closed to his op-ponent and pieces on it are immune to attack. These pieces are known as *ordi-narii,* or piled pieces.

5. Single pieces on any point are known as *vagi* (wanderers). These are vulnera-ble to attack by opposing pieces. When ''hit'' by an opposing piece a *vagus* is sent off the board and must reenter in the first quarter at the next possible throw. No other piece may be moved until the *vagus* (or *vagi*) is reentered onto the board.

6. Pieces unable to move because they are blocked by opposing forces are known as *inciti* (immovables).

7. A player is obliged to use the whole of his throw where this is possible, no matter how unfavorable or disadvan-tageous this may be.

8. The winner is the first player to bear off all his pieces.

How to Make a Tabula Board

Materials
A plywood sheet 36 cm x 45 cm x 16 mm (14³⁄₈ in x 18 in x ⁵⁄₈ in), 2.4 m (8 ft) pre-glued oak veneer strip 2 cm (¹³⁄₁₆ in) in width, 32 cm (12¹³⁄₁₆ in) pre-glued oak veneer strip 3 cm (1³⁄₁₆ in) in width, 2 sheets pre-glued mahogany veneer 18 cm x 45 cm (7³⁄₁₆ in x 18 in), varnish.

Tools
Steel ruler, pencil, hobby knife, smoothing iron, paintbrush.

Method
Using the steel ruler and pencil draw lines along the length of one of the mahogany veneer sheets at distances of 3 cm (1³⁄₁₆ in) and 13 cm (5³⁄₁₆ in) from the *top* edge. Draw two lines across the width of the sheet at distances of 21 cm and 24 cm (8³⁄₈ in and 9⁵⁄₈ in) from the left-hand edge. The "points" can now be drawn. These are positioned between the two lines along the length of the sheet and are 1 cm (³⁄₈ in) apart. The two outer points within each half of the sheet lie 2 cm (¹³⁄₁₆ in) from the edge and the center line respectively. Finally, draw a line between the two center lines across the width, at a distance of 2 cm (¹³⁄₁₆ in) from the top edge. Lay the second sheet of mahogany veneer so that the grain lies in the same direction as in the first sheet. Draw lines at distances of 3 cm and 13 cm (1³⁄₁₆ in and 5³⁄₁₆ in) from the *bottom* edge of the sheet. Complete the marking out following the instructions noting that the final line is 2 cm (¹³⁄₁₆ in) from the bottom edge. Cut out the 2 cm x 10 cm (¹³⁄₁₆ in x 4 in) strips and the center strips using a steel ruler and a sharp hobby knife. Cut along the *outside* of each line. Remove the backing from the top sheet and lay it in position on the chipboard. Iron it into place with a smoothing iron set to its medium temperature (about 60 °C or 140 °F). Lay the bottom sheet in place in the same way.
Note: If you are not used to working with veneers it is better to cut each sheet in two across the 2 cm (¹³⁄₁₆ in) bridge and lay the half sheets separately. Cut the 2 cm (¹³⁄₁₆ in) oak veneer strip into 24 lengths of 10 cm (4 in). Remove the backing and iron each strip into place. Iron in the center 3 cm (1³⁄₁₆ in) strip. Sand the board well. Make sure that remaining pencil lines are removed. Varnish to finish.

The Games of Ancient India and Ancient China

As far as games are concerned, India is perhaps best known as the country were chess was first played. This universally popular game, however, is of comparatively recent invention, appearing some thirteen or fourteen hundred years ago. But games were played in India long before chess was invented. Indeed, many scholars think that the square gaming board is also of Indian origin. In the oldest games the board had an even number of squares but in all modern games the board has an odd number. Most of the games are race games, the object simply being to enter pieces, race them along a prescribed route and take them off, all according to scores thrown by lots of one sort or another. The game shown below is the ancient game of *ashtapada* ("eight-square"). The inventor of chess used the ashtapada board to arrange his game, and Indian chessboards still bear the crosscut squares. A similar game, *dasapada*, was played on a board of 10 x 10 squares. The game shown on page 35 is still played today in India and Sri Lanka. It is called *saturankam* ("chess"), and is one of a family of games played on boards having an odd number of squares.

The Chinese are reputed to have a tendency to exaggerate the age of their inventions, and in particular the age of their games. Twentieth-century encyclopedias claim, for example, that *wei-ch'i* (*i-go* in Japan) was first played around 2300 B.C. This date is in error by some 3,000 years, for modern scholarship has established that the game dates back to not much before 1000 A.D. Before the Christian era, the only Chinese board games were simple alignment games of the Merels type. Confucius (551-479 B.C.) and Mencius 372-289 B.C.) both mention *yih*, which was the smaller Merels, known in Britain as three men's morris. The word *yih* (like the later *ch'i*) is a general word for a board game. During the first millenium A.D., Indian race games began to reach China, probably along the old trading routes from Kashmir. A written account of the game of *t'shu-p'u* can be found in *Hun Tsun Sü*, a work of the Sung period (A.D. 960-1279), which relates that the game came to China from western India in the time of the Wei dynasty (A.D. 220-265). This game (see the illustration on page 35) is an adaptation of *chatush-pada*, which is an older form of *chaupur*.

Ashtapada

How to Play Ashtapada

1. Ashtapada can be played by 2, 3 or 4 players.
2. Each player has two pieces, which are entered into one of the two crosscut central squares on his own side of the board. The pieces move along the route shown in the diagram. On reaching one of the central crosscut squares they may be taken off.
3. Four cowrie shells are thrown, the number of mouths uppermost giving the score. No mouths uppermost counts as a score of 8. Three mouths uppermost carries a "grace" of 1 point. This may be used as an extra point or to enter or take off. Pieces may only be entered or taken off by throwing a "grace" point.
4. Pieces being "hit" by any opposing piece are sent off the board and must be reentered. Pieces on any crosscut square, however, are immune from attack.
5. The winner is the first player to take both his pieces off the board.

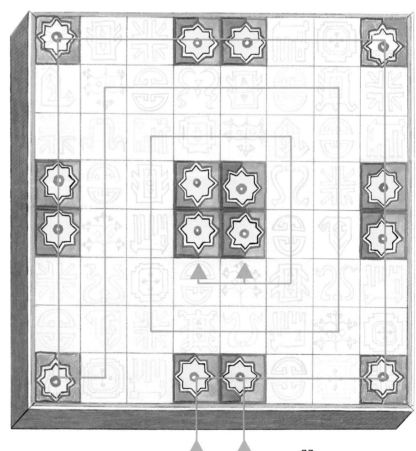

33

Right: *Two young girls enjoy an outdoor game of* sadurangam *using a board chalked on a pavement in Madras, in Southern India.*

Sadurangam

This game is for 2, 3 or 4 players and is also played in southern India and Sri Lanka. It should not be confused with *saturangam*.

How to Play Sadurangam
Equipment
Four cowrie shells (or two-sided coins or casting sticks), two pieces per player.

1. Sadurangam is played on a board of 5 x 5 cells. The middle squares along each edge and the square in the center of the board are crosscut. These are safe squares and pieces occupying them are safe from attack.

2. The object is to enter the pieces in the crosscut square on the player's own side of the board, race around along the route shown and go off from the central square. Pieces on squares other than the crosscut squares can be "hit" and must then be reentered in the starting square.

3. The scoring is very similar to that in ashtapada, described on page 33, except that it is not necessary to throw a "grace" to take a piece off the board. A throw can only be used to move one piece except when leaving the board, when it can be "split."

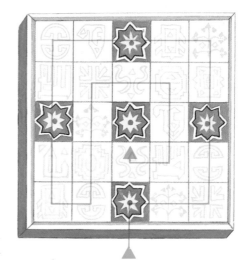

Left: *The 5 x 5 squared* sadurangam *board showing the track along which the pieces must be raced. Pieces are entered on the central crosscut squares on the sides of board.*

34

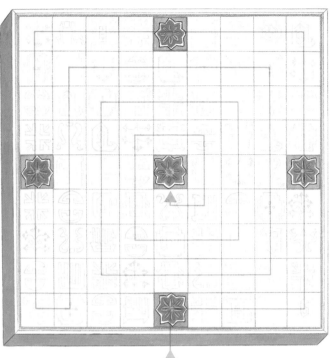

Above: *The satu-rankam board showing the track along which the pieces must be raced.*

Saturankam

How to Play Saturankam

Equipment
Two four-sided dice (marked 1, 3, 4 and 6), two pieces per player.

1. Saturankam can be played by 2, 3 or 4 players.

2. Each player has two pieces, which are entered into the crosscut square on his own side of the board. The pieces move along the route shown in the diagram. When a piece is four squares or less from the central crosscut square, it must be taken off by throwing the appropriate double.

3. Throws can be combined to move a single piece or the total can be divided in any way to move two pieces.

A player throwing a double may throw again. All throws must be used.

4. Pieces being "hit" by any opposing piece are sent off the board and must be reentered. Pieces on any crosscut square, however, are immune from attack.

5. The winner is the first player to take both his pieces off the board.

T'shu-p'u

How to Play T'shu-p'u

Equipment
Two four-sided dice (marked 1, 6, 3 and 4), a set of four pieces per player, each set being distinguished by color – say red, green, yellow and blue.

1. T'shu-p'u is a game for four players, forming two teams, partners sitting opposite each other. It is a Chinese version of the Indian game known as *chatush-pada*.

2. At start of play the pieces are placed on the board as shown in the diagram.

3. The object of the game is to race the pieces along the track indicated into the central square from where they may be taken off the board.

4. Moves are made according to the throws of the dice. One piece may be moved according to the total shown, or two pieces may be moved according to the individual numbers of each die. A piece may leap any other.

5. Pieces "hit" by an opponent are sent off the board and must be entered in one of the original starting squares on an appropriate throw of the dice. Pieces positioned on crosscut squares are immune from capture.

6. Pieces must enter the central square on an exact throw. When a 1 is thrown they are taken off the board.

7. The winning team is the first to take off all 8 pieces.

Yih

How to Play Yih

Yih is a game for two players, each of whom have three men.

1. The players enter one man at a time, in turn, on any free point, endeavoring to form a row of three along any of the eight marked lines.

2. If all the men are entered and no row has been formed, play proceeds, again alternately, by moving a man one step along any line to a neighboring empty point.

3. The winner is the first player to complete a row of three.

Note: It has been shown that the first player must win if he enters his first man on the central points.

Games similar to yih have been played (and are still played) all over the world. Only the French have a rule forbidding the first player to place his first man on the central point. In order to make the game more challenging, it is suggested that the French rule be followed in the playing of yih.

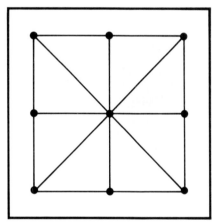

Above: *In yih players enter pieces alternately and attempt to form a* *row of three along any one of the eight marked lines.*

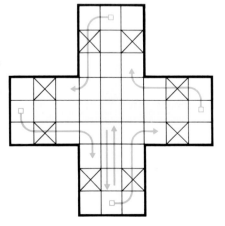

Left: *The t'shu-p'u board showing the entry squares and the track along* *which the pieces must be raced to the central square.*

Below: *Making this colorful* t'shu-p'u *board requires both accuracy and patience. However, it is a most rewarding project and one that is well worth embarking upon.*

How to Make a T'shu-p'u Board

Materials

A cardboard sheet 36 cm x 36 cm (13½ in x 13½ in), another of 36.3 cm x 36.3 cm (13⅝ in x 13⅝ in) (for the box lid), dark blue, red, yellow and white water paint, varnish, adhesive tape, 16 small pebbles.

Tools

Steel ruler, pencil, compasses, black felt-tipped pen, broad-nibbed drawing pen, paintbrushes and hobby knife.

Method

a) To make the board:
Divide the 36 cm x 36 cm (13½ in x 13½ in) sheet of cardboard into 81 (9 x 9) 4 cm x 4 cm (1½ in x 1½ in) squares using the steel ruler and pencil. Draw in the diagonals of squares 4 and 6 in the second row, 2 and 8 in the fourth and sixth rows and 4 and 6 in the eighth row.

Mark the third and sixth horizontals and verticals with heavier pencil lines, dividing the board into nine squares each consisting of nine 4 cm x 4 cm (1½ in x 1½ in) squares and forms the shape of the cross.

Right: This diagram shows the pattern that must be drawn on the board. The half-white, half-black squares are safe and pieces on them are immune from attack.

b) To draw the star: Draw it in the central 3 x 3 square. Draw the diagonals, and the horizontal and vertical lines through the center point. Set the compasses to a radius of 4 cm (1½ in) and from this point draw a circle. Draw lines from each corner of the central square to the two nearest points of intersection of the circle and that same corner 4 cm x 4 cm (1½ in x 1½ in) square. Draw lines to the two nearest points of intersection from the ends of both the horizontal and vertical through the center. Draw lines from the center of the circle to each of the 8 points of intersection (This sounds much more complicated than it actually is-if you are in any doubt, consult the diagram at top right.) Now paint your board following the color scheme of the model in the photograph. Light blue is made by mixing dark blue and white and mauve by mixing red and blue together with a little white.

When the paint has dried, draw in the black lines using the ruler and felt-tipped pen. Mark in the black points, which indicate the entry squares. Draw the yellow lines with the broad-nibbed pen. Varnish the board to give it a durable finish.
With the hobby knife cut away the four corner 3 x 3 squares to leave the cross. Turn the board over and score along the bases of the four arms of the cross. Now make a similar cross from the larger cardboard sheet. (This can be left unpainted, but it might be more attractive to paint it or decorate it with decals.) The arms of this cross and the

Right: The finished board is scored along the bases of the four arms of the cross and folded as shown. It should fit neatly inside the lid.

center square will all be slightly longer than the arms and center of the actual board.
Score in the same way as you scored the board. Fold into a box shape and secure with adhesive tape. Fold the board into a box shape and slide it into the "lid." This box structure is a convenient method of storing the playing pieces and dice.

b) To make the playing pieces:
The pieces shown in the photograph are standard and can be purchased in any shop that sells games. If you want to make your own, you need 16 small pebbles. Make four sets of four, each set painted a different color. Varnish to give a durable finish.

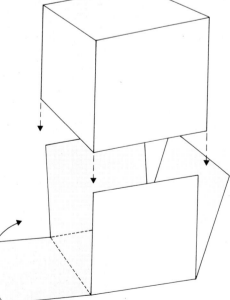

Dice Games

Left: *This drawing of Roman women casting knucklebones comes from Pompeii and can be seen in the Museo Nazionale, in Naples. Gambling with knucklebones or dice was very popular among every class in ancient Rome. Perhaps "popular" is an understatement, as the rich gambled away their fortunes and the poor their freedom on the throw of the dice.*

Dice, or to be more precise, the casting arrows or sticks that were the forerunners of dice, are undoubtedly the oldest gaming device known to man. The Greek dramaturgist Sophocles attributed their invention to Palamedes, who was supposed to have taught the game to soldiers at the siege of Troy 3,000 years ago. The historian Herodotus claimed that they were invented by the Lydians as a means of diverting themselves from a devastating famine in the days of King Atrys, and the Roman historian Plutarch gave credit to the Egyptians. Bone and ivory dice, similar to those now in use, have been found in tombs in the area of Thebes. Going much further back, we find that bones from the legs of sheep or goats were used by women and girls in Asia for playing a game of skill not unlike the present-day game of jacks. The bones were shaped like elongated dice and the men started to number the four oblong sides in order to use the bones for gambling. At a later period, cubic dice were invented, but until today in Asia these have never completely replaced rectangular dice.

The Romans used both types of dice, calling the cubic dice *tesserae* and the oblong dice *tali*. The various throws were given names, the best being named for the goddess of love and the worst being called a "dog". Gambling with dice was very popular in Rome, and wealthy men, in the latter days of the empire, sometimes staked their riches on a single throw. The barbarians, too, were addicted to the craze and they would gamble away even their freedom after having lost everything else. Dicing survived the passing of the centuries and it was still a favorite pastime in the Middle Ages, when both dicing schools and guilds

existed. One of the earliest references in English is one by Ordericus Vitalis (1075-1143): "clergymen and bishops are fond of dice-playing." References from this time are increasingly abundant, especially in the court records of the day.

Notwithstanding the conflicting claims of ancient historians, the inventor of dice was probably the same person who presided at the birth of medicine and chemistry–the witch doctor. Before dice became gambling implements, they were magical devices and they were used by primeval people to divine the future. Not only dice, but most of our other gaming implements can be traced back to the still earlier practice of divination by arrows.

Primitive tribes all over the globe have gambled with dice of many curious shapes and markings–dice made from, among other things, plum and peach stones, seeds, buffalo, caribou and moose bone, deer horn, pebbles, pottery, walnut shells, beaver and woodchuck teeth, and a wide variety of seashells.

The first home of the modern die was very probably the Orient. The Korean dice that were used in the Buddhist game of promotion bear both a magical formula and directions for the next move. Also, the game sheet with which it was played bears directions in Sanskrit, which would suggest India as the origin. There we find that the custom of fortune-telling with dice is practiced as a science under the name *ramala* and that the dice used are of a familiar pattern. They are cubical and marked with the "birds-eye" spots that some of our dice have. It is in India, too, that the first written records on dice (and on loaded ones at that!) are found in the Sanskrit epic, the *Mahabharara*, which was written about 2,000 years ago.

Below: *Over the ages, man has pressed a wide variety of objects into service as dice. Here you can see casting sticks from Egypt and Mesopotamia, pyramidal dice from Ur, Roman knucklebones, a number of teetotums, casting sticks used by the Amerindians, modern numbered dice and poker dice.*

Games Using Standard Dice

Modern dice are usually made of cellulose or some other plastic material and are marked with a number of small dots (called spots). By convention, the spots on the opposite faces total seven: 1-6, 2-5, and 3-4. There are dozens, maybe hundreds, of different dice games. Most of these are essentially gambling games, which are generally played among friends for small stakes or a round of drinks and as such are subject to certain conventions and rules that are common to all dice games.

1. Throwing: the dice are usually thrown (rolled) from a dice cup. In some games they are allowed to roll freely, in others they are thrown "under the cup" and then exposed. In both cases the dice must land flat on the throwing surface. If they do not, they must be rethrown.

2. Procedure: the first throw is to determine who plays first. Play then proceeds in a clockwise direction. The player who has lost the game usually has the option of starting the next.

Hazard

There are two games of hazard, the 800-year old version played with two dice from which craps evolved and a three-dice version played with a layout and called grand hazard. The two have long been confused and grand hazard is often mistaken for chuck-a-luck. Grand hazard is still a very popular game and known simply as hazard.

How to Play Two-Dice Hazard

Any number can play; two dice and a cup are used. Players bet against the house.

1. One of the players, known as the caster, throws two dice to determine the *main point*. This must be a 5, 6, 7, 8, or a 9; otherwise, it is *no main* and he throws again until one of the main points comes up.

2. He then throws the dice again to determine the *chance point*. This must be a 4, 5, 6, 7, 8, 9 or 10.

3. When throwing to determine the chance point, the caster loses his bet immediately if he throws an *out*.
A throw of 2 or 3 – known as *craps*–is out regardless of the main point.
A throw of 12 is out if the main point is 9, 7 or 5. A throw of 11 is out if the main point is 9, 8, 6 or 5. There are also ad-

vantageous throws known as *nicks,* when throwing for the chance point. If the main point is duplicated (i.e. if the main point is 6 and a 6 is thrown) the caster scores a nick and wins the bet. He also scores a nick on throwing 12 when the main point is 6 or 8, and on throwing 11 when the main point is 7.

4. The caster then continues to throw until he duplicates the chance point, which wins the bet, or the main point, which loses the bet. The turn then passes to the next player.

Aces

This game, sometimes called aces to the center, deuces to the left, or fives to the right, is one of the most fascinating of all dice games. It is very popular in the Far East, in particular in the Philippines, where keen players possess their own dice cup bearing their name.
Any number may play. Each player has five dice, marked conventionally except that an ace replaces the one. (Obviously "normal" dice can be used for this game, with the one standing for the ace.) If playing for money, each player puts an agreed stake into a pool and then throws his five dice. The player with the highest total takes any seat and is the first shooter, the player throwing the second highest sits on his left and shoots second, etc. Players who throw the same total throw again.

The first shooter begins by throwing five dice. Each thrown die showing an ace is placed in the center of the table; all deuces are passed to the player to the left, all fives to the player to the right. The player continues to throw until he fails to throw an ace, 2, or 5 or until he has no dice left. The player on the left then begins his turn of play. Players without any dice remain in the game as they may still receive dice from the players on either side of them.

The player throwing the last ace with the last die is declared the loser and buys a round of drinks. When playing for a wager the player throwing the last ace is declared the winner and takes the pot.

Martinetti

Any number can play this game, also called Ohio or centennial.
Three dice, a cup, a layout numbered from 1 to 12 and individual markers for each player, usually coins of different denominations, are used. Each player throws the dice from a cup, the highest scorer starting the game, while the lowest has his turn last. Ties are thrown again.
The first shooter then throws the dice. If a 1 is thrown, he places his marker on the first space (1) on the layout. If he fails to throw a 1, the dice pass to the player to his left.
If he throws a 1 and a 2 on the same throw he may advance his marker to the second space. If 1:2:3 are thrown the marker is advanced to the third space. He may also use any two or

three numbers thrown and add them together to form the number needed. For example, the numbers in a throw of 2:4:5 can be combined in various ways to produce the additional numbers: 6, 7, 9 and 11.
Each player continues throwing as long as he rolls numbers he can use. If a player throws a total that he needs but that he overlooks, an opponent who can use that number may, as soon as the shooter has passed the cup, call the number and advance his marker. If two players call the number at the same time, the one who is first on the shooter's left may use the number.
The player whose marker has first traveled from 1 to 12 and back to 1 again is declared the winner.

DEMOCRITE

*Joyeux Censeur je m'aperçois
Que tu veux compter par tes doit.
Les extravagantes sailles
Les egaremens, les folies
A' Paris chez Daumont rue de la Ferronnerie*

*Qui regnent parmi les humains
Mais tous tes efforts seront vains
Aucun nombre ne peut suffire
Crois moy, contente toy den rire*

Picard Fec.

Above: *A French
engraving, probably
from the 15th cen-
tury, around the
time of the reign of
Louis XI. Gambling
with dice was a
craze in those days.
The gentleman in*
*the picture is talking
about human weak-
nesses. It does not
make sense to try*
*and count them, he
says, because there
are too many of
them!*

Above: *These dice
in the shape of a
human figure are of
German origin.
They date from the
15th century and*
*clearly display the
bawdy sense of
humor that seems
to have prevailed in
that time.*

Thirty-six

This game is similar to the card game of twenty-one or pontoon.

Any number can play and one die is used. Each player puts an agreed stake in the pool and then throws the die to determine the order of play, the lowest score opening and the highest having the advantage of throwing last. Each player in turn throws the die, and continues to throw adding each number to his previous score, the object being to reach 36, or approach it as closely as possible without passing it.

Players throwing more than 36 go "Over the top" and are out of the game. The player nearest to 36 wins, and if there is a tie the pool is divided between the winners.

Most players throw again at 32 or less; stop at 33 or more.

Aces in the Pot

Aces in the pot is a game for any number of players, each having two counters (or coins) at start of play. The players make a single throw with two dice in turn. If a 1 is thrown, one counter is put in the pot; if two 1s are thrown, both counters must be put in. If a 6 is thrown, one counter is given to the player on the left of the thrower. If two 6s are thrown, both counters are given to the player on the left. All other throws are irrelevant.

The dice pass clockwise around the players until the pot contains all the counters except one. A player without a counter cannot throw the dice but passes them on. The player with the last counter makes three consecutive throws and if he does *not* throw a 6 he wins the game and the "pot". But if a 6 *is* thrown the counter and the dice pass to the player on the left, who also throws three times. The first player to throw three times without a 6 wins the game.

Barbudi

Barbudi of *barbotte* is a favorite gam-bling game in Canada's Toronto and Montreal and large American cities bordering on Canada, such as Detroit. Any number can play, usually as many as can fit around a regulation poker table. Each player rolls one die and the one throwing highest becomes the first *shooter.* The player on his right, known as the *fader,* bets any amount up to the house limit that the shooter will *not* win. The shooter may cover the bet, may allow other players to take all or part of the bet, or he may refuse the bet and pass the dice on. The fader can also refuse to bet. Other players may make side bets on whether the shooter or the fader will win. There is no math-ematical advantage to any player and the house takes a small percentage of each stake as its cut. Two dice are rolled and winning throws are 6:6, 5:5, 3:3, and 6:5. Losing throws are 1:2, 1:1, 2:2, or 4:4. All other combinations are meaningless.

If the fader bets and the bet is accepted, the shooter rolls the dice once. If nei-ther a winning nor a losing combina-tion is thrown the dice pass to the fader, who then throws. Throws contin-ue alternately until the shooter or the fader wins. If the shooter loses with a throw of 1:1, 2:2 or 4:4, or if the fader wins with a throw of 3:3, 5:5 or 6:6, the dice pass to the fader, who becomes the next shooter. The player on his right becomes the new fader. If, however, the shooter loses with a throw of 1:2, or the fader wins with a throw of 6:5, the shooter retains the dice. The shooter keeps the dice and continues to roll as long as he continues to win.

For a variation of this game, known as the *two-shot decision,* the following rules apply:

If either the shooter or the fader throws a 6:5, he wins only half the bet, while a throw of 1:2 loses only half the bet. At this point either the shooter or the fader may call off the rest of the bet or they can continue to shoot for it. When the shooter loses with a throw of 1:2 or the fader wins with a throw of 6:5 and the second half of the bet is refused by either player, the shooter passes the dice to the fader who then becomes the new shooter. The player on his right becomes the new fader. If, however, the players decide to shoot for the sec-ond half of the bet, they change roles, the shooter becoming the fader and the fader becoming the shooter.

Buck dice

Buck dice is one of the many dice games played to find a loser who buys the next round of drinks. Any number can play but experience suggests that four or five is ideal. If there are only two or three players the game is over too quickly, if there are more than five it is only suitable for slow drinkers! Three dice are used. Each player throws to determine the order of play. The player making the highest score throws first as this confers a slight advantage. The next highest throws second, and so on. The player throwing the lowest score then throws a single die to determine the *point number*. The first player begins by throwing all three dice and scores one point for each point number. He continues to throw as long as he throws point numbers, adding one. One point is added to his score for each one he throws. When he fails to throw a point number on any thrown, the dice are passed to the next player.

The object is to score exactly 15 points, called *buck* or game, and each player, as he reaches this score, drops out of the game until only one player remains

– the loser. Any three of a kind (not the point number) is know as *little buck* and scores 5 points. Three point numbers appearing in a single throw is known as *big buck* or *the general*. This scores 15 points and the player throwing it is eliminated from the game, no matter what score he has previously made. If a player is close to 15 and on his next throw, reaches a total above 15, the throw does not count and he must throw again.

In one popular variation, an additional rule states that when the shooter has 13 point numbers to his credit and 2 to go, only two dice are thrown, and when he has scores 14 and has only 1 to go, only one die is thrown.

The name buck dice is derived from the scoring method employed when the game is played in a bar. Three crosses, called bucks from their resemblance to the end view of a sawbuck, are drawn on the bar with chalk. The center of one cross is erased when the first point number is thrown; one arm is erased for each additional point. When all three crosses have been erased the player has scored 15 points.

Indian Dice

Indian Dice is one of the most popular bar games in the United States. Any number can play and five dice are used. The players each throw a die to decide the order of play, the player scoring the highest throwing first, the next highest throwing second, etc. Sixes are high, twos low and aces are *wild*, – they can be counted as any number desired.

1. The object of the game is to score high poker hands which rank in the following order: five of a kind (five 6s being higher than five 5s, etc.), four of a kind, three of a kind and a pair (known as a *full house*), three of a kind, two pairs, one pair. A hand without a pair or a sequence is useless.
2. The first player may throw three times but can stop after the first or the second throw if he wishes. The other players are only allowed the same number of throws.
3. After the first throw any of the five dice may be put aside. The rest are thrown again. This process of selection is repeated after the second throw, and any or all of the five dice can be thrown a third time (including those that were set aside on the first two throws).
4. Each round is called a leg. If there are only two players the winner of two out of three legs wins the game. When there are more players they all enter in two legs, and the winner in the first leg plays a two-handed deciding game with the winner in the second leg. Otherwise the two low men play off and the lose buys a round.

Example: A player throws 4:4:2:3:6. Unless he wants to throw all five dice again in the hope of throwing something better than a pair, he puts the two 4s to one side and throws the remaining three dice. If he now throws 1:3:2, he puts the 1 with the 4s to make three of a kind, since the 1 is wild. He then throws the other two dice in a final attempt to improve his hand. Theoretically, Indian dice offers exactly equal chances to each player. In practice, a knowledge of the odds against throwing any particular combination will stand you in good stead. It may, for example, be better for a player throwing first to stand pat on a good three of a kind achieved in one throw than to throw a second time – remembering that opposing players are also limited to one throw.

Sequences

Any number can play this game. Each player throws six dice once and then passes them on to the player on his left. Sequences are the important thing here.

The scoring is as follows:
5 point for a roll showing 1:2
10 points for 1:2:3
15 points for 1:2:3:4
20 points for 1:2:3:4:5
25 points for 1:2:3:4:5:6

The first player to reach 100 points wins. A roll of 1:1:1 cancels the whole score and the player has to start again.

Twenty-six

This was a favorite bar game in the 1950s in the Midwest. In many stores and taverns, customers would pay a fee, usually 25 cents, and winners were paid out in checks or tokens, which could be exchanged for drinks, cigarettes or other merchandise.
Any number can play and one of the players acts as a banker. Ten dice and a cup are used, together with counters or chips for gambling.
The player on the left of the banker chooses any number from one to six as his *point* and puts a number of counters into the center of the table. He then throws the 10 dice 13 times and totals the number of times he has thrown his point number. The object is to throw 26 or more point numbers.

The banker pays:
4 to 1 if the player scores 26 or 27 point numbers;
5 to 1 for 28 or 29 point numbers;
6 to 1 for 30 or 31 point numbers;
7 to 1 for 32 or 33 point numbers;
8 to 1 for any high point number.

The player forfeits his stake to the banker if he fails to score 26 point numbers, with two exceptions: if he throws less than 11 points, the banker pays him 4 to 1, and if he scores exactly 13, the banker pays him 2 to 1.

Ship, Captain, Mate and Crew

This game is also known as mariner, battleship, destroyer, and seaman. It is a game for any number of players who contribute equal stakes into the pot. Five dice are used. Each player throws a single die to decide on the order of

play, highest man going first, second highest second, and so on. Players tying throw again.
Play is in a clockwise direction. Each player, in turn, is allowed three throws. He first tries to get 6, 5, and 4 in that order; the 6 representing the "ship," the 5 the "captain" and the 4 the "mate." If, for example, a 5 and 6 appear on the first throw, the player puts those dice aside and rolls the remaining three dice to try to get a 4. If a 6 and 4 appear on the first throw, the 4 cannot be used until a 5 has been made; the player sets aside the 6 only and throws four dice on his next throw, trying first for a 5 and then a 4.
When the player has succeeded in getting a 6, 5 and 4 in that order, the points on the remaining two dice constitute his score, called the "crew." If he has not thrown three times he may, if he wishes, use any remaining throws to attempt to make a higher total. However, both dice must be thrown – a high number cannot be set aside and one die thrown. The player who has ship, captain and crew and whose two remaining dice show the highest score is the winner and takes the pot. If two players tie, there is no winner and another round begins. The player to the left of the first shooter in the first round becomes the first shooter in the second round.

Help Your Neighbor

This fast game for any number of players from two to six is one of the oldest dice games in existence and is once again gaining popularity. Each player throws three dice. The player with the highest score shoots first, the player with the next highest score sits on his left and shoots second, and so on. Players throwing the same scores rethrow. Each player has his own number, the first shooter being 1, the second 2, and so on. If there are only three players the first shooter takes the numbers 1 and 2, the second takes 3

and 4, the third 5 and 6. With only two players, the first takes the numbers 1, 2 and 3, and the second, 4, 5 and 6. If there are five players the 6 is ignored and if there are four players both the 5 and 6 are ignored.
Counters or chips (usually 10 to each player) are used. Each player in his turn throws the three dice and each player whose number (or numbers) appears must place one counter in the center for each such number. For example, if there are six players and the first shooter throws a 3 and two 5s, the number-3 player places one counter in the center and the number-5 player two counters.
The player who gets rid of all his counters first is declared the winner and takes the pot. The player on the shooter's left begins the following game.

Innumerable changes are possible in help your neighbor. Using one to three dice, players sometimes get rid of a chip only when they roll a number in exact rotation. Thus, until somebody rolls a 1, nobody can score, and afterward, only a 2 scores, followed by a 3, and so on. In other versions, players are permitted to add or subtract the three rolled numbers to produce whatever total is required.

Throwing Sevens

Throwing sevens is another dice game in which certain dice are set aside and the remaining points totaled. Six dice are thrown under a cup. The basic idea, as the name suggests, is to throw combinations of two dice to make seven– 6:1, 5:2 and 4:3. Any such combination is set aside and the remaining dice rethrown.
The first shooter has the option of stopping after the first throw but can also throw again, up to three times. The other players can only throw the same number of times (or fewer) as the first shooter. This gives the first player an advantage. Say he throws 1:6:2:1:1:1. Although there is only one seven combination–6:1–the total shown on the remaining dice is only five. This is a very low score and there is a good chance that one or more of the other players will be hit with 20 or more points. On the other hand, if the shooter continues to throw, not only may he end with more than five points, but he also gives the other players more throws.

The players agree beforehand to the limit to which they will play. If only two or three people play, a limit of 100 points is usual. If more than two or three play, the limit can be lowered. As always, the loser buys the drinks!

Drop Dead

Any number can play this game and five dice and a cup are used. The order of play is decided by each player throwing a single die, the man throwing low going first and the man throwing high last. Tying players throw again.

Each player in turn throws the five dice. If a 2 or a 5 appears, nothing is scored on that roll and any die showing a 2 or a 5 is set aside. If neither a 2 nor a 5 appears, the players scores the total of the numbers thrown. For example, a throw of 2:6:6:6:6 scores nothing, the 2 is set aside and the player throws four dice. A subsequent score of, say, 1:3:3:6, scores 13 points. Again, four dice are thrown. The player continues to roll and scores every time a 2 or a 5 does not appear. A turn of play ends when all five dice are "dead." The game continues until each player has

thrown. If playing for an agreed stake, the player with the highest total is the winner. If the game is played for drinks, the player with the lowest total buys a round.

Mexico

Mexico or Mexican is a bar gambling game played to decide who buys the next round of drinks. In theory any number can play, but three is generally regarded as the minimum number and six the maximum.

Each player rolls a scoring die to decide the order of play. The player throwing highest begins; play moves counter-clockwise.

Two dice are thrown under a dice cup and the usual rules apply–the dice must land flat under the cup. The highest throw is 2:1 or "Mexico"; then doubles in descending order; followed by 6:5, 6:4 etc., down to 3:1, which is the lowest throw. The first player has the option of rolling up to three times, but may stop at any time if he thinks his score is high enough. The other players can only throw the same number of times (or fewer) than the first shooter.

Above: *Gambling was a favorite pastime during the Renaissance. This illustration, after a miniature on vellum, shows a French gambling house of that period. At top left of the picture, three men are playing cards, probably three-handed whist. The two men at bottom left are engaged in backgammon and the five men around the table are gambling with dice.*

The player throwing low loses one point, unless a "Mexico" has been thrown, in which case he loses two points. The scores are recorded on scoring dice. There are various ways of doing this. But the usual method is to turn from 6 through 1 and back through 6, making a total of 10 points.

Games Using Nonstandard Dice

The Chinese, wherever they are, love to gamble, and from the long history of their gambling games it seems likely that they always have. Apart from the "Chinese finger game," a guessing game similar to (and probably the ancestor of) the *ken* games of Japan, there are innumerable card, dice and domino games. Below are a few examples of Chinese dice games. Standard Chinese dice are small cubes, usually made of bone or ivory and marked with incised pips from one to six, which are arranged so that the sum of the opposite faces is seven. The one pip is uncolored and is much larger and more deeply incised than the others. These are black except the four, whose pips are painted red, a relic of the dice that were imported from India into China many centuries ago. The dice are usually thrown from the hand into a porcelain bowl, and the players throw in turn in a clockwise direction.

Chinese Dice Games

Strung Flowers

Three dice are used and only four combinations score. These are:
1. Triples. Three 6s are high and three 1s low.
2. Strung flowers. The combination that gives the game its name. It is a sequence of 4:5:6.
3. Two alike. The highest score is two alike 6 high and the lowest is two alike 1 high (also known as the ace negative). The third dice is unimportant and does not affect the score.
4. The dancing dragons. This is a sequence of 1:2:3 and is the lowest scoring combination.

Any number can play. The players throw the dice in turn and the one with most red pips (i.e. 4s) becomes the banker. The other players place their stakes, usually divisible by three, on the table.

The banker throws until a scoring combination appears. If he throws a triple, strung flowers or two alike six high, each of the players pays him the full amount of their stakes and then the banker calls for new bets and throws the dice again. If he throws dancing dragons or an ace negative the banker pays each player the full amount of their stakes. If he throws two alike five, four, three or two high, he hands the dice to the player on his left. If this player makes a higher cast, the banker must pay him. If the player makes a lower cast, he pays the banker. If the player also throws two alike and an odd die, the amounts paid by the player or the banker are usually proportionate to the difference between the scores of the odd die; if its is 4 or 3, the full stake is paid; if 2 then 3/4 of the stake; and if 1, 1/3 of the stake.

If the banker wins, the player on his left throws against him and the game continues until someone outthrows the banker. The player on the banker's left becomes the new banker and another round begins.

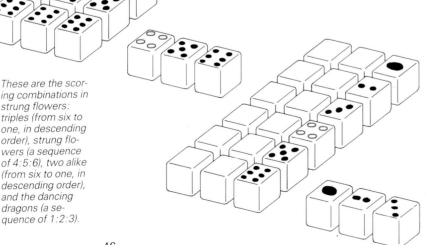

Throwing Heaven and Nine
(Chak t'in kau)

Any number can play and two dice are used. The 21 possible throws are divided into two series, *civil* and *military*. The throws, their names and their order of scoring are shown in descending scales (on the right).

Each player throws the two dice in turn; the one with the highest number of pips becomes the banker. The banker calls for the stakes and all the other players put their bets on the table in front of them. The banker then throws and his cast determines the suit; whether civil or military, for that round. The other players then throw in turn. Only throws in the reigning suit count; when a player throws in the other suit he must rethrow until he makes a cast in the correct suit. If the banker throws the highest cast in the reigning suit, that is *heaven* of the civil and *nines* of the military, each player forfeits his stake; but if the banker

Below: *In the Orient, it is still very much the custom to play gambling games on the street. These boys are enjoying a typical Chinese game, using three dice. At the beginning of the game, they each put a stake in, betting on a number representing one of the drawn figures.*

CIVIL			MILITARY		
Heaven					Nines
Earth					
Man					Eights
Harmony					
Plum Flowers					Sevens
Long Threes					
Bench					Six
Tigers Head					Fives
Red-Head Ten					
Long-Leg Seven					Final Three
Red-Mallet Six					

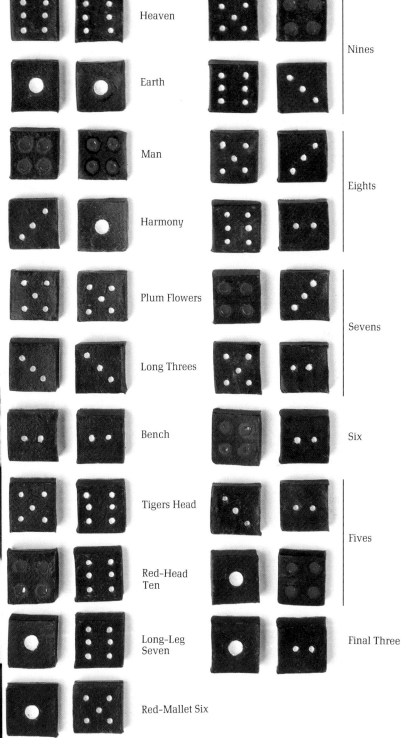

throws the lowest of the reigning suit, that is *the red-mallet six* of the civil or *the final three* of the military, he pays each player the amount of his stake. If the banker throws any pair other than the highest or the lowest of either suit, the second player gets to throw. If he throws higher than the banker, he is paid his stake, but if he throws lower, he forfeits his stake. There is no exchange if the throws are the same. The game continues until the banker is outthrown. At this point the second player succeeds him as the banker. After all the players have been banker in turn the game may finish or another round may be started. A player may withdraw at the end of each round.

Western Dice Games

For some Western dice games special dice are used. Crown and anchor, for example, uses dice with faces showing a crown, an anchor, a heart, a spade, a diamond and a club. The eight dice used for bell and hammer each have five plain surfaces and a sixth side marked with 1, 2, 3, 4, 5, 6, a bell and a hammer, respectively. Poker dice do not have pips, but have faces showing the actual ace, king, queen etc. Other games use a teetotum (a six-sided top).

Poker Dice

As the name implies, this game–similar in some ways to Indian Dice–is poker played with dice. Most often, special poker dice are used, although regular dice will do just as well. Special poker dice have faces showing the actual ace, king, queen, jack, ten and nine instead of pips. Any number can play, but the game is best for five or fewer, each with a set of dice. Each player throws one die to determine the order of play, highest man going first, next highest second, and so on.

The object is to throw the highest poker hand. These rank as follows: five of a kind, four a kind, full house, straight (any five cards or numbers in numerical sequence), three of a kind, two pairs, and one pair.

Liar Dice

Of the many variations of liar dice, the one chosen here is poker dice (described on this page) taken one step further to include the bluff element, which is so important in card poker. Each player throws five dice. The one having the highest poker hand (see poker dice) shoots first. Play proceeds counterclockwise. the first player throws the five dice under the cup, conceals them with his hand and examines them. He may then throw any number of dice a second and/or a third time, attempting to build a strong poker hand. He then announces his complete holding but he is *not* required to tell the truth! The player on his left can choose to accept the call or not. If he thinks the first player is bluffing, he lifts the cup to expose the dice. If he has correctly called the bluff, he wins the bet; if not, he loses. If he decides to accept the call, he must improve on it or bluff the player on *his* left into believing that he has improved on it.

Players generally begin with a number of chips and on losing a call put one in the pot. Play continues until all but one player has been wiped out. The latter takes the pot.

Above: *Special poker dice have faces showing the actual ace, king, queen, jack, ten and nine instead of pips.*

Put and Take

Any number can play. Each player puts an equal number of counters in the pool. The player opening the game spins a teetotum (a six-sided top) and puts counters into, or takes counters from, the pool according to the instructions on the face falling uppermost. The six faces show:

1 = Take one	4 = Put 2
2 = All put	5 = Take 2
3 = Take all	6 = Put 1

Note: 2 (All put) means that each player must put one counter into the pool. Players spin the teetotum in turn, and when a player loses all his counters he retires from the game.

Crown and Anchor

According to the American gaming expert John Scarne, this game is actually chuck-a-luck in disguise. It is a fast gambling game and used to be very popular in the British Navy and among American servicemen.

Three special dice are used. The six faces show a crown, an anchor, a heart, a spade, a diamond and a club. The players sit around a board or cloth marked with the same symbols. One

Left: *For* put and take, *spinning dice are used. They are called teetotums and can be made of different materials (ivory, wood, brass, among others), as demonstrated by these attractive examples from different countries.*

Below: *The three special dice used for* crown and anchor. *The six faces show a crown, an anchor, a heart, a spade, a diamond and a club.*

player is banker, the others bet on a the symbol of their choice. The banker throws the three dice from a cup. He pays even money on singles, 2 to 1 on pairs, and 3 to 1 on three of a kind. If the player's symbol does *not* appear, he loses his stake to the banker. The banker's advantage (approximately 8%) is such that eventually he will be far ahead and the other players will be broke. The bank, therefore, should pass to each player in turn.

Bell and Hammer

Bell and hammer, or *schimmel*, came from Germany to England, where it was played as early as 1816. It is a game for any number of people.

Equipment Five picture cards (an inn, a white horse, a bell, a hammer, a bell

and hammer); eight cubic dice, each with five plain surfaces and the sixth side marked with 1, 2, 3, 4, 5, 6, a bell and a hammer, respectively; a dicing cup; 36 counters for each player; a small wooden mallet.

How to Play Bell and Hammer

Each player throws the eight dice, the one throwing highest becoming the auctioneer. The latter takes four counters from each player to form a pool and then auctions off the five cards for counters. These counters are added to the pool. A player without a card does not take part in the round; a player out for two successive rounds is out of the game. His counters are also added to the pool.

This is the end of the first phase and the second phase begins with the the auctioneer banging his wooden mallet on the table. He is the first to throw the eight dice; the others follow in turn.

Scoring method

1. If all the dice are blanks, each player pays one counter to the owner of the white horse.
2. If a bell, or hammer, or a bell and hammer turn up, the other dice being blank, the owners of the corresponding cards pay one counter to the owner of the white horse.
3. If a bell, or hammer, or a bell and hammer turn up with one or more numbers showing as well, the auctioneer pays this number of counters to the owner of the card.
4. If only blanks and numbers are showing, the auctioneer pays the sum of numbers thrown to that player.
5. If a player throws a sum of numbers equal to the counters in the pool the game ends, but if a larger number is thrown, the player pays the difference to the owner of the inn, known as "Mine Host."

Mine Host opens the inn, which means the third phase has begun as different scoring rules apply.

6. If a player throws all blanks, the owner of the white horse pays one counter to Mine Host.
7. If a bell, a hammer, or a bell and hammer are thrown and the other dice are blanks, the owners of these cards pay one counter to Mine Host.
8. If a number is thrown with a bell, a hammer, or a bell and a hammer, the owners of these cards pay Mine Host the difference between the number thrown and the counters remaining in the pool.
9. If a player throws a number less than the number of counters in the pool, he wins the corresponding number of counters.
10. The round is won by the player throwing the same number as there are counters in the pool, which he adds to his store.

The winner of one round becomes the auctioneer in the next and the whole game ends when one player holds all the counters.

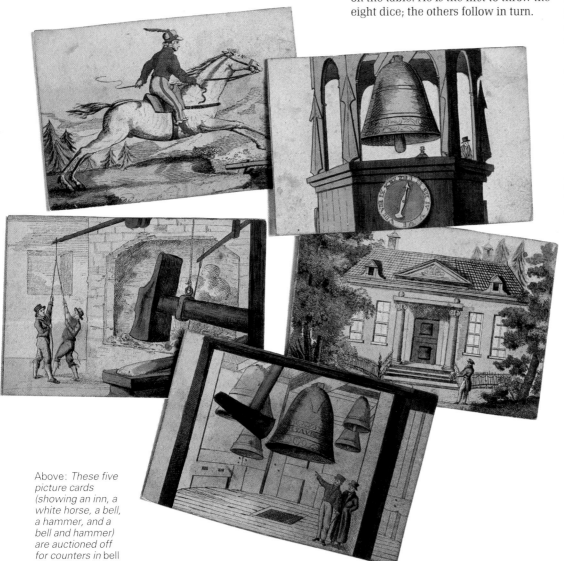

Above: *These five picture cards (showing an inn, a white horse, a bell, a hammer, and a bell and hammer) are auctioned off for counters in* bell and hammer.

Indian Chance Games with Dice

Native Americans played games of chance long before the Europeans invaded their continent. Many of these games are described in *Games of the North American Indians* by Stewart Culin. Indian games of chance can be divided into two categories: *guessing games* (discussed on page 52-53) and *dice games*. Indian dice are quite unlike the dice most of us are used to. They usually have two faces, distinguished by color or markings of some sort, and they are made of a great variety of materials–split canes, walnut shells, peach and plum stones or beaver and woodchuck teeth. Sometimes wooden or bone staves, or shell, bone, brass, or pottery discs are used. The dice are either thrown by hand or tossed in a bowl or basket, this being the difference between the two principal types of the game. Both are often found among the same tribe. Research has shown that the basket-dice game, which is most commonly played by women, is derived from the game in which the dice are thrown by hand. The method of counting varies widely, but the games can be divided into two general categories: those in which the score is kept with sticks or counters (which pass from hand to hand) and those in which a counting board or abacus is used.

Below is a description of one of the numerous versions of the basket or bowl game. This one is played by the Passamaquoddy tribe of Maine and is called *all-tes-teg-enuk*. Although it is a game of chance, skill plays an important part in it.

Below: *There are numerous versions of the* bowl *or basket game, as played by different Indian tribes. These Cheyenne women are playing the* seed game.

The Bowl Game *(All-tes-teg-enuk)*

Equipment A bowl or shallow dish; six thin bone discs, serving as dice, plain on one side and carved and colored on the other; four dozen small sticks and five larger sticks, one of which is notched.

How to Play All-tes-teg-enuk

Two players sit facing each other with the bowl containing the dice between them on a cushion. The dice are mixed

Right: *The basic equipment necessary for the* bowl *or basket game: a basket, dice and counting sticks. Here, the dice are plum pits.*

Below: *The* basket game *is most commonly played by women. This old engraving shows Indian women enjoying the* plum stone *game.*

and turned over at random. All the sticks are placed in a pile. One of the players takes the bowl and bangs it down on the cushion so that the dice jump into the air. If a player scores (see below) he has another turn, if not the bowl passes to the opponent. The players throw alternately, each winning throw being rewarded with an extra turn. If a die jumps out of the bowl the player loses his turn. The game has two phases, unless the first phase ends in a draw.

First Phase
If four of the discs are the same way up, either marked or plain, the player wins three small sticks from the pile and places them in a cache. If he does this twice in succession he wins another nine small sticks. If he throws four discs the same way up three times in succession he wins a further 12 small sticks or one big one. His turn then ceases.

If five discs are alike the player wins a big stick from the pile, or 12 small ones. If this happens twice in succession the player wins another three big sticks or 36 small ones. If he succeeds three times in a row, the player wins 16 small sticks from the opponent's cache or, if this is impossible, he turns a stick up to indicate the debt and claims his win when his opponent has enough sticks to pay him. He adds these, with the notched stick, to his own cache. When all the small sticks have been taken and there are large ones left in the pile, instead of taking three sticks from the opponent the players lay one out to show that the other owes three sticks. When a player has four sticks out, he takes a large stick from the pool and adds it to his cache, together with the four marker sticks.
The notched stick is worth three small sticks and is always the last to be taken from the pile. When it has been won, the second phase of the game begins and the sticks have different values.

Second Phase
Four alike wins four small sticks from the opponent. Four alike twice in succesion wins 12 small sticks. Four alike three times in a row wins one large stick or 16 small sticks. Five alike wins one large stick or 16 small ones. Five alike twice in succession wins three large sticks or 48 small ones. When a player has no sticks left he loses the game.

51

Indian Guessing Games

Below: *Playing gambling games was a favorite pastime among the Chippewa Indians. This photograph, taken around 1920, shows a few members of the tribe playing the moccasin game. It is a game that is usually played outdoors.*

In general, the Indians play their dice games in silence, while the guessing games are accompanied by singing and drumming. In his *Games of the North American Indians*, Culin divides guessing games into four categories: stick games, in which a bundle of sticks are divided in the hands and the opponent has to guess in which hand the odd stick or a particularly marked stick is held; hand games, in which two or four sticks, one or two marked, are held in the hands and the opponent has to guess in which hand the unmarked stick is held; four-stick games, in which four sticks, marked in pairs, are hidden together and the opponent has to guess their relative position; and

hidden-ball games, perhaps better known as moccasin games, in which a small object is hidden in one of four wooden tubes, in one of four moccasins, or in the earth, and the opponent has to guess where the object is hidden. Below follows a description of one such moccasin game, as played by the Chippewa (originally known as the Ojibway) Indians of Wisconsin (the Chippewa name is *mukesinnah-dahdewog*). In the past, the game involved quite a bit of gambling—at times the players would stake everything they had with them and come away literally stripped—but today entertainment is the prime purpose.

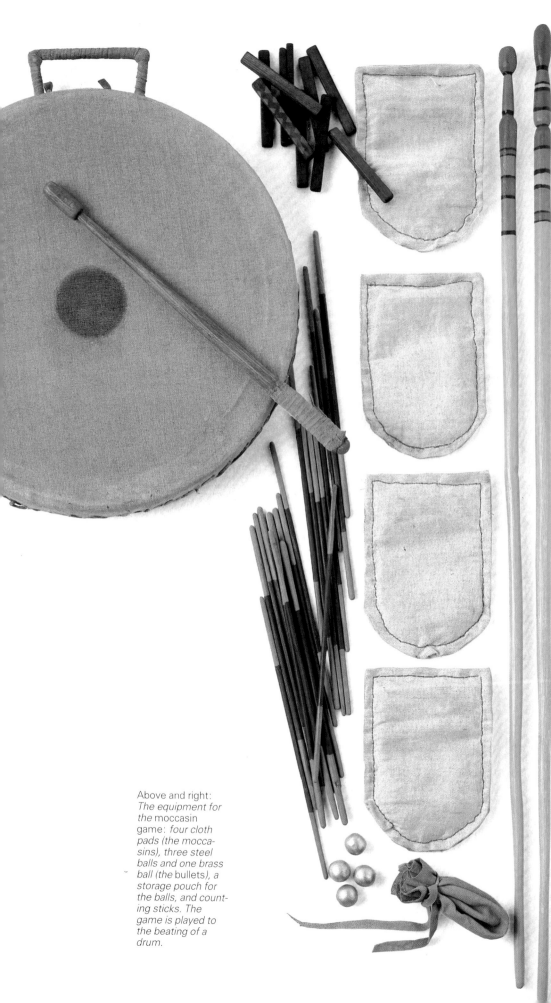

The Moccasin Game

This game is also referred to as the hidden-ball game or the bullet game by some writers. The Indians, however, still call it the moccasin game since moccasins were originally used for hiding the four bullets or balls. The bullets referred to were the round lead balls used in smooth bore muzzle-loading flintlock or percussion-cap rifles, not those used in the breech-loading weapons of today. Originally, this was probably a men's gambling game. It is still being played by older and middle-aged men, but rarely by younger men, which seems to indicate that the game will cease to be played in the near future. Drumming was and still is an important part of the game, but the singing has been more or less discontinued, apparently because most of the songs have been forgotten. Most of the time, the game is played outdoors, where a blanket or a piece of cloth or canvas is spread out on the ground and fastened down with pegs.

Equipment   the "bullets": three steel balls (plain) and one brass ball (scored face); the "moccasins": four cloth pads; 20 counting sticks for each player; a deerskin storage pouch for the balls; two striking or turning sticks. For some versions of the game, 10 additional counting sticks are used, nine plain and one notched.

How to Play the Moccasin Game

The game is played to the beating of a drum, which is passed from team to team. A knife is thrown up and when it falls on the blanket, the direction of the blade indicates which player is to start the game. He is the first to hide the four bullets, one under each moccasin. For this purpose, he holds the four bullets in his right hand and keeps his left hand moving from one moccasin to another. While moving and swaying to the beat of the drum and at the same time trying to divert the attention of the person with whom he is playing, he passes his bullet hand under the moccasins, depositing a bullet under each. The opponent, using the striking stick to strike and turn over the moccasin of his choice, has to guess where the jagged bullet is. However, contrary to what one might expect, he should not guess right the first time! For if he does so, he loses four sticks and if he makes a correct guess the second time he

Above and right:
The equipment for the moccasin *game: four cloth pads (the moccasins), three steel balls and one brass ball (the* bullets*), a storage pouch for the balls, and counting sticks. The game is played to the beating of a drum.*

loses three sticks. It is only the third time that a right guess will gain him sticks – four, to be exact. Finally, if the bullet is hidden under the fourth moccasin, the guesser loses four sticks. The game continues in this vein until the 20 sticks have passed from one hand to the other.

How to Make the Moccasin Game

Materials

a) For the moccasins: a piece of sail cloth 40 cm x 52 cm (16 in x 20 in), saddle thread;

b) For the counting sticks: approx. 1.2 m (4 ft) of very thin dowel, black and brown acrylic paint;

c) For the striking sticks: 1.6 m (5 ft) of thick dowel, beige, brown, black and red acrylic paint;

d) For the pouch and "bullets": a 28 cm x 28 cm (11 in x 11 in) square of soft leather, hobby clay, silver and gold acrylic;

e) For the extra counting sticks: 1 m

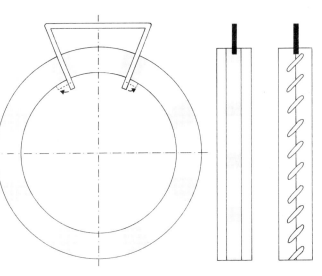

From far left to left: *The first diagram shows how the handle and the six blocks should be placed between the plywood rings. The second diagram is a side view of the assembled drum before it is covered, and the third a side view of the drum after the canvas has been stretched over the frame and stitched with leather thongs.*

(approx. 40 in) of 6 mm x 1 cm (¼ in x ⅜ in) softwood, black acrylic;

f) For the drumstick: 30 cm (1 ft) of thick dowel (min. 2 cm)–(¹³/₁₆ in), 2 m (6.6 ft) approx. leather thong;

g) For the drum: two 40 cm x 40 cm (16 in x 16 in) squares of 8 mm (⁵/₁₆ in)

plywood, 32 cm (12¹³/₁₆ in) of 3 cm x 3 cm (1⅛ in x 1⅛ in) softwood, two 44 cm x 44 cm (17⅝ in x 17⅝ in) squares of thin canvas, 30 cm (1 ft) of 6 mm (¼ in) welding wire, panel pins, U-shaped panel pins, glue, 5 m (16½ ft) approx. leather thong, shellac.

Below: *This painting, by a native artist, shows Shawnee Indians playing* the moccasin game *in Oklahoma, in the United States.*

Left: *Menomini Indians engaged in a local version of* the *moccasin game to the beat of a drum.*

Tools

Scissors, sewing needle, hand saw, scroll saw, rasp, 6 mm (¼ in) drill, hobby knife, awl, sandpaper, paint-brushes, drawing compasses, vise.

Method

a) To make the moccasins: cut the sail-cloth into four lengths of 13 cm x 40 cm (5 in x 16 in). Fold each length in half and round off the open ends with sharp dressmaking scissors. Stitch all round about 1 cm (⅜ in) in from the edge. The resulting "moccasins" should look like closed oven mitts.

b) To make the counting sticks: cut the thin dowel into 40 lengths of 3 cm 1³/₁₆ in). Round off the ends with a rasp and sandpaper. Paint them in black and brown acrylic as shown in the photo-graph on page 53.
Note: If you want to make the game so that it can be played by more than two, you need 20 additional sticks for each extra player.

c) To make the striking sticks: cut two 80 cm (32 in) lengths of thick dowel. The sticks are roughly tapered and the handles shaped with a rasp and hobby knife (see the photograph on page 53). Sandpaper smooth and paint in beige acrylic. Our model maker decorated the handles in brown, red and black acrylic but use whatever colors and pattern you like.

Note: The striking sticks in our model were made from osier wood, which was one of the materials used by the Native Americans. This is more authentic than dowel but may be diffi-cult to obtain.

d) To make the pouch and bullets: cut the largest possible circle from the square of soft leather. With and awl punch holes at 4 cm (1⅝ in) intervals around the edge of the material and about 2 cm (1³/₁₆ in) in from the edge. Thread a soft leather thong (a shoelace will serve just as well) in and out of the holes to make the drawstring. The "bullets" are made by rolling small pieces of hobby clay between the hands to make balls about 2½ cm (1 in) in diameter. When the balls have dried, paint three in silver acrylic and one in gold.
Note: One white and three black mar-bles will also serve the purpose.

e) To make the extra sticks: cut the length of 6 mm x 1 cm (¼ in x ⅜ in) softwood into ten 10 cm (4 in) lengths. Notch one of the lengths with a hobby knife. Sand and paint in black acrylic.

f) To make the drumstick: use a rasp and hobby knife to shape the drumstick (see the photograph on page 53). Bind leather thong around the handle.

g) To make the drum: draw two diago-nal lines from corner to corner on each plywood sheet. The point where the diagonals intersect is the center of the sheet. With this point as center use the compasses to draw two concentric circles of radii 40 cm and 37 cm (16 in and 14¹³/₁₆ in) respectively. Cut along the lines with a scroll saw to make two rings 3 cm (1³/₁₆ in) in width. The out-side edges should be smoothed with a rasp and sandpaper, but the inside edges do not need to be perfect as they will be hidden when the drum is com-plete.
Cut eight 4 cm (1⅝ in) blocks from the 3 cm x 3 cm (1³/₁₆ x 1³/₆ in) softwood. Drill holes through the length of two of these with a 6 mm (¼ in) drill. Push the welding wire through the holes and bend the ends round in a vise. Secure to the blocks with U-shaped pins.
Shape the wire in a vise (see diagram) to form the handle. Place the handle, together with the other six blocks (equally spaced) between the plywood rings and glue/pin them in position.
Cut circles of 44 cm (17⅝ in) diameter from the canvas squares. Lay them over the wooden framework and stitch them together with leather thong, ten-sioned as tightly as possible. Paint a black circle in the center of each side. Paint the whole surface with shellac to tension the canvas further.
Finally bind the metal handle with leather thong.

Other Dice Games

Le Jeu des Gobelets *(Thimblerig)*

Hope springs eternal–at least it does if you are the gambling type. It has already been mentioned in this book how wealthy Romans lost huge fortunes on a cast of the dice. Not much has changed in the intervening 2,000 years or so, for nowadays wealthy businessmen think little of losing similar fortunes on the dice and card tables of Las Vegas. It has been said that an inveterate gambler will wager on two flies climbing up a wall, and it is not difficult to imagine our early ancestors staking a leg of prime bronto-saurus on some equally random event. But there is gambling and, as they say, *gambling!* Knowledgeable gamblers can calculate the exact odds for and against a particular sequence of dice or a particular card turning up and wager accordingly.

Although the odds always favor the bank, at least these gamblers do have a chance. Even if you put your shirt on a three-legged horse that starts at 20:1 and is likely to come in at half past three, you have a chance–at least in theory. And *one* fly has to get there first, which is an even-money bet. So in theory a gambler always has a chance? Don't bet on it! There are so-called "gambling" games in which the chances of winning are about as remote as meeting fairies at the bottom of your garden and the "con" game described below, *le jeu des gobelets* (also known as the cup game, the shell game, and balletje balletje or little ball little ball), is a prime example.

Left: *The smaller the ball, the easier it is to conceal it between your fingers. The* shell game, *as it became known in* America, was often played with a small ball and with walnut shells instead of cups.

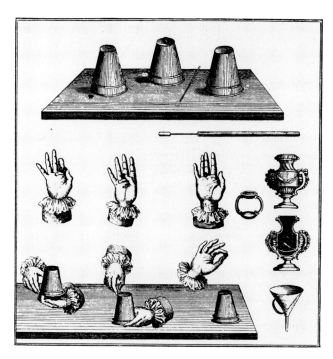

How to Play Le Jeu des Gobelets

Three cups, a little ball, practice, and a lot of nerve, and you are all set to make your fortune. "Roll up, ladies and gentlemen, find the ball and double your money!" You show the ball under one of the cups and swish them about a few times, meanwhile distracting the onlookers with convincing thief's patter. "You, Sir, you look like a good sport, find the ball and double your money!" Your "assistant" (for it is he!) has no problem whatsoever in finding the ball. Nor has he any problem finding it the second time around. By now, the assembled crowd will be fighting to force hard-earned money into your eager hand and slavering over the prospect of taking you to the cleaners. Fools, fools all of them! "Try again, Sir? Double your stakes? Why not?" After ten minutes of this, it probably is prudent to make an excuse and leave before some irate and baffled gambler—his next month's rent money is now residing in your back pocket—realizes that there is something fishy about the whole business and decides to give you a facelift. What you know, and what we know, and what the disillusioned gambler is beginning to suspect, is that the ball isn't under any of the cups at all and never was! You are, in fact, hiding it in the little pocket formed where two of your fingers meet the palm of your hand. But people fall for this kind of trick all the time, they do, they really do.

People of all ages and all walks of life have been playing games since time immemorial. *Plus ça change, plus c'est la même chose!*–the more things change, the more they stay the same! Whether it is in a bar, at home, at school, on a bus or on a train, it is an odds-on bet that you will find people playing one game or another. The pencil and paper games de-scribed below are easy to play wherever you are, be-cause they need no equipment except paper and pen-cil. What child has not at least once in his life used one of these games to while away the time during a boring lesson at school? However, these pencil and paper games are also played by adults–with dice, for amusement *and* profit–in bars and cafés.

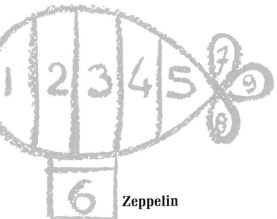

Zeppelin

Each player draws a Zeppelin and num-bers the compartments. Two dice are thrown and the numbers used sep-arately or in total to cross out com-partments. *For example:* with a throw of 3:5, the player can cross out compart-ments 3 and 5, or compartment 8. When the remaining numbers total 6 or less, only one die is thrown. A player conti-nues to throw until he can no longer cross out a compartment. The total re-maining is added to his score and the next player has his turn. Play is to an agreed number of points or turns of play. The loser buys the drinks!

Jule

Any number can play. You need a dice cup, a die and paper and pencil for each player. Each player throws the die in turn, the one throwing highest begins. Play proceeds in a clockwise direction. The first player attempts to throw a 1. If he fails it is the next player's turn. If he succeeds, he writes down "1" and throws again, this time trying for a 2. The object of the game is to throw 1, 2, 3... to 6 and 6, 5, 4... back to 1. A player continues to throw until he fails to throw the required number. When a player returns to 1 he drops out. The loser is the last person in the game.

The Pig Game

A race game that is played with two dice. The pig is drawn as follows:
(1) the body, (2) the snout, (3) the ears, (4) the tail, (5) the legs. The required throws are (in the same order) 9, 8, 7, 7, 6, 1, 1, 1 and 1. A 1:1 can be used to draw two legs.

Left: Children in Asia enjoying both a full-house type of gambling game and the attentions of the photographer.

Full House

Full House is played with three dice. Players must throw 1, 2, 3, etc. to 12, again 12 and then 11, 10, 9, etc. back to 1. Any die or combination of two or three dice counts. A player continues to throw until he can no longer move further, at which point the dice pass to the player on his left. For example, a throw of 1:3:5 can be used to form 1, 3, 4, 5, 6, 8 or 9. If a player fails to see some usable combination, players on his left have the right to claim it if they need it, preference being given to the first player, then the second and so on.

Duiven melken
(Milking the Pigeons)

This is an old Dutch country game. A cup, two dice and a field (see the diagram) are required. Each player rolls one die, lowest begins and play proceeds clockwise. An agreed stake is placed on the number corresponding to the total shown on the dice–as long as that number is open. If it is not open, the player takes the stake lying there and adds it to his cache. He continues to throw until he throws an open number. Different rules apply to numbers 2, 7 and 12. A players who throws 7 must place the agreed stake, whether the number is open or not. A player throwing 2 takes all stakes except those on 7 and 12. A player throwing 12 takes all the stakes, but he must throw again. If he now throws 2 or 12, he places the agreed stake on *every* number! Players drop out of the game when their initial stake has been lost.

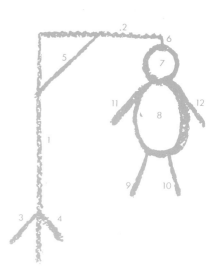

Hangman

This is another simple race game and can be played in the same way as the bug game. A variation is to draw the gallows and unfortunate victim in order following the numbers in the diagram. One die is used until the numbers 1 to 6 have been thrown, thereafter two dice are used. Each player has a pencil and paper and the last to complete his figure is the victim who buys the next round.

The Bug Game

Each player chooses a number from 1 to 6 (no two players have the same number). Players throw in turn. Each time a player's number is thrown, by himself or any other player, he draws one part of the bug on his paper. A player completing the 13 parts of his bug drops out. Last man in loses.

Knucklebones (Jacks)

Below left: *Two children enjoying a game of* knucklebones *in the Tunisian sunshine.*
Below middle: *These bronze knucklebones were made in the Netherlands in the early 19th century.*
Below right: La joueuse d'osselets, *an 18th-century engraving by Chardin.* Knucklebones *demands dexterity and a keen eye.*

Knucklebones were originally just that–the knucklebones of sheep. In ancient Greece they were known as *astralogoi* and used to prophesy the future. They were also used as gambling dice and, most frequently, for playing the game that is still known today as knucklebones. We know from paintings on amphora (vases) that the game was played by both the gods and mortals, and similar games are mentioned in the writings of Homer. The invention of knucklebones has been attributed to Palamedes who, according to legend, taught the game to Greek soldiers during the Trojan Wars. This is most unlikely, for what little evidence there is points to Asia as the place where the game originated.

Knucklebones were also much in vogue among the Romans. A fresco discovered in the ruins of Pompeii depicts a basic and ancient knucklebone game. The player tosses all five bones into the air and tries to catch them on the back of this hand. Then he throws them up again and catches them in his palm. The Romans introduced knucklebones to many countries during the course of their military campaigns. Yet the game is also traditional in parts of the world as far apart as the Soviet Union and the islands of the South Pacific, places the Romans had never even heard of let alone visited. Knucklebones has survived through the centuries and it is as popular today as it was thousands of years ago.

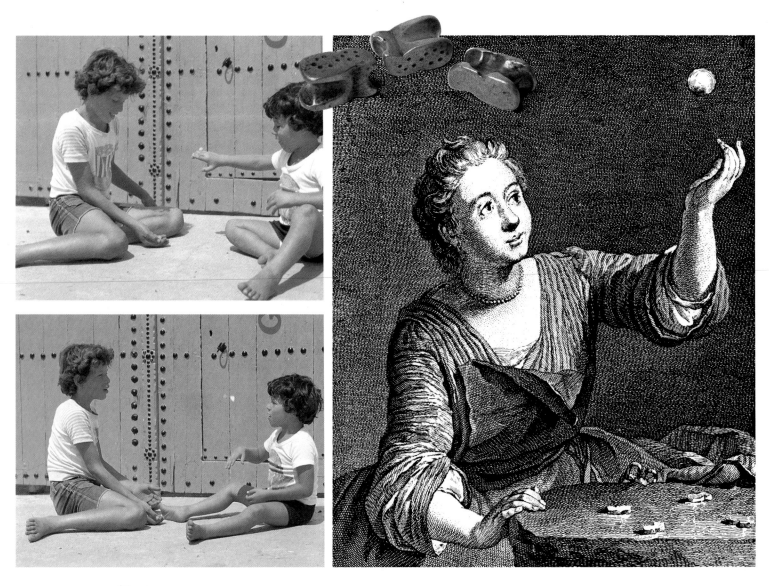

How to Play Knucklebones

Although knucklebones were used for divination in the ancient world, the modern game is basically a children's dexterity game. It can be played by any number of players, but interest is liable to flag if there are more than four. In the game, the players perform various "figures"–throws and catches of the bones–in a particular sequence. The names of the figures may differ from country to country (or even from region to region within a country) but most of the throwing and catching movements are the same throughout the world.

To begin the game, each player in turn tosses all five knucklebones into the air and tries to catch as many as possible on the back of his hand. He then throws these up and catches them in his palm. The score each player obtains determines the order of play in succeeding figures.

Ones   The first player throws the knucklebones on the ground. He picks up one of them, which is then known as the *jack*. He tosses the jack into the air, picks up one of the other bones from the ground, and catches the jack as it falls. He transfers the picked-up bone to his free hand and throws the jack again. The procedure is repeated

until all the knucklebones have been picked up. Should a player drop a bone, miss the jack or move a bone inadvertently, he is out and the next player takes his turn. When a player succeeds in picking up and holding all four bones in one turn of play, he goes on to "twos," when the bones must be picked up two at a time. When this has been achieved, he attempts to pick up first three bones and then one and finally he tries to pick up all four bones at the same time.

Under the Arch   The player throws the bones to the ground. He forms an arch by placing his forefinger and thumb downward on the ground near the knucklebones. He tosses the jack into the air and while it is in the air the flicks one of the bones through the arch, catching the jack as it falls. This movement is repeated until all the bones have been flicked through the arch. If the player succeeds, he goes on to twos, threes and fours.

Stables   Stables is a variation of under the arch. The player places his spread fingertips on the ground to form four "stables." As the jack is in the air, one bone is flicked into each stable in turn. When this has been achieved, the bones must be picked out again one by one.

Toad in the Hole   This is a similar figure to stables. The player makes a "hole" by placing one hand on the ground with the tip of his forefinger against the tip of his thumb. At each throw he must flick a bone through the hole. When all four bones have been successfully flicked, the "hole" is removed and all four bones picked up at once.

Jump the Ditch   In this game four of the bones are placed in a line a few inches apart. On the first throw of the jack the player must pick up the first and third bones. On the second throw he must pick up the remaining two.

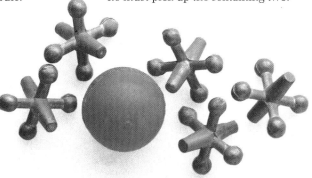

Right: *A set of star-shaped knuckle-bones.*

How to Make
Your Own Dice Collection

a) Walnut-shell dice (used by women of the Paiute tribe, Nevada, for a gambling game).
Fill eight half walnut shells with hobby clay. Press fragments of colored plastic into the clay while it is still soft. Leave to harden.

b) Split cane dice (used in *shóliwe*, a highly complex divination game, of the Zuni Indians of New Mexico). Split two 22 cm (8¾ in) lengths of cane and sand the flat sides smooth. The cross patterns are burned in with a heated knife and the holes made with a 1 mm (¹⁄₁₆ in) drill. The first has a pattern at one end only, the second at both ends, the third in the middle only and the fourth at both ends and the middle.

c) An ivory log die, used by gamblers in the United States. It is eight-sided and holes are drilled in each side in the following order: 1, 5, 3, 7, 8, 4, 6, 2.

d) A five-sided die for the Korean game of *tjyong-kyeng-to.* Notches are cut in the edges in numerical order: 1, 2, 3, 4, 5.

e) Flat, brightly painted pebbles were often used as dice and sometimes for divinatory purposes. Use acrylic paint and varnish the finished dice.

f) Long stick dice (used by the Tepehuan Indians of Chihuahua, Mexico). Four 45 cm (18 in) lengths of 5 mm x 2 cm (³⁄₁₆ in x ¹³⁄₁₆ in) softwood are painted and decorated as in the photograph. The crisscross patterns are burned in with a hot knife or a soldering iron.

g) Chair-shaped dice (used by the Haida and Kwakiutl tribes of British Columbia). If the die landed on its side, the throw was lost and the turn passed to the next player. If it landed in any of the other four possible positions the player won counters from his opponent. The dice are cut from cedar blocks 3 x 3 x 7 cm (1³⁄₁₆ x 1³⁄₁₆ x 2¹³⁄₁₆ in) with a scroll saw, and then sanded and varnished.

h) Flat wooden dice (used in a bowl game by the Zunis of New Mexico). Cut five 4 cm x 3 cm (1⁵⁄₈ in x 1³⁄₁₆ in) rectangles of 4 mm (¹⁄₈ in) plywood. The lines which form the patterns are cut with a tenon saw. Paint black and varnish.

i) Curved wooden dice (used by the Bellacoola Indians of British Columbia). Almost identical dice made of beaver teeth were widely used.
The dice are cut from 5 cm x 9 cm (2 in x 3⁵⁄₈ in) rectangles of 4 mm (¹⁄₈ in) plywood using a scroll saw. Sand smooth and paint black. The patterns are burned in with a special attachment for a soldering iron (see How to Make Seega, pages 122/123).

j) Stick dice (used by the Chippewa Indians of Minnesota).

Four 45 cm (18 in) lengths of 8 mm x 1½ cm (⁵⁄₁₆ in x ⁵⁄₈ in) softwood are roughly tapered at both ends with a rasp or hobby knife. They are then burned black on both sides with a gas burner. The set comprises two pairs of dice. One pair is patterned with four sets of double diagonal lines, cut with a handsaw. The other pair with four crosses and a 1 cm (³⁄₈ in)-wide band across the middle. The backs of the sticks are unpatterned.

k) Stick dice (used by the Shoshoni Indians of Idaho).
The stick dice were made from grooved box boards, which were a substitute for

split canes. The sticks measure 5 mm x 1 cm (³⁄₁₆ in x ³⁄₈ in) in cross section and are 25 cm (10 in) in length. Each stick is identically marked by two burned transverse marks near each end.

l) Wooden dice plus an instrument for tossing them (used by the Zunis of New Mexico). The dice are 3 cm x 3.4 cm (1³⁄₁₆ in x 1⁵⁄₁₆ in) rectangles of 4 mm (¹⁄₈ in) plywood painted red and black. The tossing peg is cut from a 2.5 cm x 9 cm (1 in x 3⁵⁄₈ in) rectangle of the same material.

m) These are Turkish fortune-telling dice. They are marked on four sides with two, three and four dots. The dowel rod on which they revolve passes through the center of the unmarked sides. The two ends are cut from softwood with a hobby knife and rasp.

Card Games

Left: *This painting by the Spanish painter Bartolomé Esteban Murillo (1618-1682) shows children playing a variety of simple games. Murillo was particularly well-known for his paintings of the street children of Seville.*

Below: *These men are deeply involved in a game using Chinese stick cards. Originally, these cards had three elements: the titles of officials in ranking order, a literary quotation, and a drinking instruction. The values of the cards appeared in the form of monetary units, thus giving them the name of money cards. The titles and drinking instructions have disappeared, but the quotations and the values still exist.*

"Cards, whether we consider them as mere merchandise or as the bond which unites people with one another, are extremely important in a state. Just think of what we would be if we had no cards! How boring and unsociable is the life of those who have to do without this invention!" This was written as long ago as 1776, in the German journal *Burgerfreund,* but in the period of more than 200 years that has since passed cards have lost none of their popularity.

According to Detlef Hoffmann's *The Playing Card* (first published in 1972 in Germany by Edition Leipzig under the title *Die Welt der Spielkarte*), "An 11th-century source reports that the game of cards appeared in the middle of the Tang period, i.e. in the 7th or 8th centuries, and that 'a certain Yang Tan-ien greatly esteemed the playing of cards.' " This seems to indicate that cards originated in China, but the history of playing cards begins, in fact, long before the 7th or 8th century, with the sticks and arrows that were used in an earlier form of divination. Games expert Stewart Culin has pointed out that the arrow shafts once used for fortune-telling in Korea bore painted emblems

denoting their rank; in time these symbols were copied, first onto gambling sticks, then onto narrow strips of oiled paper, and the result was a stylized pack of playing cards. Later Chinese cards of the same shape, called stick cards bear figures whose resemblance to those on our present court cards is remarkable. The world's oldest known playing card found in Chinese Turkestan is of this type and dates to the 11th century.

Although European playing cards seem to have undergone a separate evolution, there are a number of similarities between the (Western) playing cards we know and traditional Asian cards. For example, the Hindu deity Ardhanari is often depicted holding a cup, a scepter, a sword and a ring, and this combination suggests that the four suits of the European tarot pack–cups, batons, swords and coins–may have an Indian ancestry. Some authorities have credited the gypsies (originally an Indian nomad caste) with having brought cards to Europe, but they did not arrive in appreciable numbers until the middle of the 15th century, more than a hundred years after cards had come into general use throughout the continent.

We will probably never know exactly how and when cards were introduced in Europe, but the most probable theory is that they were brought there by the Arabs who invaded Spain and Sicily. This theory was advanced by the Italian historian Covelluzo in 1480 (*Istoria della citta Viterbo*, "History of the city of Viterbo") and also by the Italian scholar Salvini, who wrote about cards in the first decade of the 18th century. Another fact that supports this theory is that in the old sources, playing cards were called *naibi* and it is generally thought that this can be attributed to Saracen origins. Indeed, in the only early pack of cards from the Arab world there is a card with the name *naib*. Cards are called *naipes* in Spain and *naibi* in

Italy and we can safely assume that these terms are all derived from the Arabic *nabi*(prophet).

The first reliable evidence that cards were played in Europe dates from 1376. A decree of the city of Florence, Italy, forbids the playing of a game called *naibbe* and it is said there that this game had been recently introduced. Cards are mentioned in various documents of the decades following this date and many of them are government or Church decrees banning card games. (In 1423, St. Bernardino of Siena, on the steps of the church of San Petronio in Bologna, preached against games in general and against the playing of card games in particular.)

But Europe was not the only place where cards were seen as an "invention of the devil." There is a record of various people being punished for playing cards in

Above: *This set of delicately colored poetry cards dates from the 19th century and was made in Japan. These sets of cards were usually kept in beautifully lacquered and inlaid boxes such as the one shown here.*

Right above: Card-playing soldiers *by the French artist Fernand Léger (1881-1955) was painted in 1917. Léger was noted for his depictions of "man as a machine."*

Right middle: *This photograph of children playing cards in the sand was taken in Burkina Faso (Upper Volta) in West Africa.*

Right below: *On the other side of the world, these men in Peking are also enjoying a game of cards in the open air.*

66

the America of 1633. Did the Pilgrim Fathers really have playing cards in their luggage? It has been suggested that some disreputable Dutchman or a godless Englishman might have brought them. This is not known but what is certain, is that the manufacture of playing cards in America only began in the second half of the 18th century. These were very similar to the English/French type of playing cards.

Very little is known about early European playing cards. Playing cards, as objects subject to use, are usually thrown away when they are unserviceable. Some 15th-century cards have been preserved but only because paper was so expensive in that time that bookbinders used printed sheets of playing cards, i.e., printing waste, for the making of the bindings. In the course of restoration of old bookbindings, uncut sheets and, more rarely, also individual cards have been found in them. These findings–Italian, German and French cards–have shown that the type of playing cards used then has remained virtually unchanged to the present day. The four suits of early German cards were hearts, bells, leaves, and acorns. Spain and Italy retained the old division into cups, batons, swords and coins. French cards of the 16th century, however, introduced the marks still current in France and the English-speaking world: *coeur* (hearts), *trèfle* (clubs), *pique* (spades) and *carreau* (diamonds).

Most of the European cardmakers of the 17th, 18th and 19th centuries worked for a prosperous public. Cards were handpainted, printed from woodblocks or copper engravings. The oldest cards known to us were painted by artists specializing in miniatures. These are cards that were painstakingly made and so expensive that only very wealthy people could afford them.

It was the invention of xylography that first made it possible for cards to be manufactured in large numbers. The many sets that came from the workshops were so cheap that even poor people could buy them. Nowadays, the playing card is the product of a highly specialized industry. The cards are mostly machine-printed by the offset process in great quantities. Most modern playing cards are made of wood-free cardboard, but it is not absolutely necessary for playing cards to be made of this material. Any thin, stiff piece of material can be used as a playing card. In Europe there are also cards made of metal with fabric stretched over them, of leather, and of varnished wood. In India, there are cards of ivory, of stiffened fabric, and, more rarely, of costly tortoiseshell or mother-of-pearl. The leather cards of the North American Indians are also famous.

The conventional deck of 52 cards is the one most used in the games world of today. This standard deck or pack contains four suits identified by its symbol, or pip: spades (♠), hearts (♥), diamonds (♦), clubs (♣). There are 13 cards of each suite: ace (A), king (K), queen (Q), jack (J), 10, 9, 8, 7, 6, 5, 4, 3, 2. Packs of less than 52 cards are usually formed by stripping cards out of the standard deck. The various depleted packs may then be defined by the total of the cards remaining.

The annals of gamesplay contain an almost limitless selection of card games. On the following pages we describe a number of these games, combining luck and skill in varying degrees. In some, the skill and experience of the player are of paramount importance, while in others, winning or losing is only a matter of luck, or, as in a number of solitaire games, of patience.

Games Played with a 32-card Deck

Skat

Skat originated near Leipzig, in what is now the German Democratic Republic, around 1845. It was very popular, so much so that in the last two decades of the 19th century, a Skat League was flourishing in Germany. Even now it still is a leading café-bar game in that country and among German-speaking ethnic minorities in central European countries. German emigrants carried the game to many other countries, where they won numerous converts for it. An American Skat League was established in 1898 in St. Louis. Played at its highest level, skat is one of the most skilful and interesting of all card games.

How to Play Skat

Skat is one of the many games of what may be regarded as the Euchre family in which the object is to take tricks and in which one suit is nominated as the trump suit. The player who leads can play any card he likes, but the others are forced to follow suit, unless they have no such card–when they are free to discard a poor card or play a trump. The trick is won by the highest card of the suit led, unless a trump has been played. The winner of a trick keeps the three cards it contains face down in front of him, and leads to the next trick.

A 32-card deck is used (a standard 52-card deck, from which the cards below seven have been removed). The suits rank downward: clubs, spades, hearts and diamonds. The order of the cards is: A, 10, K, Q, 9, 8, 7 (seven cards). The four jacks are always part of the trump suit and they rank in the same suit order. Thus, the ranking order of the trump suit is: J of clubs, J of spades, J of hearts, J of diamonds, A, 10, K, Q, 9, 8, 7 (11 cards).

Skat is a game for three, four or five people, but only three play on any one deal. If four players are involved, the dealer gets no cards. If five people play, the dealer and the third player to his left remain out of the hand. To determine the dealer for the first hand, cards are dealt out one at a time, one to each player. The first person to get a jack is the dealer. Dealer shuffles and the opponent to dealer's right cuts. Dealer deals 10 cards to each player, clockwise starting with the player on his left: three cards to each player, then two to the *skat* (also known as *blind* or *widow*) in the center of the table, then four cards each, then three. The deal moves round to the left on subsequent hands. The person to dealer's left is called *forehand* or *leader,* next comes *middlehand,* and finally *endhand.*

The Bidding

The objective of the bidding is to win the right to name the game that will be played.

Each bid names merely a number of points, without specifying the intended trumps or game. The lowest possible bid is 10. It is customary to bid up in twos–10, 12, 14, and so on. The size of the bid depends on the player's estimation of the points that can be won by various types of play and by holding–or capturing–certain cards. (For the values, see under Scoring.) If someone else eventually gets to name the game then there is no obligation on the bidder. And if the bidder who becomes the declarer makes a higher score than the bid there is no problem–he scores the higher number.

Middlehand is the first to bid. If he chooses to pass, it is endhand's turn to bid. If both middlehand and endhand pass, leader is obliged to name the game and play the hand. If middlehand bids, the response comes from leader, who says "Yes," if he feels he can equal or exceed middlehand's bid. The latter then has to increase his bid. This continues until one of them decides to pass, at which time endhand enters the bidding against the survivor. He who finally wins the right to name the game is then called *player* (who is contracted to score the number of points he has bid), and the other two become the *opponents.*

The Skat

The player begins by deciding if he wishes to pick up the two cards that form the skat. If he picks up the skat, he must then discard any two cards from his hand. These discards will eventually count towards his final score . (One does not always discard "junk." It is often sensible to put high-point cards into the skat, especially 10s, which are unlikely to win tricks but count heavily when time comes to add up the score.)

If he does not pick up, this is referred to as "handplay" or playing "in hand." The skat is then set aside for the duration of play. At the end of the hand, the fate of the skat depends on the game that has been played.

Naming the Game

The player can choose to play with or without a trump suit, with or without using the skat, or choose to use only the four jacks as trump. He can contract to win all of the tricks in process of achieving the score he has bid, or he can contract to win no tricks at all. And he can attempt various combinations of the aforementioned propositions. Whatever plan he chooses has a specific name and is worth a specific number of points. If he succeeds, the final value of his hand is based on that established value, multiplied by other values that are derived from the kinds of cards held and captured and the number of tricks taken.

The Basic Games

Tournée (known in the United States as *second turn*): The player looks at the top card of the skat, concealing it from his opponents. If he likes the suit, he displays it to identify trump, then puts it into his hand with the other skat card (which he keeps concealed). If he dislikes the suit of the first card, he puts it in his hand without exposing it. He then must turn up the second skat card, which establishes trump. (This game costs the player double penalties if he fails to make his bid.) Having picked up the skat cards, the player discards any two cards from his hand. They are later used in calculating his score.

If the exposed skat card is a jack, the player may play *grand tournée,* with only the four jacks as trumps.

Solo: Without looking at the skat the player names a trump suit. He plays the hand in that suit, without using the

Above: *Six examples of hand-painted ganjifa, the traditional playing cards of India. Whereas the typical form for playing cards in the West is rectangular, playing cards in India are usually round.*

Above right: *Although the Chinese have always been famous for their love of gambling, this game in Canton is played purely for pleasure in much the same way as skat in Germany or hearts in America.*

skat. However, the skat cards will be included in his score. The player also may choose to play *grand solo,* with only the jacks as trumps and without using or looking at the skat cards.

Guckser (also known as *gucki grand*): The player picks up both skat cards at once. After the discards, play proceeds as in all *grand* games, with only the four jacks as trumps.

Nullo: When declaring *nullo* or *null,* the player contracts to lose all the tricks without looking at the skat. There is no trump suit and the four suits each have eight cards: ace, king, queen, jack, 10, 9, 8, 7, in that order. The hand stops immediately if declarer takes a trick–he has lost.

Ouvert: Before the opening lead, player exposes his hand and contracts either to win all the tricks with the four jacks as trump *(grand ouvert)* or to lose all the tricks *(null ouvert).*

Ramsch: When middlehand and endhand do not bid, the hand must be played by leader. He may choose this

game, which plays like a grand, with only the four jacks as trumps. The object is to win no tricks. Skat cards are not used in play, but go to whoever wins the last trick of the hand. In another version of skat, ramsch is played only when all three participants refuse to make a bid. Each plays for himself and tries to take in as few points as possible.

Grand: In all games called *grand,* the four jacks are the only trumps.

Bidding and Playing Strategy
When bidding, one should not count on too much from the skat. With a declaration of tournée in mind a hand should at least contain one jack to be considered biddable–in which case the other nine cards should be divided evenly among three suits. With two jacks, two-card suits in all four denominations are acceptable (as is one three-card suit, two two-card suits and a singleton). For solo, a five-card suit is considered essential. Side cards should include two aces, or the ace-king of one suit and the 10 of another. With two jacks and two aces or any four cards made up of jacks and aces, the leader may consider declaring a grand. In other positions, it is best to have a total of five such cards.
When playing with a solid trump holding, it is very important to flush out the opponents' trumps by leading one's own. If the trump holding is less impressive, it is usually wise to force out the opponents' trump winners early by leading one's own low ones.

Scoring
The value of the cards

Ace	= 11 points
10	= 10 points
King	= 4 points
Queen	= 3 points
Jack	= 2 points
9, 8, and 7	= 0 points

This makes a total of 120 points in one pack. The object of the game is to capture half of these card points in tricks. Declarer needs 61 points to win, defenders 60 to beat him. (The skat cards count as part of the declarer's tricks.) Note that the jacks, which are the most powerful cards for winning tricks, are not in themselves worth many points.

The basic value of the games

Tournée

with diamonds as trumps	5 points
with hearts as trumps	6 points
with spades as trumps	7 points
with clubs as trumps	8 points

Solo

with diamonds as trumps	9 points
with hearts as trumps	10 points
with spades as trumps	11 points
with clubs as trumps	12 points

Grand

tournée	12 points
guckser	16 points
solo	20 points
ouvert	24 points
ramsch	10 points

Null

simple	20 points
ouvert	40 points

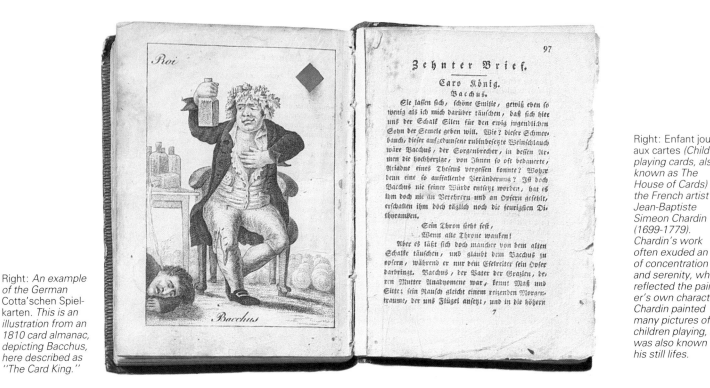

Right: *An example of the German* Cotta'schen Spiel-karten. *This is an illustration from an 1810 card almanac, depicting Bacchus, here described as ''The Card King.''*

Right: Enfant jouant aux cartes *(Child playing cards, also known as The House of Cards) by the French artist Jean-Baptiste Simeon Chardin (1699-1779). Chardin's work often exuded an air of concentration and serenity, which reflected the paint-er's own character. Chardin painted many pictures of children playing, but was also known for his still lifes.*

Penalties and Errors

The slightest deviation from the rules can cause havoc in a game as complex as this. Therefore, punishment can be harsh.

When playing tour-née, failure to show the second skat card before putting it in the hand costs the player a 100-point loss of game. Anyone who acci-dentally looks at the skat before quali-fying to do so is fined 10 points. And if the player playing solo looks at the skat, he loses im-mediately, unless the opponents require him to conti-nue play so they can amass points. A player's failure to follow suit costs him the game. But no player can win because of an error made by an oppo-nent. Revokes and all other errors by opponents must be corrected, even if portions of the hand must be replayed.

The Multipliers

The point value of each game has to be computed for scoring as well as bidding purposes. Except when nullo or ramsch is being played, the score for a fulfilled contract is arrived at by adding the applicable multipliers (which always total at least two, because of the inevi-table matador and game credits), and then multiplying the basic game value by the total multiplier. The multiplier depends mostly on the number of the top trumps the player holds, but va-rious bonuses have been added.

At nullo, no multipliers are used. For that reason, a player who bids more than 20 is forbidden to declare nullo. If he has bid more than 40, he may not declare null ouvert. When playing ramsch, the player taking the fewest points is the winner and gets 10 points. If he has taken no tricks at all, he gets 20 points.

In case all three players tie, the leader gets 10. If a player has taken all tricks, he loses 30 points.

Matadors: If player holds the jack of clubs (the highest trump), he is ''with'' as many matadors–or multipliers–as he holds trumps, in sequence from the J of clubs down. If player does not hold the jack of clubs, he is ''without'' as many matadors as the trumps he is missing, in sequence from the J of clubs down.

Schneider: Player makes schneider when he takes 90 or more card points in his tricks and this achievement mul-tiplies his score, as shown in the table below.

Schwarz: To win all the tricks is to score schwarz or *grand slam*. For the multi-plier, see the table below.

Announcing: Before the opening lead, player may multiply his potential win-nings (or penalties) by announcing that he expects to score schneider or schwarz.

Value of the multipliers

Making game (61 to 90 points)	1 point
Schneider without announcement	2 points
Schneider announced and made	3 points
Schwarz without announcement	3 points
Schneider announced, schwarz made	4 points
Schwarz announced and made	5 points
Each matador, ''with'' or ''without''	1 point

Other scoring

If a player makes his contract and the full value of his game equals or ex-ceeds his bid he scores that full value. If a player does not make the necessary points for game, he loses the basic value of the game. The penalty is doubled at guckser or tournée. If the player fulfills his declaration yet amasses fewer points than his bid, he loses whatever multiple of his declared game's basic value exceeds his bid. For example: the player has declared a heart solo and has bid 22. The 72 points he has taken in high cards are enough for game, and he is ''with'' one mata-dor. Thus, his game is worth 20–not enough. His penalty is computed by multiplying the basic value of his de-clared game (10 for heart solo) by whatever number it takes to exceed his bid. This means multiplying 10 by 3, because 30 is the first multiple of 10 that exceeds the bid of 22. The penalty, therefore, is 30.

At guckser or tournée, it would be doubled: −60.

Melds (Sequences) Three or more cards of the same suit and in sequence have potential scoring value. In *klaberjass,* such a sequence is called a *meld.* The player with the highest meld scores the points. For the purposes of sequence, all suits rank downward: ace, king, queen, jack, 10, 9, 8, 7. A trump meld outranks one in a side suit. A sequence of three cards scores 20, four cards or more scores 50. To settle the issue, nondealer declares first. If he has no meld, he says ''No meld'' or ''May I lead?'' Dealer gives the appropriate reply, ''Lead'' if he has no melds in his hand, or ''No'' if he does. In the latter case, dealer declares his points. If nondealer does have one or more sequences he names the point value of his best one. If this beats the dealer's best, dealer says ''Good.'' If dealer holds a meld of higher value, he says ''No good'' and makes a declaration of his own. If the matter is in doubt, dealers asks ''How high?'' Nondealer then reveals the rank of his sequence's highest card and if another question is asked, he discloses whether the sequence is in trumps. The player with the highest sequence scores the point for this and any other sequence he holds. He must expose his sequence(s) after the first trick has been played. The opponent who holds the inferior meld scores nothing, but he does not have to show his meld; nor is a player obliged to show a meld he does not wish to receive point credits for.

Klaberjass

Klaberjass is known by various names and spellings: clabber, kob, klab, clubby, Indiana clobber, etc. Its origin has been variously claimed by the Dutch, Hungarians, Swiss, and French, but two facts point to the Hungarians as the most likely candidates: first, klaberjass means ''jack of clubs,'' which used to be the highest trump card in central European card games; second, the game first became popular in Jewish ''goulash joints'' (card rooms) in Hungary. Two-handed klaberjass is almost identical with the popular French game belotte.

How to Play Klaberjass

For two players, a 32-card deck is used. In the trump suit, the cards rank as follows: jacks, 9, ace, 10, king, queen, 8, 7. The jack of trumps is known as the *boss* or *jass,* the nine of trumps is called *menel* and the seven of trumps is called *dix.* In the other suits they rank: A, 10, king, queen, jack, 9, 8, 7. Players cut for the deal and the player who draws the lower card becomes the dealer for the first hand. Thereafter, the deal alternates. The dealer shuffles the cards and offer them to his opponent to cut. He then deals six cards to his opponent and himself, three at a time. The next card of the pack is turned face up and placed partly underneath it. This is the so-called trump card.

The Bidding Dealer's opponent declares first. He has three choices: he can say *take,* thereby accepting the exposed card as trump and becoming trump *maker.* He can declare *schmeiss,* which means he is proposing to abandon the deal. If his proposal is accepted, the cards are thrown in. If it is refused, the *schmeisser* is obliged to be the trump maker and the exposed card establishes trump. And he can say *pass,* whereupon dealer becomes the bidder and can choose to declare take, schmeiss, or pass. If both players pass, the first bidder (non-dealer) may name any other suit as trumps, or he may pass again. In the latter case, dealer has the same options. If both pass a second time, the deal is abandoned.

After the trump suit is decided, dealer gives a batch of three more cards to each hand. By custom, he then turns the bottom card of the pack face up. (Thus, two cards not in play are known

to both players; these two cards often influence the playing strategy.) If the exposed card has been accepted as trumps, a player who has the *dix* may exchange it for the trump card, thereby obtaining a higher trump. He may not make this exchange after playing to the first trick.

Object of the game The object of the game is to try and score 300 or 500 points (as agreed beforehand) before your opponent does. This is done by scoring points for melds (see margin) in the hand and by winning tricks which possess point value (see Scoring).

Regardless of who made trumps, nondealer makes the opening lead. He may play any card he chooses. His opponent must follow suit. If he is not able to do so, he must trump if he can. If a trump has been led, he must play a higher trump if he can. A trick is won by the higher trump, if any, or by the higher card of the suit led. The winner of the trick leads to the next.

Bella If a player holds the king and queen of trumps, he may score 20 for them by calling ''bella'' on playing the second of the two. The call is not obligatory, and indeed is omitted when this player sees that he is going to lose.

Scoring The object of play is to win specific cards rather than tricks as such. But winning the last trick called *stich* scores 10 points. High cards won in tricks count as follows:

Jass	20 points
Menel	14 points
Each ace	11 points
Each ten	10 points
Each king	4 points
Each queen	3 points
Each jack	2 points

At the end of play, each player counts what he has taken in tricks, together with any due score for stich, meld and bella. If the trump maker scores a higher total, each player scores his total. If the totals are equal, only the opponent of the trump maker scores. If the trump maker has a lower total, he is *bête* and his opponent scores the sum of the two totals.

Fly from Spain

Three to six can play. If there are three people playing, a 32-card deck is used. If four play, four sixes are added to the deck, if five play, four sixes and four fives, and if six play, four sixes, four fives, and four fours are added. All face cards are worth ten points.

How to Play Fly from Spain

Players toss up to determine who will be the dealer. Each player is dealt five cards–first two, then three–and the remaining cards form the stock, which is placed face down in the middle of the table. The top card of the stock is exposed and this card indicates the trump suit.

The picture cards are worth 10 points in this game, the other cards retain their own value.
The object of the game is to make a ''fly,'' i.e., have five cards of the same suit, but if no one succeeds in making a fly, the hand is played for tricks, the object then being to collect as many points as is possible.

After the top card of the stock is exposed, a player may exchange any number of his cards for stock cards if he thinks it will improve his hand. If a player likes his hand so much that he does not want to exchange any of his cards, he announces that he ''plays.'' If, on the other hand, he feels his cards are so bad that even exchanging would not help sufficiently, he passes. In that case, his five cards are placed at the bottom of the stock.

The player should not automatically announce the fly the moment he has one, because it can be advantageous to wait until there is more money in the kitty (see below). The highest ranking fly wins; i.e., if there is a fly in the trump suit, it always beats the others; if there is no ''trump fly'' the one that contains the most points wins.

Each player in turn–every time he exchanges a card–decides how much he wants to wager on the basis of his hand. The betting continues until a fly is announced. If no one manages to compose a fly, the hand is played for tricks. The winner of the round is not the player who wins the most tricks, but the player who wins the most points. He gets the kitty.

Three-handed Klaberjass

The rules are the same as for the two-handed game, except that the player at the dealer's left is dealt to first and he is also the one who starts the bidding. Furthermore, the bidder must score more than both opponents combined. If he loses, opponents divide his points between them and each also scores whatever points he made on his own melds and play.

Four-handed Klaberjass

This is a good partnership game. The rules for the two-handed game apply, except that the turn to deal, bid, meld, and play passes to the left, beginning with the dealer's left. When one player establishes the best meld, his partner may also score for his meld(s). Partners keep their tricks and score together.

Swimming

1. This game is for three to nine players and a 32-card deck is used. Each player has three matches as his "starting capital" and the object is not to lose this capital.

2. After it is decided who will be the first dealer and the cards are shuffled, everyone is dealt three cards. The next three cards are placed face down on the table and the rest of the pack is put aside.

3. The dealer may now pick up the three cards from the table and, if he wishes, exchange them for his own cards, which are then placed face up on the table. However, if he prefers his own hand, he puts the cards back on the table, but face up this time.

4. The object of the exchange is to better the hand by collecting high cards of the same suit or cards of the same value in different suits. (For the scoring, see right.)

5. It is now the turn of the player to the left of the dealer (and after that, the player to the left of him, and so on) to decide whether to exchange his cards for those on the table (he may exchange one or three, but *not* two cards). He must place the cards he wants to exchange face up on the table before picking up the cards he needs.

6. The player who does not want to exchange any more cards knocks on the table. Now the other players all have one more chance to exchange, or knock on the table. After the last player has done this, everyone lays his cards down, face up on the table.

7. The player who has three aces, or one ace and two face cards in the same suit, should knock on the table immediately, and call out "fire." He has won the round and all the other players lose one match, which they place on the table.

8. If a player has two or three cards in the same suit, his score is the point value of these cards added up. A player who has three cards of the same value scores 30½ points. The player with the lowest score loses a match, which is placed on the table. If there is more than one player with the lowest score, they all lose a match.

Scoring for Swimming:

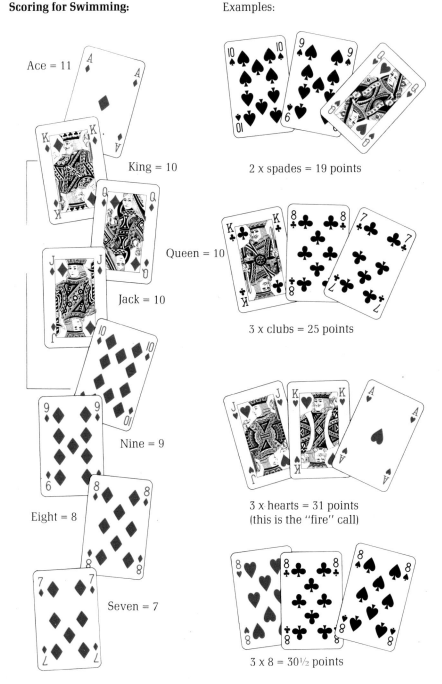

Ace = 11

King = 10

Queen = 10

Jack = 10

Nine = 9

Eight = 8

Seven = 7

Above: *Swimming or* Schwimmen *is an old German bar and tavern game, always accompa-* *nied by impressive quantities of good German beer, paid for by the losers.*

Examples:

2 x spades = 19 points

3 x clubs = 25 points

3 x hearts = 31 points (this is the "fire" call)

3 x 8 = 30½ points

9. The player who has lost his capital (all three matches) is "swimming." If he loses one more time, he is out of the game. The others continue to play until half of the players (or half + one, if an uneven number is playing) are out of the game.

10. And now the payoff: the losers pay for the next round. If there is an even number of players, this can be done fairly and squarely: each loser pays for one winner and for himself. If there is an uneven number of players, the last one out of the game is in luck: he only has to pay for himself.

Point value of the cards in Twenty-one

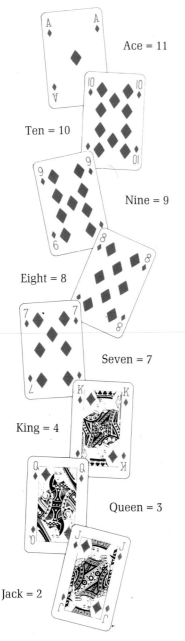

Ace = 11

Ten = 10

Nine = 9

Eight = 8

Seven = 7

King = 4

Queen = 3

Jack = 2

Twenty-one
(Blackjack)

1. A game played with a 32-card deck, for two to seven players.

2. One player is designated to be the banker. He shuffles the cards and deals to everyone, including himself, one card.

3. Each player looks at his card, decides on the amount of money he wants to wager, and puts this down in front of him on the table.

4. Each player may now ask the bank for one to four cards. The object is to collect exactly 21 points, or a point total as near to 21 as is possible. However, the player who ends up with more than 21 points is "dead"–his stake is appropriated by the banker. (For the point value of the cards, see left.)

5. When everyone has decided he has enough cards, the banker also picks up one to four cards. He calls his point total, and the number directly above it. For example: "20, 21 wins."

6. Each player lays down his cards in front of him so that the accounts can be settled.
a) If the banker has exactly 21 points, he gets the stake of the players who also have 21, and double the stake of the players who have less than 21 points.
b) If the banker has less than 21 points, the players who equal his score or have less must pay him their stake. The player who has more points than the banker gets double his stake from the banker.
c) If the banker has more than 21 points– which means he is "dead"–he has to pay all those still in the game twice the amount of their stake.

The Last Trick

1. This is a game for three to eight players. If three or four play, a 32-card deck is used, and for five to eight players two 32-card decks are used.

2. After it is decided who will deal first, the cards are shuffled and dealt one by one. If, at the end, there are not enough cards to give everyone his last card, the remaining cards are put aside.

Ranking order of the cards in the last trick:

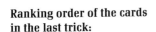

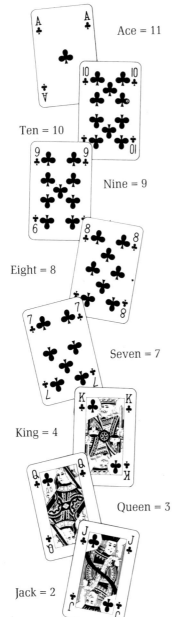

Ace = 11

Ten = 10

Nine = 9

Eight = 8

Seven = 7

King = 4

Queen = 3

Jack = 2

Right: The last trick is a very simple but original game, its most unusual aspect being the ranking order of the cards, Ace is high, jack low.

Six of nine hand-painted cards known as the "goldsmith" cards because of their gold-leaf back- *grounds. They were probably produced during the 15th century in Pro-vence, France. Apart from the five* *of "clubs" they all depict cryptic versions of the classic tarot trumps. From what we know we assume that the* *man with the dog represents the tarot "magician" and the crowned sea-monster, the devil.*

3. The player to the left of the dealer leads a card. The others have to follow suit and if they cannot do so may "dump" any card. There are no trumps in this game.

4. The player with the highest card in the suit led wins the trick. (For the ranking order of the cards, see left.)

5. The player who has won the trick leads to the next.

6. The player who wins the last trick has won the game and may stop playing. The others continue playing, until there is only one player in the

game left. Het is the big loser and... buys a round for everyone.

This simple but original game has confused many an experienced card player, because of the unusual ranking order of the cards and because it is not that easy to figure out how to win the last trick. It is wise to lead low in the beginning and keep the high cards for later. It also pays to think of a tactic by which the opponents' high cards are forced out as early in the game as possible. The fact that one is obliged to follow suit plays in important part in this.

Games Played with a 52-card Deck

Rikken

1. A game for four players, using a standard deck. Anyone can be the dealer and cards are dealt three, three, three, three and one. The dealer keeps his last card face down on the table until the bidding is finished. (For some games, this card will determine the trumps.) At the beginning of the game, the players each put an agreed number of their chips or counters in the pot–20, for example.

2. The ranking order of the cards is the usual one (ace, king, queen, jack, ten, etc.), except for the trump suit, were they rank downwards: jack, nine, ace, king, queen, ten, eight, seven, etc.

3. The player to the left of the dealer is the first to bid or pass. Next, it is the turn of the player to the left of him, and so on. The player who bids the highest ranking game wins the bidding.

4. Nine different games can be bid, all with different values. *Rik* has the lowest value, *open misère* the highest.

Rik   The player has to take at least five tricks. If he wins the bidding, he can form a partnership with one of the other players by asking for an ace "to go with him."

Example   The bid is "I rik, spades are trumps and ace of clubs goes with me." The player who holds the ace of clubs then takes the first trick won by the bidder, thereby indicating to the others that he is the bidder's partner. Together, the players have to take eight tricks to make rik.

Plus one   The player must take six tricks to win this game. He can, if he wishes, get himself a partner by asking for an ace. If played by two, nine tricks have to be made.

Troela   A player who holds three aces may bid troela. The player holding the fourth ace becomes his partner and he decides what will be trumps. If the player holds all four aces, he asks for a king "to go with him"; the owner of this king determines the trump suit. Eight tricks have to be won to make the game.

The Losers
The players who do not make the game they bid have to pay out exactly what they would have received if they had won.
Example: Avandans has been bid and the player has only made five tricks. He has to pay the pot 10 chips and each of the others 4 x 2 = 8 chips (two chips for every undertrick).

Pic   When bidding pic, the player commits himself to lose all but one trick. Pic is played without a trump suit.

Seven tricks   As can be deduced from the name, the bidder of this game has to win seven tricks. The player plays solo and the trump suit is determined by the last card the dealer gave himself.

Misère   Misery probably is an apt name for this game: the player may not win *any* tricks. There is no trump suit in misère.

Eight tricks   Also a solo, and eight tricks have to be made. The trump suit is determined by the dealer's last card.

Avandans   The player commits himself to win nine tricks. (Avandans is a corruption of the French word for abundance.) A solo game; trumps are determined by the dealer's last card.

Open misère   The highest ranking game. The player lays down his cards face up on the table as soon as the first card is led. As in misère, he may not win any tricks.

5. Scoring for Rikken:

Rik   The two players each receive two chips from the pot. If there are over-tricks, they each get two chips per trick from the opponents.

Troela   For making eight tricks, the players each receive four chips from the pot and four chips from the opposition for every overtrick.

Pic   If the player has succeeded in not winning more than one trick, the three others each have to pay him four chips.

Seven tricks   The winner of seven tricks receives four chips from the pot and two chips from each of the three other players for every overtrick.

Misère   The player receives six chips from each of the three others.

Eight tricks   The winner receives six chips from the pot and two chips from each of the other players for every overtrick.

Avandans   For winning nine tricks, the player gets 10 chips from the pot and two per overtrick from each of the opponents.

Open misère   The three opponents each have to pay the winner eight chips.

Hearts

This popular game evolved in the 19th century and since then many interesting variants have appeared. It is a non-partnership game that provides an opportunity for skill in the play of cards. It is the ultimate application of the *nullo* idea in games like euchre, whist, and skat (see page 68) in that it is based on the principle of not winning tricks. In fact, hearts may very well be the answer to people who often complain about their poor hands, for in this game the premium is on holding poor cards.

How to Play Hearts

1. Three to seven people can play, each playing solo. A standard deck is used. Twos are removed as follows: if three play, one black two is stripped from the deck, if five play, both black twos, if six or seven play, three twos are removed (the heart two is retained).

2. Cards are drawn and the player with the low card is the first dealer. He deals out all the cards one at a time and face down, beginning with the player on his left and going clockwise.

3. There is no bidding and no trump suit is used. The player to the dealer's left leads to the first trick. Thereafter the winner of one trick leads to the next. Players must follow suit it they can. If they cannot, they may play any card they like.

4. The object is to avoid winning any tricks that contain one or more hearts.

5. Each player scores one penalty point for each card of the heart suit contained in the tricks taken by him. The winner is the player with the fewest penalty points after an agreed number of hands.
Alternatively, the winner is the player with the fewest penalty points when one player reaches a set number of points (usually 50).

6. If a player revokes–i.e., fails to follow suit when he is able to–he may correct his mistake without penalty if he does so before the trick is picked up. Otherwise the penalty is severe: he scores all the penalty points in the hand: 13.

7. In one version of basic hearts, players are rewarded for taking all the hearts in the game. A player with a

Right: These photographs were all taken in the last years of the 19th century and depict North American Indians of three different tribes playing cards out in the open. Top: Apaches, 1884. Middle: Taos, 1898. Bottom: Havasvpai, Cataract Canyon, Arizona.

hand free or almost free of any losing tricks can be certain that he will not be able to avoid winning tricks and he may feel he has a good chance at "take-all." If he succeeds in winning all the tricks containing hearts, he is "clean" and has zero penalty points.

Two-handed Hearts

Using a full deck, 13 cards are dealt to each player; the remainder is placed face down as a stock. Nondealer leads. After each trick, the winner takes the top card from the stock and the loser takes the next. After the stock is gone, the final 13 tricks are played. Otherwise, the principles of basic hearts apply.

Black Lady

This is the most popular version of hearts. Here, the queen of spades is an extra penalty card, scoring 13 penalty points. After inspecting the hand, each player passes three cards face down to the player to his left. The queen of spades is usually disposed of in that way, unless it is guarded by at least two smaller spades. In some games, a player unable to follow suit must play the "black lady," and is charged with a revoke for failing to do so.

In black lady, the "take-all" version can also be played. The passing feature makes it more difficult, of course, but not impossible. After having passed his only losers to the opponent on his left, the player may discover that he has received three high cards from his opponent on the other side. If he receives three losers, however, he should abandon the idea of a take-all at once.

Spot Hearts

This game is played like basic hearts, except that the ace counts 14 penalty points, the king 13, the queen 12, the jack 11, and the other cards as many penalty points as their face value. Almost any hearts variant can be scored this way. Many people feel this added feature makes hearts more intricate and interesting.

War

This simple but amusing game probably orginated in France, where it was played as early as the last decades of the 14th century. It was a favorite at the French court. Charles VI (popularly called Charles the Fool) is reputed to have been absolutely crazy about the game. To play war well, skill is not required, but speed is extremely important, otherwise the game is no fun.

1. Two people play and a standard deck is used. Ranking order of the cards is the usual one.
2. Each player draws a card from the pack. Highest card deals. After shuffling, the cards are dealt one at a time, face down, on top of each other (the players are not allowed to look at them). After all the cards have been dealt, nondealer takes the top card from his pile and places it on the table, face up. Dealer does the same.
3. The player with the highest card now is obliged to pick up both cards and add them to his pile (at the bottom, face down). He then leads the next card. The object of the game is to get rid of all the cards as quickly as possible. If the two players play cards of the same value, they continue drawing cards from their pile until one of them has a higher card than the other. The unfortunate "winner" of this "war" has to pick up all the cards on the table.

Games played with two 52-card Decks

Canasta

Canasta originated in South America (Uruguay) in the beginning of the 20th century and spread rapidly around the world soon after the Second World War. In North America it became a big fad in the 1950s and its sudden vogue there probably was the most spectacular in the history of cards. Although it has declined in popularity, it is still played widely in the United States. Canasta is an entertaining game; it is easy to learn and not nearly as complicated as it may seem at first acquaintance.

1. *The players and the cards* This is a game for four players, divided into two partnerships, but it can also be played by two or three players (two or three play individually).
Two standard decks plus four jokers are used–108 cards in all. There are 12 *wild cards*– all eight deuces and the four jokers–which can be given any denomination that the holder wishes. Wild cards are also used as stoppers in play (see below).

2. *Preliminaries* Unless partnerships are already established, each player draws a card from the deck and the two highest play against the two lowest. For this purpose, cards rank normally (ace high) and suits rank downwards: spades, hearts, diamonds, clubs. Players who draw a joker or exactly equal cards draw again.
The highest card is the first to play and the player to the right of the highest card is the first dealer.

3. *Dealing* After shuffling, cards are dealt one at a time and face down, in the usual clockwise direction. Everyone gets 11 cards and the remaining cards are placed face down on the table as a *stock*. The dealer turns the top card of the stock face up and places this card next to it to start the discard pile (the *pot* or *pack*).

4. *Start of play* Play begins with the player to the dealer's left, who picks up the top card from the stock and then discards a card from his hand face up on the discard pile, trying to form his hand into melds while doing so. Then each player in turn draws and discards.

5. *The object of the game* The goal is to be the first partnership to score 5,000 points over a series of hands. This is done by capturing as many cards as possible, particularly those of scoring value, and making as many *melds* as possible.

6. *The melds* Melds are sets of at least three cards of the same rank. They can be all natural cards or a mixture of natural and wild cards. But no matter how many cards there are in the meld, there must be at least two natural cards and it may not contain more than three wild cards. A partnership is not allowed to meld more than one group of the same rank–all additions must be laid off the original meld. Melds score according to the cards they contain (see Scoring).

The first time the player lays down a meld on the table, it must total at least a certain number of points. This minimum value of the initial meld depends on the score of the partnership so far (see below). Once either partner has laid down his first meld, both partners can make new melds of any value. They also may add to their melds that are already on the table (a player may add to his own or his partner's melds).

7. *The value required for the initial meld* depends on the accumulated score of the partnership as follows:

Negative score	0 points
0-1495	50 points
1500-2995	90 points
3000 or more	120 points

8. *Canasta*
a) A natural (or pure) canasta is a meld of seven cards of the same natural rank. It is worth 500 bonus points on top of the card score.
b) A mixed canasta is a meld of seven cards of the same rank. It contains at least one wild card, but not more than three. It is worth 300 bonus points on top of the card score.
c) A golden canasta is a meld of seven deuces and is worth 1,000 bonus points on top of the card score. During play, cards may be added to a canasta. But a mixed canasta my not receive a fourth wild card and a natural canasta loses its value if a wild card is added.

9. *Frozen discard pile*
a) The discard pile is frozen for both sides at start of play and players must take cards from the stock until it is unfrozen. The discard pile remains frozen for each partnership until one of the partners has made his *initial meld.*
b) The discard pile is also frozen for both sides at any stage of the game if the top card is a *wild card* or a *red three*. In this case further discards are placed crosswise on top of the "freezing card" and the discard pile remains frozen until one player is able to use the freezing card at once in a meld that includes two cards of the same natural rank.
c) The discard pile is frozen if a *black three* is the top card. In this case it is no longer frozen after the player has drawn from the stock and discarded.

10. *Taking the discards* Instead of taking from the stock, a player may take the top card from the discard pile if he has in this hand at least two natural cards of the same denomination, two natural, or one natural and one wild card. First he displays the cards with which he plans to meld the top discard. He then takes the card and completes the meld on the table. He then also takes the remainder of the discard pile and adds it to his hand. He immediately uses as many cards as possible by adding to existing melds or laying out new ones. Any cards that he cannot use become part of his hand. The player ends his turn with a discard, beginning a new pile.

11. *Red treys* Whenever a player has a red three in his hand he must lay it face down on the table, as if it were a meld, and draw another card from the stock. If he has more than one red three, he must do the same. However, if he takes a red three from the discard pile, he need only place it face up on the table without an extra card being drawn from the stock.

Red treys are bonus cards, counting 100 points each. They cannot be melded. If a partnership holds all four treys they are worth 200 points each. If a partnership has made no melds, each red three counts as minus 100 points, all four red treys count as minus 800 points.

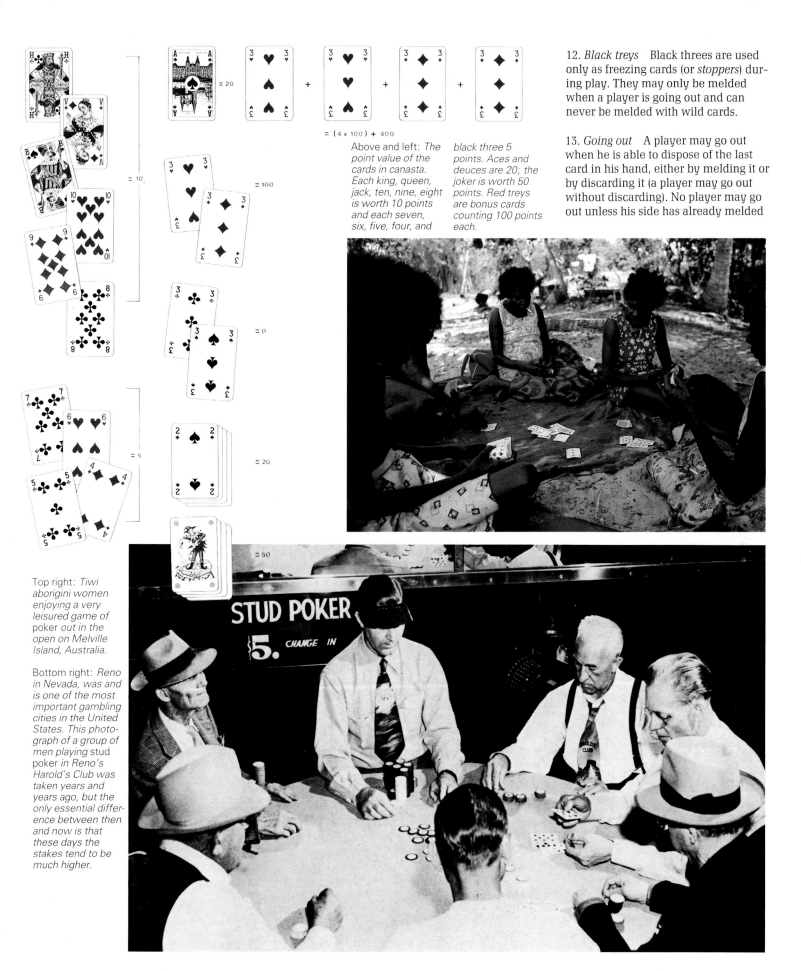

= 10.

= 20

= (4 x 100) + 400

= 100

= 0

= 20

= 50

= 5

Above and left: *The point value of the cards in canasta. Each king, queen, jack, ten, nine, eight is worth 10 points and each seven, six, five, four, and* black three 5 points. Aces and deuces are 20; the joker is worth 50 points. Red treys are bonus cards counting 100 points each.

12. *Black treys* Black threes are used only as freezing cards (or *stoppers*) during play. They may only be melded when a player is going out and can never be melded with wild cards.

13. *Going out* A player may go out when he is able to dispose of the last card in his hand, either by melding it or by discarding it (a player may go out without discarding). No player may go out unless his side has already melded

Top right: *Tiwi aborigini women enjoying a very leisured game of poker out in the open on Melville Island, Australia.*

Bottom right: *Reno in Nevada, was and is one of the most important gambling cities in the United States. This photograph of a group of men playing stud poker in Reno's Harold's Club was taken years and years ago, but the only essential difference between then and now is that these days the stakes tend to be much higher.*

STUD POKER
5. CHANGE IN

one canasta. Permission is usually asked to go out, in the form of "May I go out, partner?" He is required to abide by his partner's yes or no, but if the answer is no, he need not ask the question at his next turn. The player is not obliged to ask permission, but he usually does so as a tactic. He warns his partner to meld as many cards as possible and then goes out in his next turn.

A player is said to have gone out *concealed* when he has not previously melded any cards and does so in one fell swoop. Concealed going out is worth extra bonus points.

Play continues even after the last card of the stock is gone. At this stage, *forcing* occurs. It consists of making a discard that the next player *must* take if he is able to add it to one of his side's existing melds. If the player refuses the card although he is able to add it to a meld, the hand ends at once and the score is computed. Play also ends if the last card of the stock is a red three. The player who draws it may not meld or discard.

14. Scoring
The point value of the cards:

Each joker.............................	50 points
Each ace................................	20 points
Each deuce (2)......................	20 points
Each king, queen, jack, ten, nine, eight....................	10 points
Each seven, six, five, four...	5 points
Each black three (see text)	5 points
Each red three...........................	see text

Bonus points:

Golden canasta	1,000 points
Natural canasta...................	500 points
Mixed canasta.....................	300 points
Going out	100 points
Concealed going out...........	200 points
Red three	100 points
All four red treys.................	800 points

When a player goes out, each side counts the total point value of all melded cards, plus the total of all bonus points, less the value of any cards remaining in the hands of either partner. Hands continue until one side has made a total of 5,000 points and wins the game. For each sucessful hand the deal passes clockwise.

15. Errors and penalties
a) If a player neglects to declare a red three at his first turn after getting it and the hand ends before he corrects his error, he is penalized 500 points.

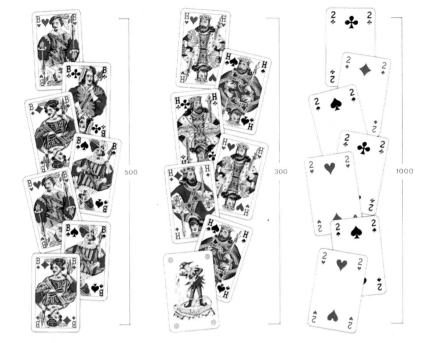

Top right: A canasta is a meld of seven cards. A natural canasta (left) has a bonus value of 500 points, a mixed canasta (middle) is worth 300 extra points, and a "golden" canasta–seven twos–gives 1,000 bonus points.

Bottom right: A painting from the 19th century by Abraham Soloman (1824-1862). The lady sitting at the table is practicing the art of fortune-telling with cards (and it looks as if she has not had good tidings for the girl standing on the left!).

b) If a player lays down an initial meld containing insufficient points according to the rules he restores the cards to his hand and the minimum required value of his partnership's initial meld is increased by 10 points.

16. Variant rules   The following two variations on the standard rules are widely accepted:
a) A player may not use the top card of the discard pile to add it to a completed canasta even if the discard pile is not frozen.
b) When taking the top card from the discard pile to make a new meld, a player must always have a natural pair to match it (i.e., not a matching card and a wild card).

Two-handed Canasta

Each player is dealt 15 cards. To go out, the players must have melded two canastas. In taking from stock, each player gets two cards per turn but discards only one.

Three-handed Canasta *(Cutthroat)*

Each player is dealt 13 cards. In taking from stock, player takes two cards per turn and discards only one. Players play individually. To go out, a player must have melded two canastas.
In another version of cutthroat canasta, the foregoing rules are modified and added to as follows:
a) During play players form sides of two against one. The player who first takes the discard becomes the *lone hand*. The other two form a partnership, combine their melds and help each other against the lone hand where possible.
b) If a player goes out before the discard pile is ever taken, he becomes the lone hand and the other two play as partners.
c) The initial meld requirement for a player depends on his individual score. Hence, it may happen that one partner has a higher requirement than the other.
d) If no one goes out, play ends with the player who drew the last card from the discard of the stock.
e) A red three counts only for the owner, plus or minus, according to whether or not his side has made any melds. All other partnership scores are totaled and each partner receives the total plus or minus his own red treys.

Cooncan

Cooncan is also known as conquian and in some places as rum poker. (In its native Spanish, it was called *con quien*–"with whom"). It is probably the oldest surviving ancestor of modern rummy. Very little is known about the original game, however, as it has undergone a great number of adaptions over the years. Below, one of the many variations of cooncan.

1. A game for two to eight players. Two standard decks are used plus two jokers–106 cards in all. The jokers are *wild cards*. If four or fewer play, each player gets 13 cards, if five play 12 cards each, if six play 11 cards each, if seven play 10 cards each, and if eight play nine cards each. The remainder is placed face down on the table as a stock.

2. The point value of the cards is the usual one: ace counts for 11 points, all face cards for 10 points, nine for 9 points, eight for 8, etc.

3. This game is usually played with chips. Each player begins with the same number of chips, to be decided on beforehand.

4. Each player in turn takes a card from the stock and discards a card from his hand. The discard is placed face up next to the stock and becomes part of the "open stock." If the player is able to lay down a meld, he must do so before discarding.

5. The player who holds a three of hearts or draws one from the stock must show this card to his opponents, whereupon he receives a chip from each of them. If he is dealt two treys of hearts, he receives four chips from each player. Once "paid for," the three of hearts is considered a regular card.

6. The object of the game is for the player to get rid of all the cards in his hand as quickly as possible.

7. To achieve this, each player first must lay down a meld that counts for at least 40 points. The meld can consist of a sequence of three or more cards in the same suit, or three or more cards of a kind (the same ranking but in different suits), or a combination of both.

8. Once a player has laid down his 40-point meld, he may also draw from the open stock, i.e., he may draw two cards at the same time.

9. When a player has a 40-points meld on the table he may in his next turn meld cards from his hand or cards drawn from the stock with his meld(s) on the table. If other players lay down a 40-point meld, he may use his cards also to "build on" those melds.

10. The winner is the first player to be rid of all his cards. He receives from each of the other players as many chips as the number of cards the player has in his hand.

Example
The first player who lays down a meld does that with queen of hearts, queen of clubs and queen of spades (30 points) and four, five, six of diamonds (15 points). The second player lays down ace of spades, ace of hearts, and a joker, which he calls ace of diamonds (33 points), plus three treys (nine points). The second player then adds a diamond queen to the three queens of the first player and a diamond three to the latter's sequence. Play continues in this fashion. A player who holds or draws the ace of diamonds may exchange this card for the joker on the table. He then gives the joker any denomination that he wishes.
A player is not obliged to lay down the 40-point meld as soon as he has one and it is not always wise to do so. If, for example, his meld contains a joker, it may be advantageous for him to first try and make a "normal" meld and keep the joker in his hand for "hard times," i.e., the moment when most of the players have melds on the table and one of them may go out at any time.

Cribbage

Cribbage is one of the oldest card games in existence today. The board used for scoring in cribbage was evidently adapted from earlier dice-game scoreboards and the rules of play seem to owe much to an old English game called noddy. The invention of cribbage has been popularly accredited to the English poet and courtier Sir John Suckling, who lived from 1609 to 1642. Early English settlers brought cribbage to America, where its popularity still endures, especially in New England. Modern six-card cribbage is basically a two-handed game, but it can also be played three-handed and four-handed, partnership style. Played either with or without stakes, two-handed cribbage is a fast, absorbing game.

1. *The players and the cards* Two players, using a standard 52-card deck. Ace is low (1 point), King is high. Picture cards and tens are worth 10 points, the other cards retain their face value.

2. *The deal* Each player cuts the deck. Low draw deals six-card hands, one at a time. The remaining cards go face down as a stock, which is placed next to the scoring board.

3. *The crib* After the cards have been dealt, each player selects two cards from his hand and places them face down to the dealer's right. These four cards are known as the *crib* and form an extra hand that belongs to the dealer but is not used while the hand is played. At the end of the hand, the crib is added to the dealer's score. As compensation for the dealer's crib, the non-dealer is given three points at the start of the game and may advance his peg three holes on his outer row.

4. *The board* Score is kept on a special cribbage board. There are four rows of 30 holes, two rows for each player, and usually there are additional game holes at one or both ends of the board. Each player has two pegs (each pair of a different color, usually black for one player and red for the other) and each player moves his pegs up the outer row and down the inner row on his side of the board. When there are four game holes, the players put their pegs in them for the start of play. To mark his first score, the player moves one peg that number of holes from the start.

Below: *A beautifully carved cribbage board made of walrus bone. During the 19th century, Eskimos made this and other gaming boards to sell them to whalers.*

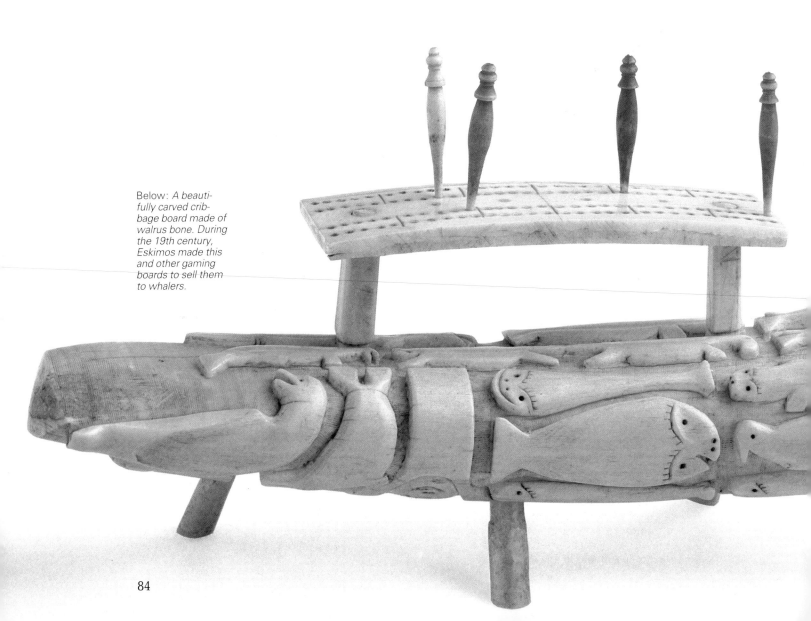

Above: *This simple but elegant cribbage board, inlaid with ivory, was made in England in the time of Queen Victoria (1837-1901).*

His second score is marked by placing his second peg that number of holes beyond his first peg. He marks his third score by placing his first peg that number of holes beyond his second peg, and so on.

5. *Object of the game* The objective is to score 121 points, i.e., to go "twice around the board."

6. *Scoring during play* Before cribbage can be played seriously and enjoyably, the players must be aware of the scoring during play, as the credits to be accumulated are the basis of all strategy and tactics.

His heels = 2 points
(for dealer when starter card is a jack)
Fifteen = 2 points
(for any combination of cards totaling fifteen)
One pair = 2 points
(for two cards of the same rank)
Pair royal = 6 points
(three cards of the same rank)
Double pair royal = 12 points
(four cards of the same rank)
Sequence or run, each card = 1 point
(series of cards in sequence, not necessarily of the same suit)
Flush, each card = 1 point
(four or five cards of the same suit)
Last card = 1 point
Last card and 31 = 2 points.
Thirty-one = 2 points
(for player whose card brings total to 31)
Closest to 31 = 1 point
(for player whose opponent is unable to play and says "Go".)

7. *The Play* Nondealer cuts the stock and dealer picks up the top card of the lower part of the deck. Nondealer puts the top half of the stock back and dealer places the card face up on top of the stock. This is the *starter* and will be used at the end of the hand, when both players tally their scores. If the starter is a jack, dealer announces "two for his heels" and advances his peg two holes. Nondealer chooses one of the four cards in his hand, places it face up on the table directly in front of him and calls its value. Dealer now also lays down a card and calls out the total value of his card plus his opponent's. (On all subsequent plays, the total value of the card played is called out.) On this play, dealer tries either to match his opponent's card and make a pair or to add to it so that the total is 15.

(If he succeeds, he advances his peg two holes for two points.) The nondealer, in his turn, now attempts to build on the cards already played. Besides trying for a 15 or a pair, each player can now try for any of the other combinations mentioned under "Scoring during play." For example, if a pair was scored and the next player is able to lay down a third card of the same rank, he will score for a royal pair, etc.
A sequence of cards scores regardless of the order in which it is played. Thus, if cards are played in the order ace, 2, 5, 4, 3, the player putting out the 3 can count a run of five cards. Should the second player be able to lay down a 6, he can count a run of six cards, etc.

The players continue to lay down cards in turn as long as the total value of the cards does not exceed 31. If a player at his turn is unable to play a card that is within the limit of 31, he says "Go." His opponent then plays any of his cards that are low enough to be within the limit. If they make 31 he scores two points, if less than 31 he scores one point and also says "Go." When the count during play reaches 31, the cards are turned face down to prevent confusion. The remaining cards in hand are played, the called score starting with the next card. Play continues until all the cards are played or until another 31 limit is reached. The player discarding the last card in the hand wins a point, or two points if he is able to score 31 with the last card.

8. *Scoring in showing* In cribbage, the melds are scored after the play of the hand. That is, all the cards in a player's hand are tallied for the scoring combinations possible. (This score is then added to whatever is already pegged on the board.) In scoring, the starter is considered the fifth card in each hand. There are slight variations in scoring double, triple and quadruple runs, depending on where the game is played. This method is the one most commonly used in the USA.

Scored points when melding:
Fifteen = 2 points
Pair = 2 points
Royal pair = 6 points
Double royal pair = 12 points
Run, each card = 1 point
Double 3-card run = 8 points
Double 4-card run= 10 points
Triple 3-card run = 15 points
Quadruple run = 16 points
Four-card flush = 4 points
(all in hand of the same suit)
Five-card flush = 5 points
(with starter–the crib cannot score for a four-card flush)
His nobs = 1 point
(if hand or crib contains jack of same suit as starter)

Nondealer shows and scores first, which gives him an advantage if he is very near reaching 121. Each score should be announced by name and points so the opponent can verify it. Experienced players sometimes use the "Muggins" rule, which allows a player to call "Muggins" and score for himself any points his opponent missed in melding.
A card may be ranked for scoring in any number of different combinations. For example, two 10s and two 5s would score eight points for four 15s and four points for two pairs–a total of 12 points. The highest possible count while showing is 29–when the hand contains J-5-5-5, and the starter is a 5 of the same suit as the jack. After taking one point for His nobs, player would then score eight points for four 15s, (formed by the jack with the 5s), eight more for four more 15s (formed by the 5s), and 12 more points for the double royal pair, for the total of 29.
After the nondealer has declared his score, the dealer shows and scores his own hand. The crib is scored in the same way as the hands, except that the only flush allowed is a five-card one. The deal alternates between the players from hand to hand. After each hand, the cards are shuffled. The loser of a game deals first in the next game.

Games of Solitaire

The earliest known references to solitaire–or patience, as it is known in Europe–date from the 18th century and were found in northern Europe. Since then, it has become popular throughout Europe, Britain and North America. "Patience is the mental equivalent of jogging: its purpose is to tone the brain up and get rid of unsociable mental flabbiness." This is the opinion of David Partlett, a well-known author on card games *(The Penguin Book of Patience)*, but to many other people a game of patience is simply a form of relaxation and has little if anything to do with mental exercise. This difference of opinion is not surprising, for the gamut of patience games ranges from the facile to the very complex; some are simply games that require patience rather than skill while others call for a high degree of judgment and analytical power.

Below: La belle Lucie *is one of the many solitaires in which the hand is also the tableau. It begins with a display of 17 three-card columns (all cards visible), with the last card also exposed.*

Belle Lucie

Belle Lucie, also called Alexander the Great, midnight oil and clover leaf, belongs to the largest group of solitaire games, the *building games* or *packers*. The games of this group involve a *tableau* (a center-table arrangement) and a *foundation*. The idea is to develop arrangements on the tableau from which individual cards may be conveyed to the foundation. Visually, belle Lucie has an attractive feature: the tableau consists of cards dealt face up in sweeps of three at a time, forming what look like fans rather than columns.

Layout Using a standard 52-card deck, deal all the cards in 17 fans of three cards each, with one left over (see diagram).
The simplest method of dealing is to count off three cards at a time and turn them face up, overlapped.

Foundations Play to release the aces, place them in a row and built up in suit to kings.

Play Move only one card at a time. Top cards are available for building on foundations, or for building on each other in suit and descending sequence. A space formed by removal of an entire fan is never filled.

Redeal Two redeals are permitted. When stuck, gather up the cards of the tableau (not the foundations) and shuffle them thoroughly. Then deal again in fans of three, with an odd fan of one or two cards on the side if necessary.

Draw or Merci After two (or even three!) failed redeals, some players grant themselves a feature called *merci*–a "free draw" – which permits transfer of any tableau card to the foundation or, for that matter, to any convenient position on the tableau. (After which, it should not be too difficult to conquer la belle Lucie!)

Trefoil or Les Fleurons

This game is played exactly the same way as belle Lucie, except that the aces

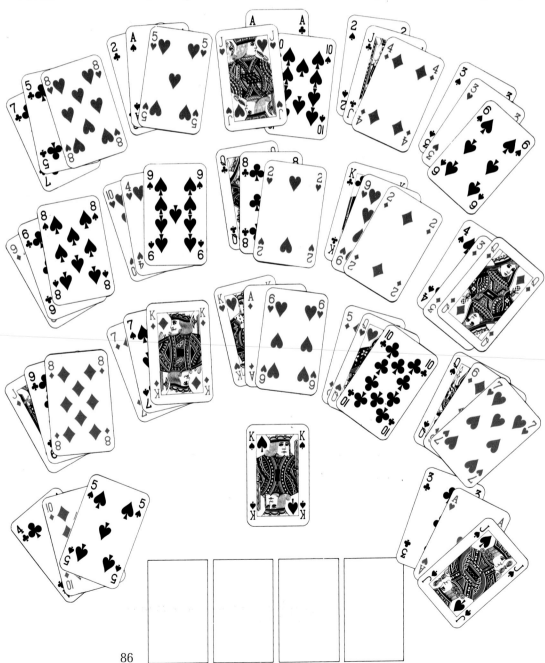

Above: *A colorful, cheerful painting by the Italian master Niccolo dell'Abate. While the tarot cards displayed here are relatively simple, most Italian playing cards of the 15th and 16th century were lavishly decorated.*

are removed from the pack and founded to start with, and the rest dealt in 16 fans of three.

Carré Napoleon is played with two complete 52-card decks and without jokers. The position of the columns of cards resembles the famous carré of Napoleon's army... hence the name of the game.

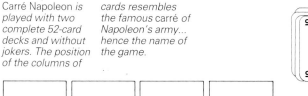

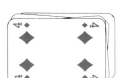

Carré Napoleon *(Napoleon's Square)*

This is another member of the solitaire building games. It is very much like the solitaire game Napoleon at St. Helena, except that it has twelve columns instead of 10. Much time–and patience– is needed for this game and it also requires considerable space on the table. It is called carré Napoleon–or so the story goes–because of the way the cards are arranged. This is in the shape of one of the famous Napoleonic military stratagems.

Object of the game   To build the eight aces up in suit to the kings.

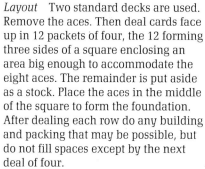

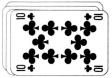

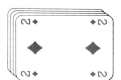

Layout   Two standard decks are used. Remove the aces. Then deal cards face up in 12 packets of four, the 12 forming three sides of a square enclosing an area big enough to accommodate the eight aces. The remainder is put aside as a stock. Place the aces in the middle of the square to form the foundation. After dealing each row do any building and packing that may be possible, but do not fill spaces except by the next deal of four.

Play   The top card of each pile of four is available to be played on foundations or built on other piles. Turn cards from the stock pile and play them if possible or else discard them face up to a single "wastepile," which may be spread so that all cards can be read. Pack the tableau in suit and descending order. Move only one card at a time. A space made by clearing out a column may be filled by any available card from the stock, the tableau or the wastepile.

Redeal   There is no redeal.

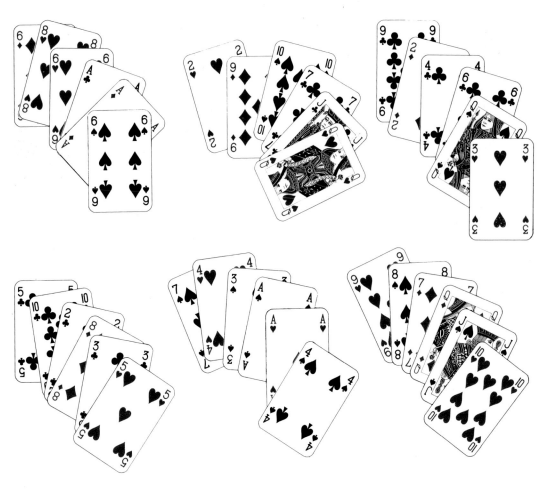

Play Pack the tableau in descending sequence regardless of suit. Move only one card at a time. An empty space may be filled with any available card. All exposed cards and all those of the tableau are simultaneously available for packing and building. The bouquet cards are not replaced when used.

Example To release the aces in the situation shown in the diagram, take the four of spades and put it on the five of hearts. Both the ace of hearts and the ace of spades can now be moved to the foundation. Then remove the king of hearts and the king of spades from the bouquet (not pictured) and cover the respective aces with them. Now the queen of hearts can be transferred to the foundation and the jack is taken from the bouquet and is placed on top of it, followed by the 10 of hearts from the tableau. Take the three of hearts and put it on the four of spades. Now the jack of clubs can go on the queen of spades, the six of spades on the seven of clubs, and both the ace of clubs and the ace of diamonds are released. Take the respective kings from the bouquet and transfer them to their place on top of the aces in the foundation. We confidently leave the rest up to you.

Above: *For parterre, a 52-card deck is used, without jokers. All the cards are visible. The four aces are the "base" cards.*

Parterre

No one knows where the name parterre came from, but the two other names for the game, bouquet and flower garden, seem more appropriate.

Apparently, the tableau represents the flower garden and the reserve cards in the hand form the bouquet. Well, with a bit of imagination...

Layout One standard 52-card deck is used. Deal six overlapping rows of six cards each and regard the tableau as six columns of six. The other 16 cards form a reserve, which is held in hand so that all are visible.

Right: *Playing cards in modern-day Egypt. Some of the oldest games known to us have been traced to Egypt.*

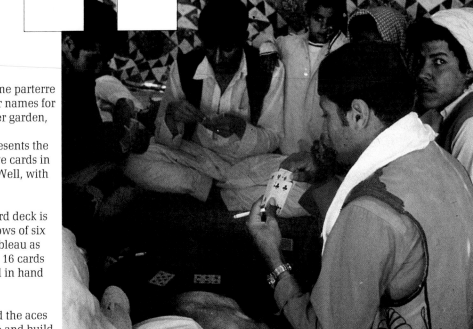

Object of the game To found the aces when they become available and build them up in suits to kings.

Stacking

Layout Two standard decks are used, without the jokers. Remove the eight kings and place them on the table as shown in the diagram. Shuffle the two packs. Now deal 13 cards, one at a time, in two horizontal rows of six with the 13th card apart below them. Cover these cards with another 13 cards, and so on. Only the top card of the pile should be visible. However, before you do this, read the following carefully. As you see in the diagram, each stack has its own number. You are not allowed to place a card on a stack if that stack has the same number as the card you are about to place there (the cards are numbered in ascending order from ace = 1 to king = 13). Such a card is laid aside to be part of the stock. If, for example, you are about to deal a card to "pile 13" and this card turns out to be a king, it is placed on the stock pile, not on pile no 13.

Object of the game To build on the eight kings. Four are built up in suit (ace, two, three, etc. up to the queen) and four are built down in suit (queen, jack etc. down to the two).

Play The top cards of the piles are available for packing on the tableau in descending order and in alternating colors and for building on the kings as described above. The stock pile is only available when there is no playable card left. When that moment has arrived, take the top card of the stock and place it at the bottom of the stack with the corresponding number (for example, a queen should go at the bottom of pile no. 12). Now take the top card of that particular stack and place it at the bottom of the stack that has the corresponding number. You now have a new card to play with. The next time you are "stuck," follow the same procedure. Continue playing in this fashion until there are no more stock cards left. If, at that time, the game is not finished, take the 13 piles, shuffle them well and start all over again.

Redeal Three redeals are allowed.

Above: Solitaire *(or* patience*)* in its many different forms has been popular all over the world since time immemorial and is played by young and old alike.

Right and below: *For* stacking, *two complete decks are used, without jokers. Here, the eight kings are the "base" cards.*

1	2	3	4	5	6

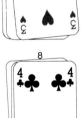

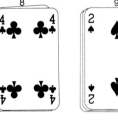

7	8	9	10	11	12

Below: *Early sets of dominoes were made of bone. Later the bone strip was glued to an ebony backing and* fixed in place with brass sprigs.

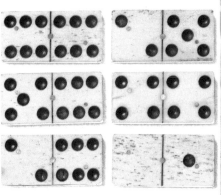

Below: *East African tribesmen playing the block game with wooden dominoes. And why not make your own set of dominoes? You need about 1.12 m* (3 ft 10 in) of 2.5 cm x 8 mm (1 in x ⁵⁄₁₆ in) softwood for 28 dominoes 4 cm (1⁵⁄₈ in) in length. The ''spots'' are drilled out with a 4 mm (⅛ in) drill.

Domino Games

In *Sports and Pastimes of the People of England*, published in the early years of the 19th century, the author, J. Strutt, wrote that dominoes "is a very childish sport, imported from France a few years back, and could have nothing but the novelty to recommend it to the notice of grown persons in this country." This comment was both disparaging and unfair, for dominoes is far from being simply a game for children, as Strutt implies. Like many card games, domino games call for calculation and strategy and some of them are extremely complex.

Dominoes are direct descendants of the ordinary six-sided dice, and although a very similar game was played in ancient Egypt, the domino appears to have been invented independently in Europe and China. Where the Chinese have played domino games for several centuries, the European game seems to have orginated in Italy as recently as the beginning of the 18th century. It quickly spread throughout Europe and towards the end of the 18th century it was brought to England, probably by French prisoners of war. Since then, domino games have become known throughout most of the world.

The Chinese domino set differs markedly from the set used for Western games. Individual dominoes (also known variously as tiles, bones or stones) represent the possible throws of a pair of dice–6:6, 6:5,... 2:1, 1:1–giving a total of 21. In addition, Chinese sets contain 11 duplicates, making 32 dominoes in a complete set. In contrast, the standard Western domino set, the *double-six* set, has only 28 tiles and does not contain duplicates. In the Western set, 21 of the tiles are the same as those in the Chinese set and represent all the possible throws of two dice. Six of the seven remaining tiles contain a *blank* (representing zero) combined with one of the numbers, and the seventh has two blanks (or double zero). Some of the games require sets of dominoes going up to double nine (55 tiles) or –in certain American games–to double 12 (91 tiles).

A typical domino is a rectangle which is twice as long as it is wide. Originally, they were made in two layers: an upper layer of white bone or ivory and a bottom layer of ebony or black-colored bone (hence the name "bones"). Most of the time, modern dominoes are made of plastic. The white top is divided across the middle to form two *ends*. Each of these carries a number of dots, which are usually black. Dominoes having the same number of dots at each end are known as *doublets* (or doubles). There are seven of these running from double blank to double six.

The derivation of the names of most games is well known, but the name "dominoes" seems to be one of the exceptions. The word *domino* as the name of the game as well as of the bones was accepted in 1798 by that arbiter of the French language, the Académie Française, in 1798. Some entymologists suggest that the name is derived from the domino, a hooded cape, black with a white lining, which was worn by priests–but this is only a guess.

The game achieved great popularity during the 18th and 19th century when it was widely played in coffee houses. As is the case with most popular café and salon games, it proved profitable to cheat, so much so that in the Netherlands in 1820 a book was published, entitled *Het bedrog, hetwelk men met het zogenaamde Domino-spel pleegt, ontmaskerd* (The deceits which people commit at the so-called game of dominoes, unmasked), as a warning to those unwise enough to play with strangers! Dominoes had retained much of its popularity as a café game, in particular in Britain where it is widely played in pubs and social clubs. Not only is it played, like dice, to find a loser to buy a round of drinks, it is also played in competition between individuals and teams within a pub and against other pubs.

In this section, games played with both Chinese dominoes and Western dominoes are discussed, together with the highly sophisticated Asian domino game, mah jong, which is played with a set of special tiles.

Left: *These desert tribesmen in southern Tunisia are playing the most basic form of dominoes, the* block *game, in which a chain is formed.*

Below: *An arrangement of dominoes in the* block *game.*

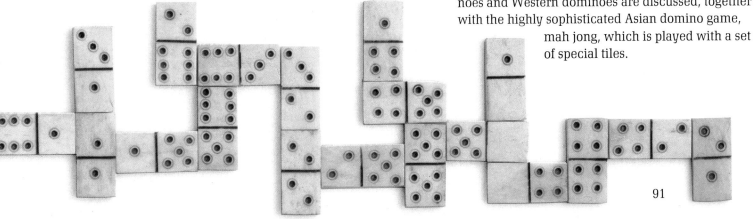

Chinese Domino Games

Chinese dominoes are made of ivory, bone or wood and are known as *kwat p'ai* (bone tablets). They usually measure about 7.2 cm x 2.1 cm (approximately 3 in x 1 in), which makes them longer than Western dominoes. The tiles have the same names as the corresponding dice throws (see Chinese dice games, pages 46-47), and they are divided into the same civil and military series. All the tiles in the civil series are duplicated.

The spots are incised: the one and four spots are marked in red, the others in white, except for the double six tile, which is half red and half white. Identical tiles of the civil series pair together, while those of the military series pair in total counts. The 2-4 and 1-2 tiles form the *supreme pair*, which is the highest in the military series, although separately they rank as the lowest tiles.

Tiu-ü *(Fishing)*

This simple game involves matching two tiles having the same number of spots, irrespective of whether they belong to the civil or the military series. The two tiles forming the *supreme* (2:4 and 1:2) mate with each other and form the single exception to this rule.

1. Tiu-ü is played by two or three players with two sets of dominoes. The tiles are well mixed and placed in a *woodpile* four tiles high and 16 tiles long. Four stacks of four are drawn from one end of the pile and placed face up on the table.
If two players are playing, each draws three stacks (12 tiles) from the same end of the pile. If three are playing, each draws two stacks (eight tiles).
2. The players then examine their tiles. Any pair of double-sixes in a player's hand is laid out in front of him immediately. The first player then attempts to match one of the tiles in his hand with a tile on the table that has the same number of spots. If he succeeds, he lays out the matched pair on the table in front of him. Whether a player succeeds in making a matched pair or not, he draws the top domino of the stack at the end of the woodpile–from which the tiles were originally drawn–

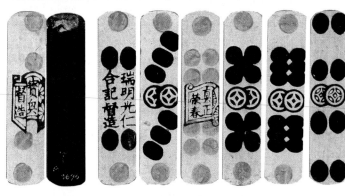

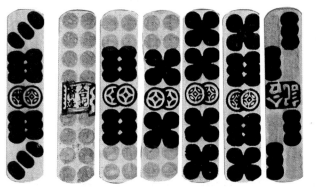

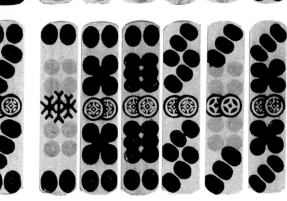

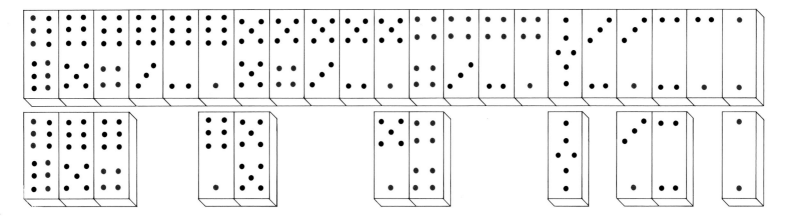

Above: *A set of Chinese dominoes. The doubled dominoes are the eleven pairs that form the civil series. The single dominoes are those of the military series.*

and tries to match this new tile with one of those on the table. If he succeeds he takes the pair; if he cannot match the tile drawn, he places it face up with those already on the table.

3. The next player at his turn tries to match one of his tiles, and also draws one from the pile and tries to match it. Play continues in this way until the pile is exhausted.

4. If a player holds a tile in his hand that is identical to two of the tiles on the table, and if the fourth tile of the same kind has not been played, he may, in his turn of play, pile the three tiles that are alike one on top of the other face up, at the opposite end of the stack from which tiles are being drawn. The player who lays down the fourth tile then takes the other three.

5. After the last tile has been drawn from the stack, the players count their scores. Tiles with eight or more spots are called *large fish* and count two points for each spot of either color. The tiles containing less than eight spots are known as *minnows* and count one point for each red spot only. The score of minnows is always taken to the next ten–i.e., a score of 6 counts as 10, a score of 13 counts as 20.

6. The player with the highest score is declared the winner. Each player pays a previously agreed stake for each point the winner has in excess of his own total.

Note: It is not too difficult to visualize a similar game for which European dominoes are used.
For three or four players four sets would be ideal, although two players could play with only two sets.
Scoring would be simplified by counting each spot as one point, perhaps counting a bonus point for each set of doubles.

Tau Ngau *(Bullfighting)*

This is a game for three to six players and any number of onlookers can place stakes alongside those of a player of their choice.

How to Play Tau Ngau

1. Dice are thrown to decide who will be the banker. The tiles are shuffled and each player draws five. The players place their stakes (up to a limit imposed by the banker) before seeing their tiles.

2. When all stakes have been placed, the players examine their tiles. The value of each tile is the number of spots, except that 2:1 may count as three points or six points and 4:2 as six points or three points.

3. Each player must discard three tiles with a total value of 10 points, or a multiple of 10 points:
4:1 + 2:1 + 1:1 = 10 (2:1 = 3)
4:4 + 2:1 + 3:3 = 20 (2:1 = 6)
6:6 + 6:5 + 4:3 = 30 etc.

4. After each player has discarded three tiles, he exposes the other two and scores the total of their spots. If this total reaches double figures the first figure is ignored (i.e., 16 or 26 counts as 6). If a player has a lower score than the banker, he loses his stake. If his score is more than that of the banker, the banker must pay him his stake. If their scores are the same, no money changes hands.

5. If a player cannot discard three tiles, he loses his stake. If the banker cannot discard, he pays the stakes to all those players who have been able to discard. There is no exchange between a player who cannot discard and a banker who is in the same position. If the banker scores points, the player on his right becomes the new banker. If the banker fails to score, he retains the bank.

Pai Kow

Pai kow is a popular gambling game in which the players try to form two pairs of dominoes both of which are higher in value than those of the banker. Before the game can start, the players must learn the ranking order of all the possible pairs. For this, see page 94. The highest ranking pair, supreme, is at top left. Values of the pairs then diminish from left to right and from row to row. Below mixed fives, which is the lowest pair shown, there are four other pairs. These are, in descending order: 6:6 and a nine; 1:1 and an eight; 4:4 and a seven; and 3:1 and a five. Pairs 2 (heaven) to 12 (spinning six) are made of matching dominoes in the civil series, while the remainder are made of dominoes in the military series.

How to Play Pai Kow

1. Pai kow is a game for four. The tiles are shuffled and stacked face down in two piles of four rows of four. Each player throws a die. The player throwing high becomes banker. The banker deals the first pile of dominoes counterclockwise and the first tile is for the player with the lowest throw.

2. The players each form two pairs, designed to beat the two pairs held by the banker, and place them face down on the table. They then place their stakes (usually chips representing different denominations) beside their pairs. The banker may impose a limit on the stake if he so wishes and onlookers are allowed to bet on the outcome. They do this by placing a stake next to the pairs of a chosen player.

3. When all stakes have been placed, each player in turn shows his first pair, the banker showing last. Finally, the second pairs are exposed.

4. To win a round the same player or

the banker must win *both* exposures. If a player wins both, the banker must pay him his stake as well as the stake of any onlooker who may have bet with him. The banker also pays the stakes of any other players (and onlookers) if both their pairs are higher than both of his. If the banker wins both exposures, he takes all the stakes on the table. In the case of two players (or one player and the banker) each winning one exposure, the round is drawn and no stakes change hands.

5. The banker then deals the second pile of 16 tiles, after which the second round is played in the same way. The dominoes are reshuffled and restacked when both rounds have been played. The player on the banker's right becomes the new banker and the game continues. Players may drop out of the game at the end of any round and onlookers may take their place.

Tien Kow

Tien kow is a popular gambling game in Hokien. It is a game for four players and its object is to score points by taking tricks made up of single tiles or pairs of tiles.

How to Play Tien Kow

1. The tiles are well shuffled and stacked. Dice are thrown to decide who is to be the first banker. The player with the highest score wins and then deals eight tiles to each player. The banker leads.

2. The banker plays the first tile; the other players follow in turn, playing tiles from the same series, military or civil. If a player has no tile in that series he may discard a tile from the other series. The player with the highest ranking tile in the correct series wins the trick and takes over the lead.

3. At his lead, a player may play either a single tile or one or two pairs. If one or two pairs are led, the other players must also play one or two pairs.

4. If one pair is led, the trick is won by the player who lays down the highest ranking pair. Pairs rank as shown in the illustration, with additional pairs, described in pai kow on the previous page. If two pairs are led, the trick goes to the player who plays the highest pair of all, regardless of what pair is played with it.

Supreme   Heaven   Earth   Man

Goose   Plum Flower   Double Three   Double Two

Axe Head   Red Ten   Long Legs Seven   Spinning Six

Mixed Nines   Mixed Eights   Mixed Sevens   Mixed Fives

Note: In this game the supreme pair (4:2, 2:1) only scores highest when it is led. In all other instances it is the lowest ranking pair.

5. The game continues until all the tiles have been played. The player who wins the last trick becomes the new banker.

6. *Scoring*
a) A player who has failed to win any tricks pays four points to the player taking the last trick. The exception to this rule is when the banker wins the last trick and so retains the bank. In this case the player who has failed to win a trick pays eight points the first time, 12 the second and so on, until the bank changes hands.
b) A player with one, two or three tricks deducts his number of tricks from four and pays the difference to the winner of the last trick.
c) A player who has more than four tricks deducts four from his total and claims the difference from the winner of the last trick.

d) If the banker leads the supreme pair, he claims four points from each player. If a player leads the supreme pair, he claims four points from the banker and two points from each of the other players.
e) If the banker leads two of the following pairs: 6:6 and a mixed 9, 1:1 and a mixed 8, 4:4 and a mixed 7, 3:1 and a mixed 5, he wins eight points from each player.
f) Any other player claims eight points from the banker and four points from each of the other players if he leads two of the above pairs.

7. A game ends by mutual consent or after an agreed number of hands.

Mah Jong

The history of *mah jong* is long, puzzling and clouded by legends. It has for centuries been the favorite game of the Chinese. According to some authorities, its name refers to the sound made by the tiles clicking together during the game. *Mah* means flax or hemp plant and is said to recall the rustling of the plant's leaves in the wind, while *jong* is the Chinese word for sparrow and supposedly recalls the bird's chattering. Whatever its early history, mah jong found its way from China to America in the early 1920s. There, the rules were altered and amended to make the basically simple game more interesting and more acceptable to Western tastes. It has been said that the rules were elaborated to the point of absurdity. Whether that is true or not, it is a fact that the game became much more complicated and was played in many different ways. (A Chinese businessman visiting America once remarked, ''We Chinese have played mah jong one way for a thousand years, but you foreigners have played it a thousand ways in one year.'')

In the United States, mah jong experienced a boom that lasted well into the thirties, after which it more or less faded from the scene, although it retains a small following. It is extremely popular in Japan, where it was also introduced in the 1920s. Only recently is the game again being played to any extent in Europe.

Below: *Mah jong is played with fervor throughout the Far East by young and old, male and female. This photograph was taken in a Philippines gambling den. In such establishments, huge sums are won and lost on the fall of one tile.*

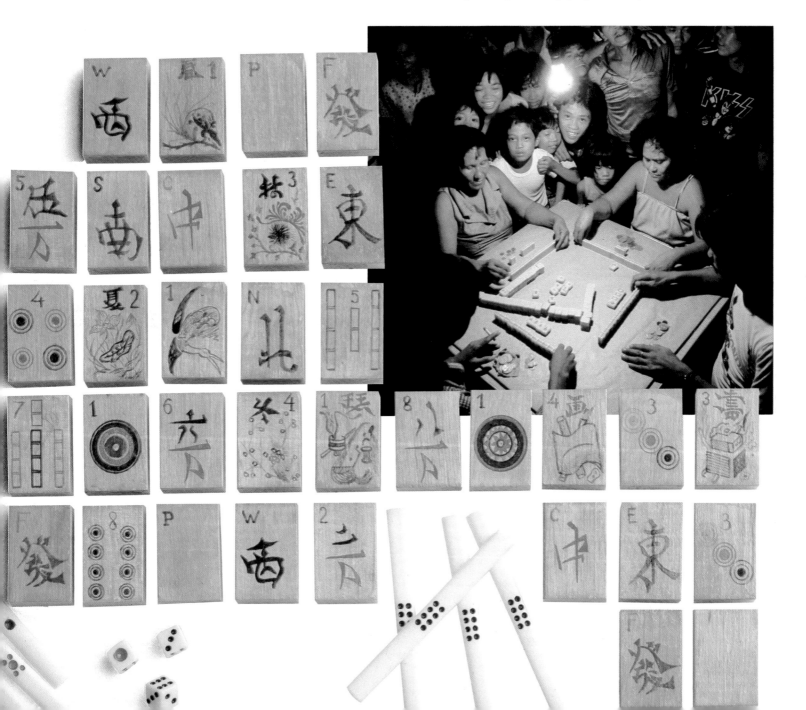

Below: suit tiles. *There are three different suits: circles (or dots), bamboos (or bams) and characters (or craks). Each suit comprises tiles numbered 1 through 9, and there are four of each type of tile. The 1 bamboo usually shows a bird; all other tiles have symbols.*

Below: wind tiles. *East, south, west and north winds are represented. Again there are four of each type of tile.*

Far below: dragon tiles. *There are three different dragons: white, red and green. There are four of each type of tile.*

The Mah Jong set
A mah jong set comprises 144 tiles, four racks for the players to keep their tiles on, tallies for scoring, a wind indicator and dice. Tiles are made of ivory, bone, bamboo, wood or plastic. The designs vary. Sets sold in the West usually have Arabic numerals in one corner of the suit tiles, and letters denoting the four winds.
Of the 144 tiles, 136 are playing tiles and 8 are flower and season tiles (see below). Of the 136 playing tiles, 108 are suit tiles (see illustration) and 28 are honor tiles. Suit tiles numbered 1 and 9 usually are given higher point values than others. They are called *terminals*, whereas 2 through 8 are *simples*. There are four each of seven honor tiles—red, green and white dragons and East, North, West and South winds.

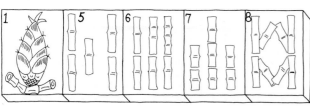

Bamboos

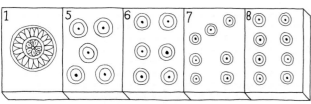

Circles

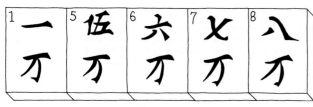

Characters

Winds

Below: terminals. *In scoring, the 1s and 9s of the suit tiles are of higher value than the tiles 2 through 8. They should be thought of in a separate category, as the terminals. The tiles 2 through 8 are known as the simples.*

Dragons

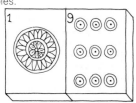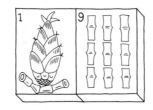

Terminals

How to Play Mah Jong

Mah jong is best played by four players, each player playing for himself.

Deciding the winds The players determine their seats by throwing in turn two dice and adding the numbers shown on the dice together, the highest total having choice of seats. This having been done players in turn again throw two dice and the highest total becomes *East Wind*. The player on East Wind's left is *North Wind* and the player opposite East Wind is *West Wind*. If the player who is East Wind does not win the first hand, the winds pass counterclockwise around the table. Thus East becomes North, South becomes East, West becomes South, and North becomes West. If the player who is East Wind wins a hand, the players retain the same winds for the next hand. The East player wins or loses double.

Prevailing wind East Wind prevails during the first deal, South Wind in the second, West Wind in the third, North Wind in the fourth. A player who obtains a set of tiles of the prevailing wind scores more for it than another wind.

Shuffling the tiles The winds thus being allocated, the tiles are now shuffled *(washed)*, which is done with them face downwards, a procedure in which East does not take part. This shuffling is known as "the twittering of the sparrows."

Building the wall The players, without looking at the tiles' faces, then proceed to build the tiles into four walls, each 18 tiles long and two tiles high (with the long sides of the tile touching). These four walls must be pushed into the center so that they touch the walls on either side to "keep the devils out." The square thus formed is called "The Great Wall of China."

Breaching or opening the wall This takes place once the wall is built. East throws the dice to determine where this will take place. If he throws two 1s, he must throw again.
Otherwise he takes the total thrown and, starting with his own wall as no. 1, counts the total counterclockwise around the table. (Thus, if the dice result was six, South Wind's wall would be opened—South being no. 2, West no. 3, North no. 4, and East no. 5.) The player whose wall has to be opened now throws the dice and adds his total to the total previously thrown by East. The new total is used to determine where exactly the opening will be made. He counts clockwise along the top of his tiles, beginning at the right-hand corner. For this purpose, each stack of two counts as one. If the total is more than 18 he continues along the next wall. The player then removes the stack indicated by the throws and places the two tiles on top of the wall to the right of the breach (see drawing). These tiles are known as *loose tiles*.

Drawing of the hands East Wind then proceeds to draw four tiles (two stacks) from the opposite side of the opening to the loose tiles. South then takes the next two stacks, West the next two, and North the next two. The draw continues until each player has 12 tiles. East Wind takes the first and third tiles from the top row of the wall and the other players, in turn as before, each take one more tile. At the end of the initial draw East has 14 tiles and the other players have 13 tiles each. The tiles are placed on the racks and examined. They should of course be concealed from the other players.

Far right: *After a day's work, mah jong is a favorite form of relaxation in China and many other Far Eastern countries.*

Right: *Antique hand-painted mah jong cards. Cards are often used instead of the domino-like mah jong tiles.*

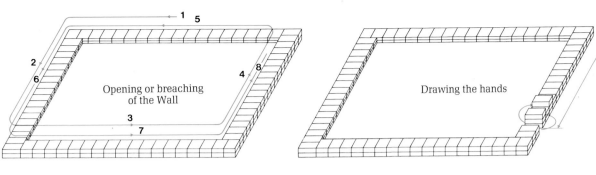

Opening or breaching
of the Wall

Drawing the hands

Mah Jong Scoring

Basic Score

Pairs

Dragons	2 p.
Player's wind	2 p.
Prevailing wind	2 p.
Player's wind if prevailing wind	4 p.

Sets

Pung (exposed):	4 p.
Honors or terminals	2 p.
Simples	2 p.
Kong (exposed):	8 p.
Honors or terminals	16 p.
Simples	8 p.

Pung or kong (concealed): double the above points

Bonus tiles

Flower or season	4 p.

Player going mah jong

Going mah jong	10 p.
Final tile from wall	2 p.
Mah jong with only possible tile	2 p.

Scoring

Doubles
One double of basic score for each of the following:

Mah jong hand only
All chows
No chows
All sets concealed

One-suit hand (one suit and honor tiles only)
Robbing the kong

All hands
Pung or kong of following:
Dragons
Player's wind
Prevailing wind
Player's flower and season (pair)
Set of flowers (4)
Set of seasons (4)

Loose tiles Loose tiles are used as replacement tiles during play, to make a player's hand up to the correct number of tiles – after a flower or season tile has been drawn or after a *kong* (see below). The tile farthest from the opening is used and then the other loose tile. After both tiles have been used they are replaced by the two tiles at the end of the wall–the top tile going farthest from the opening.

Flower and season tiles drawn in the initial hand or later in the game must be placed face up in front of the player and replaced by a loose tile. Replacement at the start of the game must be in rotation, with East playing first.

The object of the game is to "go out" by completing a hand composed of four *sets* (see below), each of three or four tiles, plus a pair. The first player to achieve this announces "mah jong." A *pair* may be any two identical tiles. A *chow* is a run of three tiles in the same suit. A *pung* is a set of three identical tiles. A *kong* is a set of four identical tiles. *Mah jong* is a complete hand, usually composed of four chows, pungs or kongs, plus a pair.

Playing procedure East starts play by discarding a tile; he places it in front of him face up. Play proceeds to East's right, each player in turn drawing one tile from the wall and discarding one by placing it face up in front of him—except when a player interrupts the order to claim a discarded tile.

Discarding and claiming When a player discards a tile he must always call out its name (for example: green dragon, three characters, five bams etc.). A discarded tile may be claimed by any other player to form a set, but only the tile that was last discarded may be claimed. Claims may be made even after the next player has taken a new tile from the wall–in which case the tile taken from the wall must be replaced. Claims are not allowed if the next player has already made his discard.
If no player claims the tile that was last discarded, the player to the right of the last player to discard now takes a tile from the wall. The new tile is taken from the end of the wall without the loose tiles. The player may conceal the tile's face from his opponents. If he wishes to keep the new tile, he does so and discards another from his rack.

Otherwise he discards the new tile. If more than one player claims a discarded tile, the player who wants it for mah jong has precedence. If two players require the same tile for mah jong, but one needs it for a pung and the other needs it for a chow, the player with a pung has precedence over the one with a chow. In other words, the ranking of the set for which the tile is claimed determines the order of precedence.

Claiming a chow Only the player sitting to the right of the player who last discarded is permitted to claim for a chow. To claim a chow, the player must already hold in his rack the two other tiles needed for the set. To claim the discard the player must call "chow," pick up the tile, and then expose the complete chow by laying it face up in front of him. The player ends his turn by discarding a tile from his rack.

Claiming a pung A player who wishes to claim the last discard for a pung must hold in his rack two tiles identical with the one he is claiming. If he has failed to "pung" that same discard, he must have played an intervening turn before being permitted to claim his pung. To claim the discard he must call "pung," pick up the tile and expose the pung. He then ends his turn by discarding a tile from his rack.

Claiming a kong Any player may claim the last discard for a kong if he holds in his rack three tiles identical with the tile he is claiming. To claim the discarded tile the player must call "kong," pick up the tile and expose the complete kong. He then draws a loose tile before discarding in the usual way. (A loose tile is always drawn after a kong because a complete hand has one extra tile for each kong it contains.)

Concealed chows or pungs If a player has a chow or pung in his original hand or he completes a chow or a pung with a tile drawn from the wall, he may keep these tiles concealed on his rack.

Concealed kongs If a player has all four tiles needed for the kong in his original hand, this kong is concealed. A kong is also concealed if the player has a concealed pung in his original hand and then draws the fourth similar tile from the wall. A player may lay his concealed kong on the table at any time when it is his turn to play. The

loose tile needed to bring his hand up to the number of tiles required to go mah jong may only be drawn after the player has laid his concealed kong on the table.

Converting an exposed pung into a kong An exposed pung may be converted into a kong if the player draws the fourth similar piece from the wall. After having made a kong out of his exposed pung, the player ends his turn by drawing a loose tile and then discarding in the usual way. (This is the only time that an exposed set of tiles may be interfered with.) It is not permitted to claim a discarded tile to convert an exposed pung into a kong.

Robbing the kong A player who is fishing (see below) may complete his hand by "robbing a kong"–i.e., claiming a tile drawn from the wall by another player who uses it to convert an exposed pung into a kong.

Fishing If a player requires only one tile to go mah jong, he is said to be "fishing" and must announce this. A player who is fishing has prior claim on any discard even to complete a chow or a pair though he may of course draw the desired tile from the wall. A player who is fishing may also "rob the Kong" (see above).

A standing hand East Wind may declare a "standing hand" if he is fishing after making his first discard. Any player may declare a standing hand if he is fishing after drawing and discarding for the first time in a hand. A player who has declared a standing hand may not change any of the 13 tiles then in his hand. At each turn, he draws a tile from the wall and then discards it if it is not the tile he needs to go mah jong. Completing a standing hand earns the player extra bonus points (see Scoring).

Last 14 tiles A hand is declared "dead" if no player goes mah jong before play reaches last 14 tiles in the wall (including the loose tiles). There is no scoring and a new hand is played with the same player as East Wind.

European Domino Games

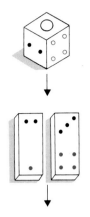

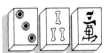

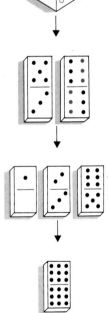

The earliest record of dominoes in Europe comes from early 18th-century Italy, although the game may well have been introduced earlier—perhaps it was brought back from the East by some traveler. It quickly became popular and soon spread to France and Britain. Nowadays, many different domino games are played throughout the world; in many countries they are particularly popular as pub games.

The standard Western set is the double-six set containing 28 tiles, but for some games larger sets are necessary, particularly when there are several players. These larger sets go up to double-nine or even double-twelve. Before the game can start the dominoes must first be shuffled. This is done by placing them face downwards on the playing surface and mixing them thoroughly.

The Block Game

Together with its many variations, the block game is one of the most popular and simplest domino games.

How to Play the Block Game

1. The tiles are shuffled and each player draws one. The player with the highest double starts the game and play proceeds in a clockwise direction. If no double is drawn, the player drawing the domino with the highest number of spots begins.
2. The tiles are returned to the pool and reshuffled. If there are two players, each draws seven tiles. If more than two are playing, each draws five.
3. The first player plays a tile and the next player tries to match one end of it. If he cannot do so, his turn is forfeit and the next player tries. Play continues until no one is able to match either end of the sequence.

The game is now *blocked* and each player counts the spots on the tiles remaining in his hand. The player with the lowest total wins the hand and scores his own total plus those of his opponents. The first player to reach 121 points is the winner.

Note: In several variations of the block game, the tiles are drawn and the player with the highest double lays it down to begin play.

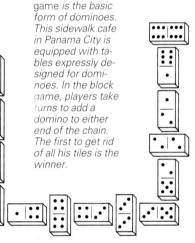

Below: The block game *is the basic form of dominoes. This sidewalk cafe in Panama City is equipped with tables expressly designed for dominoes. In the block game, players take turns to add a domino to either end of the chain. The first to get rid of all his tiles is the winner.*

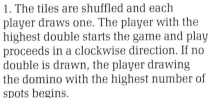

Far above: *Mah jong tiles developed from Chinese dominoes, which themselves developed from Chinese dice.*

Above: *European dominoes descended from dice in the same way. European dominoes are shorter than Chinese.*

Cyprus

Cyprus is very similar to the block game. The main differences are that it is played with a double-nine set and there are eight "ends" to choose from instead of two.

How to Play Cyprus

1. The tiles are shuffled and drawn, the number varying according to how many are playing: four players draw 13 tiles each; five draw 11; six draw 9; seven draw 7; eight or nine draw 6; and 10 players draw 5. The remaining tiles are left face downwards and not used.
2. The player holding double-nine puts it face up on the table. If no one has the double-nine, the tiles are reshuffled and redrawn. Play proceeds in a clockwise direction, the players either placing nines to form a star or playing tiles to match the ends of tiles already played.
3. The first player who can place his last tile calls "domino" and wins the hand. He scores one point for each spot held by his opponents.
4. If no one is able to play a nine or match and end, the game is blocked and the player who holds the lowest number of spots wins, again scoring the spots held by his opponents. If two players end up with the same low score, the game is drawn and no one scores any points.

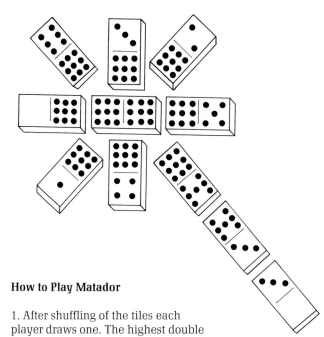

Left: *This typical layout shows how the game of* cyprus *is played. It is similar to the block game except that in* cyprus *there are eight ends.*

Matador

Matador is another game in which a double-nine set of dominoes is used. Tiles are added to either end of the domino row to form 10s rather than matching pairs: a 1 is added to a 9, a 2 to an 8, etc. The tiles that themselves add up to 10 (9:1, 8:2, 7:3, 6:4 and 5:5), together with 0:0, are known as *matador* tiles. The matador is the only tile that can be played on a blank, but matadors can also be played at any time if a player cannot make a 10.

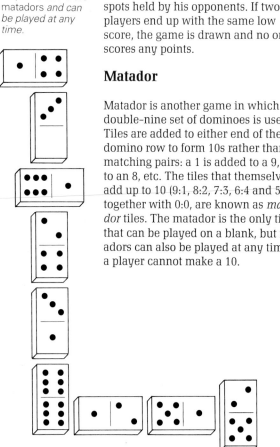

Below: *A typical matador layout, using a double-six set. Dominoes are laid so that spots on adjacent half tiles sum to seven; 6-1, 5-2, 4-3 and 0-0 are* matadors *and can be played at any time.*

How to Play Matador

1. After shuffling of the tiles each player draws one. The highest double begins the game (or the highest number of spots if there is no double). The tiles are returned to the pool and reshuffled. If there are six or fewer people playing, each draws 7 tiles. If more than six are playing each draws 5 tiles.
2. The first player plays a double if possible; if not he plays his highest tile. The player on his left plays a tile so that a 10 is formed. If he cannot do this he must play a matador or draw from the pool until he draws a tile he can use. Play continues in a clockwise direction.
3. If a player cannot make a 10 and does not wish to play a matador, or hasn't got one, he must draw until he can play or until there are only two tiles left in the pool. If he has failed to draw a playable tile he must then play a matador–if he has one.
4. If he still cannot play, he says "pass" and the next player gets his turn. When no one can play the game is *blocked*. The player with the lowest number of spots then scores the spots held by his opponents.
5. If a player plays his last tile, he calls "out" and again scores all the spots held by his opponents.
6. A game is played to a previously agreed total–usually 200 points.

Bergen

This is a game for between two and four players and a double-six set is used. The tiles are shuffled as usual. If there are no more than two or three players each draws six tiles, and if there are four players each draws five tiles.

How to Play Bergen

1. Tiles are matched to either end of the domino row. The object of this game is to make as many *double headers* and *triple headers* as possible. Double headers are formed by matching a tile at one end of the domino row so that the exposed number is the same at both ends. For example, if the exposed numbers are 5 and 2, a player needs the 2:5 tile to make 5:5 or 2:2 as he chooses. A triple header is formed by adding a double to match the other end of the domino row. If there is a double at one end, the triple header is formed by adding a tile so that the exposed number matches the double. If 5 and 5 are exposed, for example, a double 5 is needed to make a triple header. If double 5 and 2 are exposed, the 2:5 tile is required. Double headers score 2 points, triple headers score 3 points.

2. The player who has the lowest double leads and scores 2 points for a double header. If no one holds a double, the lowest tile is led. Play continues in a clockwise direction. If a player cannot match a tile, he draws one from the pool. If he still cannot match, the turn passes to the next player.

3. If there are only two tiles left in the pool and no player can match either end of the row, the game is blocked. The player with no doubles in his hand is the winner, scoring 2 points. If no one has any doubles the player with the lowest number of spots wins. If more than one player has a double in

Right: *A scene in a Cairo back street. Dominoes is a game that makes you thirsty – perhaps because the loser makes the coffee instead of standing a round of drinks!*

his had, the player with the fewest doubles wins. When a player plays his last tile he calls "domino" and wins.

4. Three or four players play to 10 points; two players play to 15. Within 3 points of game, a triple header scores only 2 points. Within 2 points of game, both double and triple headers count only 1 point.

Tiddlywinks

How to Play Tiddlywinks

1. A double-nine is required for this game. Each player is dealt an equal number of tiles and any tiles remaining are left face down on the table and not used.

Right: *A similar back-street scene, this time in Jacmel, Haiti. No, we don't know what the tin and string contraption is either! Our best guess is that it is a device to make sure the players do not cheat by looking at their opponent's dominoes.*

2. The dealer calls for the double nine and the player holding it leads. If the double nine is not in play, the next highest double is played. Any player playing a double at any point in the game (also when leading) has a second turn of play. Play proceeds in clockwise direction, each player attempting to match an exposed end of the domino row.

3. A player unable to match either end calls "pass" and the turn passes to the next player.

4. The first player to play his last tile calls "tiddlywinks" and wins. If no one is able to play a tile the game is blocked and the player with the lowest number of spots wins. If two players have the same number of spots, the player holding the lowest number of tiles is the winner and he scores a point for each spot held in his opponents' hands.

5. The game is usually played to a total of 200 points.

Blind Hughie

This game for two to five players was very popular with the miners in the south of Scotland. Each player has five tiles, face downwards (see the illustration). The players draw a tile to decide who starts, high tile beginning. The first player plays his *left-hand* tile into the middle. The next player turns his left-hand tile and if he can match one end of the exposed tile, he does so. If he cannot, he places the tile face up at the *right-hand* end of his pile. Play continues, each player playing the tile on his

left-hand side, until one player has played of all his tiles. Each player pays the winner the spot value of the tiles left in his hand. When the game is blocked, the player with the lowest number of spots is paid the difference between his hand and each individual opponent's hand by that opponent.

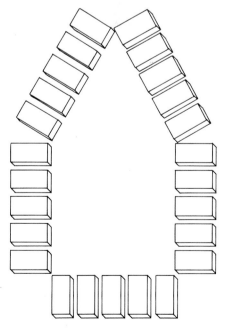

Right: *Dominoes laid out face down ready for a five-handed game of blind hughie.*

101

These children in Swaziland are playing twelve men's morris on a board scratched into the sandy ground.

Modern Board Games

Games of Alignment and Configuration

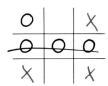

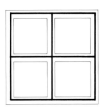

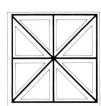

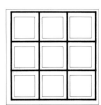

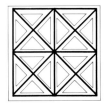

Above: *Boards for three-in-a-row games.*

The aim of alignment games is to enter pieces on the points of the playing board so that a number of them, generally three, form a row. Games of this type have been played for thousands of years and are among the oldest we know. Boards for these games have been discovered incised into the roofing slabs of the temple at Al-Qurna in Egypt. These were probably carved by the masons who helped to build the temple nearly 3,500 years ago. Confucius described a simple alignment game known as *yih*, which was played in China as long ago as 500 B.C. This was the game, that we now know as tic-tac-toe, or three men's morris.

In Sri Lanka, two other boards were found, cut into the great flight of steps that leads to the 2,000-year-old shrine at Mihintale. Traces of boards have been found in Crete, in Rome and in a Bronze Age burial site in Ireland. A fragment of a nine men's morris board was found among a royal burial hoard in a funeral ship at Gokstad, in Norway.

Below left: Three men's morris *in Senegal, in West Africa.*

Below right: *This fragment of a medieval French manuscript shows a* couple playing a game of nine men's morris.

Noughts and Crosses

Generations of schoolchildren have enjoyed a surreptitious game of noughts and crosses while their teachers' attention was diverted. A variation of tic-tac-toe, it is perhaps the simplest of the three-in-a-row alignment games. It is a game of entry only and once entered the men have no power of movement. The game is usually played on a board drawn on a scrap of paper or scratched on the ground with a sharp stick. The first player enters an X on any one of the nine squares and the second player enters a O on any other square. Play continues alternately, the object being to form a row of three X's or O's, either vertically, horizontally or diagonally. The first player to do so

wins. Analysis has demonstrated that the second player can never win, unless the first player makes a mistake–something that does not seem to have deterred children from carrying on the noughts and crosses tradition.

Tic-Tac-Toe

Tic-tac-toe is played throughout the world under a variety of names. In Britain it is generally known as three men's morris, "morris" being a corruption of the old English word *merels*, which was derived from the Latin *merellus*, meaning a "counter" or "token." This game was known in ancient Egypt and was also played in China 500 years before the birth of Christ. (See: p. 35, for the method of play of yih.) In his *Ars*

Amatoria (Art of Love), Ovid mentions tic-tac-toe, and several wooden or stone Roman boards have survived. The game was very popular in 14th-century England. Boards for both this game and the larger nine men's morris were cut into cloister seats in many large cathedrals and abbeys and these were sometimes used by the monks to while away the long hours they should have been spending at their devotions.

Three-in-a-Row

In Egypt, children play a form of tic-tac-toe on a board having 3 x 3 cells. Each player has three pieces that are placed on the board at the start of the game. The players move alternately. In each turn any piece can move one square in any direction, including diagonally, like the king's move in chess. Each player tries to make a row of three anywhere on the board, except on his own starting position. The first player to do this successfully is the winner.

103

Five or Six Men's Morris

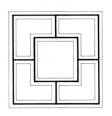

The board for nine men's morris.

This game was popular in England, France and Italy during the Middle Ages but has not been played much in Europe since the late 16th century. However, an almost identical game, differing only in that there is an additional method of capture, is still played in West Africa.

How to Play Five Men's Morris

The game is played by two players. They each have five (or six) pieces. These are entered, one at a time, alternately, each player attempting to form a row along one of the lines marked on the board. If a player succeeds in making a row, he may remove any opposing piece he wishes. When all the pieces have been entered, a piece may be moved along any line to an adjacent empty point. Pieces removed from the board are not allowed to reenter. The player whose pieces are reduced to two has lost.

Nine Men's Morris

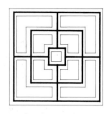

The board for five or six men's morris.

Nine men's morris in its various forms has been enjoyed since the earliest civilizations by princes and peasants alike. The oldest morris boards, found in Upper Egypt, were much like the ones still used today. They consisted of three concentric squares with intersecting lines joining the center points of the sides. Almost 3,000 years later an almost identical board was illustrated in King Alfonso's classic 13th-century *Book of Games*. In Europe, from the 14th century on, combined boards were frequently used. These took the form of a shallow box with a hinged lid. When the box was closed, one surface carried a chessboard and the other a merels (nine men's morris) board. When open, the box revealed a tables or backgammon board. These days, particularly in Germany and Italy, nine men's morris boards are often set out on the back of chessboards.

How to Play Nine Men's Morris

In this game for two players, each has nine black or nine white pieces. All the pieces are off the board at the start of the game. The game is played in two phases.

Right: *This painting over a doorway in the Castello di Issogne, Val d'Aosta, in Italy, shows a late 15th-century café scene. The men on the left are playing an early form of* backgammon. *Those next to them are playing* nine men's morris. *Both games appear to have reached an exciting stage for no one is taking any notice of the poor fellow on the right who is being attacked with a sword.*

Phase 1

1. The players toss a coin or draw lots to decide who begins. They enter their pieces, alternately, onto any vacant point. The object is to form a row of three pieces along a line. This is known as a *mill*.

2. When a player has formed a mill, he may remove one of his opponent's pieces from the board. Pieces in a mill are immune from attack. When all the pieces have been placed the game enters its second phase.

Phase 2

3. The players continue to play alternately, moving a piece along any line to an adjoining vacant point, attempting to make a mill and capture an opposing piece.

4. If a player forms a mill and all the opposing pieces are already in mills, play continues without loss to the opponent.

5. Double mills are five pieces so placed that each time a mill is broken, another is formed (see the diagram), an opposing piece being captured each time.

6. When a player has only three men left on the board and these form a mill, he must break the mill when it is his turn to move, even if it is disadvantageous to him.

7. The game is won by the player who reduces his opponent to two pieces *or* blocks all his opponent's pieces, preventing them from moving.

Twelve Men's Morris

This variant of nine men's morris first appeared sometime during the 14th century. Diagonal lines were added to join the corners of the squares. Early English settlers took the game to North America; it still enjoys a certain popularity in the United States today. Each player begins with twelve pieces. Mills can be formed horizontally, vertically or diagonally. Otherwise the game is played in the same way as nine men's morris.

Nine Men's Morris with Dice

Alfonso X's wonderful 13th-century manuscript describes a variant of nine men's morris using three cubic dice. During the first phase of the game–the entry phase–throws of 6,5,4, or 6,3,3, or 5,2,2, or 4,1,1 gave the thrower the right to break into an opposing mill and capture a piece, in addition to entering one of his own pieces onto the board. If a mill was formed with this piece, two opposing pieces were removed. With any throw other than those mentioned, only a single piece could be entered. The dice were discarded at the end of the first phase of play and then the game continued in the usual manner.

How to Make Twelve Men's Morris

Materials

A plywood sheet 35 cm x 35 cm x 8 mm (14 in x 14 in x ⁵/₁₆ in), a thin sheet of black formica (or some similar opaque plastic material) 35 cm x 35 cm (14 in x 14 in), a roll of 2 mm (¹/₁₆ in) yellow adhesive tape, a roll of 1 cm (³/₈ in) yellow adhesive tape, glue suitable for bonding formica to wood.

Tools

Pencil, ruler, hobby knife, pencil eraser, sandpaper.

Method

Glue the sheet of plywood and the sheet of formica together. It may be necessary to place weights (heavy books, for example) on the formica to ensure a good bonding. This depends on the type of glue used.

When the glue has dried, smooth the edges with sandpaper, taking great care not to damage the corners of the formica.

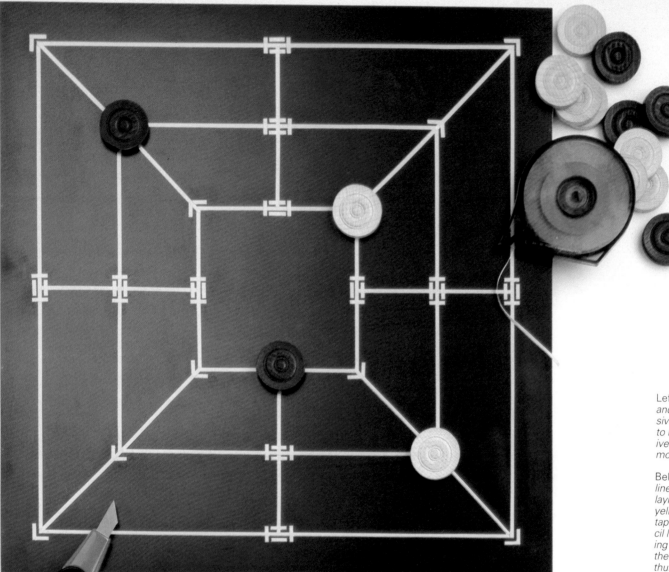

Left: *Black formica and yellow adhesive tape combine to make an attractive twelve men's morris board.*

Below: *The playing lines are marked by laying 2 mm (1/16 in) yellow adhesive tape along the pencil lines and pressing it in place with the index finger or thumb.*

The edges must now be covered with the 1 cm (3/8 in) adhesive tape. The easiest way to do this is to unroll the tape as you go, smoothing it flat with your thumb. The surplus tape is then folded under the board and smoothed to bond it. If there is insufficient tape to ensure a good bond, an extra strip can be stuck to the underside.

The next step is to mark out the playing lines using a ruler and pencil. First draw the diagonals. Next divide the board in half both vertically and horizontally. The sides of the three squares are respectively 2½ cm, 7 cm and 12½ cm (1 in, 2¾ in and 5 in) from the edge of the board. Measure these and draw them in. Finally, erase the unwanted lines from the center square and from around the edge of the board. The playing lines are now followed in

2 mm (1/16 in) yellow adhesive tape, as shown in the drawing, far right. The easiest way to do this is to follow each line, unrolling the tape as you go and pressing it onto the board with your index finger or thumb, in much the same way as you applied the 1 cm (3/8 in) tape to the edges. Each line is laid down separately and the tape cut with the hobby knife when it is position. When this is done, the points of intersection are decorated as shown in the photograph.

Note: It is not essential to follow the black and yellow color scheme suggested here. Formica and similar plastic materials are available in a wide range of colors, as is adhesive tape. Also, the decoration at the points of intersection can be varied to suit your own taste.

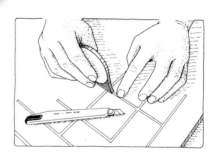

When you have made this board, you may like to use the diagrams on the previous pages to make boards for the games of five men's morris and nine men's morris. Follow the same principles as described above. The only difference is in the positions of the playing lines, but these can easily be worked out.

Five-in-a-Row Games

Go-moku

Go-moku, which is an adaptation of the complex Japanese game of *i-go* (known in China as wei-ch'i), is probably the most popular of the five-in-a-row games. The game was introduced into Europe during the 1880s and is also known in Britain as spoil five. It is played on an i-go board, which has 18 x 18 cells. Each player has a set of 100 pieces, known as stones. One set is black and the other white.

Go-bang

It is often said that *go-bang* is merely an alternative name for go-moku. On the other hand, some people think that go-bang is similar to the morris games and that opposing pieces must be captured in order to win. In the latter case, it is played with no less than 100 stones per player on an 18 x 18 i-go board! However, the game can be simplified by using a smaller board and fewer pieces, as is shown in the version below.

How to Play Go-moku

1. At the start of play, the board is empty. Black has the opening move and introduces a stone on any point (line intersection).
2. Players enter stones alternately and attempt to form an uninterrupted row of five stones–horizontally, vertically or diagonally. The first player to do this wins the game.
3. If all the stones are entered before either player has succeeded in forming a row of five, the game can be declared drawn. Another possibility is for the players to move one stone one point in an orthogonal (horizontal or vertical) direction until a five is formed.

How to Play Go-bang

1. Go-bang is played on a checkers board. Each player has 12 white or 12 black pieces.
2. The players enter their pieces alternately and attempt to form a row of five horizontally, vertically or diagonally. When this is achieved an opposing piece may be removed from the board.
3. When all the pieces are entered onto the board, each player moves one piece at a time to any adjacent vacant square, still attempting to form a row of five. Each time this is achieved, an opposing piece is removed from the board.
4. The winner is the player who reduces his opponent to four pieces, thus making it impossible for him to form a row of five.

Right: *These Japanese ladies while away the time playing* go-moku.

108

Exchange Games

Salta and Pyramid

Salta and pyramid are clever variations of checkers. But while checkers is a war game–in which the object is to capture opposing pieces–both salta and pyramid are essentially games of configuration in which the object is to occupy the opponent's initial squares with your own pieces. The origins of pyramid are unclear, but we know that salta was invented around the turn of the century and first shown at the Monte Carlo Chess Tourney in 1901.

How to Play Pyramid

1. The game is played on an 8 x 8 chessboard, each player having 10 white or 10 black pieces. At start of play the pieces are positioned as shown in the diagram.
2. Black begins and subsequent moves are made alternately. A piece may be moved one square diagonally onto a vacant square, as in checkers, and a piece may be jumped over an opposing piece–by a *short leap*–onto an empty square. Players are allowed to make more than one leap in a single turn of play.
3. A piece that is leaped is *not* removed from the board; all 20 pieces remain on the board at the end of play.
4. The player who first occupies all 10 of his opponent's initial squares is the winner.

How to Play Salta

1. The game is played on the black squares of a 10 x 10 checkerboard, each player having 15 white or 15 black pieces. At start of play, the pieces are positioned as shown in the diagram. The pieces in the first row are stars, those in the second row are moons and those in the third are suns. In each row the pieces are numbered one to five from left to right.

Note: The symbols and numbers serve only to individualize the men and confer no special power of move.

2. Black begins and moves are then made alternately. A piece may be moved one square diagonally, backwards or forwards. A piece can jump a piece of either color by a *short leap*. A player may make more than one leap in a single turn of play. Pieces leaped are *not* removed from the board but remain in play.

3. The object of the game is to occupy the squares held by the opponent at start of play, placing on each square a piece with the same symbol and number. For example, the piece marked with a star and a 2, which begins the game on square 1c, must finish on square 10h. The first player to move all 15 of his pieces to the correct squares is the winner.

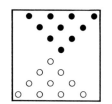

Above: *The positions of the pieces at start of play in pyramid.*

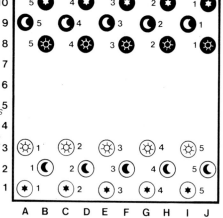

Right: *The positions of the pieces at start of play in salta. Note: The numbers beside the pieces serve to differentiate them. In fact they appear on the actual pieces.*

Halma

Halma derives its name from the Greek and means "jump" or "leap". According to most authorities the game was devised in England in about 1880, although Pick in his *Dictionary of Games* (J.M. Dent & Sons Ltd., 1952) states that it was invented in 1883 by George H. Monks of Boston, Massachusetts.

Halma was originally known as "hoppity" in Britain and, like salta and pyramid, it is a game of configura-tion. The object is to occupy the position originally occupied by the opposing forces. The game can be played by either two or four players. If there are two players, each has 19 pieces or counters of contrasting color. If four people play, each player has 13 pieces. Halma is played on a checkered board of 16 x 16 squares and each corner is a "camp," the boundaries of which are marked with thicker lines. At start of play the pieces are arranged as in the diagram.

How to Play Halma

1. At start of play the pieces are arran-ged in *camps,* as shown in the diagram. A coin is tossed or dice are thrown to decide which player moves first, play continuing alternately. If four people are playing, turns pass clockwise around the board.

2. There are two types of move:
a) a *step* in which a player moves a piece in any direction into a vacant adjoining square, and
b) a *leap* in which a player jumps a piece over a piece in an adjoining square into a vacant square directly behind it.

3. A player may leap over his own piec-es or those of an opponent. (He is not required to leap if he does not wish to.) A player may make several leaps in one move but he may not combine a step and a leap.

4. Pieces that have been leaped remain on the board.

5. A player may block an opponent's attempt to form a *ladder*. (A ladder is a series of pieces on alternate squares enabling a piece to be moved several squares in a turn of play.) A player may also make use of an opponent's ladder to advance his own pieces.

6. The winner is the first player to move all 19 of his pieces into the opposing camp.

Above: The position of the pieces at start of play in halma. If two are playing, each player has 19 pieces. If four are playing, each has 13 pieces.

Left: *The playing pieces are cut at an angle of 45° to the center line.*

Right: *A grid to enable you to make the template for the four sides.*

How to Make a Halma Board

Materials
a) For the board:
a plywood sheet 40 cm x 40 cm x 8 mm (16 in x 16 in x 5/16 in),
2 plywood sheets 14 cm x 40 cm x 5 mm (5 5/8 in x 16 in x 3/16 in),
2 plywood sheets 14 cm x 41 cm x 5 mm (5 5/8 in x 16 3/8 in x 3/16 in),
2 plywood sheets 12 1/2 cm x 12 1/2 cm x 8 mm (5 in x 5 in x 5/16 in), a plywood sheet 7 1/2 cm x 10 cm x 8 mm (3 in x 4 in x 5/16 in),
a sheet of thin cardboard 14 cm x 41 cm (5 5/8 in x 16 3/8 in),
3 sheets of adhesive plastic–blue 40 cm x 50 cm (16 in x 20 in), yellow 50 cm x 60 cm (20 in x 24 in) and green 20 cm x 50 cm (8 in x 20 in),
a roll of 4 mm (3/16 in) black adhesive tape, wood glue, 1 cm (3/8 in) panel pins, black acrylic paint, paintbrush.
b) For the playing pieces: 2 x 40 cm (16 in) lengths of 1 1/2 cm (5/8 in) dowel in contrasting woods, teak oil, varnish. Note: if you make pieces for 4 players, 2 x 30 cm (12 in) lengths of 1 1/2 cm (5/8 in) dowel in other woods are also needed.

Tools
Pencil, steel ruler, hobby knife, com-passes, scroll saw, sandpaper, square file, handsaw, vise, hammer, mitre box and scissors.

Method
1. To make the terraces: divide the 7 1/2 cm x 10 cm (3 in x 4 in) plywood and both pieces of the

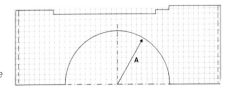

12 1/2 cm x 12 1/2 cm (5 in x 5 in) plywood into 2 1/2 cm (1 in) squares. Mark the cutting lines in heavier pencil accord-ing to the diagram in the margin. Cut along these lines with the scroll saw. Clean the corners with the file and sandpaper if necessary.
2. To make the sides: first, a cardboard template has to be made, the dimen-sions of which are shown in the dia-gram below. Draw it out using the ruler, pencil and compasses. Cut the template out using a steel ruler and hobby knife. Lay it on one of the 41 cm (16 3/8 in) lengths of 5 mm (3/16 in) ply-wood and draw round it. Cut out with a scroll saw, cleaning the corners if ne-cessary. Repeat to make a second side. Turn the template over so that it be-comes a "mirror image." Place the template on the 40 cm (16 in) lengths of plywood so that the dotted lines fall at the ends. Draw, cut out and clean as before.
3. To assemble: apply glue to one edge of the 40 cm x 40 cm (16 in x 16 in) square. Lay one of the longer sides on this edge so that the lowest center part is flush with the top surface and each end protrudes 5 mm (3/16 in). Fix in place with panel pins. Repeat for the opposite side. The shorter sides can now be slotted in, glued and pinned. Apply glue to the undersurfaces and straight edges of the pieces which make up the terraces and fix them in position. Sand down the whole board.
4. To finish: paint the edges of the side panels and the terraces in black acrylic paint. This can be done roughly as any errors will eventually be hidden. The top surface of the board, including the terraces but *not* the painted edges, should now be covered with the blue adhesive plastic sheet. (You may find it easier to do this in smaller areas as a large sheet is difficult to handle.) Now cut the green sheet into 2 1/2 cm (1 in) strips using a steel ruler and a hobby

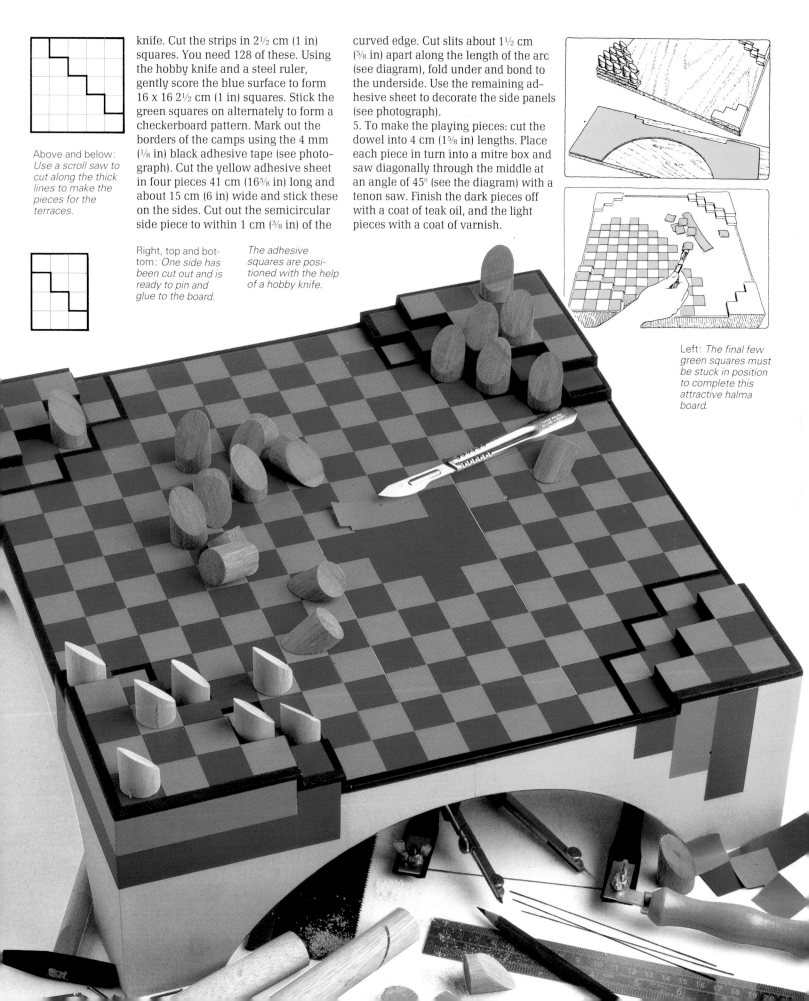

knife. Cut the strips in 2½ cm (1 in) squares. You need 128 of these. Using the hobby knife and a steel ruler, gently score the blue surface to form 16 x 16 2½ cm (1 in) squares. Stick the green squares on alternately to form a checkerboard pattern. Mark out the borders of the camps using the 4 mm (⅛ in) black adhesive tape (see photograph). Cut the yellow adhesive sheet in four pieces 41 cm (16⅜ in) long and about 15 cm (6 in) wide and stick these on the sides. Cut out the semicircular side piece to within 1 cm (⅜ in) of the

curved edge. Cut slits about 1½ cm (⅝ in) apart along the length of the arc (see diagram), fold under and bond to the underside. Use the remaining adhesive sheet to decorate the side panels (see photograph).

5. To make the playing pieces: cut the dowel into 4 cm (1⅝ in) lengths. Place each piece in turn into a mitre box and saw diagonally through the middle at an angle of 45° (see the diagram) with a tenon saw. Finish the dark pieces off with a coat of teak oil, and the light pieces with a coat of varnish.

Above and below: Use a scroll saw to cut along the thick lines to make the pieces for the terraces.

Right, top and bottom: One side has been cut out and is ready to pin and glue to the board.

The adhesive squares are positioned with the help of a hobby knife.

Left: The final few green squares must be stuck in position to complete this attractive halma board.

War Games

Most games, board games included, are imitations of real-life situations. Not surprisingly, therefore, games based on various aspects of warfare have been popular all over the world since time immemorial. Most war games are designed for two players, each the leader of his own forces and the originator of strategic operations against the opponent. There are a number of different types of war game and they are based on the different types of strategic operation we know in real warfare. Murray, arguably the best authority on board games, has classified war games under four headings:

a) *battle games,* in which the object is to capture or immobilize all the opposing pieces–chess is a typical game of this kind;

b) *territorial contests,* in which the object is to gain control of a larger portion of the board–the Chinese game of wei-ch'i and the Japanese game of i-go are examples of territorial contests;

c) *blockade games,* in which the object is not to capture enemy pieces but to immobilize them–the game mu-torere, played by New Zealand Maoris, is a good example of this type;

d) *clearance games,* in which the only moves are captures and the object is to make the larger number of captures–leap-frog and solitaire are two examples of clearance games.

The typical battle game is one in which opposing players direct a conflict between two armies of equal strength upon a circumscribed battlefield. These two armies are differentiated in some way, usually by color. Experience accumulated over the centuries has demonstrated that a field of 8 x 8 cells is the optimum for this type of game, although many battle games are played on larger or smaller boards. The games can be further distinguished by the moves allowed and the methods of capture employed, and it is the combination of the allowable moves and the method of capture used that gives a particular game its unique character.

In games played on latticed boards pieces can be moved in only three basic ways: orthogonally (horizontally or vertically), diagonally or a combination of these two (the knight's move in chess, for example).

Right: *This French cartoon,* Le délasse-ment des politiques *(The relaxation of politicos), is a cynical comment on the characters of the politicians of the day. The players in the foreground seem to be playing* checkers–except *that the board has 10 x 18 cells. This is not surprising as the satirists of the time were more concerned with the broad view and often paid little attention to detail.*

In some games, pieces can only be moved one square, in others they can be moved any number of squares. Sometimes pieces can only be moved in a forward direction, other times they can be moved forwards or backwards. In some games leaps are permitted, in others not. In games such as checkers each piece has the same power of move and in other games, such as chess, different pieces have different powers of move.

There are several methods of capture; the three most often employed are replacement, interception and the short leap. Replacement capture is employed in all race games and in chess. A player reaches a square occupied by his opponent by a legal move, removes the occupying piece and takes its place. Interception captures are the oldest form of capture and take place by enclosing an opposing piece between two of your own pieces on three consecutive squares, in a direction in which a legal move can be played.

This method of capture was used in latrunculi, the Roman game described on page 26. The third common method of capture is the short leap in which a piece leaps an opposing piece in a legal direction of play and lands on a vacant square immediately next to the opposing piece. A fourth method, the huff, is employed in some games in which capture is compulsory. If a player overlooks a possible capture, his opponent *huffs* a piece and removes it from the board.

In this chapter, examples of all four types of war game are offered: battle games, territorial contests, blockade games and clearance games. The moves allowed and the methods of capture are illustrated where necessary. For many of these games, boards are not readily available and in such cases simple instructions on how to make your own board are given.

Left top: *Throughout history invading armies have taken games with them on their conquests and this has been one way in which games have spread all over the world. Many games played in North Africa were first introduced by the French and Spanish. This game* of checkers *is being played in Casablanca, Morocco.*

Left middle: *Board games are very popular in the countries of West Africa, where boards are often scratched into the sand and the playing pieces consist of whatever comes to hand. These tribesmen in Mali are playing a game called* yoté *on a board of 5 x 6 cups. The playing pieces are sticks and what appear to be fruit stones.*

Left, bottom: *Chinese* chess (choohong-ki) *still displays most of the characteristics of its ancestor, the ancient Indian game of* chaturanga. *It is played on the intersections of the lines of an 8 x 9 celled board. The middle horizontal row separates the domains and represent the Hwang-ho—the great Yellow River.*

113

The Alquerque Group of War Games

In peralikatuma, each player has 23 pieces, the extra pieces filling the seven points in the extra triangles to the left and right. The games are identical in all respects to alquerque. Players move alternately and a piece may be moved in any direction to any adjacent vacant point. Capture is by the short leap and any number of pieces may be captured in a turn of play. The first player to capture all the opposing pieces is the winner.

Right: This diagram of the alquerque board shows the position of the pieces at start of play.

Below and next page, top left: Sixteen soldiers and peralikatuma are played in Sri Lanka and are both forms of alquerque. In sixteen soldiers, each player has 16 pieces, which are arranged as shown in the diagram below.

Battle games of the alquerque type date back to at least 1400 B.C. This is indicated by a replica of an alquerque board cut into a roofing slab of the great temple at Al-Qurna, on the west bank of the Nile, in Egypt. It seems safe to assume that this and the other gaming boards found at the temple were engraved by the stonemasons working on the construction of the temple and that they used them to while away their leisure hours. The game has been played throughout the area we now know as the Middle East for centuries. The Arabic name is *elquirkat;* it is mentioned in a 10th-century work known as the *Kitab al-Aghani.* When the Moors invaded Spain, they took the game with them and its name became *alquerque.* Several versions of this game are described and illustrated in Alfonso X's magnificent *Libro de Juegos* (Book of Games). One of these versions, *alquerque de doce,* (twelve-man alquerque) is very similar to the game that is still played in Spain today. The basic alquerque board and the method of play have provided the basis for several other battle games that have been developed in countries all over the world.

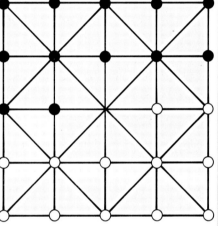

Alquerque

How to Play Alquerque

Alquerque is basically an early form of checkers. Each player has 12 pieces, black or white. They are arranged on the board as shown in the diagram. A coin is tossed to decide which player moves first. A piece may be moved from its position along any marked line to any adjacent empty point. If a piece is next to an opposing piece and the point behind that piece is vacant, the opposing piece can be captured by the short-leap method. Where possible, a series of short-leap captures can be made; change of direction during a series of captures is permitted. If a possible capture is overlooked, the offending piece is huffed and then removed from the board. The first player to capture all his opponent's pieces has won. The Alfonso manuscript notes that the advantage lies with the player moving second, but if played by two players of equal skill the game will always end in a draw.

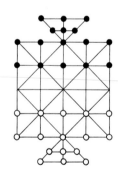

Right: A variation of sixteen soldiers or mogol putt'han, played in Pakistan. The players in the background are playing nine men's morris.

114

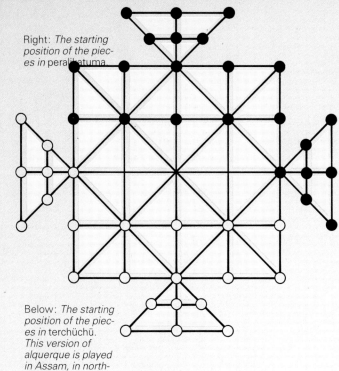

Below: *The starting position of the pieces in* terchüchü. *This version of alquerque is played in Assam, in northeast India. The eight triangles are*

refuges to which men can retire.

Fanorona

Fanorona dates from about A.D. 1680 and comes from Madagascar. It was adapted from alquerque by doubling the size of the board, increasing the number of pieces on each side to 22 and changing the method of capture. The game played an important role in the Malagasi rituals and seems to have been invested with divinatory properties. In 1895, when the French stormed the capital, the then queen, Ranavalona III, had more faith in the result of an

official fanorona match than in her army commanders, allowing the outcome of the game to influence her military strategy. This turned out to have been something of a mistake, for the French conquered the island, the monarchy was abolished and the queen spent the rest of her life in exile.

How to Play Fanorona

1. There are two distinct phases, or games, which are played alternately. A match consists of an agreed number of games. The winner is the player who gains the majority of games in the match.
2. At start of play the pieces occupy the nine points of intersection on each of the two rows nearest each player. Four pieces of each color are placed alternately on points in the middle row. The center point is empty. White moves first, and play proceeds alternately. Pieces may be moved one step along any line to an adjacent vacant point.
3. *Approach* and *withdrawal* are two methods of capture that have not yet been discussed in this book. In approach capture, when a move ends on a point, and then the following point or points in unbroken sequence along the line of movement are occupied by opposing pieces, those pieces are captured and removed. In withdrawal capture, when a piece moves away from a point or points occupied by opposing pieces in the same line of movement,

those pieces are captured and removed.
4. Captures are compulsory, but on the first move by each player only one such sequence can be taken. In subsequent moves, a player may make several capures providing each move is along a different line. The piece changes direction to make each capture.
5. If capture is possible in two directions, the player may choose in which direction to capture. He cannot capture in both directions. There is no obligation to capture the larger number of pieces.
6. When one player has captured all his opponent's pieces, the game ends.
7. When one player has suffered defeat, the following game is played in a different way. The player who lost begins and the previous winner sacrifices piece after piece until he has lost 17 pieces. This phase is known as *vela;* during play the winner cannot capture opposing pieces. His opponent can only capture one piece at a time. When 17 pieces have been lost, normal play is resumed, using rules 1 to 6.
8. The third game is played like the first and the fourth game is a vela-game again. In this fashion both openings are played in turn until the agreed number of games has been reached.

Below: *Use the methods and materials given on pages* 144/145 (mu torere) *to make this clay fanorona board.*

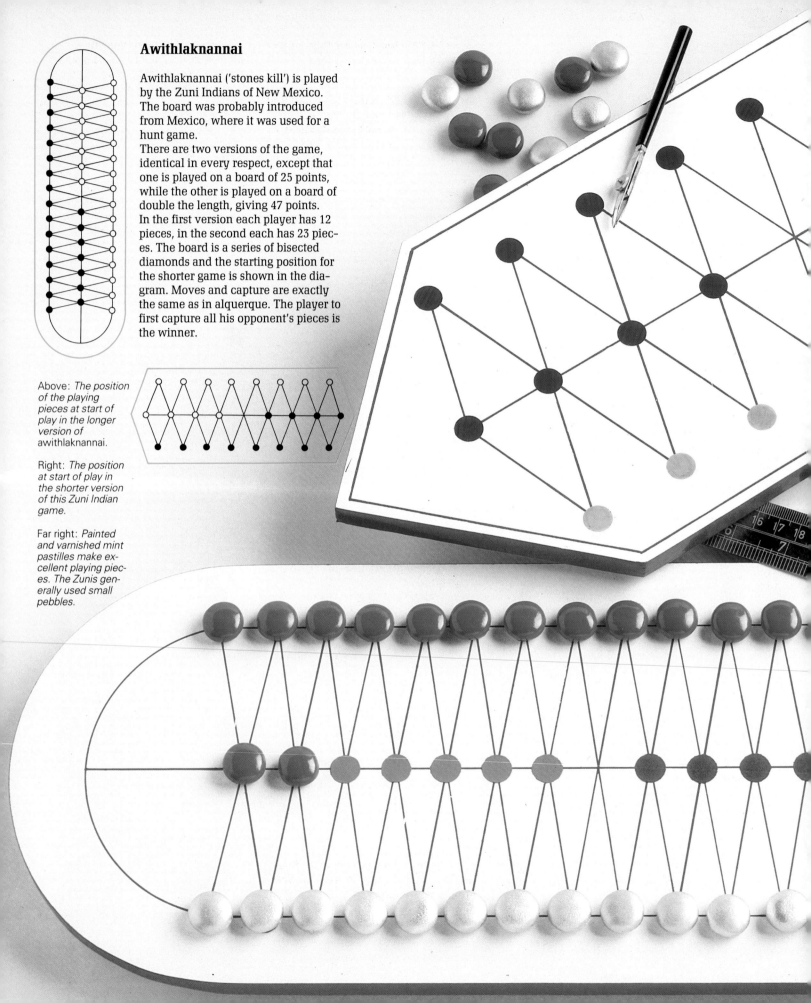

Awithlaknannai

Awithlaknannai ('stones kill') is played by the Zuni Indians of New Mexico. The board was probably introduced from Mexico, where it was used for a hunt game.

There are two versions of the game, identical in every respect, except that one is played on a board of 25 points, while the other is played on a board of double the length, giving 47 points. In the first version each player has 12 pieces, in the second each has 23 pieces. The board is a series of bisected diamonds and the starting position for the shorter game is shown in the diagram. Moves and capture are exactly the same as in alquerque. The player to first capture all his opponent's pieces is the winner.

Above: *The position of the playing pieces at start of play in the longer version of awithlaknannai.*

Right: *The position at start of play in the shorter version of this Zuni Indian game.*

Far right: *Painted and varnished mint pastilles make excellent playing pieces. The Zunis generally used small pebbles.*

How to Make an Awithlaknannai Board

Materials

A sheet of white plasticized chipboard 20 cm x 50 cm x 1 cm (8 in x 20 in x ⅜ in), a roll of blue adhesive tape, 23 red and 23 blue stickers 1 cm (⅜ in) in diameter, blue oil-based paint.

Tools

Compasses, pencil, ruler, scroll saw, rasp, pencil eraser, drawing pen, hobby knife, sandpaper.

Method

Mark the center line along the length of the plasticized chipboard using the ruler and pencil. Mark a point on this line 10 cm (4 in) from one end. Set the compasses to a radius of 10 cm (4 in) and with this point as center draw an arc as shown in the diagram. Cut along this arc with the scroll saw and take care not to cut inside the line. Smooth the edge with a rasp, keeping exactly to the line so that you achieve a perfect curve. Finish with sandpaper.

Now repeat the entire operation at the other end of the board.

Apply the adhesive tape to the edge of the board, making sure it bonds well to the chipboard. The tape is wider than the board is thick. The surplus can be folded underneath the board or carefully trimmed off with a hobby knife. Now draw lines across the width of the board at right angles to the center line and through the points 10 cm (4 in) from each end of the board. Set the compasses to a radius of 7 cm (2⅘ in) and with these same points as centers draw arcs at each end of the board to meet the marked lines.

Draw lines along each side of the board between the marked lines to join the ends of the arcs. These lines should be 30 cm (12 in) in length.

Using a ruler and pencil mark points at 2 cm (⅘ in) intervals along these lines. Mark points on the center line 1 cm (⅖ in) inside each of the lines across the width of the board. The distance between these points should be 28 cm (11⅕ in). Mark points at 2 cm (⅘ in) intervals along this length. The points can now be connected as shown in the diagram to form a series of triangles. Use a pencil eraser to erase the lines across the width of the board and those parts of the center line that lie outside the end arcs.

Paint over all the remaining lines with blue oil-based paint using a ruler and drawing pen. A standard drawing pen can be mounted in the compasses to enable you to point the arcs at each end of the board.

When the paint is dry the stickers can be applied. The easiest way to do this is to take them on the tip of a hobby knife, position them carefully and press them into place with the thumb. Red stickers are applied to the points on the near side of the board and to the first seven points to the right on the center line. The middle point on the center line and the two points where the center line intersects the arcs have no stickers. Blue stickers are applied to the remaining points.

The board for the shorter version of awithlaknannai is made in a similar way. The eight points along the outer lines and the nine along the center line are placed at 4.5 cm (1¾ in) intervals.

Below: *A scroll saw is used to cut the curved ends of the board.*

Below center: *Draw the arc with the compasses at a radius of 7 cm (2⅘ in).*

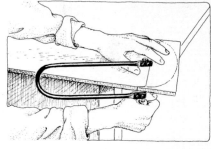

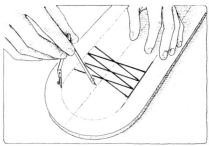

Below: *The initial positions from which the points are marked and the diagonals are drawn.*

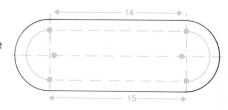

Zamma

Right: Zamma *is played on a modified quadruple alquerque board. The second, fourth, sixth and eighth rows and columns are omitted, reducing the power of movement. The position of the pieces at start of play is identical in both games.*

Zamma is sometimes also called quadruple alquerque. It is a game from the Sahara desert and is played on a modified quadruple alquerque board. The second, fourth, sixth and eighth rows and columns are omitted, which reduces the power of movement of pieces from these points. Most of the time, the board is scratched in the sand; short lengths of stalk and pellets of camel dung are used as pieces. As we assume that few of our readers will have access to an incontinent camel, we suggest using plastic counters of different colors instead.

How to Play Zamma

1. Each player starts with 40 pieces, which are arranged as shown in the diagram. Black moves first.

2. A piece moves one point directly or diagonally forwards.

3. The captures are made by the short leap method in any direction: straight or diagonally, forwards, backwards or sideways. Capture is compulsory and failure to capture results in the offending piece being huffed and removed from the board.

4. When a piece reaches the opposite back row it is promoted and becomes a *mullah*. It can be distinguished by turning it or marking it in some way. A mullah has special powers of move and capture. It can move any distance along any marked line through the point it occupies and in any direction. A mullah can capture either by the short leap or the *long leap* (a leap which allows a piece to jump over intervening vacant squares in order to capture). Captured pieces are not removed from the board until the move is complete and the mullah may not leap a piece a second time.
This rule is designed to restrict the otherwise enormous powers of the promoted piece.

5. The winner is the player who captures all his opponent's pieces.

Right: *These Saharan desert dwellers use stones and pellets of camel dung as playing pieces in* zamma.

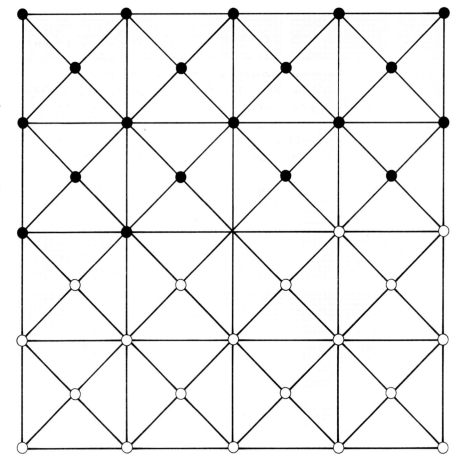

118

Hnefatafl or Alea Evangelii

A fragment of a hnefatafl board found in a Roman Iron Age grave in Denmark shows that this game was played in Scandanavia before A.D. 400. Norsemen took *hnefatafl* to Iceland, Britain and Ireland, where it became the only board game played by the Saxons. It retained its popularity until the introduction of chess in the 11th century. The game is mentioned in many of the later Icelandic sagas and also in a number of Celtic manuscripts. In a 10th-century English manuscript, written in Latin during the reign of King Athelstan, the board and the arrangement of the pieces are used to set out a harmony of the Gospels–a rather curious attempt to give a scriptural meaning to hnefatafl.

The text of this manuscript begins with the words *Incipit alea euangelii quam Dubinsi...*, from which the name "Alea Evangelii" is taken. The manuscript is useful in that it gives the game–as it was played in the 10th century–an account that is consistent with both older and later descriptions. The following reconstruction is based on a translation of this manuscript by J. Armitage Robinson (*Time of St. Dunstan,* Oxford, 1923). There is only one basic difference: in the modern version the pieces move on the squares and not on the points.

Left: *This wooden board was discovered in 1932, during the excavation of a lake dwelling at Ballinderry, West Meath, in Ireland. Dating from the 10th century A.D., the board is made of wood and is 9½ in (23 cm) square. There are 7 x 7 holes for the pegged men and the center hole, intended for the king, is circled. The decoration round the frame indicates that the board was made in the Isle of Man.*

How to play Hnefatafl

1. The game is played on a latticed board containing 18 x 18 cells. One player has a king and 24 black pieces, the other player has 48 white pieces. At start of play the pieces are positioned as shown in the diagram on this page. The king is on the central square.

2. The king's forces move first and then play proceeds alternately.

3. Any piece can move any number of vacant squares orthogonally–the rook's move in chess.

4. Capture is by the interception method–trapping an opposing piece between two of your own pieces in rank or file (but not diagonally). It is, however, possible to move a piece between two opposing pieces without being captured.

5. The king is only captured when it is surrounded on all four sides by opposing pieces.

6. Black wins if the king succeeds in reaching any square on the edge of the board. White wins if the king is captured.

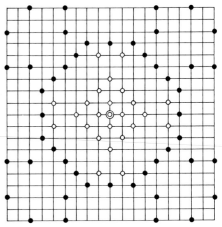

Left: *A version of hnefatafl that is akin to the game of tablut, described on the opposite page.*

Note: *These boards are in the collection of R.C. Bell MB FRSC, and we are indebted to him for permission to reproduce them.*

Above: *A reproduction of a hnefatafl board and bone pieces. Here the game is played on the squares and not the intersections. The board is 19 x 19 squares, therefore, not 18 x 18.*

Right: *The first two pieces are of jet and were found in Warrington in the north-west of England. The third piece, which is made of bone, was found in Woodperry, a village in Oxfordshire.*

Tablut

The game of tablut bears a great resemblance to hnefatafl, although it is played with fewer pieces and on a smaller board. The starting layout of the pieces is also different, but the powers of move and the objectives are the same as in the Norse game. Tablut originated among the Lapps in the far north of Scandinavia. It was first described by the Swedish botanist Carolus Linnaeus–who later became famous for his system of classification of plants and animals–in a diary he kept during a six-month journey through Lappland in 1732. This diary not only contained descriptions of Lappland's flora and fauna, but also copious notes on the Lapps and their customs, among which were a description of the game and an illustration of a board made of embroidered reindeer skin. Linnaeus was still a young unknown student at the time of his arduous and dangerous journey and nobody was interested in publishing his account.

It was not until the 19th century, years after his death, that this fascinating diary, containing his account of the ancient Scandinavian game of tablut, was finally published.

How to Play Tablut

Tablut is played on a board of 9 x9 cells, marked as shown in the diagram. The central cell represents the *konakis*, or throne, and only the Swedish king may occupy this square. In the game described by Linnaeus, one player held the king–shaped like its counterpart in chess–and eight Swedish soldiers, which were pawn-shaped and had pyramidal heads. The opposing player held 16 Muscovites. They were also pawnshaped, but had two heads. These pieces being difficult to obtain, the game can be played using a chess king and chess pawns or checkers pieces.

1. At start of play the pieces are placed on the board as shown in the diagram.

2. All pieces have the same power of move–any number of vacant squares in an orthogonal direction. This is the rook's move in chess.

3. Capture takes place by the interception method–that is, by enclosing an opposing piece between two of your own pieces in a row or a column. Any piece moved deliberately between two opposing pieces is, however, immune from capture.

4. The king is captured if all four surrounding squares are occupied by opposing pieces, or if the fourth square is the konakis. In this event, the game is won by the Muscovites.

5. The Swedish forces are victorious if their king reaches any square on the edge of the board.

When there is a clear route for the king, the player calls out "raichi!" (check!). If there are two clear routes, he calls "tui-chi!" (checkmate). He is the winner, as the opponent cannot block two routes in a single move.

Left: *The Saxon hnefatafl board and opening position of the pieces. The game was sometimes known as alea evangelii because of a Latin text that describes the game as a religious allegory.*

Far Right: *The board for the Scandinavian game of tablut. The king occupied the konakis, or central throne, and was surrounded by his bodyguard. The enemy, comprising 16 Muscovites, was positioned at the four cardinal points of the board.*

Right: *The Swedish botanist, Carolus Linnaeus, who first described the Lapp game of tablut.*

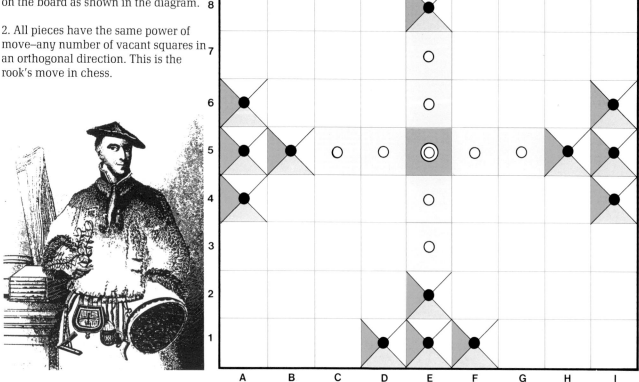

121

Seega

The origins of this Egyptian game are shrouded in mystery, although most authorities agree that it must be very old. It was described by Lane more than a hundred years ago and both Falkener (1892) and Murray (1951) offer methods of play and rules. Seega seems to have been the "poor man's game"; it was usually played on a lattice scratched in the sand. Arab guides found more durable boards scratched at the summit of the Great Pyramid and on fallen roofing slabs in the temple at Al-Qurna. The latter are inferior to the gaming boards that were originally cut by the masons who worked on the temple thousands of years ago, and Murray is of the opinion that they are of comparatively recent origin. Seega seems to have lost its popularity in Egypt, but is still enjoyed farther south in Somalia. There are several varieties, differing only in the size of the board and the number of pieces (*kelb*, "dog") employed.

Here, we offer the basic game. It is played on a board of 5 x 5 cells and each player has 12 pieces of a distinctive color.

More complicated forms of the game can be played on boards of 7 x 7 or 9 x 9 cells, using 24 and 40 pieces per player respectively.

Children enjoying a game of seega *on a board scratched into the dust of a Dakar street. Seega spread to Senegal and other countries in West Africa from Egypt and Somalia.*

Below: *The method of capture employed in* seega. *The piece on the top row moves one square vertically downwards and has the choice of capturing either of the white pieces to the left or right by the method of interception.*

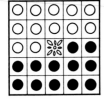

How to Play Seega

Seega is played in two phases.

Phase 1–The Placement Phase
1. A coin is tossed to determine which player is the first to play. Play proceeds alternately. In each turn of play, each player places two pieces on any vacant square other than the central square. The latter is left empty until the second phase of the game.

2. When all the pieces are in position, the player placing the last two begins the second phase.

Phase 2–The Capture Phase
1. A piece can be moved on any adjacent vacant square, including the central square, orthogonally but not diagonally.

2. Capture is by the interception method: enclosing an opposing piece between two of your own pieces. A player may continue to move a piece as long as it can capture.

Above: The starting position for a variation of seega *known as* high jump. *This game is popular in Somalia. Moves are the same as in* seega *but capture is by the short leap method.*

3. Capture of offered pieces is compulsory, but a player can choose between two captures where this is possible. A piece moving voluntarily between two opposing pieces is *not* captured, but if an attacking piece is moved away and then back again, a capture *is* made.

4. A piece on the central square is immune from attack.

5. If a player's pieces are blocked, the opponent must take an extra turn and make an opening.

6. A player achieves a "major" win if he succeeds in capturing all the opposing pieces.

Seega has a number of weaknesses. One of them is that a stalemate can be easily created by building a *barrier* along a row or column behind which only pieces of the same color are placed. Then an attack is no longer possible. If a barrier is built, the player having the most pieces on the board achieves a "minor" win. If both players have the same number of pieces, the game is drawn.

How to Make a Seega Board

Materials
A piece of 5 mm (³/₁₆ in) thick saddle leather measuring 35 cm x 35 cm (14 in x 14 in).

Tools
Steel rule, pencil, soldering iron with two branding attachments, one for the straight lines, the other for the central pattern of concentric circles.

Note: These attachments can be bought in shops specializing in leatherwork and in many hobby shops.

Top right: *Pieces can easily be made by painting small pebbles in contrasting bright colors.*

Method

Ask your supplier to cut the leather sheet to size.

Note: If you already have a sheet of leather, the board can be cut using a sharp hobby knife. Some shops may only sell saddle leather in certain sizes. While they will certainly cut it for you, you may have to pay for the surplus.

First draw the grid using the ruler and pencil. The sides of the outer square are 4½ cm (1¹³⁄₁₆ in) from the edge of the sheet, those of the inner square are 5 cm (2 in) from the edge. Divide the inner square into a grid of squares each measuring 5 cm x 5 cm (2 in x 2 in).

Burn all the pencil lines using a steel ruler and a special branding attachment fitted to your soldering iron. The pattern of concentric circles is also burnt into the leather with a branding attachment. The lines joining the

circles and completing the pattern are burnt using a steel ruler and the original branding attachment.

Note: Branding attachments can be obtained in a variety of patterns.

Above: *The board is marked out and decorated with a soldering iron fitted* *with special attachments for burning the pattern.*

Gala

Gala, also known as farmer's chess, used to be popular in the West German farming villages of Schleswig-Holstein. Even today boards can still be found in remote farmhouses, although the game has long since lost its popularity.

Gala is played on a board similar to a 10 x 10 checkerboard, the main difference being that the gala board has a central cross marked on it. This is important because pieces entering the cross are deflected and change their direction of move. Each player has 20 pieces–two kings, five rooks, five bishops and eight pawns–which at the beginning of the game are arranged as shown in the diagram.

In the original game the pieces were of identical shape, rather like small skittles, the kings being slightly larger than the other pieces. They were differentiated in terms of color, the upper half of both black and white kings being painted gold, rooks green, and bishops red. The pawns were left unpainted. Nowadays, the game can simply be played with ordinary chess pieces. The object is to capture both opposing kings and all capture is by the replacement method, as in normal chess.

How to Play Gala

1. Pawns move diagonally up to the deflection line, or one square beyond it. This means that the central pawns may move two squares on the first move. After crossing the deflection line they can move one square in any direction, including backwards. If a pawn returns to its original row it can only move diagonally, as on its first move.
2. Bishops move any number of squares in any diagonal direction until crossing the deflection line. After the first square beyond the deflection line, they move orthogonally–horizontally or vertically–until crossing a second deflection line. At this point, they again move diagonally.
3. Rooks move any number of squares in any orthogonal direction until crossing a deflection line. When crossing a deflection line, the rook moves diagonally in any direction to the next deflection line–thus assuming the move of the bishop in "ordinary" chess. When crossing another deflection line, the rook resumes its orthogonal movement.
4. Kings move one square in any direction and are not affected by the deflection lines. When a king has reached one of the four central squares, on the next move it can be placed on any free square on the board, excluding the 40 "starting squares". At certain stages of the game this can yield great tactical advantage.

How to Capture

1. Kings, rooks and bishops capture when they pass over any deflection line.
2. The bishop's powers of capture are limited. If it is standing on a square next to a deflection line, it cannot capture a piece on an adjacent square on the other side of the line.
3. Pawns cannot capture when crossing a deflection line, but can on the following move.
4. If the king is threatened, the attacking player calls "Gala" and his opponent must defend the king or move it to safety. If he cannot do so, the threatened king is removed from the board at the next move. When one player has lost both his kings the game is over. If a state of play is reached in which only two opposing kings are left on the board, the game is drawn.

How to Make a Gala Board

Materials
a) For the board: a plywood sheet 30 cm x 42 cm x 8 mm (12½ in x 17½ in x 5/16 in), 1.5 m (5 ft 3 in) of softwood 2 cm x 6 mm (13/16 in x ¼ in), a 54 cm (22½ in) length of plywood 6 cm x 8 mm (2 5/16 in x 5/16 in), 30 cm x 30 cm (12 in x 12 in) black felt, 25 cm x 30 cm (10 in x 12 in) green felt, 12 cm x 30 cm (5 in x 12½ in) red felt, glue, panel pins;
b) For the playing pieces: 2.1 m (7 ft) of 16 mm (5/8 in) dowel, white and black acrylic paint.

Tools
Pencil, steel ruler, sandpaper, hand saw, hobby knife (or scissors), mitre box and paintbrushes.

Method
a) To make the board: Draw three lines across the plywood sheet 12 cm (5 in), 24 cm (10 in) and 30 cm (12½ in) from one end. Draw two lines along the sheet 12 cm (5 in) and 18 cm (7½ in) from one side. This produces a 30 cm x 30 cm (12½ in x 12½ in)

Above: From the top down are the king, bishop, rook and pawn.

Below: At start of play the pieces are arranged as shown.

Below: The diagram in the center column shows how the pieces change direction on crossing a deflection line.

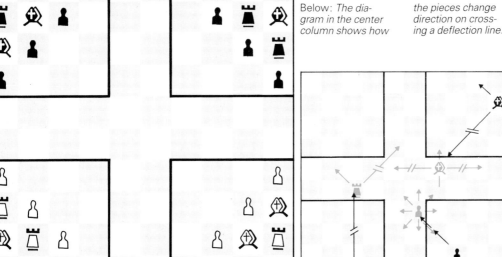

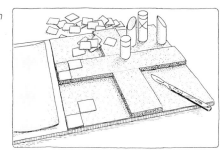

Right: *This diagram shows the raised center cross glued in position. The next step is to cut the black felt and glue it in place.*

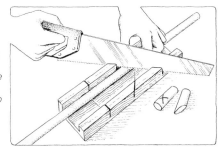

Right: *A mitre box is used to ensure that the saw cuts for the bishops' mitres and the tops of the rooks are at an angle of 45°. The cross that decorates each king is also cut like this.*

Below: *The finished board and playing pieces. This project is not one of the easiest in this book, but perhaps it is one of the most rewarding.*

playing area containing a central cross, and a 12 cm × 30 cm (5 in × 12½ in) area for captured pieces.
Cut a length of 30 cm (12½ in) and two lengths of 12 cm (5 in) from the 8 mm (⁵⁄₁₆ in) plywood strip. Sandpaper the edges smooth and paint them black. These three pieces form a raised central cross and should be glued between the marked lines.

Cut two lengths of 30 cm (12½ in) and two of 43.2 cm (18 in) from the 6 mm (¼ in) softwood strip. These pieces form the frame and should be glued and pinned flush with the upper edge of the board.
Draw a 30 cm x 6 cm (12½ in x 2½ in) cross on the black felt and cut it out using a hobby knife and steel ruler. Glue the five pieces to the board. Mark the board in 3 cm (1¼ in) squares, scoring the lines gently with a hobby knife. Fifty squares of 3 cm x 3 cm (1¼ in x 1¼ in) should now be marked and cut from the green felt. These are glued on alternate squares on the board to produce a checkerboard pattern. Glue the red felt to the remaining area of the board. This area is decorated with green felt shapes (see photograph).

b) To make the playing pieces:
1. pawns: Cut a length of 64 cm (24 in) from the 16 mm (1¼ in) dowel. Make a pencil mark 3 cm (1³⁄₁₆ in) from one end of the dowel and further marks at intervals of 4 cm (1½ in) from the first. Place the dowel in the mitre box and using a tenon saw, make shallow cuts at right angles to the dowel at each marked point.

These should be about 3 mm (⅛ in) in depth and are made by rotating the dowel as you cut. Cut the dowel into sixteen 4 cm (1½ in) lengths.
2. rooks: Cut a length of 60 cm (24 in) from the dowel. Mark and cut it at intervals of 6 cm (2²⁄₅ in). Shape one end of each piece by cutting it at an angle of 45°.
3. bishops: Cut a length of 50 cm (20 in) from the dowel. Make a pencil mark 3½ cm (1¼ in) from one end and further marks at intervals of 5 cm (2 in) from this point. Cut grooves at these points in the same way as for the pawns. Cut the dowel into ten 5 cm (2 in) lengths. At one end of each piece make two cuts at 45° angles to form the mitres.
4. kings: Cut a length of 28 cm (11 in) from the remaining dowel. Make a groove 6 cm (2¼ in) from one end and further grooves at intervals of 7 cm (2¾ in) from the first. Cut into four 7 cm (2¾ in) lengths. On each king make two cuts at angles of 45° to form a cross.
Sand each piece smooth. Paint half of each set white and half black.

Chess

The game of chess is rather like the violin; almost anyone can learn to play it, but only a gifted few can do so supremely well. This has never discouraged people from playing, however, for at any level it is an intellectually demanding and elegant game.

The original form of chess was invented in India more than 1,300 years ago and ever since it seems to have exercised an uncanny fascination over virtually everyone who has played it seriously. Over the course of the centuries, chess has become the undisputed queen of all board games. It has been subject to more exhaustive analysis and it has had more books and articles written about it than all the rest of the board games put together.

It was once calculated that—on a worldwide basis—an average of more than one book a day is published on some aspect of the game or another!

In more than one country chess is regarded as the national game. In the Soviet Union, for example, clubs and individual players are heavily subsidized and the country's players have dominated the world rankings for years. The better players can earn large sums in prize money and receive many special privileges. They are just as much celebrities as, say, baseball or basketball stars in the United States or the best soccer players in Europe or South America.

At its highest level chess has become a full-time occupation. The physical and mental demands of top tournament play are such that the players must be supremely fit. Mental training is just as rigorous and players study, analyze and refine the endless variations in strategy.

The 1986 World Championship series between the two famous Soviet players, Anatoli Karpov and Gari Kasparov, offered an interesting insight into the upper echelons of the chess world. The challenger, Karpov, not only had three world-class players to support him as seconds, but was also accompanied by his personal doctor, translator/secretary and physical trainer! Furthermore, a Yugoslav press secretary was attached to his entourage and the whole show was masterminded by a delegation chief. (Not that this did him a lot of good: he lost.) Kasparov, on the other hand, made do with only two seconds, his mother and a few friends.

The modern game of chess, however, bears little relation to the original game invented in India. That game was called *chaturanga*, a Sanskrit word that literally means "four limbs".

Above: *Medieval chess pieces were sometimes works of art in their own right. This king belongs to a set of chess pieces made in Germany and is carved from ivory.*

Right: *You can almost feel the concentration exuding from the player on the left in this painting by the French master Daumier.*

Above left: Players and onlookers alike enjoying an open-air game of chess under the palm trees of sunny southern Spain.

Above right: Chess is played through-out the world. This picture was taken in Sumatra, one of the largest islands of Indonesia.

Above: Bone chess pieces, Egyptian or Arabic in origin and dating from the 9th century A.D. They can be seen in the Germanisches Nationalmuseum in Nuremberg.

This word refers to elephants, horses, chariots and foot soldiers, the four components of an army in those days. From India, the game made its way to Persia, where it was known as *chatranj.* Persia was later invaded by the Arabs who quickly took to this new game and became the first people to study and play it in a scientific way. After the Moors (as the Arabs were known in Europe) had conquered Spain, they introduced the game there and from Spain chess spread north into France. It was very popular among the Vikings, who may well have learned the game from the Persians, with whom they had trade links. The Vikings were probably responsible for introducing chess into much of northwest mainland Europe and into the British Isles.

As the game spread from the Middle East to Europe, the names and character of the pieces and moves were changed to adapt to the different cultures. The Persian "shah" acquired the name "king," and *shah-mat* (translated: "the shah is helpless"), became *check-mate.* The "vizir"–or counselor–who occupied a position next to the shah, became the queen. Elephants and their use as instruments of war were practically unknown in Europe; the piece underwent several changes until it eventually became the modern bishop. This is not so strange as it may appear at first: in the Middle Ages, bishops often combined their religious duties with more warlike behavior. It was easy to identify the original horse with the knight who fought on horseback. The *baidag* (foot soldier) has remained more or less unchanged as the pawn. The last piece, the original chariot, has become the modern castle or rook, but how this metamorphosis took place remains something of a mystery. Some experts seem to think that the rook symbolizes the *howdah* on

the back of the elephant (from which the archer's arrows were loosed). If that is true, it was the chariot that somehow became the modern bishop.

In its early form, chess was a slow and ponderous game, particularly in its opening phases, but toward the end of the Middle Ages important changes were made in the rules governing the moves of the queen and bishop. The queen, formerly the humble counselor with severely limited powers, became the most versatile and influential piece on the board. The powers of the bishop were also considerably increased and pawns were allowed to move two squares instead of one on the opening move. These changes not only increased the tempo of the game, they also changed the entire strategy. The opening moves became much more important for they now had a more decisive effect on the outcome of the game.
The end of the 15th century marked the completion of these changes. Since then, the game has in effect remained unchanged.

As the popularity of chess increased, some players began to display exceptional ability. As early as the 15th century, the party trick of playing chess blindfolded was performed by a Mogul player. The first professional players also appeared around the same time. It was, however, only in the mid-19th century that the greatest players began to achieve world fame. Nowadays, "grandmasters" of all nationalities play tournaments throughout the world, and millions follow their exploits eagerly.

Left: *From the 17th century onwards, the rich commissioned the best craftsmen of the day to produce ornate and beautifully worked games boards. They sometimes had a backgammon board inside and a chess board and a nine men's morris board on the outside.*

Above: *Wherever it is played chess seems to attract spectators of all ages. This game, played in Manila in the Philippines, is in its final stages.*

Right: *Large-scale chess, played in the open air, is becoming a common sight in many Western cities. This game is taking place in Zurich, in Switzerland.*

Above: *As long as no gratuitous advice is offered, spectators are tolerated by most chess players.*

How to Play Chess

All the novice player needs to know is the basic rules. With practice he will soon become fluent in the game, but if he wants to master the fine points and become a serious player he should study some of the many excellent chess books that have been published for both masters and novices. Joining a chess club is also very helpful. The rules given here are an authorized translation of Part One of the official FIDE (Fédération internationale des échecs) Laws of Chess. This extract is reproduced by kind permission of the British Chess Federation.

Article 1 Introduction

The game of chess is played between two opponents by moving on a square board called a "chessboard."

Article 2 The Chessboard and Its Arrangement

1. The chessboard is made up of 64 equal squares in colour alternately light (the "white" squares) and dark (the "black" squares). 2. The chessboard is placed between the players so that the square in the corner to the right of each player is white. 3. The eight rows of squares running from the edge of the chessboard nearest to the other player are called "files." 4. The eight rows of squares running from one edge of the chessboard to the other at right angles to the files are called "ranks." 5. The rows of squares of the same color touching corner to corner are called "diagonals."

Article 3 The Pieces and Their Positions

At the beginning of the game one player has 16 light colored pieces (the "white" pieces). The other has 16 dark colored pieces (the "black" pieces).

These pieces and their symbols are as follows:

A white King   ♔
A white Queen   ♕
Two white Rooks   ♖
Two white Bishops   ♗
Two white Knights   ♘
Eight white Pawns   ♙

A black King   ♚
A black Queen   ♛
Two black Rooks   ♜
Two black Bishops   ♝
Two black Knights   ♞
Eight black Pawns   ♟

The initial positions of the pieces are as follows:

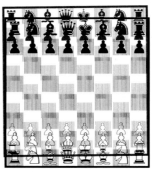

Article 4 The Method of Play

1. The two players must play alternately and make one move at a time. The player who has the white pieces commences the game.
2. A player is said "to have the move" when it is his turn to play.

Article 5 The Move in General

1. With the exception of Castling (Article 6), move is the transfer of one piece from one square to another square which is either vacant or occupied by an opponent's piece. 2. No piece, except the Rook when Castling or the Knight (Article 6), can cross a square occupied by another piece. 3. A piece played to a square occupied by an opponent's piece takes it as part of the same move. The captured piece must be immediately removed from the chessboard by the player who has made the capture. See Article 6(b) for taking "en passant."

Article 6 The Moves of individual Pieces
The King.

Except when Castling, the King moves to an adjacent square that is not attacked by an opponent's piece. Castling is a move of the King and a Rook, reckoned as a single move (of the King), which must be carried out in the following manner–the King is transferred from its original square to either one of the nearest squares of the same color in the same rank; then that Rook towards which the King to the square has been moved is transferred over the King to the square the King has just crossed. Castling is permanently impossible (a) if the King has already been moved, or (b) with a Rook that has already been moved.
Castling is prevented for the time being–(a) if the original square of the King or the square which the King must cross or that which it is to occupy is attacked by an opponent's piece or (b) if there is any piece between the Rook and the King involved in the move.

The Queen.
The Queen moves to any square on the file, rank, or either of the diagonals on which it is placed.

The Rook.
The Rook moves to any square on the file or rank on which it is placed.

The Bishop.
The Bishop moves to any square on either of the diagonals on which it is placed.

The Knight.
The Knight's move is made up of two different steps. It takes one step of one single square along the rank or file, and then, still moving away from

the square it left, takes one step along the diagonal.

The Pawn.
The Pawn can only move forward. a) Except when making a capture it advances from its original square either one or two vacant squares along the file on which it is placed, and on subsequent moves it advances one vacant square along the file. When making a capture it advances one vacant square along either of the diagonals on which it is placed. b) A Pawn attacking a square crossed by an opponent's Pawn which has been advanced two squares on the previous move can capture the opponent's Pawn as though the latter had only been moved one square. This capture can only be made on the move immediately following such advance and is known as taking *"en passant."* c) On reaching the end of a file a Pawn must be immediately exchanged, as part of the same move, for a Queen, a Rook, a Bishop, or a Knight at the player's choice and without taking into account to other pieces still remaining on the chessboard. This exchanging of a Pawn is called *"promotion."* The promoted piece must be of the same color as the Pawn and it's action is immediate.

Article 7 The Completion of a Move

A move is completed: a) In the case of the transfer of a piece to a vacant square, when the player's hand has quitted the piece; or b) In the case of a capture, when the captured piece has been removed from the chessboard and when the player, having placed the piece on it's new square, has quitted the piece with his hand; or c) In case of Castling, when the player's hand has quitted the Rook on the square crossed by the King; when the player's hand has quitted the King the move is still not yet completed, but the player no longer has the right to make any other move except Castling; or d) In case of the promotion of a Pawn, when the Pawn has been removed from the chessboard and the player's hand has quitted the new piece after placing it on the promotion square; if the player's hand has quitted the Pawn that has reached the promotion square the move is still not yet completed, but the player no longer has the right to move the Pawn to another square.

Article 8 Touched Piece

Provided that he first warns his opponent, the player whose turn it is to move can adjust one or more pieces on their squares.
Apart from the above case, if the player whose turn it is to move touches one or more pieces, he must make his move by moving or taking the first piece touched which can be moved or taken; and if he touches pieces of opposite colors, he must take the enemy piece with his own touched piece, or if this is not possible, with another piece. If none of the touched pieces can be moved or taken, the player is free to make any legal move he chooses. If a player wishes to claim a violation of this rule, he must do so before he touches a piece himself.

Article 9 Illegal Positions

1. If during the game it is ascertained that an illegal move has been made, then the position shall be set up again as it was immediately before the making of the illegal move. The game shall then continue in accordance with the rules given in Article 8 as regards the move replacing the illegal move. If it proves impossible to set up the position again then the game must be annulled and a fresh

game played. 2. If, in the course of a game, one or more pieces have been accidentally displaced and are not correctly replaced, the position must be set up as it was immediately before the mistake and the game continued. If it proves impossible to set up the position again then the game must be annulled and a fresh game played. 3. If, after an adjournment, the position is incorrectly put up, then the position as it was on adjournment must be set up again and the game continued. 4. If during the game it is ascertained that the initial position of the pieces was incorrect, then the game must be annulled and a fresh game played. 5. If, during the game it is ascertained that the initial position of the chessboard is incorrect, then the position that has been reached must be transferred to a chessboard that has been correctly placed and the game continued.

Article 10 Check

1. The King is in check when the square which it occupies is attacked by an opponent's piece; in this case the latter is said to be "checking the King." 2. The check must be met on the move immedi-ately following. If the check cannot be met then it is called "mate" (see Article 11,1). 3. A piece that intercepts a check to the King of its own color can itself give check to the opponent's King.

Article 11 Won Game

1. The game is won for the player who has mated the opponent's King. 2. The game is considered won for the player whose opponent declares he resigns.

Article 12 Drawn Game

The game is drawn: 1. When the King of the player whose turn it is to move is not in check, and such player cannot make a move. This is called "stale-mate." 2. By agreement between the two players. 3. At the request of one of the players when the same position appears three times, and each time the same player has had the move. The position is considered the same if pieces of the same kind and color occupy the same squares.

This right of claiming the draw belongs to the player: a) who is in a position to play a move lead-ing to such repetition of the position, if he declares his intention of making this move; or b) who is about to reply to a move by which such repeated position has been produced. If a player makes a move without having claimed a draw in the man-ner prescribed in (a) or (b) he then loses his right to claim a draw; this right is however restored to him if the same position appears again with the same player having the move.

4. When the player whose turn it is to move proves that at least fifty moves have been played by each side without a capture of a piece and without a Pawn move having been made. This number of fifty moves can be increased for certain positions providing that this increase in number and these positions have been clearly laid down before commencement of the game.

Below: *The charac-ters in this lovely set of hand-made and painted chess pieces are all from* Alice's Adventures in Wonderland *and* Through the Look-ing Glass, *which were written in the late 19th century by Lewis Carroll.*

English Checkers or Draughts

The origins of many board games are shrouded in mystery and checkers, or draughts as it is known in Europe, is no exception. It is generally believed that the game may have been invented as long ago as A.D. 1000, although some experts think it is of more recent origin, maybe early 13th century. Most authorities are of the opinion that draughts was invented in southern France, although again, not all agree, some believing that the game originated in Spain. One intriguing theory, put forward by Pennycook, is that the inventor was probably trying to figure out how to play alquerque on a chessboard while using "tablemen," or backgammon pieces. Whatever the accuracy of this theory, checkers became a very popular game. The precise form of play varied then and varies now, different versions of the original game being played in different countries. The English version, which was later adapted by North America, was fixed by about 1800. This is the basic game described here.

How to Play English Checkers

1. Each player has 12 pieces, which are arranged at start of play on an 8 x 8-celled checkered board, as is shown in the diagram. The pieces are usually flat, round, wooden disks, 12 white and 12 black.
Note: The white corner square should always be to the player's right; the pieces should only be moved on the black squares; black always begins and players change pieces at the end of the game.

2. Pieces move diagonally one square forward. They do not move in a backward direction unless they have been "crowned" as kings (see Rule 6).

3. An opposing piece is captured by the *short leap* method, that is, by leaping diagonally over it into a vacant square immediately beyond.

4. A series of captures can be made in one turn of play, the capturing piece leaping opposing pieces one by one, diagonally forwards, until no further legal leaps are available. When a piece is captured it is taken from the board.
Note: The last rule is important for removing pieces *as they are taken* as

opposed to at *the end of a turn of play* can make a difference to the result of the game. This will be seen later when Polish checkers and its rules are discussed.

5. If an enemy piece is at risk and a player omits to capture it, his opponent can choose between three courses of action. He can a) insist that the moved piece be returned to its original position and the proper capture made; b) accept the move if it is to his advantage to do so (in which case the capture must be made on the next move, if this is still possibble); c) *huff* the piece which should have made the capture and remove it from the board. Huffing does not count as a move.

6. When a piece reaches the opposing back row it is "crowned" and becomes a king–and then has the powers of both forward and backward movement. Crowning ends a turn of play and the king cannot be used until the next move. There can be several kings on the board at the same time.

7. The first player to capture or immobilize the 12 opposing pieces is the winner of the game.

Above: *The checkers playing pieces were made in a variety of materials, including metal, wood, bone and ivory. Sometimes they were elaborately carved, showing people engaged in different activities. Three of the above pieces (two white and one black) seem to belong to the same set.*

Polish Checkers

In the original game of checkers, capture was optional, as it is in modern chess. Compulsory capture was introduced early in the 16th century–if a player neglected to capture, he was penalized by being "huffed." This "new" game became known in France as *jeu forcé*, and it is this game which is usually known today as English checkers. In France, *jeu forcé* was replaced by another form of checkers known as *le grand forçat*. This, too, became obselete and in the 1720s it was replaced by the game we now know as Polish or continental checkers and which is played throughout mainland Europe. Once again, various authorities offer slightly different theories as to the origins of this version of checkers. Most of these theories, seem to have been derived from Murray's extended discussion of the game's beginnings. He suggests that most of the circumstantial evidence points to the fact that Polish checkers was devised at the court of Philippe II of Orleans (regent from 1713-23) by an officer of the court. The latter collaborated with a Polish gentleman, who thought the game could be made more interesting if a piece could take diagonally backwards as well as forwards. The officer then suggested that the game might become still more interesting if it were played on a bigger board. Further modifications, mainly concerning the powers of movement and capture by the king, were later made. The end result, as shown here, is a game that can certainly be considered one of the great board games of the present day.

Right: *At start of play the pieces are arranged as shown.*

Far right: *A little advice from your friends is sometimes welcome. These tribesmen from Mauritania, in West Africa, seem to be taking the game very seriously.*

Below: *You are never too young to learn–or at least to watch! These Bangkok children obviously find the game fascinating.*

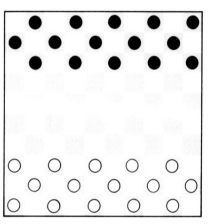

How to Play Polish Checkers

1. Each player has 20 pieces, which are arranged at start of play on a 10 x 10-celled checkered board as shown in the diagram.

2. Pieces move diagonally one square forward.

3. An opposing pieces is captured by the short leap method, *forwards* or *backwards.* Capturing is obligatory.

4. If a player has a choice between captures, he must choose the one in which the greatest number of pieces are captured. If equal captures can be made, then the strongest pieces (i.e., a king) must be taken.

5. Captured pieces are only removed from the board at the end of a turn of play; a "dead" piece cannot be leaped a second time.

Above: Checkers has always been a popular game in bars and cafés. These two Panamanians are preparing to play a game in one of the many open-air cafés in Panama City.

Above: *The two characters in this painting by the French artist Gustave Courbet seem to be enjoying themselves immensely. Courbet was a founder of the Realist School and his paintings are very true to life.*

6. A piece is "crowned" and becomes a king only when he reaches and *remains* on the opposing back line. If further enemy pieces can be captured after a piece reaches this line, the move must be completed.

7. A king can move diagonally any number of unoccupied squares, exactly like the bishop's move in chess (but without the bishop's power of capture).

8. The king may land any number of vacant squares beyond the opposing piece.

9. Rules 7 and 8 may occur together. This method of capture is known as a *long leap.*

10. The winner is the first player to capture or immobilize all 20 opposing pieces.

Note: The increased powers of capture, particularly by the king, make Polish checkers a more tactical game than most other variations of checkers. This is indicated by the fact that the game is organized on the lines of chess, with clubs and competitions at various levels up to, and including, a world championship.

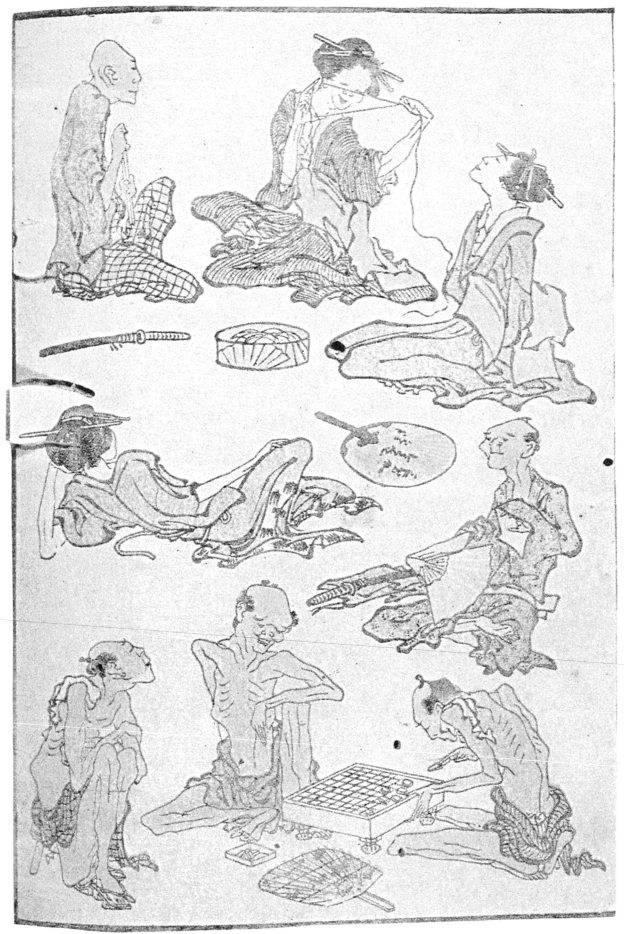

136

Shogi or Japanese Chess

Over the years, the basic game of chess, invented in India during the sixth or seventh century, developed and changed into many different forms as it spread throughout the world. One of the most modified and unusual forms of the game is shogi, the generals' game, which is commonly known as Japanese chess. There are few reliable records, but from what we know shogi entered Japan from Korea around the eigth century A.D. and the several forms of the game were played on latticed boards of various dimensions.

The most complex of these was tai-shogi, played on a 25 x 25 celled board with no less than 354 pieces! The first rank contained gold, silver, copper, iron, stone and clay generals. The next four ranks were a veritable menagerie of furious dragons, raging tigers, soaring phoenixes, blind boars, hard-biting wolves, thrashing serpents and even an odd cat or two and an old rat. In the rear stood the commander, who was probably as confused as everybody else by the proliferation of pieces. (As the Duke of Wellington is reported to have said on reviewing his troops before Water-

loo: "I don't know what effect they'll have on the enemy, but I think I'll go and have a lie down.") It is recorded that this super-heavyweight of a game was actually played! On September 12, 1142 to be precise. At least a courtier recorded as much in his diary, adding sadly "I lost." Towards the end of the 16th century the game was standardized to a 9 x 9 celled board and 40 pieces. This standardization is traditionally ascribed to the Emperor Go-Nara, who is also believed to have introduced the rule by which a captured piece can be enlisted in the army of the player making the capture. The game rapidly attained great popularity and it became to the Japanese what chess later became to the Russians. The Japanese government instituted shogi schools, employed teachers and sponsored annual tournaments. Such tournaments still exist and the best of an estimated 10 million players compete for the title of *meijin*, supreme master.

The object of the game is to checkmate the king of the opposition–i.e., place him in a position in which he is under attack and unable to escape. Shogi differs from chess in two basic aspects: firstly, in that most pieces can be promoted and assume wider powers of movement (in chess only the pawn can be promoted) and secondly, in that captured pieces can be returned to the board and enlisted in the army of the player who has captured them (in chess pieces are not returned into play). Some see this as a disadvantage–a player loses his castle and his opponent suddenly has two of them! Others see it as adding to the excitement and interest of the game. Whatever view one takes there is no denying that shogi is a game which involves dramatic and rapid changes of fortune.

The ramifications of shogi are such that it would be impossible to adequately describe the strategy and methods of play in a book such as this. The basic rules are given, but for someone who wishes to learn more about the game and play it seriously, Trevor Leggett's *Shogi: Japan's Game of Strategy*, published by Charles E. Tuttle Company in 1966, is highly recommended.

Below: *The one who is playing up the board is in trouble. He has lost four pawns and a bishop and a promoted bishop lie next to the king on his back row. Only his gold general on the second row can save him from imminent checkmate.*

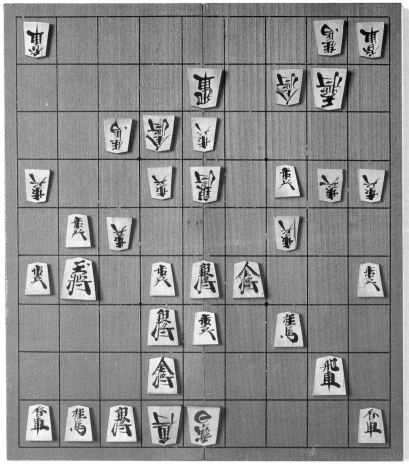

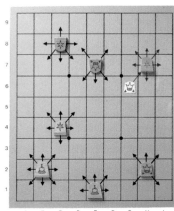
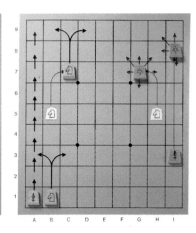
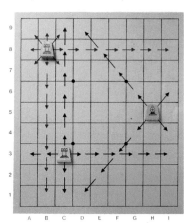

1   2   3   4

1. At start of play the pieces are arranged as in this diagram. The pieces point in the direction of play.

2. The king and the gold and silver generals may move one square at a time in the directions shown by the arrows. After promotion, a silver general becomes gold (top right).

3. The spear and knight have limited powers of movement, but after promotion (right) they become gold generals and can move accordingly.

4. A promoted castle (known as a crowned castle) retains its own powers of movement and also assumes the powers of movement of king. The bishop (right) moves exactly as it does in the game of chess.

The Board and the Pieces

Shogi is played on a 9 x 9-celled board. Each cell is oblong in shape. Two intersections on the fourth and two on the seventh line are marked with dots, dividing the board into three strips of 3 x 9 squares. The strip nearest a player is "home" territory; that nearest his opponent is "enemy" territory. Most pieces entering this enemy territory can be promoted.

The pieces of the two players are not differentiated by color. Pieces are pointed at one end and ownership is shown by the direction in which this end is facing–i.e., towards the enemy! Each player starts with 20 pieces, which at start of play are arranged on the board as shown in the diagram. These pieces are:

1. *Yari* (pikeman or spear). This piece can move any number of squares in a forwards direction only. When promoted it becomes a *kin-sho*, or gold general.
2. *Kei-ma* (honorable knight or horse). The knight's move is restricted to the equivalent of the two forward leaps of the knight in chess. It is the only piece which can leap other pieces. On promotion it becomes a gold general.
3. *Gin-sho* (silver general). This piece can move one square straight forward, diagonally forward or diagonally backward, but not sideways or straight backward. On promotion it becomes a gold general.
4. *Kin-sho* (gold general). This piece can move one square straight forward, diagonally forward, sideways or straight backward, but *not* diagonally backward. It is not promoted on entering enemy territory.

5. *O-sho* (jeweled general or king). This piece has the same powers of move as the king in chess–i.e., one square in any direction. The king is also not promoted–but then, where does one go from being a king?
6. *Kakko* (angel-going or bishop). The bishop's move is the same as the bishop's move in chess–i.e., any number of squares along any of the diagonals. On promotion the bishop acquires the powers of move of the king in addition to its own. It is then called *ryo-ma* or dragon horse.
7. *Hisha* (flying chariot or castle). This piece has exactly the same powers of move as the chess castle–i.e., any number of squares forwards, backwards or sideways. On promotion it becomes *ryo-wo,* or dragon king, and acquires the powers of move of the king in addition to its own.
8. *Fu-hyo* (soldier or pawn). The pawn moves one square forward. There is no option of moving two squares on the first move, as there is in chess. The pawn also captures as it moves, in a straight line, and not diagonally. On promotion the piece becomes a gold general.

Promotion of Pieces

Each piece bears its original rank on the top surface and its promoted rank on the bottom. On promotion the piece is simply turned over to show its new rank. A piece can be promoted when it enters, leaves or moves within the enemy territory–i.e., rows 7, 8 or 9. These is no obligation to promote a piece immediately. It can be promoted later when the player in question considers it an advantage. For example, a knight, with its leaping power, may be

more advantageous at that point in the game than a gold general. In general, pawns, bishop and castle can only gain by promotion so it is sensible to promote these pieces at the earliest opportunity. However, a player may wish to retain the powers of movement of a knight or a spear, but if these pieces arrive on the enemy's back row they are "dead" until promoted. Once a piece has been promoted it retains its new rank until it is removed from the board. It cannot be demoted.

Capture of Pieces

For capture, the replacement method is used, as in conventional chess. But here we come to perhaps the most important difference between these two fascinating games. On any turn, instead of making a move, a player is allowed to bring a captured piece "out of the blue" into play *as part of his own forces.* This privilege is subject to certain limitations, however. The piece can only be placed on an unoccupied square and it assumes its original rank–*not* its promoted rank–although it can be repromoted later. Also a player cannot place the piece on a square from which it is unable to move–a pawn or spear cannot be set on the opponent's back row, for example. Extra restrictions apply to pawns. "Doubled" pawns are not allowed and therefore a captured pawn cannot be brought into the game on any vertical row occupied by allied pawns. Pawns that have been promoted to gold generals are, however, allowed on the same line. A pawn may not be brought back into play on a square on which it checkmates the opposing king.

5

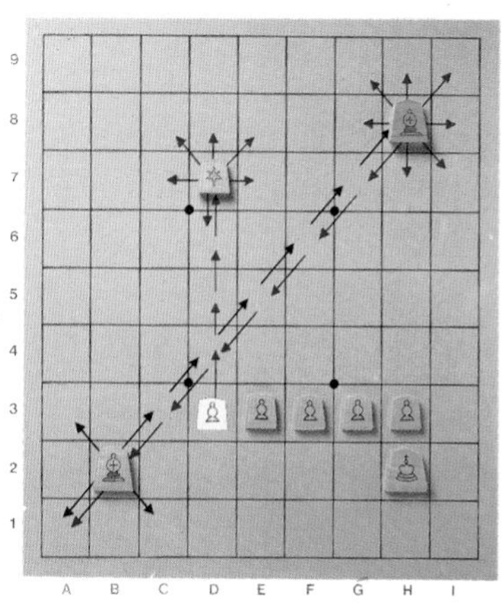

5. A promoted (or crowned) bishop may move one square forwards, backwards or sideways as well as along the diagonals. A promoted pawn becomes a gold general.

Far right: *The shogi pieces, their promoted values and how many are required. From the top down: king (2x); castle (crowned, 2x); bishop (crowned, 2x); gold general (4x); silver general (gold, 4x); horse (gold, 4x); spear (gold, 4x); pawn (gold, 18x).*

How to Make the Game of Shogi

Materials

a) For the board: a plywood sheet 27 cm x 33½ cm x 16 mm (12¼ in x 14½ in x ⅝ in), black acrylic paint, varnish;

b) for the playing pieces: three slanted molding strips all 6 mm (¼ in) thick at the wider edge: one 3 cm x 15 cm (1 3/16 in x 6 in), one 2½ cm x 32 cm (1 in x 14 in) and one 2 cm x 27 cm (13/16 in x 11¼ in), black and red acrylic paint, varnish.

Tools

Sandpaper, steel ruler, drawing pen, paintbrush, handsaw.

Method

a) To make the board:

Sand the plywood sheet thoroughly. Using the steel ruler, drawing pen and black acrylic, draw lines 1 cm (½ in) from each side of the sheet to form a rectangle measuring 27 cm x 31½ cm (11¼ in x 13½ in). Mark points at intervals of 3 cm (1¼ in) along the shorter sides of this rectangle and at intervals of 3½ cm (1½ in) along the longer sides. Join opposite points to form a 9 x 9 grid of 3 cm x 3½ cm (1¼ in x 1½ in) squares. Mark the four points of intersection shown in the diagram. Varnish to finish.

b) To make the playing pieces: Place the 3 cm x 15 cm (1 3/16 in x 6 in) strip on the work table with the wider edge towards you. Mark points at 2½ cm (1 in) intervals along this wider edge. Mark a point on the top edge of the strip 4 mm (3/16 in) from the left side. From this point mark further points at alternate intervals of 1.7 cm (⅝ in) and 8 mm (⅜ in) respectively: i.e., at 1.7 cm (⅝ in), 2.5 cm (1 in), 4.2 cm (1⅝ in), 5 cm (2 in), etc. Draw a line joining the bottom corner with the first point on the top edge. Join the first point on the bottom edge with the second and third points on the top edge. Join the second point on the bottom edge with the fourth and fifth points on the top edge, etc. Cut the strip along the drawn lines with a handsaw.

This procedure is repeated with the other two strips. The wider edge of the 32 cm (14 in) strip is marked at intervals of 2 cm (⅞ in) A point is marked 3 mm (⅛ in) from the left side on the top edge. From this point further points are marked at alternate intervals of 1.4 cm (⅝ in) and 6 mm (¼ in): i.e., at 1.4 cm (⅝ in), 2.0 cm (⅞ in), 3.4 cm (1½ in), 4.0 cm (1¾ in) etc. Draw and cut as before.

The wider edge of the 27 cm (11¼ in) strip is marked at intervals of 1½ cm (⅝ in). A point is marked 2 mm (1/16 in) from the left side on the top edge. From this point further points are marked at alternate intervals of 1.1 cm (½ in) and 4 mm (⅛ in): i.e., at 1.1 cm (½ in), 1.5 cm (⅝ in), 2.6 cm (1⅛ in), 3 cm (1¼ in), etc. Draw and cut as before. Sandpaper each half of the narrow top edge of each piece at a slight angle, so that the middle point is peaked.

Using the drawing pen and black and red acrylic paint, mark the pieces as shown on the right. The black markings show the normal values and the red the promoted values. The largest pieces comprise two kings, two castles and two bishops; The middle-sized pieces comprise four gold generals, four silver generals, four horses and four spears. The smallest pieces comprise 18 pawns.

When the acrylic has thoroughly dried, varnish the pieces to finish.

Below center: *The board showing the points that mark the lines of promotion.*

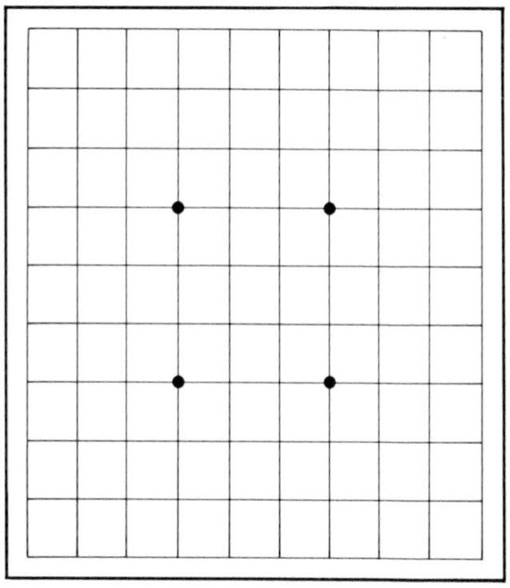

Below: *Use this template to help in the marking and cutting out of the pieces.*

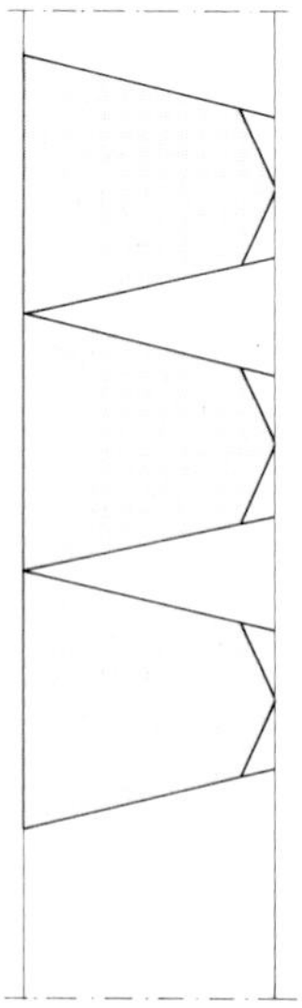

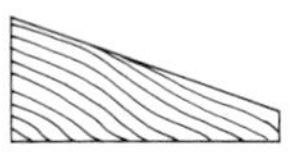

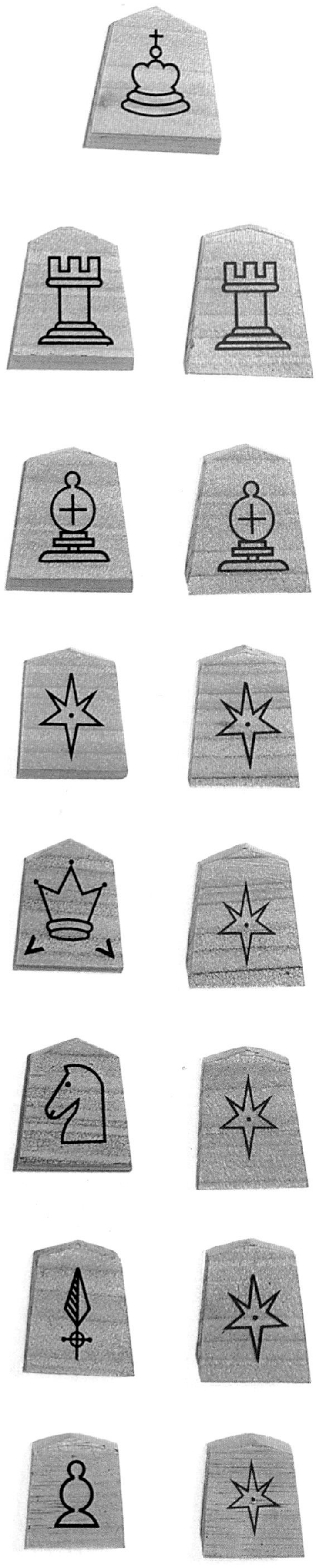

Wei-ch'i

Until now in this section all the games we have mentioned have been battle games, in which the object has been to wipe out the opposing forces. This game is somewhat different. *Wei-ch'i* is the Chinese name and i-go (usually shortened to go) the Japanese name for a fascinating war game in which the primary object is not to capture enemy pieces, but to enclose the largest possible areas of territory. It is very much an Eastern game, reflecting unique cultural values little known in the West. For this reason there are few wei-ch'i experts in Europe or North America, outside the large Chinese and Japanese minorities there. The principles of wei-ch'i are deceptively straightforward: the players in turn each place a stone on the intersecting points of a latticed board so that a "string" of stones encloses opposing stones and/or territory. This would not appear to be very difficult, yet players who are familiar with both games say wei-ch'i is at least as taxing and complex as chess.

Most authorities are of the opinion that the game was invented in China as many as 4,000 years ago, although Murray puts the true "date of birth" at about A.D. 1000. Whatever the truth of the matter, it is certain that the game spread first to Korea, where it acquired the name pa-tok, and after that to Japan, where it became known as i-go, or go.

The Japanese quickly took to the game when it was introduced into their country. In the beginning it was only played in court circles, but by the 13th century go had become very popular among the *samurai*, or warriors. Go boards and stones were as essential to a campaign as weapons and armor, and once the bloodletting was over, go contests began! In the 16th century, go was a compulsory course at the military academy. Later, private schools were set up and professional players frequently toured the country, playing challenge matches and giving lessons. A *dan* system was created, the highest grade being *Kudan*, an honor granted only to the very best players.

When the shogunate fell in the late 19th century, go lost some of its popularity. This did not last for long and a few years later there was a revival of interest in the game. Today there are at least 8 million players in Japan and probably about 400 professionals.

Right: *Two Japanese ladies engaging in the opening phases of a game of* wei-ch'i *(or go, as it is known in Japan). This tinted plate dates from the early years of this century.*

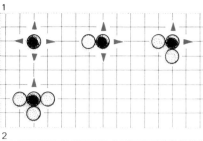

1. The black stone has four freedoms—it is connected by lines to four empty points. Each time a white stone is placed on one of these points, the black stone loses a freedom.

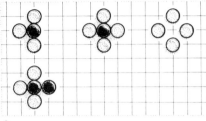

2. White places a stone so that the black stone loses its last freedom. The black stone is captured and taken from the board. Black can avoid capture by forming a chain, which must be captured as a unit.

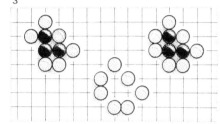

3. A chain is captured in the same way as a single stone—by losing its last freedom. Here white places a stone on black's last freedom: the chain is killed and taken from the board.

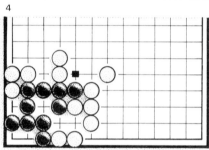

4. A chain is not necessarily made stronger by adding more stones. Here black can place a stone on seven different points, but only a stone placed on the marked point gives his chain more freedoms.

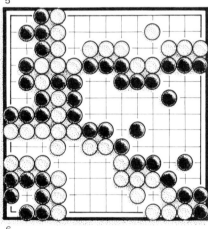

5. At the end of play, each player counts the number of points in the territory he has surrounded. Here, black has encircled 45 points and white 41 points and black is therefore the winner.

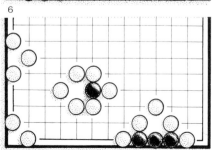

6. If black placed a stone on any of the surrounded points (marked by squares), he would be committing suicide. The stone would be immediately captured and taken from the board.

How to Play Wei-Ch'i

Equipment

Wei-ch'i is played on a board marked out by thin black lines to form a grid of 18 x 18 cells, giving 361 intersection *points*.

Nine of these are marked to assist in handicapping. One player has 180 white stones and the other has 181 black stones. Traditionally, these are kept in wooden bowls.

While learning the game, we suggest that you confine play to a 13 x 13 section of the board and play with 84 and 85 stones respectively. This limitation enables novice players to learn the rules and strategies much more quickly.

Rules and Method of Play

1. All the stones are off the board at the start of play.
2. Black plays first by placing a stone on any point, including those at the edge of the board. It is probably best to give the privilege of playing black to the weaker player, as starting the game gives a slight advantage.
3. Players then place the stones, one at a time, alternately on vacant points. A player has the option of *passing* or missing a turn, but this only makes sense in the final phases of the game.
4. Stones cannot be moved once they have been placed and they remain in position until the end of the game, except when they are captured—then they can be taken from the board and retained by the captor.
5. The primary object of the game is to capture territory rather than opposing stones. However, captures can be made and count towards the final total of points scored. Captures are made by enclosure, i.e., by completely encircling opposing stones on adjacent points (connected only along the marked lines and not along the unmarked diagonals).

A vacant adjacent point is known as a *freedom* and a stone or a *chain* of stones is captured when it loses its last freedom.

6. A chain does not necessarily have to be totally "killed." A threatened stone or chain is sometimes allowed to retain its last freedom, but in that case it remains on the board as a *prisoner*. This occurs when the player does not wish to waste a move to complete the capture. Prisoners are removed from the board at the end of the game and

counted as captured stones.

7. Whenever a stone or a chain of stones is captured and removed from the board, either player can occupy the vacated point or points.
8. In placing stones, remember that danger exists if: a) the chain is too small or too compact, or b) the space inside the chain is so large that opposing stones can attack it from within.
9. The building of a secure or *live* chain is based on the formation of *eyes*. Making eyes or preventing them from being made is the basis of the game. An eye is a vacant point (or freedom) controlled by stones of one color. A group with two eyes (two enclosed vacant points) is virtually safe from attack, because if the opponent attempted to enter a stone on one of these points he would be committing suicide. This is forbidden, unless the player in so doing also makes a capture. Nor can a stone occupy the last freedom in one of its own groups, unless opposing stones are thereby captured.
10. A situation in which capture followed by recapture would result in the same formation that existed before the first capture is known as a *ko* situation. This is not allowed, and the second player must make a different move. At the next move the opponent may fill the ko, thus ending the situation. If for some reason he decides not to do this, the second player can return to the ko in the following turn of play and recapture the opposing stone. As this would again result in a ko situation, the other player must wait one turn as well before capturing in return. Ko situations are very important. The player who is fighting for a vital ko will attempt a threatening move elsewhere on the board against which his opponent will be forced to defend himself, thus allowing the first player to recapture the ko. A ko ends when one player runs out of threatening moves or a threat is ignored in order to fill the ko.
11. The game is drawn if there are three ko situations on the board at the same time.
12. A *seki*, or stalemate, situation occurs when opposing stones are so interlocked that neither player can attack his opponent without seriously endangering his own formation. These situations are left untouched until the end of the game and the area enclosed cannot be claimed by either player.

The End of the Game

A game comes to an end when it is no

7/8. It is not, however, suicide when a stone is placed on an enclosed point so that it deprives an enemy chain of its last freedom. In the first situation shown here, black places a stone on the corner intersection and captures three white stones. In the second situation black places a stone on the empty point of intersection capturing two white stones.

9. This group of white stones contains two vacant points (eyes). If black attempts to enter either of them he commits suicide and therefore the group is completely secure from capture. Such a group is known as a "live" group.

10. The first stone to be placed on the central vacant point is decisive. If white places a stone on this point, two eyes are formed and the group becomes live. If black places a stone on the point, white has no chance of saving his chain.

11. Black kills the white stone and turns position (a) into position (b). If white captures in turn, the original situation would be re-created. This is known as ko and white cannot recapture until he has made a move elsewhere on the board.

12. A This is not a ko situation. Black and white can capture but the original position is not repeated after two moves.
B Neither player can attack without putting his own stones in danger. This is seki, or deadlock.

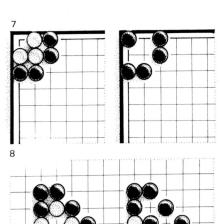

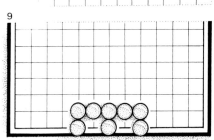

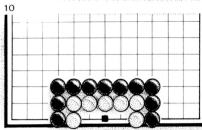

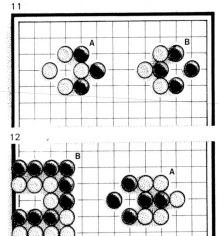

longer possible for either player to capture further territory or when it is no longer possible to capture any opposing stones that can affect the final score. At this stage isolated vacant points between opposing chains–so-called *dameh* points–are occupied, so that hostile chains are joined without interruption. When the last dameh point is filled, the game is finally over. Any prisoners are then taken from the board. Players now begin to tally their scores. Captured stones and prisoners are counted, together with the number of territorial points enclosed, so giving the total score. Counting can be simplified by placing captured stones in opposing territory. This does not influence the score, as a player loses a prisoner with each stone, while his opponent loses a point of territory.

How to Make the Game of Wei-ch'i

Materials
a) For the board: a plywood sheet 48 cm x 48 cm x 16 mm (19¼ in x 19¼ in x ⅝ in), varnish, black acrylic paint, a roll of 1 cm (⅜ in) black adhesive tape;
b) For the playing pieces: approx. 100 white and 100 colored "flying-saucer" shaped mint pastilles, an aerosol spray can of varnish.

Tools
Sandpaper, paintbrush, steel ruler, drawing pen.

Method
Sand the plywood sheet thoroughly and seal with a coat of varnish. When the varnish has dried, sand again with fine grade sandpaper.

Using the steel ruler, drawing pen and thick black acrylic paint draw lines along each side of the board, 1½ cm (⅝ in) from the edges, to form a 45 cm x 45 cm (18 in x 18 in) square. Mark points at 2½ cm (1 in) intervals along the sides of this square. Using the ruler, pen and acrylic, connect opposite points both vertically and horizontally to make a grid of 2½ cm x 2½ cm (1 in x 1 in) squares.

In black acrylic, mark the nine "handicap points" at the points of intersection shown in the diagram.

Handicapping
Games between beginners are usually decided by chance, but games between more experienced players are a very different matter. Even a slightly better player will win consistently. The difference in ability can be resolved by giving the weaker player a handicap of between two and nine stones. (The weaker player plays black and in effect always receives a handicap of one stone.) He is not obliged to place this on any fixed point. If a higher handicap is given, black places the initial stones on the points indicated in the diagram. This is considered to be his first move and white then proceeds to play.

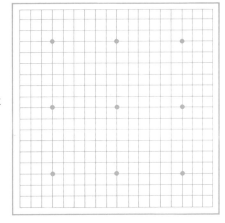

Above: *The layout of the board showing the nine handicap points.*

When the paint has dried thoroughly, give the board a coat of varnish. The edges can then be masked with black adhesive tape. Any excess tape can be folded under the board and pressed into place with the thumb or it can simply be trimmed off with a hobby knife.

The temptation to eat the "stones" in course of play might prove too strong—especially if the game is a lengthy one. This could clearly lead to confusion as to the result, if not to accusations of cheating. To prevent any possible problems, coat the "stones" with varnish from an aerosol spray can. This not only gives them a foul taste but ensures that they are more durable.

Mu Torere

Mu torere is an example of a *blockade game*, in which the object is not to capture the opponent's pieces, but to immobilize them. The game is played mainly among the Ngati Porou tribe who live on the east coast of North Island (New Zealand), although it can sometimes be found among other Maori tribes. It is the only native Maori board game, but action games and cat's cradle are also popular.

The mu torere board consists of an eight-pointed star with cells *(kewai)* at the ends of the rays and a central cell *(putahi)*. Each player has four pieces *(perepere)*, which are of a distinctive shape or color.
When played by the Maoris, the board was usually scratched on the ground with a sharp stick or drawn in charcoal on a large flat stone. More permanent boards were made from the bark of the evergreen Totara tree; these had sticks at either end to prevent warping as the bark dried.

Some authorities are of the opinion that the word "mu" is derived from the English word "move." For this reason it is sometimes thought that the game is an adaptation of checkers, taken from the early British settlers. This appears to be a farfetched idea because the two games are so dissimilar. It is much more likely that mu torere is a board game of pure Maori origin.

Right: *A Maori couple playing* mu torere *in the sunshine. The object is not to capture the opposing pieces, but to immobilize them.*

How to Play Mu Torere

1. At start of play the pieces are placed on the board as shown in the diagram.

2. Black begins and the players move one piece alternately.

3. A piece may be moved:
a) from a *kewai* to the *putahi,* but only if one or both of the adjacent cells are occupied by an opposing piece or opposing pieces;
b) from a *kewai* to a vacant, adjacent *kawai;*
c) from the *putahi* to a vacant *kewai.*

4. Only one piece is allowed on any cell at one time.

5. A piece is not allowed to leap any other piece, friendly or enemy.

6. The player who blockades the opposing pieces with the result that it is impossible for them to move is the winner of the game.

An Example of Play
Murray quotes Elsdon Best, who offered the following sequence of moves (black moves first):
1. 5–9, 4–5;
2. 9–4, 3–9;
3. 4–3, 9–4;
4. 3–9, 2–3;
5. 9–2, 4–9;
and a win for white.

How to Make a Mu Torere Board

Materials
a) For a board that does not need to be fired: ½ kg (1 lb) of hobby clay, a chipboard sheet 30 cm x 30 cm (12 in x 12 in), yellow ochre, orange and red acrylic paint, varnish.

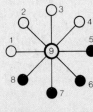

Above: *At start of play the pieces are arranged on the board as shown here. The center hole (the* putahi) *is empty.*

Below: *Original Maori boards were usually scratched on the ground with a stick or drawn in charcoal on a flat stone. More permanent boards were sometimes made from the bark of trees. The model shown here was made in clay and the pattern incised with a hobby knife and a wooden spatula. The pieces are dried kidney beans that have been painted in acrylic and varnished.*

b) For a board which must be fired: ½ kg (1 lb) of modelmakers' clay, yellow ochre, orange and red glazing powder.

Tools
Rolling pin, hobby knife, spatulas, paintbrushes.

Method
First soften the clay by kneading it in your hands for a few minutes.
Note: It is most important to knead modelmakers' clay thoroughly. This removes the tiny air bubbles in the clay which can cause it to explode during the firing process.
When the clay has been softened, place it on the chipboard base and using the rolling pin roll it out flat to cover an area of a little more than 25 cm x 25 cm (10½ in x 10½ in). If the clay tends to stick, moisten it with a little water. Use a steel ruler and a hobby knife to trim the board to a size of 25 cm x 25 cm (10½ in x 10½ in). Smooth off the edges by molding them with wet fingertips.
Note: If modelmakers' clay is used the board is rolled out on a flat surface and not on the chipboard!

The positions of the holes for the playing pieces and the pattern which decorates the board are shown in the gridded diagram. This diagram is enlarged by drawing a 21 x 21 grid of 1 cm (½ in) squares on a 21 cm x 21 cm (10½ in x 10 ½in) sheet of tracing paper and copying the pattern square by square.
It must then be transferred to the surface of the clay by tracing over the lines with the back of a hobby knife. This produces indentations that are then deepened using the blade of a hobby knife. The smaller details of the pattern can be altered or amplified, if wished. The holes are made by scooping out the clay with a spatula. Use the end of a scrap piece of large-diameter dowel to smooth out their bottoms and sides.

The board should now be left to dry out thoroughly in a warm, airy place for two or three days.

When the board has dried, paint it following the color scheme used in the model in the photograph. Give the completed board a coat of clear varnish to finish it off.
Note: If you have used modelmakers' clay the board must be fired before it is glazed. After firing, brush on the glaze following the color scheme used in the model in the photograph. The board must then be refired.

Mu torere is played with eight playing pieces, four being of one color and four of another. These can be almost anything as long as they fit the holes. Small pebbles, for example, painted in contrasting colors and varnished, make excellent playing pieces. Small discs cut from two contrasting woods are also easy to make.

Below: *Use a 21 x 21 grid of 1 cm (½ in) squares to* help you transfer the pattern to the surface of the clay.

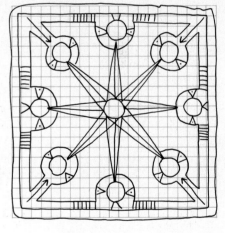

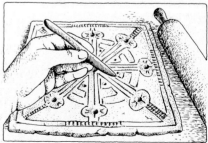

Above: *After you have transferred the pattern, deepen* the lines using a hobby knife or a wooden spatula.

145

Hunt Games

Hunt games were developed somewhat later than war games. They have always been extremely popular in Asian countries, where a war game and a hunt game are often played on the same board. Hunt games are generally played by two people. One player has a large number of pieces, the other player a much smaller number. The larger body represents a group of hunters that attempts to track down and kill the quarry (or alternatively to immobilize it). The smaller body represents the quarry, a number of dangerous beasts that attempts to isolate and pick off the hunters, one by one, and remove them from the board. In most earlier hunt games, the quarry was a single piece and its capture was not difficult, provided the hunters advanced methodically. Later, however, the number of the quarry increased to as many as four, all of which have to be cornered. This development made the games much more even and therefore increased their interest.

Below: Tunisians playing an alquerque *game amid the ancient ruins of Carthage.*

The Alquerque Group of Hunt Games

The earliest example of a hunt game in European literature occurs in the 1283 Alfonso manuscript. It is included among the alquerque games and is played on an alquerque board. Its inclusion in the Alfonso manuscript suggests that the game was of Arab origin, because the games mentioned in this manuscript were all games brought to Spain by invading Moors. On the other hand, hunt games are played in most Asian countries but not in Africa, which prompts Murray to suggest that they originated in Asia. If he is right about this, we can surmise that the Arabs adapted at least one hunt game to an alquerque board during their numerous forays to the East. The first game described here is that which appeared in Alfonso's manuscript.

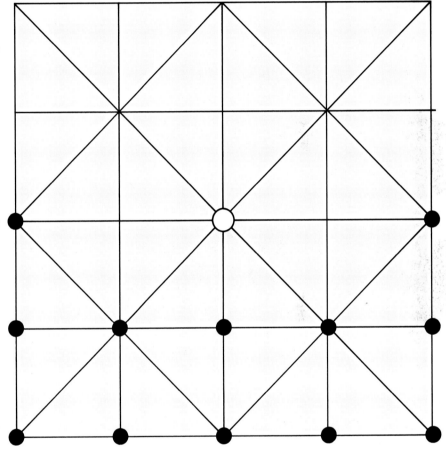

Right: The board used for the ancient game of de cercar la liebre (catch the hare), *showing the starting positions of the hare and the hunters.*

De Cercar La Liebre
(Catch the Hare)

De cercar la liebre, or "catch the hare," was included in Alfonso X's *Libro de Juegos* (1283). This is the first known description of a hunt game in European literature.

How to Play Catch the Hare

1. For this game the latticed board shown to the right is used. At start of play one player has a "hare," which is situated on the central point, and the other player has twelve "hunters," who are arranged on the first and second rows and the end points of the third row.

2. Both the hare and the hunters have the same power of move–one step along a marked line in any direction to a vacant point.

3. Only the hare can capture and he does so by the multiple short leap method, as in checkers.

4. The object of the hunters is to enclose the hare so that it is impossible for him to move or capture. The object of the hare is to capture enough hunters to make it impossible for those remaining to corner him.

5. The game is biased in favor of the hunters. A good player can lose one or two men and win comfortably.

6. Over the centuries the board was simplified by omitting the diagonals and by a corresponding reduction in the power of move. The modern *juego de la liebre* is played on the board shown at bottom right.

Bottom right: Coyote. This variation of the hare game is from Mexico. Only the major diagonals are marked, which means the powers of move are restricted. Otherwise the game is identical.

Bottom far right: Ko-app-paw-na or "Indian and jackrabbits" is a game played by the Tigua Indians of New Mexico. Small stones are used for the rabbits and the position of the Indian is indicated by pointing a stick.

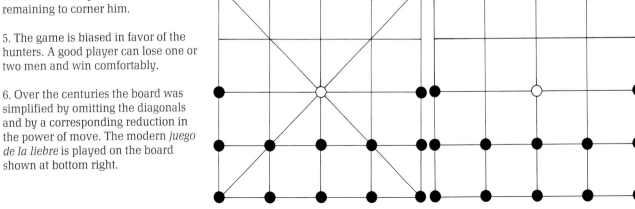

147

Shap Luk Kon Tseung Kwan

Shap luk kon tseung kwan can be roughly translated as "sixteen pursue the general." This Chinese game is played on an alquerque board that is enlarged by the addition of a triangular section from the three center points at one end of the board (see the diagram in the left-hand margin). The German scholar Himly wrote in the 1870s that the board was often scratched out in the surface of dusty country roads and that the game was very popular among "laborers and children." In this game the general is taken by interception—occupying the points on either side of him along any marked line. This is a primitive method, which suggests that the game may very well be older than the others described in this section.

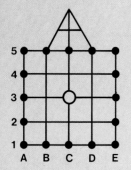

Above: *At start of play the general is in the central hole and the rebels occupy the holes around the edge of the board.*

Above: *This is the template used to mark the four foam pieces that fit into the triangular area at the top of the board.*

How to Play Shap Luk Kon Tseung Kwan

1. In this game for two players, one player has 16 rebel soldiers; the other has a general. At start of play the pieces are arranged on the board as shown in the diagram. The soldiers make the first move.

2. All the pieces have the same power of move–one step along any marked line to an adjacent vacant point.

3. Only the general is allowed to enter the triangular sanctuary. If, however, he is trapped there and cannot move out, he loses the game.

4. Both the general and the soldiers can capture, but they use different methods to do this.
a) The general does so by the method of *intervention*–i.e., by occupying a point immediately between two soldiers on the same marked line. If he does this, the general captures both opposing pieces.
b) The soldiers do so by the method of *interception*–i.e., by occupying the points immediately on both sides of the general on the same marked line. If two solders do this, the general has lost the game.

Example:
In this very simplified example, soldiers play first and move A2-B2. The general seizes the opportunity to capture two soldiers by moving C3-D2, thus capturing C1 and E3 by intervention. If Napoleon had been as short-sighted as the general in this game, he would certainly never have reached Paris (not to speak of Moscow!), for B2-C2 uses the method of interception to capture the general and wins.

How to Make Shap Luk Kon Tseung Kwan

Materials
a) For the board: A plywood sheet 32 cm x 45 cm x 8 mm (12¾ in x 18 in x ⁵/₁₆ in), 15 cm x 30 cm (6 in x 12 in) sheet 5 mm (³/₁₆ in) foam board, 5 furniture-leg studs, glue, primer, red and black acrylic paint, a roll of 5 mm (³/₁₆ in) black adhesive tape;
b) For the playing pieces: approx. 115 cm (44 in) of 6 mm (¼ in) dowel, thumb tacks with heads of approx. 1 cm (³/₈ in) diameter, green and yellow acrylic paint.

Tools
Steel ruler, pencil, handsaw, 6 mm (¼ in) drill, 6 mm (¼ in) round file, sandpaper, hobby knife, hammer, paintbrushes.

Method
a) To make the board:
Using a ruler and pencil, draw the center line along the length of the plywood sheet. Draw a line across the width of the sheet 13 cm (5³/₁₆ in) from one end. Mark points on this line 7½ cm (3 in) from each side and join them to the end of the center line to form a triangle. Erase the line that forms the base of the triangle. Cut away the corners with a handsaw.

Mark a grid on the board following the diagram in the margin. The sides of the squares and the distance between points on the sides of the triangle are 7½ cm (3 in).

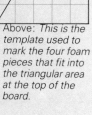

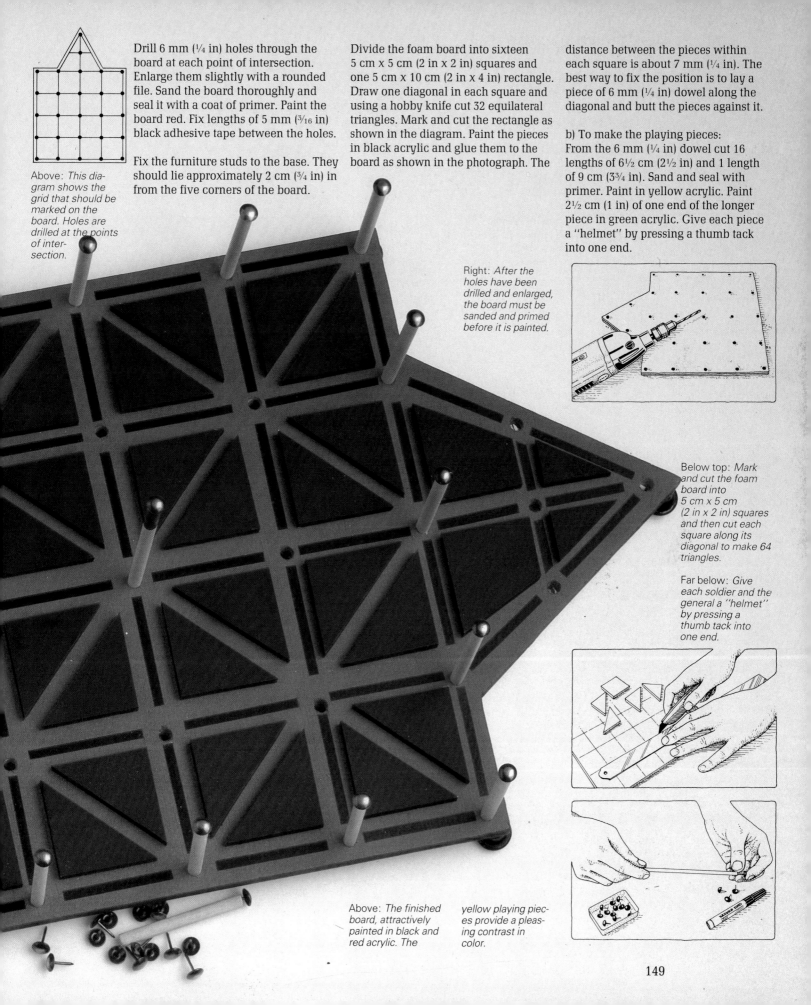

Drill 6 mm (¼ in) holes through the board at each point of intersection. Enlarge them slightly with a rounded file. Sand the board thoroughly and seal it with a coat of primer. Paint the board red. Fix lengths of 5 mm (³⁄₁₆ in) black adhesive tape between the holes.

Fix the furniture studs to the base. They should lie approximately 2 cm (¾ in) in from the five corners of the board.

Above: This diagram shows the grid that should be marked on the board. Holes are drilled at the points of intersection.

Divide the foam board into sixteen 5 cm x 5 cm (2 in x 2 in) squares and one 5 cm x 10 cm (2 in x 4 in) rectangle. Draw one diagonal in each square and using a hobby knife cut 32 equilateral triangles. Mark and cut the rectangle as shown in the diagram. Paint the pieces in black acrylic and glue them to the board as shown in the photograph. The

distance between the pieces within each square is about 7 mm (¼ in). The best way to fix the position is to lay a piece of 6 mm (¼ in) dowel along the diagonal and butt the pieces against it.

b) To make the playing pieces:
From the 6 mm (¼ in) dowel cut 16 lengths of 6½ cm (2½ in) and 1 length of 9 cm (3¾ in). Sand and seal with primer. Paint in yellow acrylic. Paint 2½ cm (1 in) of one end of the longer piece in green acrylic. Give each piece a "helmet" by pressing a thumb tack into one end.

Right: After the holes have been drilled and enlarged, the board must be sanded and primed before it is painted.

Below top: Mark and cut the foam board into 5 cm x 5 cm (2 in x 2 in) squares and then cut each square along its diagonal to make 64 triangles.

Far below: Give each soldier and the general a "helmet" by pressing a thumb tack into one end.

Above: The finished board, attractively painted in black and red acrylic. The yellow playing pieces provide a pleasing contrast in color.

149

Yeung Luk Sz'Kon Tseung Kwan

This is a Chinese game which was first mentioned by Hyde (1694), who came across it in Nanking.

The central point of a rectangular lattice is occupied by the general point, while the remaining points of the three middle columns (see photograph) are occupied by the 26 rebels (kwan)–the forces of the pirate Yeung luk sz'.

The rules are identical in every respect to the rules for shap luk kon tseung kwan. Pieces move one step at a time, along any marked line, to a vacant point. Only the general can enter the triangle, and if confined there, loses the game. The general captures by intervention and the rebels do so by interception.

How to Make the Game of Yeung Luk

Materials
A split bamboo placemat measuring approx. 36 cm x 36 cm (14½ in x 14½ in), green, blue and yellow acrylic paint;

Tools
Pencil, steel ruler; fine paintbrush.

Method
Draw the grid on the mat following the diagram. The central cells measure 3 cm x 3 cm (1¼ in x 1¼ in) and the distance from the base of the triangle to the apex is 11 cm (4½ in).

Paint carefully over the outside lines of the grid in blue acrylic and the inside lines in green.

Complete the board in yellow acrylic. (Following the color scheme in the photograph of the model.)

Note: An additional project might be to make a set of four split bamboo placemats, each showing one of the four hunt game boards described in this section. The dimensions of the boards for shap luk kon tseung kwan, fox and geese, and rimau rimau may need to be reduced to fit the mats.

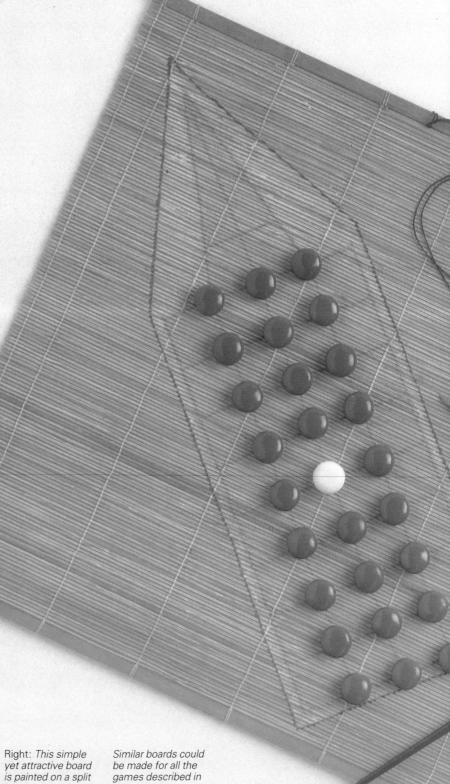

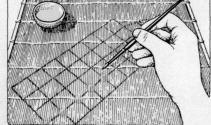

Right: *This game is played on the inter-sections of the lines. These are marked with blue acrylic—except the center spot, the starting point of the general, which is marked in yellow.*

Right: *This simple yet attractive board is painted on a split bamboo placemat.*

Similar boards could be made for all the games described in this section.

150

Fox and Geese

Fox and geese first appeared in northern Europe during the Viking period. One of the earliest references can be found in the *Grettis Saga*, which was written in Iceland around the end of the 12th century and another one is in the accounts of the royal household of Edward IV of England. In the latter, it is mentioned that "two foxis (sic) and 26 hounds of silver overgilt" were purchased to form two sets of "Marelles." Ancient boards that were scratched on stone have been found in places as far apart as Norwich Castle in eastern England and the cloisters of a church in Rome. There have been many varieties of fox and geese over the centuries. The size and shape of the board, the number of pieces and the powers of move differ from country to country and from century to century. The version offered here is *lupo e pecore*, which appeared in a 16th-century compendium of games from Venice.

Below right: This version of fox and geese *appeared in a 16th-century book of games that was published in Venice, Italy.*

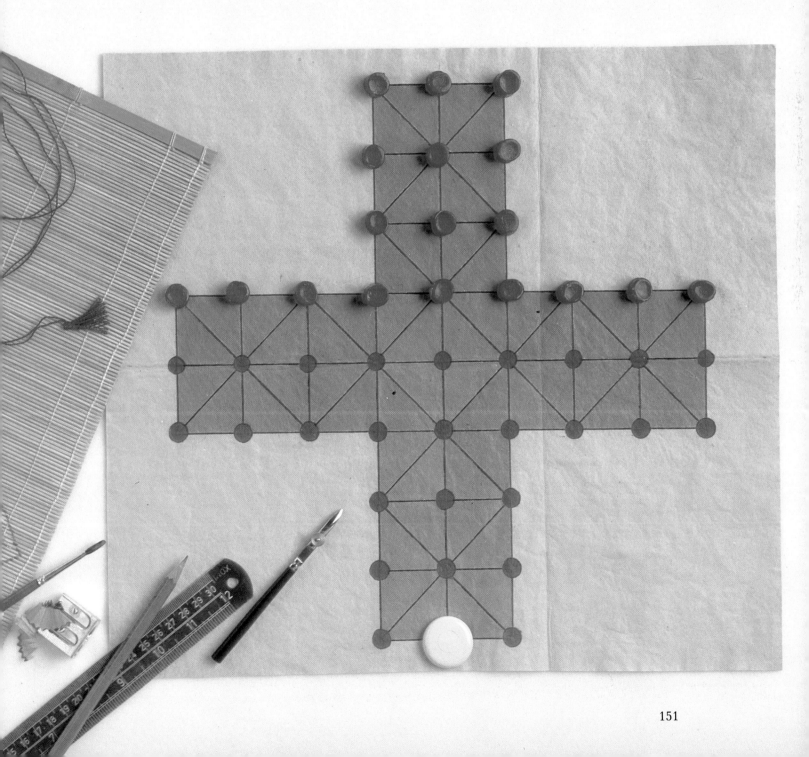

Above: Le jeu du roi (the king's game) first appeared in 1664 as the frontispiece of a treatise on chess and other board games. The game being played is a rather complex form of fox and geese.

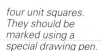

Below: *Note that the diagonals are those of the larger squares made up of* *four unit squares. They should be marked using a special drawing pen.*

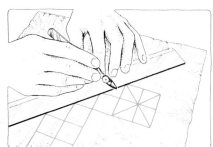

Right: *Painting the board is a painstaking and time-consuming job but the end result makes it worthwhile.*

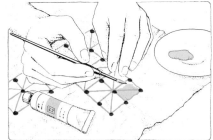

How to Play Venetian Fox and Geese

1. This is a game for two players. One player has 18 geese, the other a single fox. At start of play the geese are arranged so that they fill one limb of the cross and the row of points adjoining this limb, as shown in the photograph on p. 151. The fox can be placed on any one of the remaining points, but it is agreed by most authorities that placing the fox on the central point offers the best chances. The aim of the geese is to crowd the fox into a corner and so immobilize him. The aim of the fox is to take enough geese to prevent this happening.

2. Players move alternately. The player holding the geese opens the game by moving a goose forwards onto an adjacent vacant point. On subsequent turns of play the geese may move forwards or sideways to any vacant point, but they *cannot* move back backwards or diagonally.

3. The fox is allowed to move in any direction–forwards, backwards or diagonally–along a line to any vacant adjacent point.

4. Geese are captured by the short leap method–the fox jumping over a goose on an adjacent point onto a vacant point immediately beyond. Multiple captures can be made, in the same way as they can be made in checkers. Captured geese are removed from the board.

5. Geese cannot capture the fox, but they attempt to force him into a corner so that he can neither move nor capture. If the geese manage to do this they win the game. The fox wins the game if he captures enough geese to make it impossible for them to immobilize him. This is unlikely, however, because a weakness of this and similar hunt games lies in the fact that optimum play will result in a win for the geese. The fox can only win if the opposition fails to play correctly.

How to Make the Game of Fox and Geese

Materials
A piece of chamois leather measuring approx. 36 cm x 36 cm (14½ in x 14½ in), green, red and black acrylic paint.

Tools
Steel ruler, pencil, drawing pen, compasses, and paintbrush.

Method
First draw the grid shown in the diagram using a ruler and pencil. The four limbs of the cross measure 3 squares by 2 squares and are set around a central 2 x 2 square. Use a unit of 4 cm (1⅝ in) for the squares. Note that the diagonals are not those of the 4 cm x 4 cm (1⅝ in x 1⅝ in) squares, but are the diagonals of the 8 cm x 8 cm (3¼ in x 3¼ in) squares made up of 4 of the basic squares. When the grid has been drawn accurately, go over each line in black acrylic paint with a drawing pen.
Note: It is possible to draw the grid directly on the chamois leather in black acrylic. We suggest pencil first in case of a drawing mistake, which, if acrylic were used, would ruin the chamois leather.

Use the drawing pen and compasses to draw the circles at each point of intersection including those along the sides of the cross.

Paint the areas between the playing lines in green acrylic and the areas inside the circles in red. This is a painstaking and time-consuming task, but the end result makes the trouble and time worthwhile.

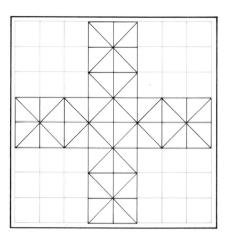

Right: *The board is laid out as shown in this diagram.*

Leopard Games

Leopard games are a small group of games played on triangular boards. They are found throughout India and in Sri Lanka, Thailand and Indonesia. Both the Thai game of *len choa* and the Sri Lankan game of *hat diviyan keliya* are played on a triangle, dissected by one vertical and two horizontal lines to form a lattice of 10 points. The only difference between these two games is that in len choa, one player has a tiger and the other six leopards; in hat diviyan keliya the first player also has one tiger, but the second has seven leopards.

How to Play Leopard Games

1. All these games are played in the same way, the only differences being in the numbers of tigers and/or leopards employed.

2. The tigers are placed on the board as shown by the black dots in the illustrations. The leopards are entered one at a time, in alternate moves with a tiger.

3. All pieces move in the same way—one step along a marked line—but leopards cannot move until they have all been entered.

4. Only a tiger can capture, and he does this by the method of the leap. The

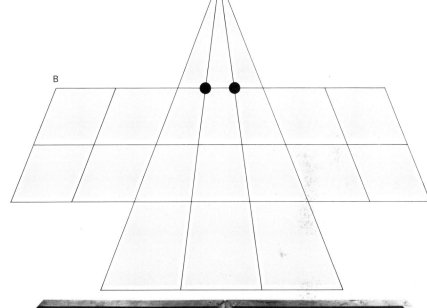

Far right and below: Both boards A and B are used for leopard games: the only difference is that board B has six more points, which prolongs the game somewhat.

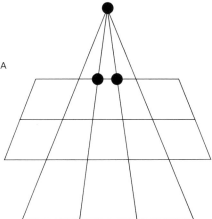

leopards try to immobilize the tigers; the tigers attempt to capture so many leopards that immobilization becomes impossible.

Pulijudam (India):
Played on board A with three tigers/leopards and 15 "lambs."
Rafaya (India) or *Demala diviyan keliya* (Sri Lanka):
Played on board A or B with three tigers/leopards and 15 "dogs."
Meurimûeng-rimûeng-do' (Sumatra):
Played on board A with five tigers/leopards and 15 "sheep."

Right: This folding wooden board, inlaid with mystic symbols, is Indian in origin. Clockwise from the top left, the boards are for (1) a single track race game, (2) pera-likatuma, (3) the leopard game, and (4) a pentalpha placement game.

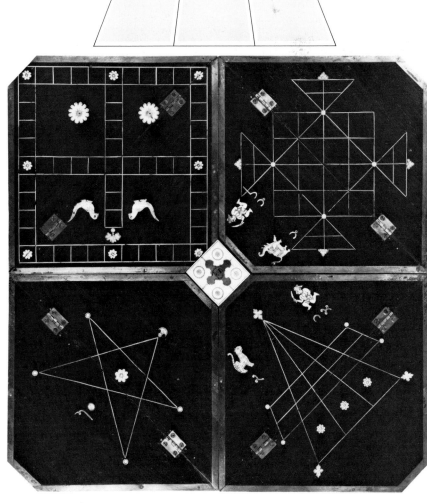

Tiger Games

The main difference between leopard games and tiger games lies in the fact that the latter are played on enlarged alquerque boards. Tiger games are popular in parts of India, Burma, Thailand, Malaysia and Indonesia. Although they are similar to the European and Chinese games played on the alquerque board (and to games derived from them), tiger games seem to have developed independently.

Many versions of the basic game exist. The numbers of tigers and opposing pieces (men, goats, cattle, sheep, etc.) vary. Also, the opening arrangement, methods of play and rules of capture differ from game to game. In general, however, the aim of the tiger is always to capture enough opposing pieces to make it impossible for the remaining pieces to immobilize him. Rimau is one of the tiger games.

Below: Tiger games are played on enlarged alquerque boards. This photograph shows the starting position for rimau.

How to Play Rimau *(Tiger)*

1. This is a Malaysian game. One player has the *rimau* (tiger) which is placed at the vertex of either triangle (in Malay it is known as *gunung*, "mountain"). The other has 24 *orang-orang* (the plural of *orang*, "man"), nine of which are placed on the square's central points.
2. All pieces move one step along a marked line to a vacant point.
3. Only the tiger can capture. If the tiger has a man or a series of an *odd* number of men next to him along a marked line and the point beyond is

Rimau-rimau:
In this variation of the game, one player has two tigers and the other has 22 men. A tiger can only take one man at a time, using the short leap method. At start of play, eight men are placed on the eight points surrounding the central point. The tigers may be placed on any vacant points or they may both be placed on the central point. To begin the game, a tiger takes one man from any point and places himself on any other vacant point. Play then continues as already described.

vacant, he can leap this man or row of men. He then removes them from the board.

Note: Capture is not compulsory.

4. At the beginning of the game, the tiger removes any three men from the board (whether they form a row or not) and places himself on any vacant point. For the next 15 moves, the opponent enters his remaining men on vacant points as play suggests, the tiger moving and capturing as chance arises when it is his turn of play. In this phase of the game, no man may be moved. Power of move is acquired only when all 15 men have been entered.

5. If the tiger is forced into a position in which he can neither move nor capture he loses the game. If the opponent is reduced to 10 or 11 men he usually resigns because this is an insufficient number of men to immobilize the tiger.

How to Make the Game of Rimau

Materials
a) To make the board: Scrap hardwood of any sort to make a board of approx. 30 cm x 45 cm (12 in x 18 in); glue, primer, red, black and yellow ochre acrylic paint; varnish;

b) For the playing pieces: a short dead branch of any sort of tree, 1 cm (3/8 in) approx. in diameter; a similar piece of branch, 3 cm (1 3/16 in) approx. in diameter, dark wood stain.

Tools
Handsaw, sandpaper, ruler, pencil, protractor, compasses, paintbrushes, fine-mesh metal gauze, toothbrush. Note: Other tools—a smoothing plane, a pair of wide-jawed clamps, etc., may be necessary depending on the type and size of wood available.

Method
a) To make the board:
In practice gaming boards in most third world countries are marked in the sand or earth, or made from whatever materials come to hand. The model in the photograph was made by glueing two 45 cm (18 in) lengths of oak cut from an old floorboard. Any hardwood is suitable, although it is probably better to choose one where the grain is not too prominent.

If it should be necessary, the wood is first prepared by removing any paint or varnish, planing smooth and sandpapering. If more than one piece of wood is used, the edges forming the join must fit snugly. Glue the pieces and clamp them together.

Seal the surface with primer and paint in thinned-down yellow ochre acrylic. Hold the gauze over the board and brush red acrylic over it using the toothbrush. This produces a very fine spray and gives a warm, glowing appearance to the board.

In the center of the board lightly draw a 4 x 4 grid of 5 cm (2 in) squares. Draw the diagonals as shown in the model in the photograph. Place the protractor on the midpoint of the side of the grid at one end of the board and mark points at 45° on each side of the center line. Draw lines 10 cm (4 in) in length through these points from the same midpoint. Set the compasses to a radius of 5 cm (2 in) and with the midpoint as center describe an arc between the 10 cm (4 in) lines. Set the compasses to a radius of 10 cm (4 in) and draw an arc between the ends of the 10 cm (4 in) lines. Repeat this process at the other end of the grid.

Now paint the whole grid roughly in black and red acrylic and decorate following the scheme used in the model in the photograph. Varnish.

b) To make the playing pieces:
Cut 24 discs, about 5 mm (3/16 in) thick, from the 1 cm (3/8 in) diameter wood. Cut 2 similar discs from the 3 cm (1 3/16 in) diameter wood. Stain the larger discs. Varnish all the discs to finish.

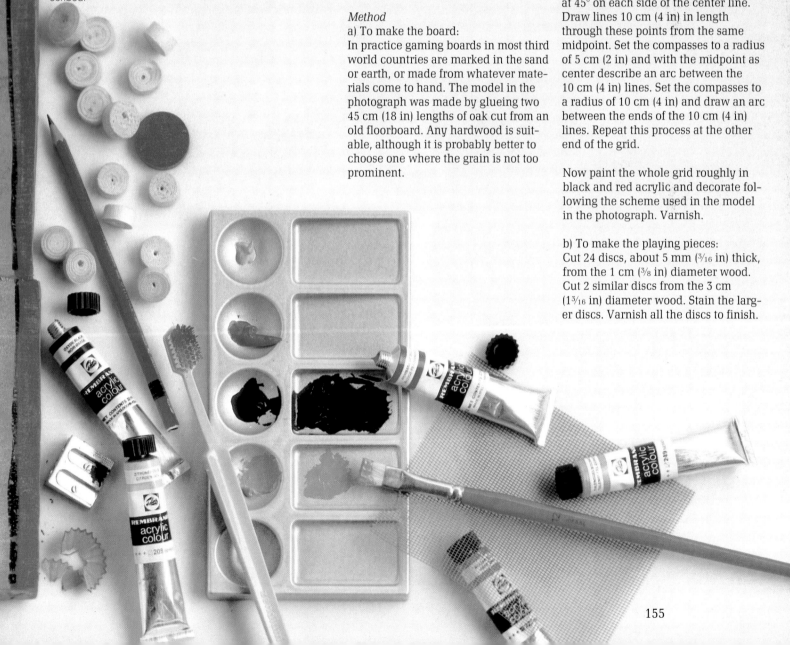

Race games

Race games are the oldest type of board game and in one form or another have been played by young and old alike for thousands of years. The ancient Egyptian games of senat and hound and jackals, the Royal Game of Ur and the Roman games of duodecim scripta and tabula, described in the opening chapter of this book, were all games of this type. Race games have always remained popular games and even today new ones regularly appear on the market–although the great majority of these new games are variations of existing ones.

Murray describes a race game as "a game in which teams of equal size race one another along a given track, and the first player to complete the course with his team wins." The "course" varies widely, some race games being played on square boards, some on cruciform boards and others on single-track boards. In all race games the moves are controlled by throwing "lots," which can be various kinds of dice, knucklebones, seeds, sticks or shells.

Race games are played throughout Europe, North and South America, Africa, Australia and in most Asian countries. Although some of them (backgammon, for example) are universally popular, others are only found within very narrow geographical limits. One good example of the latter is *totolospi*, which is only played by the Hopi Indians of Arizona in the United States. The games described in this section were selected from literally hundreds and are intended to provide an historical and geographical cross section of this universally popular type of board game.

Kerala

Kerala appears to be a much modified member of a subgroup of race games known as cross and circle games. This subgroup includes games like *nyout*, which has been played in Korea for centuries, and *pachisi*, which is the national game of India. Many scholars believe that the original inhabitants of North America came from Northeast Asia. This view is supported by the fact that incised boards for cross and circle games that are similar to nyout and pachisi have been discovered in Mayan as well as Aztec ruins. Unfortunately, not much is known about kerala and even its country of origin is a mystery. We offer a method of play here adapted from that given in Bell's *Board & Table Games 2.*

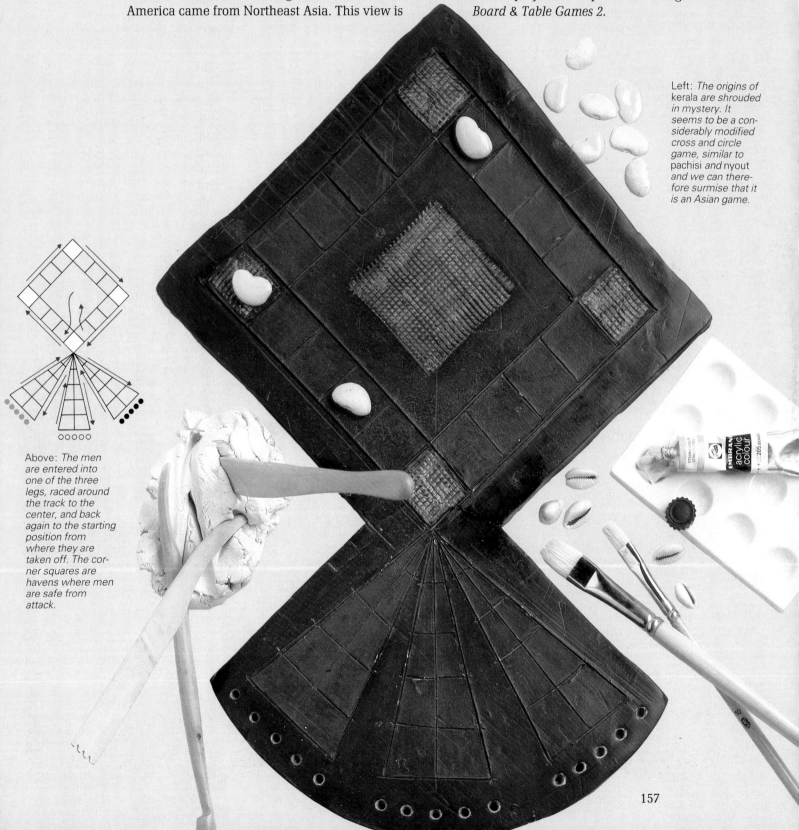

Left: *The origins of* kerala *are shrouded in mystery. It seems to be a considerably modified cross and circle game, similar to* pachisi *and* nyout *and we can therefore surmise that it is an Asian game.*

Above: *The men are entered into one of the three legs, raced around the track to the center, and back again to the starting position from where they are taken off. The corner squares are havens where men are safe from attack.*

157

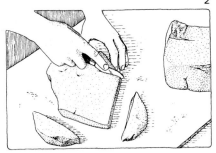
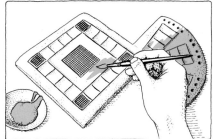

Right: *1. Roll out the clay to a thickness of about 2 cm (¹³⁄₁₆ in).*
2. Cut out the basic shape of the board using a hobby knife.
3. The tracks are incised with a spatula or the back of a hobby knife. The five holes at the ends of the entry tracks are made with a scrap of 3 mm (⅛ in) dowel. The squares forming the rest of the track are made by pressing a 3 cm x 3 cm (1³⁄₁₆ in x 1³⁄₁₆ in) square of plywood into the clay. The stippled effect in the 6 cm x 6 cm (2⅜ in x 2⅜ in) central square, the corner squares and the edges of the board was produced by scraps cut from a stippled rubber bathmat. When the patterns have been incised, the board is left to dry. The final step is to paint it in acrylic.

How to play Kerala

Equipment   Board, five distinctive stones for each player, five cowrie shells (or two-sided dice). Kerala is played by two or three players.

Scoring system   To enter a stone, one of the following throws must be made: Five backs up, scoring 5 points, four backs up, scoring 1 point. When a stone is on the board, the moves depend on the number of *mouths* up. 5, 4, 3, 2, 1 and 0 mouths up score respectively 10, 4, 3, 2, 1, and 5 points.

Method of Play
1. All stones are off the board at start of play. The stones are entered and moved according to the throws of the five cowrie shells or two-sided dice.
2. Each throw can only be used to move one stone. If a 5 is scored, the player has a second throw, which he can use to advance the same stone or a different one. A subsequent 5 gives a third throw on which a third stone can

be moved. When a throw cannot be used it is lost.
3. All five stones must reach the center before any stone can start the return journey. A stone hit by any other (including one of its own color) on its way to the center must begin again. When a stone is hit on the return journey, it must go back to the center.
4. Any stone on a marked square is immune from attack. Each player is allowed to have one stone on a safe square at the same time.
5. The first player to get all his stones off the board is the winner.

How to Make the Game of Kerala

Materials
1½ kg (3¼ lb) of hobby or model-makers' clay, a chipboard sheet 30 cm x 40 cm (12 in x 16 in) (if using hobby clay), black and green acrylic paint (or glazing powder), varnish.

Tools
Rolling pin, hobby knife, paintbrush, scrap dowel, plywood etc. to make the incised patterns of the track.

Method
For the general methods of making the basic board and painting or glazing it, follow the descriptions on p. 28 (duodecim scripta) and p. 145 (mu torere), and the photograph on this page, during the making and finishing processes.
Note: The sides of the square part of this board are approx. 17 cm (6¾ in) long. The straight sides of the fan-shaped part are approx. 12 cm (4¾ in) long. The entry tracks are formed using a spatula or the back of a hobby knife. The holes are made with a scrap of 3 mm (⅛ in) dowel. The squares forming the rest of the track are made by pressing a 3 cm x 3 cm (1³⁄₁₆ in x 1³⁄₁₆ in) square of plywood into the clay. The stippled effect in the 6 cm x 6 cm (2⅜ in x 2⅜ in) center square, the corner squares of the track, and the board's edges was produced by scraps cut from a rubber bathmat.

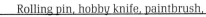

Right: *This totolospi board is carved into a sandstone slab and can be seen in the Southwest Museum, Los Angeles.*

Totolospi

In terms of scholarly research, Stewart Culin's outstanding book *Games of the North American Indians* ranks alongside Murray's *A History of Board Games*. But for Culin's work, conducted in the latter years of the last and the early years of the present century, countless traditional Indian games would have vanished and been lost forever.

Two of the games Culin collected were known as *totolospi*. One was played by the Moki Indians of New Mexico and appears to have been a little like checkers. The other totolospi game is the one described below. It was the most modified of the cross and circle games and used to be popular among the Hopi Indians of Oraibi, Arizona.

How to Play Totolospi

Equipment
A board scratched or chalked on a large, flat stone; one stone for each player; three throwing sticks, each having one face flat and plain and the other face curved and marked with a pattern of dots. Totolospi is a game for two or four players.

Method of scoring
The only scoring throws are when all the sticks fall the same way–either flat side up or curved side up. These throws allow the stone to be moved one point. The reward for a successful throw is a second throw. The player continues to throw until he fails to score, at which point the turn passes to the next player.

Unfortunately, this is the sum total of information provided by Culin. It seems reasonable to assume that the stone was moved to the center circle and back again and that some form of capture was involved. But we leave you, the reader, to invent this part of the game for yourself!

How to Make the Game of Totolospi

Materials
a) For the boards: a thin sheet of slate, approx. 15 cm x 30 cm (6 in x 12 in), a similar sheet approx. 30 cm x 30 cm (12 in x 12 in). (Note: Suitable sheets can often be found at the site of an old slate quarry; otherwise they can be bought at a garden center), green and red wax crayons, varnish;
b) For the playing pieces: a few small rounded pebbles, yellow and black acrylic paint, varnish;
c) For the throwing sticks: three pieces of half-round dowel approx. 8 cm (3¼ in) in length, black and dark blue acrylic paint, varnish.

Tools
Paintbrushes.

Method
a) To make the board:
The models in the photograph show the grid patterns that must be drawn in wax crayon on the slate. They should be drawn roughly, in the manner in which a child chalks out a hopscotch diagram. Varnish the top surface to finish.

b) To make the playing pieces:
Paint half the pebbles in black acrylic and half in yellow. When dry, paint a band around each pebble in the opposite color. Varnish.

c) To make the throwing sticks:
Paint the dowels in black acrylic paint. When dry, paint a pattern of dots on the curved sides of each stick in dark blue acrylic. Varnish to finish.

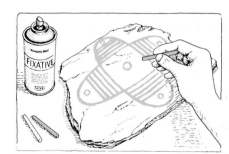

Left: *These simple totolospi boards are made by chalking the plain lines on thin sheets of slate.*

Above: *The chalk (or wax crayon) must be "fixed" with an aerosol varnish spray.*

Patol and Similar Games

Most Native American tribes used to play a race game that was originally divinatory. These games varied from tribe to tribe, but the basic idea was always to enter a man or men—usually known as *horses*—and race them around a circular or square track a certain number of times before taking them off. Horses were entered and moved according to the throws of three or four throwing sticks. These were usually flat on one side and round and colored on the other. In some games one of the sticks was notched. A larger stone, known as the *ahl* stone, was placed in the center of the track and the sticks were thrown so they hit this stone and bounced off. Most often the board was set out on the ground with small stones, although sometimes it was marked on cloth or hide. An entry "gate" (also called a river, door or creek) usually appeared at each quadrant and often entailed a penalty to players landing there. In some of the games captures were allowed, in other games not. The number of players also varied. Usually two or four people played, but in some games any number could play. Here we describe two of the dozens of versions of this game; *patol*, which was played by the Tigua Indians and *tasholiwe*, which was played by the Zuni Indians, both from New Mexico.

Right: This variation of patol is called Hue-ta-qui-chi-ka, and is being played by a group of girls from the Hauasupai tribe. The photo was taken in 1898.

How to Play Patol

Equipment
A board consisting of 40 stones arranged in four quadrants of 10 divided by four rivers *(p'ayhiah)*; a larger center stone (the ahl stone) against which the sticks are thrown; a horse *(kahniddeh)* for each player; three flat throwing sticks painted red on one side. One stick has 15 notches cut in the unpainted side.

How to make the stick dice: Cut three 10 cm (4 in) lengths from a strip of 2 cm x 6 mm (¹³⁄₁₆ in x ¼ in) plywood. Paint one side of each piece in red acrylic. Use a hobby knife to cut 15 notches on the edges of the un-painted side of one stick—10 on one edge and five on the opposite edge (see the photo).

Method of Scoring
Two red sides up together with the notched side of the third stick scores 15 points. Three unpainted sides up scores 10 points. Both these throws win an additional throw. Two red sides with a non-notched side scores 3 points; one red side with two unpainted sides scores 2 points and three red sides up scores 5 points.

1. Patol is a game for any number of players, playing individually. Each player chooses his river of entry and the direction of play. A player cannot change direction during the course of a game.

2. Each player enters and moves his horse according to the throws of the sticks against the ahl stone.

3. When an opponent plays to the point on which his horse stands, a player must return to his starting point and

begin again. There is no penalty for falling in a river.

4. The winner is the first player to successfully complete the course.

How to Play Tasholiwe

Tasholiwe is played in exactly the same way as patol except that:

1. Each player (two or four play) has a colored chip, which is entered at one of the gates: yellow at north, white at east, red at south and blue at west. Yellow and blue move from right to left and red and white move from left to right.

2. Each player makes four complete circuits of the board.

Far right: This picture dates from 1890 and shows Pueblo Indians engaged in a game of patol. Most Indian tribes had their own versions of this race game.

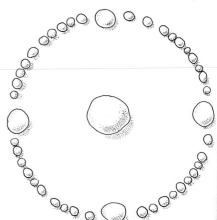

Above: The four large stones placed at the four cardinal points represent the rivers or gates.

The stone in the middle is the ahl stone on which the sticks are thrown.

Grand Jeu de l'Histoire Ancienne de la Grèce

(Great Game of the History of Ancient Greece)

This game is an excellent example of how the spiral race game was adapted for educational purposes. The board is divided into a number of adjacent rectangles; each carries an illustration and text describing an event in the history of ancient Greece.

Literally hundreds of similar games were published during the 18th and 19th centuries, and for decades they were very popular. They were used to teach a variety of subjects, but history, geography and natural history were the most common.

The rules for all of them were almost identical. The players moved around the track according to the throws of two dice. Certain places carried some kind of forfeit–the player might lose one or two turns; pay a token intro a pool; move back two or three places or even return to the beginning and start again. If a player landed on other places he might be rewarded by an another throw; by receiving a token from the other players or by doubling the original throw.

The grand jeu was developed from a game called "Royal Game of Goose," which was invented in Florence, Italy, during the time of Francesco di Medici (1574-87). From Spain, it went on to Britain, where it was first registered in 1597.

Originally it was simply an amusing race game played on a board consisting of 63 spaces. Players landing on a goose were allowed another turn and other squares carried penalties. A player had to land exactly on the 63rd place in order to win the pool and end the game. Failure to do this meant he had to start again.

It was probably around the mid-18th century that manufacturers first began to see the educational potential of this simple game. Modern educational theorizers and teachers are well aware of the important function of games play in the learning process, not only in the process of learning skills, but also in the process of learning facts.

It is interesting that even in the repressive educational systems that prevailed 200 years ago, games like this were used to instill knowledge into the young.

Right: *Spiral race games have been very popular since the end of the 16th century. At first they were played for amusement, but later they were used for educational purposes. This French board–for the* grand jeu de l'histoire ancienne de la Grèce–*shows events in the history of ancient Greece.*

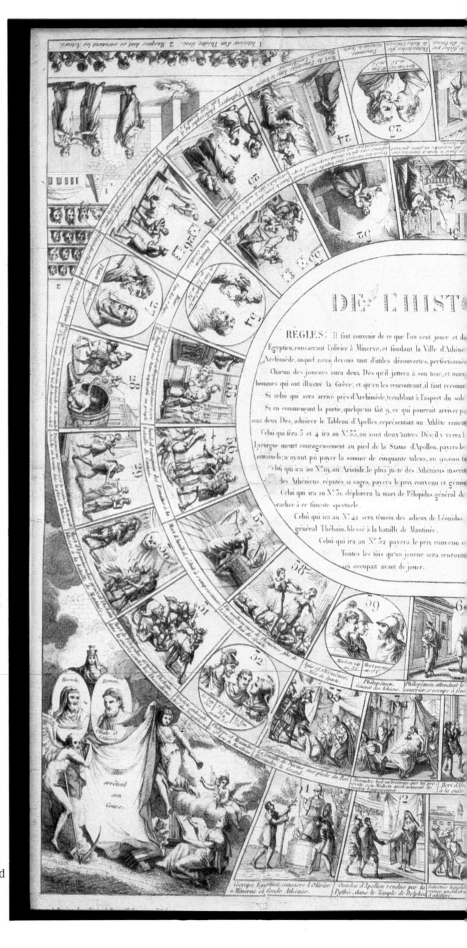

Coan Ki or the Bottle Game

Coan ki was originally a Chinese race game. The first description in the West appeared in *De Ludis Orientalibus Libri Duo,* one of the pioneer works on board games. It was published by the Oxford University press in 1694 and written by the scholar Dr. Thomas Hyde. Unfortunately, Hyde's work, like so much of the classical literature of that time, is written in vulgar Latin. Because of this, his meaning is not always as clear as it might be. Furthermore, his description of the game is incomplete: the opening phase is not described, nor is there any mention of what happens to throws that cannot be utilized.

Despite these difficulties, however, it is still possible to construct a very playable game on the basis of the available evidence. The result is a little like backgammon, but it is lent an extra dimension by the range of possible combinations that can be computed from most throws. This, in addition to the fact that there is an escalating scale of penalties on certain throws, makes this game a most exciting one.

How to Play the Bottle Game

Equipment
An eight-track board; two dice; 16 green and 16 red pieces in the shape of a bottle.

1. At start of play, the bottles are arranged on the board as shown in the diagram. Each player throws the dice. The player throwing the highest total score utilizes this to begin the game.

2. The bottles move around the board–in a counterclockwise direction–across the tracks, along the eighth track to any vacant space in the opposing home position (this counts as one space), back across the board to the player's own side. Finally, the bottles move along the board back to the starting position (also counting as one space). The bottles must be brought home with an exact throw and the first player to get his bottles back into their original configuration wins the game and takes the pot.
Note: Bottles starting on track 2 must still be brought back to track 1 before going to row 2. Once home, bottles are turned over to differentiate between those not yet moved.

3. Once the bottles have left the two home tracks (marked with lines), they do not have to stay "in line" and can fill any available space in the track where they land.

4. The players throw the dice alternately and bottles are moved according to the scores achieved.

Method of scoring
a) 1:1 is a penalty throw. Players throwing this must pay a penalty of 10% of the total pot (see margin) and lose a bottle, which must be returned into the first home track on a throw of 1 before other bottles can be moved. Alternately, a player can elect to pay a penalty of 20% of the pot, in which case he does not forfeit a bottle. This can offer tactical advantages, particularly in the end game.

b) If a double is thrown the player may *either* move one bottle half the total shown *or* two bottles the whole number thrown.
Example: on a throw of 4:4, one bottle could be moved four spaces, or two bottles could each be moved eight spaces.

c) If a run is thrown the total can be split in any way possible. Two bottles may be moved by the higher number and one by the lower.
Example: if 4:3 is thrown (4 + 3 = 7) the following combinations are possible: 2 x 6 and 1 x 1; 2 x 5 and 1 x 2; 2 x 4 and 1 x 3.

d) On all other throws, one bottle can be moved by the total score, or two bottles can be moved by the higher score and one by the lower.
Example: When the score is 6:2, one bottle could be moved 8 spaces, or two bottles could be moved, one bottle 6 spaces and one 2 spaces.

5. Only eight bottles can be in any one track and in any one half of the board at the same time. Therefore it is possible to form a tactical block to prevent an opponent's advance. The one exception to this rule is that eight bottles in the two home tracks are deemed *not* to be blocks and an opponent can bypass them.

Note: A player who is new to the bottle game might be forgiven for thinking that it would be logical to work out the highest possible combinations and so take the greatest number of steps, but a few sample games will be enough to convince him that this is not at all the case.

As is the case with backgammon, it is sometimes prudent to spread the playing pieces judiciously–particularly when trying to form a block or when nearing home. If the bottle game is played at speed, it can be even more complex and demanding than backgammon.

How to calculate the wagers in the bottle game.	Pot	20.00
(A) = the first player	(A) 10%	2.00
(B) = the second player		22.00
10% = a player throws 1:1 and elects to reenter.	(A) 10%	2.20
		24.20
20% = a player throws 1:1 and elects to keep the bottle in play and pay the heavier penalty.	(B) 10%	2.42
		26.42
	(A) 10%	2.66
		29.28
	(B) 20%	5.96
The players agree to play for a stake of 10 units each–a pot of 20 units.		35.24
	(A) 20%	7.05
		42.29

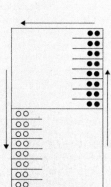

Above: *At start of play the bottles are positioned as shown. The arrows indicate the direction of play.*

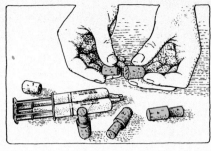
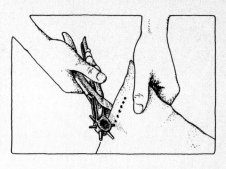

Note: Near the end of the game, both players calculate that they have winning chances and elect to pay the higher penalty rather than send a bottle back to the beginning. In this example the winner takes the pot of 42 units—or, to to put it another way, the loser pays the winner 32 units.

How to Make the Bottle Game
Materials
a) For the board: a plywood sheet 32 cm x 41 cm x 16 mm (13 in x 16½ in x ⅝ in), 1.65 m (66 in) pre-glued oak veneer 4 cm (1⅝ in) wide, 1.65 m (66 in) pre-glued birch veneer 4 cm (1⅝ in) in width, 2 mm (1/16 in) brown adhesive tape, varnish; b) For the playing pieces: 32 small and 32 large corks, glue, green and red acrylic paint.

Tools
Steel ruler, pencil, hobby knife, smoothing iron, sandpaper.

Method
a) To make the board:
Cut each veneer strip into 4 lengths of 41 cm (16½ in). Remove the backing from an oak strip and lay it along one side of the board. Iron it in place with a smoothing iron set to its medium temperature (about 60° C [140° F]). The other strips are laid alternately across the width of the board. Make sure that the grain of each strip lies in the same direction. Sand thoroughly.

Using a steel ruler and a pencil, mark seven lines at one corner of the board across the first two veneer strips at distances of 2½ cm (1 in). Mark seven similar lines in the diagonally opposite corner. Mark the two center lines, each 2½ cm (1 in) from its last adjacent short line. When the lines have been drawn, cover them with brown adhesive tape. Varnish the board to finish.

b) To make the playing pieces:
You need 32 playing pieces and each is made by glueing a small cork to a large one. Paint 16 in green acrylic and 16 in red.

Below: *The board and playing pieces for this unusual game are quite simple to make.*

Backgammon

No one knows for certain where or how backgammon originated and the existing legends only serve to confuse the issue. What we do know for certain is that the Romans were avid players of a game called duodecim scripta and that this was similar to modern backgammon in its basic rules and methods of play. Duodecim scripta was later modified and became known as tabula, which was even closer to the present-day game. This game spread across Europe under the name of *tables*.

The first of the Sassanian kings, Ardshir, ruler in Persia during the third century A.D., is one of several people credited in legend with the invention of backgammon. According to an Indian legend, a gentleman by the name of Qaflän created the game. Whatever the truth, or otherwise, of these legends, it is interesting to speculate that the inventor was perhaps influenced by the cycle of the year. The backgammon board has 24 "points," which correspond to the 24 hours of the day; the 12 points in each half of the board represent the 12 months of the year; the 30 playing pieces the days of the month. This analogy can be taken further. Day and night can be said to correspond to the two dice that are thrown to indicate the moves, while the seven days of the week (and also the seven planets that were known at that time) are represented by the total of the dots on opposite faces of the die (1 and 6, 2 and 5, 3 and 4).

All this, however, is pure speculation. Wherever and by whomever the game was invented is not of utmost importance. Suffice it to say that over the centuries backgammon has spread to every corner of the globe and that it is probably more popular today than it has ever been.

Right: *This diagram shows the position of the stones at start of play. The arrows show the direction of play. Note: Many players prefer to play using the left-hand side of the board as the home table, in which case the stones are set out the other way around.*

How to Play Backgammon

1. Backgammon is played on a board divided into 24 triangular *points*, 12 on each side of the board. They are marked in two alternating and contrasting colors to facilitate counting. The *bar* further divides the 24 points into four *tables*, each of six points. Thirty *stones* (15 of one color and 15 of another–usually black and white, or red and white) are used. Two dice are thrown from a dice cup to determine moves. Many players prefer to play for a small stake and for this purpose a special die, with faces showing, respectively, 2, 4, 8, 16, 32 and 64 is used. The use of this die, the *doubling die*, will be discussed later.

2. At start of play the stones are arranged as shown in the diagram. Table 1 is black's *inner table*. Black must move all his stones–in a clockwise direction–from tables 4, 3 and 2 into his inner table, from where they may then be *borne-off*.
Table 4 is white's inner table, and he must move his stones counterclockwise from tables 1, 2 and 3 into this table before he can bear off. The winner is the first player to bear off his stones.

3. To begin play, each player throws one stone. The player throwing high begins by using the combination of the two dice thrown. For example, 5 and 3

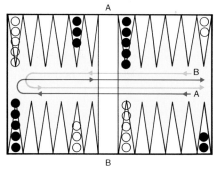

are thrown. The player who has thrown the 5 begins with 5:3.

4. Advancement of the stones is determined by the throws of two dice (the moves are subject to certain restrictions, which will be discussed later). By convention the dice are thrown in the area of the board to the right of each player. They must both land flat–a throw is not valid if a die comes to rest "tipped up" against the edge of the board or a stone. If this occurs both dice must be rethrown.
Say, for example, 6:3 are thrown. The thrower has two choices. He may move a stone 6 points and another stone 3 points; he may also move a single stone by the total shown on the dice–in this case 9 points. If a double is thrown the player may move twice the total shown. With a throw of, say, 4:4, he may move one stone 16, one stone 12 and another 4, two stones 8, two stones

4 each and another 8, or four stones 4 points. This sounds much more complicated than it actually is.

Restrictions: 5. The principal restriction on a move is that each point played onto must be *open*–that is, it must not contain two or more hostile stones. If a point has two or more of these hostile stones on it, it is said to be *closed*. An opposing stone or stones may leap the closed point, but may not land on it. If, however, a point is empty or contains only one stone the point is said to be *open* and the single stone is vulnerable to attack. Such a stone is known as a *blot*; if an opposing stone lands on this point the blot is *hit* and removed from the board to rest on the bar. A player with a stone on the bar cannot move any other stone until this stone is returned into play on an open point in the opponent's inner table. This can only be done on an exact throw; if this is not possible the throw is lost. For example, if points 1, 2, 4, and 6 are closed, a stone can only be reentered on a throw of 3 or 5. If the opponent manages to close his entire inner table, the other player cannot throw until a point becomes available. It is a good tactical move to close off the inner table, as it often results in a win. A throw is also lost if a player has no legal move because all possible landing points have been closed by his opponent. It often happens that the throw

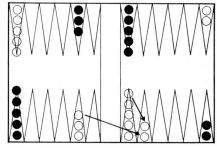

Right: *White's first throw is 1:3 and he decides to make his five point. This is a good defensive move as the point is now closed to black.*

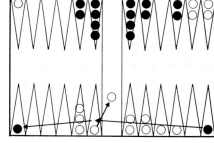

Right: *A single stone on a point (a blot) can be hit and sent to the bar. Black throws 6:5, hits the blot on white's seven point and moves on five spaces.*

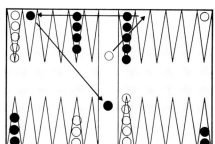

Right: *A stone reentering can also hit a blot. White has a stone on the bar and throws 6:5. He enters on five and moves six, thus hitting black's blot on his eleven point.*

shown by one die can be used, while the other is forfeit.

6. A player is not allowed to bear off any stones until all his stones are in his inner table. A stone is borne off by throwing the relevant score on the die. A throw of 6, for example, can be used to bear off a stone on point 6. If there is no stone on this point a stone on the next available point can be borne off. Bearing off is optional. If a player has a legal move within his inner table, he can elect to make this move rather than bearing off a stone. If there is no legal move within the inner table, a stone must be borne off if possible, even if this is to the detriment of the player–if bearing off would leave a blot, for example.

If during the process of bearing off a player's stone is sent to the bar, no further stones may be borne off until that stone is returned into play in the opponent's inner table, and is brought back into the home inner table. Once borne off men are "dead" and take no further part in the play.

The Doubling Die 7. Many players prefer to play for a stake–so much per point. At start of play the doubling die

is set on 64 (representing 1) between the two players. Either player can "double"–i.e., turn the die to 2, when it is his turn to throw. The opponent then has the choice of accepting the die and so doubling the original stake, or rejecting it and conceding the game. If he accepts, the die remains with him until the end of the game or until his position improves to a point where he feels strong enough to redouble to 4. The first player then accepts or rejects the offered die. This process continues until the doubling die is on 64, when the players are playing for 64 times the original stake.

The game can be even more expensive, however. If a player bears off all his stones before his opponent has borne off any, his win is a *gammon*, and this means that the loser pays double the stakes.

If a player has the bad luck to end up with a stone on the bar or in his opponent's home table after all the opposing stones have been borne off, it is a *backgammon*, which means that triple stakes are paid.

(Theoretically, this could lead to a loss of 192 times the stake, but this rarely, if ever, happens.)

Left: *The local policeman enjoying a game of* backgammon *in this Turkish village.*

Below: *This 17th-century print shows two men playing* trictrac, *a simplified form of backgammon.*

The Backgammon Players. *A late 19th-century watercolor by Giulio Rosati.*

Giulio Rosati

How to Make a Backgammon Board

Materials
Two plywood sheets
34 cm x 34 cm x 8 mm
(12¾ in x 12¾ in x ⁵⁄₁₆ in); 2.75 m
(8 ft 6 in) of 5 cm x 16 mm
(1⅞ in x ⅝ in) planed softwood;
4 sheets pre-glued mahogany veneer
34 cm x 34 cm (12¾ in x 12¾ in);
1.92 m (6 ft) pre-glued mahogany
veneer strip 16 mm (⅝ in) wide, 2.72 m
(8 ft 6 in) same strip 24 mm (¹⁵⁄₁₆ in)
wide, 2.8 m (9 ft 3 in) pre-glued oak
veneer strip 3 cm (1⅛ in) in width,
92 cm (34 in) pre-glued teak veneer
3 cm (1⅛ in) in width, a roll of 2 mm
(¹⁄₁₆ in) white adhesive tape, glue, panel
pins, varnish, 2 brass hinges 3 x 1 cm
(1³⁄₁₆ x ⅜ in) with screws.

Tools
Sandpaper, tenon saw, mitre box, vise,
hammer, steel ruler, pencil, hobby
knife, smoothing iron, paintbrushes,
screwdriver.

Method
The board consists of two identical halves hinged to form a box in which the
stones and dice can be kept. The instructions below refer to one-half of the
board only. The other is made in
exactly the same way.
Using the 45° slot in the mitre box and
a tenon saw, cut four lengths from the
5 cm x 16 mm (1⅞ in x ⅝ in) planed
softwood. These lengths should be
34 cm (12¾ in) on the longer side and
24 cm (9 in) on the shorter (see diagram). Cut four 24 cm (9 in) lengths
from the 16 mm (⅝ in) mahogany veneer strip and remove the backing.
Clamp each piece of softwood in a vise
and glue the veneer strips along the
shorter edges using a smoothing iron
set at medium temperature. Fix each
piece in position on a 34 cm x 34 cm
(12¾ in x 12¾ in) plywood sheet using
glue and panel pins.

Above: *Gouge out
the 2 mm (¹⁄₁₆ in)
surplus strips with
the point of a small
screwdriver.*

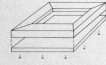

Above: *The mitred
side pieces are
glued and pinned to
an 8 mm (⁵⁄₁₆ in)
plywood sheet to
form one half of the
board.*

Mark an inner square at a distance of
5 cm (1⅞ in) from the edge of a sheet of
34 cm x 34 cm (12¾ in x 12¾ in)
mahogany veneer. Using the grid as a
guide, draw the patterns according to
the diagram. The easiest way is to draw
lines along the full length and width of
the sheet and erase surplus lines when
the pattern is complete. Now draw further lines at a distance of 2 mm (¹⁄₁₆ in)
outside each existing line. Using a steel
ruler and hobby knife, cut out the inner
square and remove the backing. Fix it

to the board by pressing the tip of a
smoothing iron at the corners. Then cut
out the three center shapes and the six
shaded triangles (see diagram) along
the *inner* lines. Cut two 3 cm (1⅛ in)
lengths and six 9 cm (3⅜ in) triangles
from the 3 cm (1⅛ in) oak veneer strip
and iron in place. Cut a 14 cm (4⅞ in)
length from the 3 cm (1⅛ in) teak veneer strip and iron in the place. Iron
over the entire inner board.
Remove the backing from the outer
square and iron it in place. Cut out the
shapes along the *inner* lines. Cut four
8 cm (3 in) lengths from the teak veneer
strip and iron in place. Cut eight 10 cm
(4⅛ in) lengths from the oak veneer
strip. Mitre one corner of each at an
angle of 45° and iron in place. Then
iron the entire outer board again.
Iron a 34 cm x 34 cm (12¾ in x 12¾ in)
sheet of mahogany veneer to the back
of the board. Cut four 34 cm (12¾ in)
lengths from the 24 mm (¹⁵⁄₁₆ in)
mahogany veneer strip and iron these
to the edges of the board.
Now cut along all the pencil lines remaining on the board. This will give a
series of 2 mm (¹⁄₁₆ in) strips. Gouge out
these strips with the point of a small
screwdriver. Fill the grooves with 2 mm
(¹⁄₁₆ in) white adhesive tape. Press the
tape in place with your thumb as you
unroll it and cut with a hobby knife.
Re-iron the board. Finally, sand
thoroughly and varnish.
When both halves of the board have
been made, position the hinges 4 cm
(1⅝ in) in along the
upper inside edges.
Draw round them
and cut away the
veneer. Screw on the
hinges.

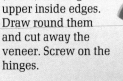

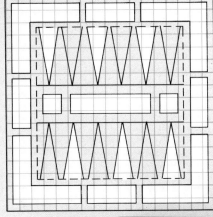

Above: *This
2 cm x 2 cm
(¾ in x ¾ in) grid
will assist in the
laying out of the
veneer pattern. All
the strips are 3 cm
(1⅛ in) width. The
"points" are also
cut from 3 cm
(1⅛ in) veneer strip.*

Right: *The lighter
veneered areas on
the boards are of
oak. The darker
strips on the edge
and in the center
are of teak. You can
clearly see how the
2 mm (¹⁄₁₆ in) white
adhesive tape sets
off the contrasting
veneers.*

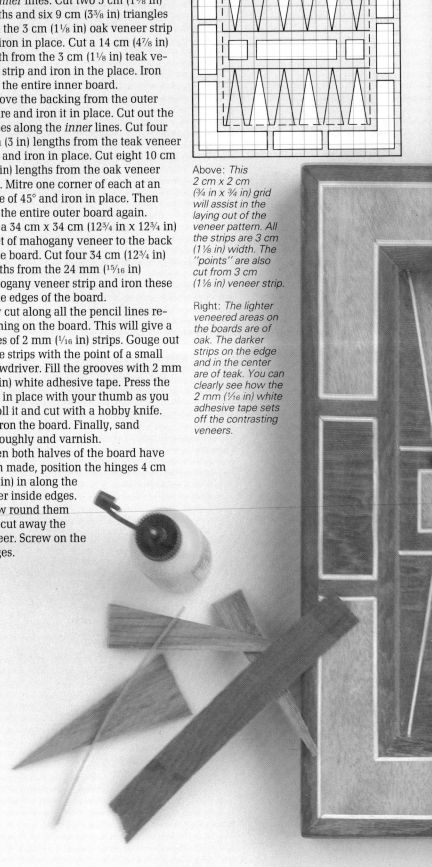

Right: *The adventurous (or the masochistic!) may be tempted to use the same veneer techniques to make boards on the outer surfaces. The board on the left is for nine men's morris, that on the right is for solitaire.*

Race Games on Cruciform Boards

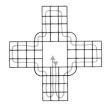

Above: *The playing pieces begin in the central square and race along the track according to throws of the cowrie shells.*

Below: *A variation of asi keliya played on the street in a town in southern India.*

The group of race games played on cruciform boards are essentially of Indian invention, but over the centuries they have spread to many other countries, including Sri Lanka, Burma, Iran, Syria, Spain and Somalia. One such game, *ludo,* was introduced into Britain at the end of the last century and became extremely popular, particularly among children. It was also widely played, as a gambling game, in the British Royal Navy under the name of uckers.

One of the most popular of these games in India today is known as *pachisi,* which, translated, means "twenty-five." This game is played on a board consisting of a cross, each arm having 3 x 8 cells arranged around a large central square known as the *char-koni,* or throne. (The boards are often made of embroidered cloth.) Each player has four distinctively colored pieces, which he races around the board in accordance with the throws of six cowrie shells or coins. In the 16th century the Mogul emperors often had large boards marked out in the courtyards of their palaces and they used slavegirls dressed in suitably colored saris as playing pieces. In palaces in Agra, Allahabad and Fatehpur-Sikrim traces of these boards can still be seen.

A great number of games is played on cruciform boards and they are all basically the same. They differ in the number of cells in each arm of the cross (3 x 4, 3 x 5, 3 x 6, 3 x 8, etc); in that some of the games have a number of crosscut cells on which pieces are immune from attack; in the numbers of lots (usually shells) thrown and also in the scoring. The game chosen to be described here is *asi keliya* (the shell game), also called *sonaru* (four-four), which is played throughout Sri Lanka.

How to Play Asi Keliya

Equipment
A cruciform board (as illustrated); four sets of 4 men, differentiated by color or pattern; six cowrie shells, of which five *(bella)* are the common yellow cowries and the sixth *(so-bella)* is a white cowrie. (It is allright to use six two-sided dice or coins, as long as one is different from the others.)

1. At start of play the men are in the center square. After entry they are raced counterclockwise along the track as shown in the diagram. When they arrive back in the center square they are taken off the board.

2. Each player in turn throws the six cowrie shells, the value of the throws

being given by the number of mouths that fall upward. A throw of four mouths upward, when the white cowrie falls mouth *down,* is known as *so-hatara.* So-hatara, or a throw of 1 or 5, gives an additional throw. Otherwise there is only one throw in each turn of play. So-hatara may also be subdivided into 1, 1, 1, 1, but all other throws must be used as a whole to move a single man.
(This is also the case with a throw of four mouths upward that *includes* the white cowrie shell–this throw is simply a 4.)

3. A throw of 1 (or so-hatara) is needed to enter or reenter a man. When a man has reached the middle row and is moving up it to be taken off, it can only be moved one cell at a time by a throw of 1.

4. So-hatara is also the only throw that allows a man to jump over an enemy man, due to its alternative value of 1, 1, 1, 1, which allows it to take the enemy man and move on beyond. Otherwise a man is only captured when an enemy man lands on the cell that it occupies. Doubled men are not immune from capture, but two men so taken can be reentered as one. All the captured men must be reentered from the central square.

5. The winners are the pair who first take off all their eight men.

Materials
A sheet of red cotton tentcloth 60 cm x 60 cm (24 in x 24 in), a piece of black imitation leather 25 cm x 25 cm (10 in x 10 in), a piece of this material 10½ cm x 10½ cm (4¼ in x 4¼ in), glue, gold felt-tipped pen, green acrylic paint.

Tools
Steel ruler, protractor, pencil, hobby knife, a small potato.

Method
Using the steel ruler, pencil and protractor, construct a 15 cm x 15 cm (6 in x 6 in) square in the center of the tentcloth. To form a cross, construct 15 cm x 20 cm (6 in x 8 in) rectangles on the sides of this square. Divide each of the four rectangles into a grid of 5 cm x 5 cm (2 in x 2 in) squares. Draw a grid of 3½ cm x 3½ cm (1⅜ in x 1⅜ in) squares on the leather sheet. (Note: there will be ½ cm (⅜ in) of waste material along two edges.) Cut out the squares using a steel ruler and hobby knife. Cut 20 of them in half and 4 in quarter, both diagonally. Glue them to the tentcloth following the pattern in the model. Glue the 10½ cm x 10½ cm (4¼ in x 4¼ in) piece in the center square of the cross. Draw over the entire grid with the gold pen and mark the pattern of dots on the black squares. Cut the potato in half. Cut away the outer edge to leave a raised circle. Cut a cross within this circle to leave four raised quadrants and use this to print the pattern in green paint.

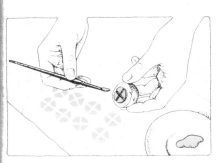

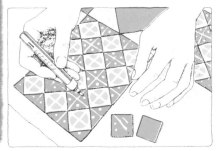

Mancala Games

The name *mancala* is from the Arabic word *manqala*, which is derived from the verb *naqala*, "to move." There are hundreds of mancala games, all of which are similar in their basic goals and methods of play, though they differ in detail. Mancala games are usually games for two players, although there are often so many onlookers discussing the moves, giving advice and even interfering with play, that an uninitiated bystander might easily be forgiven for thinking he was watching a team game!

The boards for these games consist of a number of rows, each containing a number of cups. These are sometimes made of wood, but just as often cut into stone, or simply pressed into the dry earth. The number of rows can be two, three or four, and the number of cups also varies, from as few as three for simple children's games to as many as 28 for several of the more complex games. Small objects, such as beans, seeds or nuts, are arranged in various ways in the cups. There is no differentiation between those pieces. The aim is to redistribute them according to certain rules and in such a way as to capture as many "pieces" as is possible. All this sounds reasonably simple, but the speed at which these games are played and the complexity of most of them are such that they should present a challenge to almost anyone. Most authorities agree that the birthplace of the mancala games lies in the region around the Red Sea. Indeed, boards that are almost 3,500 years old have been found at Al-Qurna, Luxor and Karnak, all of which are in Egypt. These are the earliest mancala boards we know, a fact which not only supports the theory that the game originated in Egypt, but also puts it among the oldest games we know.

Right: *This form of mancala is known as* mweiso. *It is played in Tanzania and many other East African countries and is one of the most complex forms of the game. Mweiso is played on a 4 x 8 celled board and captures are reentered into play.*

Wari

Right: *Diagram 1. To begin the game, player A sows the beans from the third cup from his left.*

Right: *Diagram 2. Player B begins by sowing beans from the second cup on his right.*

Wari, or games very similar to it, is played among many African tribes. The wari board consists of two rows of six cups and there is a reservoir at each end to hold captured pieces. At start of play, the 12 cups all hold four similar-sized objects, such as nuts, dried beans, seeds or fruit pips, etc. Here we use beans.

How to Play Wari

The first player removes the beans from any one of his cups and sows them, one by one, counterclockwise into the next four cups. An example: if he begins with the third cup from his left, after his move the board will be like the upper diagram left. If his opponent then begins with the second cup from his right, the board will be like the lower diagram right after his move.

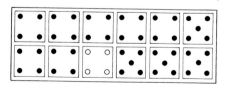

Diagrams 1 and 2

Play continues alternately. The aim of each player is to capture beans in his opponent's cups. This occurs when the *last* bean sown falls into a cup on the opponent's side that already holds one or two beans. With the sown bean, the total is then two or three beans. These are captured, removed from the board and deposited in that player's reservoir. In the diagram below, one possible capture is shown.

Note: Once play has started there is no differentiation in beans. Those beans captured may have started play on either side of the board.

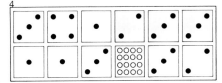

Diagram 3

When a player has made a legal capture, he can also remove beans from the immediately preceding cup and also from cups consecutively before that, provided (a) the cups are on the opponent's side of the board and (b) each cup originally contained only one or two beans. It frequently happens in wari that at a certain point in the game one cup is heavily loaded and this means that beans may go around the board more than once. Because of a rule that states that if this occurs no beans may be sown in the cup just emptied, a well-timed move from a heavily loaded cup can result in the capture of several beans. Such a situation is shown above:

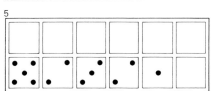

Diagram 4

A game ends when all the cups on one player's side of the board are empty and it is his turn to play. A player may *not* leave the cups of his opponent empty if he can still move into them. Nor can a player make a move by which he would capture every opposing bean and leave the opponent with nothing to play. The strategy is, therefore, to get all the beans on your side of the board in such a way that nothing can be passed to your opponent. When this situation occurs, the remaining beans are regarded as captured.

Diagram 5

When all possible moves have been exhausted, any player who still has beans in his cups removes them and adds them to his reservoir. If very few beans remain, the players may agree to end the game and remove any beans remaining on their own sides. The winner is the player who holds most beans at the end of play.

Diagram 6

Player A can defend himself by moving one of his single beans to another cup or by sowing the three beans so that an attack launched from B's six cup overshoots the target. If A makes either of the moves shown below, only the single bean can be taken. However, by electing to move the three A gives B a loaded square and this may cause problems later in the game.

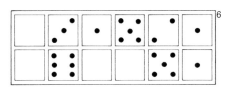

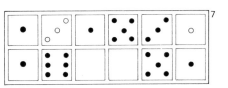

How to Play Kiuthi

Kiuthi is played among the Masai of East Africa. The board consists of two rows each of eight holes and there is a reservoir at each end. At start of play four beans are placed in each player's six center cups.

Until the player makes a capture, play is counterclockwise except to make a *ram* (see below). After a capture has been made, play is alternately counter-clockwise and clockwise. Single beans cannot be moved.

Rams: If the last bean is sown in an opposing cup that contains three beans, that cup becomes a ram. Beans in a ram cannot be lifted and sown. If, later in play, the last bean is sown into a ram by the player who originally made it, he captures the beans in the ram. If the ram remains at the end of the round, the contents belong to the player on whose side of the board it lies.

Moves and captures: A move may begin from any of the player's loaded cups, but must extend to his opponent's row. If the last bean is sown in a loaded cup, the contents of that cup are lifted and sown in the opposite direction. A turn of play continues, in alternate directions, until the last bean falls into an empty cup. If this cup lies in the opponent's row, the move ends. If it lies in the player's own row any beans in the opposite cup are captured, together with the last bean. If the next cup on either side is empty, beans in cup(s) opposite are also captured. The round ends when both players have only singletons or uncaptured rams left. Each player now adds his singletons (and any rams) to his reservoir. If both players have the same number of beans, the game is drawn. If this is not the case, the player with the fewer beans arranges them in any way he likes providing there is at least one in every cup. The other player copies this arrangement returning any surplus beans to his reservoir. If the losing player has few beans, the board can be shortened to 2 x 3 or 2 x 2 cups. Rounds continue until one player can no longer move or until one player has captured all the beans.

Kiuthi, *a mancala game played on a 2 x 8 celled board,* *is a favorite game among the Masai of Kenya.*

Mefuhva

Right: *This* mancala game, which is played in Malawi, is a form of bao kis-wahili bao bau, where captured pieces are re-entered. It is not played on the normal 4 x 8 celled board but on a larger 4 x 24 celled mefuhva board.

How to Play Mefuhva

Mefuhva is played in the northern Transvaal and boards can consist of 4 x 6, 4 x 8... up to 4 x 28 cups with reservoirs at each end. Usually the boards contain at least 4 x 16 cups. At start of play there are two beans in each cup except for the end left-hand cup in each player's front row (which is empty), and the next cup to it, which contains one bean.

Moves: Play is counterclockwise around each player's own two rows. A move may begin from any loaded cup. Further moves can be made and a turn of play ends when the last bean in hand is sown in an empty cup. Single beans can only be moved if a player has no loaded cups, and then only into an empty cup.

Captures: When a player's last bean in hand is sown into an empty cup on his front row, and the opponent's opposite front-row cup in the same file contains beans, these beans are captured. If both of the opponent's opposite cups, front and back rows, contain beans, these are captured.
Only men play mefuhva and it is taboo to play with fruit pips as beans in the rainy season as this is considered to invite thunderstorms.

How to Make a Mancala Board

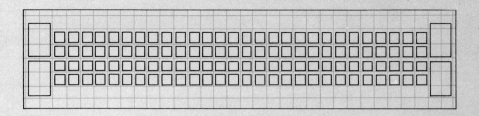

Materials
A large piece of old timber, approx. 1.30 m (4¼ ft) in length, 30 cm (12 in) in width and 10 cm (4 in) in thickness. The piece used to make the model in the photograph was originally part of a workbench in a car-repair shop.

Tools
Smoothing plane, sandpaper, steel ruler, pencil, 3 cm(1¼ in) straight chisel, 3 cm (1¼ in) half-round firmer gouge, wooden mallet.

Method
The board consists of 4 rows each containing 28 shallow cups with 2 larger cups at each end. The smaller cups should be at least 3 cm x 3 cm (1¼ in x 1¼ in), and the larger 5 cm x 10 cm (2 in x 4 in). The cups are approximately 1 cm (½ in) apart along the length and 3 cm (1¼ in) apart across the width, but the exact measurements will depend on the length of the piece of wood you use.

First check to make sure that there are no old nails or screws in the wood. Choose the side that is in the best condition and plane it smooth. Sand thoroughly.

Mark out the positions of the cups using a steel rule and pencil.

Make shallow cuts round the four edges of each cup using a 3 cm (1¼ in) straight chisel and a wooden mallet. This prevents the wood from accidentally splitting as you cut out the cups. Cut the cups with a half-round firmer gouge. They must be cut as smoothly as possible and should be about 1 cm (³⁄₈ in) in depth.

Sandpaper the cups and then varnish the board to finish.

Above: *This grid will assist in laying out the positions of* the holes before cutting.

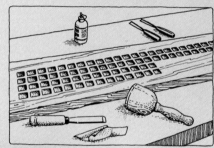

Below: *A larger piece of wood and a great deal of patience are all that* are needed to make this splendid mefuhva board.

Right: *A half-round firmer gouge and a wooden mallet are used to chisel out* the holes. The board is then sanded down and varnished.

Modern Board and Computer Games

Right: *A variety of modern games including Risk, Monopoly and the perennial children's favorite, battle-ships.*

Below: *Cheap pocket electronic games have flooded the market in recent years.*

Below: *Video-games have also become widely popular during the last few years.*

So far in this book, two groups of board games have been discussed: that small group of forgotten games, mostly race games, which were played thousands of years ago in the ancient world; and a somewhat larger group of games collected from all over the world, many of which are hundreds of years old and most of which are still played today.

We have already said elsewhere that man has played games in one form or another almost since the dawn of time. It has also been mentioned that although the classic board games of today—chess, backgammon, wei-ch'i, Polish checkers and pachisi—have their origins in the mists of antiquity, they have nonetheless been played in their modern forms for hundreds of years.

Two other groups of games, however, have not so far been mentioned. The first of these two groups can loosely be described as "modern." A number of these games are based on older games—snakes and ladders and ludo, for example. Others are more original and

have become classics in their own right—Monopoly, Diplomacy and Scrabble, for example. The reason why these games have not been included in this book is simply that they are readily available commercially and rules of play are always included with the game.

In recent years a new phenomenon in games play has appeared—computer games. The first games of this type were chasing games, in which the player tried to race round a course, while keeping ahead of a pursuer and avoiding obstacles, or simple games like tennis, in which a light spot was deflected back and forth between two controlled bars. These games were more a test of dexterity and reaction speed than true games.

Later, more sophisticated software led to the creation of programs based on existing board games. Not surprisingly, chess was the leader and although the first programs were quite crude, such has been the technological progress that today computers can be programmed to play chess, as well as many other board games, at world-class level.

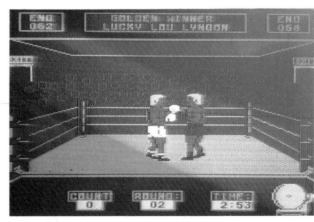

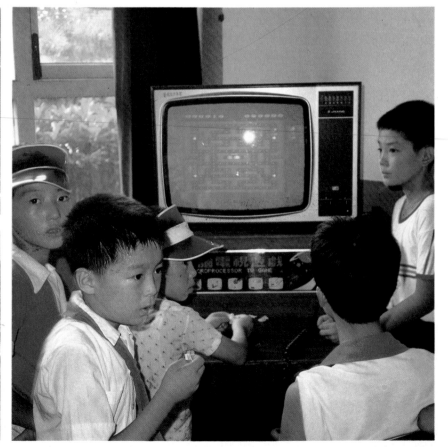

Activity Games

We have discussed those games–board games, card games, dominoes and dice– that could generally be described as "passive"; passive in the sense that they do not require any great exertion of physical energy. These games are usually played indoors (at least in Europe and North America) between a limited number of players (usually between two and four). In this last section we shall look at a few of the hundreds of other games and pastimes enjoyed by teams or by individual players in different parts of the world. The games included fall broadly into seven categories: bowling games, darts games, games played by the Indians of North America, ball games, children's games, kites and kite flying, and lastly a section containing a few interesting and brain-teasing puzzles.

Bowling games, in which a bowl is rolled towards a target, are popular in many parts of the world. They fall generally into two categories–those that are played on an alley (usually of polished wood) and those that are played on grass. Games in the first group are descended from the ancient French game of *quilles*, which became very popular in England under the name of skittles. This game is still popular, although the "bowl" is now a cheese-shaped disc. Tenpin bowling, in which a heavy wooden bowl is rolled down a polished wooden lane with the object of knocking over 10 pins, is extremely popular in Europe and even more so in the United States. The Canadians have their own version of this game known as fivepin bowling. Skittles, tenpin and fivepin bowling are played indoors on specially built surfaces. The most popular outdoor bowling games are flat green bowls (here called bowling on grass), which originated in Britain, and jeu de boules and boccie, which are played mainly in Italy and in French-speaking countries.

Darts games, which were originally a form of target practice using cut-down spears or arrows, have been played in British pubs and in North American bars for decades. In the last few years–largely because of the influence of television–darts has also spread to many European countries.

Long before the settlers brought darts–among other games–to the North American continent, the Native Americans played a variety of games. Many were basically tests of hunting and fighting skill, others were pure gambling games. Two of their most important games were shinny and racket and ball, respectively the forerunners of the modern games of hockey and lacrosse.

Ball games have been popular for hundreds of years among both children and adults alike. Some of the more unusual traditional games are discussed in this chapter, including an old Japanese religious rite, an American game played with a giant ball, tennis played with the feet and a hair-raisingly dangerous game once played by the Aztecs of Central America.

Kites and kite flying have also been popular in many countries for centuries. In Japan, flying kites is a cross between an art form and a war game. In this section, you can learn how to make several different traditional kites.

Puzzles of various types have always fascinated people. In the final section of this last chapter, there are instructions on how to make five handsome mechanical puzzles. There are, however, no instructions on how to solve them–we leave that for you to puzzle out for yourself!

Below: Marbles has been played since the time of the ancient Egyptians. These little glass, clay, metal or alabaster spheres still fascinate children (of all ages!) in countries all over the world.

Right: *Making games materials from scraps has always been fun. This Tanzanian boy has made a car out of old wire and wood and will derive hours of pleasure from racing it against the cars of his friends.*

Below: *His elders are engaged in a more vigorous game. Many tribal peoples have traditional games that were designed to improve hunting and fighting skills.*

Above: *Spinning tops is another pastime that has fascinated children (and adults) for centuries.*

Bowling Games

Bowling games in which the target is another bowl or ball, rather than a number of pins, have been played for more than 2,000 years. The Greeks considered that throwing balls through the air was an excellent physical and mental exercise. The Romans had a similar game and they introduced it to many other countries during the course of their military expeditions. This Roman game was the forerunner of jeu de boules and boccie, both of which are particularly popular in Mediterranean countries. These two games are generally played on sand or gravel "pitches," but in Britain bowling games have traditionally been played on grass–on a crown green, which has a raised center, or on a green, which is perfectly flat and level.

It is said that the green of the Southampton Town Bowling Club, in southern England, was laid down during the reign of Edward I (1272-1307) and has been played on ever since. This may well be true as the game certainly existed in the 13th century. At first it was played in the turfed alleyways of the towns and villages and had a cone as marker instead of the modern-day jack. Biased bowls were introduced in the 16th century when it was recorded that "A little altering of the one side maketh the bowl to run biasse waies." By the beginning of the 19th century the game had rolled "biasse waies" into obscurity, however, and it was only revived in its present form during the 1880s in Scotland.

Right: *A typical tranquil English rural scene.* Bowling on grass, *long regarded as a simple game for the middle-aged and elderly, is in fact a game that requires great skill and cunning, and nowadays is played by people of all ages.*

Bowling on Grass

How to Play Bowling on Grass

The game
Bowling on grass is played by two players or by two teams of up to four players. The object of the game is to place the bowls as close as possible to the target bowl, which is known as the *jack*. One point is scored for each bowl nearer to the jack than the opposition's best bowl.

The green and the rinks
The green is a level turf square or rectangle bounded by a ditch and a bank. The sides of the green must be between 33 and 44 yd (approx. 30/40 m) in length. The green is divided into rinks 19 ft (5.80 m) in width (the width can vary a foot or two either way). Rink boundaries are marked, usually by string attached to pegs at the corners. The center line of each rink is marked on the bank at each end by a peg or similar object. White markers on the side banks indicate a distance of 27 yd (24.70 m) from each end ditch.

The bowls and the jack
The bowls are slightly flattened spheres and are biased on one side so that they move along a curved path. They are tested and stamped with the degree of bias. They can be made of wood, rubber or composition and are either black or brown in color. Wooden bowls have a maximum weight of 3½ lb (1.57 kg) and a maximum diameter of 5¾ in (14.6 cm). Rubber and composition bowls are a little smaller and can be a little lighter. The jack must be white. It has a diameter of 2⅝ in (6.5 cm) and weights between 8 and 10 oz (224-280 gm). The jack is not biased.

Duration and scoring
Games are divided into *ends*, which are played alternately in opposite directions. Play is for a specified period of time, a specified number of ends or until a specified number of points has been scored. A point is scored for each bowl nearer to the jack than the opposition's best bowl.

The types of game
a) Singles: Two players each have four bowls, which they deliver alternately.

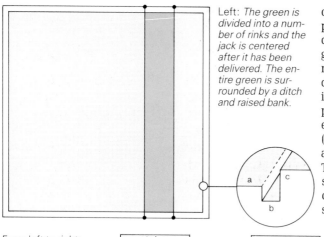

Left: *The green is divided into a number of rinks and the jack is centered after it has been delivered. The entire green is surrounded by a ditch and raised bank.*

c) Triples: Opposing players play in pairs, bowling alternately. Each player delivers two or three bowls. A game is generally played over 18 ends, the winners are the trio with the highest score.

d) Fours: This is the true form of bowling on grass. Each of the four players plays two bowls, singly and in turn, and each has special duties. The first player (lead) is responsible for placing the mat and delivering the jack (see below). The second player (second) acts as scorer. The third player (third) is the one who has to measure any disputed shots. The fourth player *(skip)* is a man for all seasons. He is the captain, tactician, father-figure and despot. A game is over 21 ends; the highest score wins.

Starting the game

a) Placing the mat: The black rubber mat measures 2 ft x 1 ft 2 in (61 cm x 35.5 cm). A player's back foot must be on or above the mat at the moment of delivery. At the start of play, the mat is placed lengthwise along the center line of the rink with its back edge 4 ft (1.22 m) from the rear ditch. In subsequent ends the mat is placed 4 ft (1.22 m) from the opposite ditch *or*

From left to right:
For the first end the mat is positioned 4 ft (1.22 m) from the rear ditch (A). For subsequent ends the mat must not be less than 27 yd (24.70 m) from the front ditch (B).

The jack must travel at least 25 yd (27.87 m) to be valid (B). If it stops less than 2 yd (1.83 m) from the ditch it is centered on the 2 yd line (A).

Any bowl failing to travel 15 yd (13.72 m), stopping outside the boundary, driven off by another bowl, ending in the ditch without having touched the jack or rebounding from the bank without having touched the jack is regarded as dead.

All other bowls, including "line bowls," are regarded as live.

A jack becomes dead if a bowl drives it: over the bank, over the boundary, so that it rebounds to within 22 yd (20.13 m) of the mat. Jacks marked A are live, jacks marked B are dead.

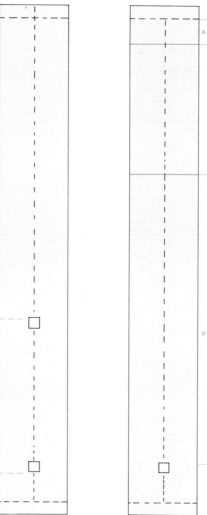

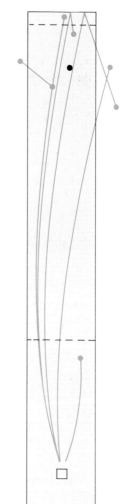

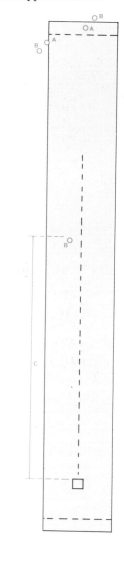

The score is tallied after each end. The winner of an end plays first in the next. The first player to score 21 points is the winner.

b) Pairs: Two opposing players bowl two, three or four bowls alternately (the number is decided beforehand). Their teammates then bowl the same number of bowls alternately. A game is played over 21 ends, the winners are the pair with the highest score.

Left: *A bowl may have a maximum diameter of 5¾ in (14.6 cm) (A). The maximum diameter of the jack is 2⅝ in (6.5 cm) (B).*

This series of diagrams shows the various shots in *bowling on grass*.

1. *The draw*, close to the jack.
2a. A bowl delivered to guard the jack.
2b. A bowl delivered to guard a teammate's bowl.
3. *The trail* that knocks the jack towards friendly bowls.
4. *The tap* knocks away an opposing bowl.
5. *The rest*, where the bowl takes the place of an opposing bowl.
6. *The yard on* breaks up an enemy formation.
7. *The follow on* bowl knocks an enemy bowl away and runs on towards the jack.
8. *The cannon-off* uses an opposing bowl as an aid to approaching the jack when other routes are blocked.

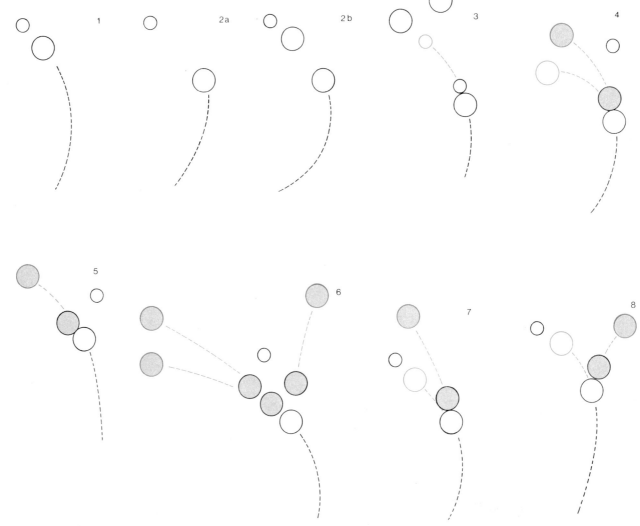

Right: *A jack on the boundary line is live. Players may play to it from either side, even though the bowl passes outside the boundary. A bowl stopping within the rink is live, even if it misses the jack. A bowl stopping outside the rink is dead, even if it has touched the jack.*

between ditch and the position of the jack at the close of the preceding end, provided the front of the mat does not lie less than 27 yd (24.7 m) from the opposite ditch. (These limits are indicated by white markers on the side banks).

b) Delivering the jack: The lead of the team to play first delivers the jack, which must travel at least 25 yd (22.87 m) from the mat. It is then centered in the rink. If it comes to rest less than 2 yd (1.83 m) from the ditch, it is centered 2 yd (1.83 m) from the ditch. If the jack travels less than 25 yd (23 m) or comes to rest outside the rink, it is redelivered by the opposing lead.

Below: *At the moment of delivery, the rear foot must be on, or above, the mat.*

Right: *This medieval manuscript shows an early form of bowling on grass. The young apprentices are using a feather to mark the target.*

The shots in bowling on grass
This is a game of great skill and subtlety, interspersed with sheer brutality. The main shots are:
1. *The draw*–where the bowl is placed as close to the jack as possible. In fours this shot is lead's speciality.
2. *The guard*–where the bowl is placed to block the opponent's path to the jack or to guard a friendly bowl.
3. *The trail*–where the bowl carries the jack to a position where bowls belonging to teammates will score.
4. *The tap*–where the bowl knocks away an opposing bowl which is close to, or touching the jack.
5. *The rest*–where the bowl pushes an opposing bowl through and takes its place.
6. *The yard on*–a heavy shot designed to break up the arrangement of bowls.
7. *The follow on*– where a leading bowl is knocked on past the jack and the player's own bowl runs close in.
8. *The drive*–where a bowl is picked off and struck hard.
9. *The cannon-off*– where a bowl strikes another bowl and rebounds favorably.

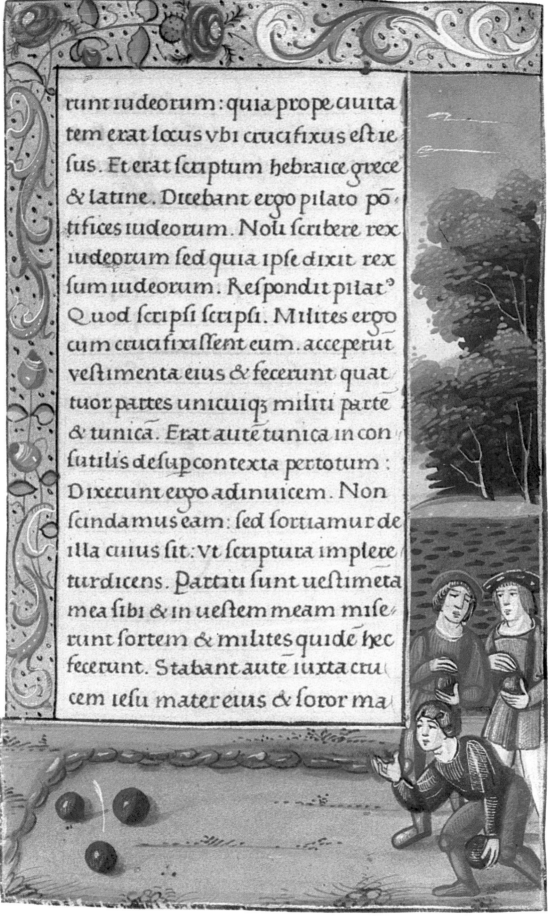

Responsibilities and tactics: In fours play, the prime object is to build up a *head* (an arrangement of bowls) round the jack.
Lead must draw his shot as near to the jack as possible. The cardinal sin is to play a short bowl as this leaves the jack wide open for the opposing lead. *Second* must consolidate a good draw or rectify lead's mistake. *Third* must be an expert in every shot and his play is dictated by the position in which he finds himself. *Skip* is in over-all control and dictates strategy and tactics. He, too, must be an expert in every shot.

Jeu de Boules

Anyone who has visited *la place,* that shady square in the center of French towns and villages, has certainly observed the ritual of boules. Although the game is also played in other countries, it is as closely associated with France and the French way of life as bullfighting is with Spain.

To the casual onlooker, boules may appear to be a simple enough game–rolling or tossing metal balls towards a tiny *cochonnet* or target ball. But like flat green bowls, boules is a game that demands a high level of concentration, skill and devious cunning. The French think that a *bouliste* reaches his prime in middle age, for only by then has he acquired the cunning and experience to play the game well. This may be so, but boules can still be enjoyed by all age groups.

Both jeu de boules and its close relation, the Italian game of boccie, are undoubtedly derived from an old Greek exercise that was practiced by older men. According to the writings of Oribasius, a physician who lived in the fourth century A.D., the men would meet at some appointed time in a gymnasium and throw balls of different sizes as far as they possibly could. This was regarded as an excellent exercise for both the mind and body. The practice was adopted by the Romans, who threw or rolled balls along the ground towards a target. The Roman armies took this game with them on their travels and it soon became popular in many parts of their empire. Centuries later, the French introduced the game to the countries of *their* empire, and today boules is still played in many of these places.

Below left: *Local children enjoying a game of* jeu de boules *in the Isles du Vent, French Polynesia, in the Pacific Ocean.*

Below right: *A Maltese version of bocce or boccie, which itself is an Italian form of* jeu de boules. *In this version the players are playing with weighted cylindrical "boules."*

How to Play Jeu de Boules

The game   Jeu de boules is played by two players or by two teams of up to four players. The object of the game is to place the boules nearer to the cochonnet (jack) than the opposition.

The pitch   For official matches, the pitch is between 24.5 m and 27.5 m (27 yd and 30 yd) in length. The minimum width is 3 m (3.3 yd). The pitch is marked at each end by lines at 2 m (2.2 yd) and 7 m (7.7 yd). The 7 m (7.7 yd) lines are the footlines, which must not be crossed when throwing the boules; the 2 m (2.2 yd) lines are the out of play lines. When the cochonnet

is thrown at start of play, it must come to rest within the rectangle formed by these lines and the sides of the pitch. Most boules games are "unofficial" and are played on any patch of open ground that happens to be available. Players usually scratch the playing lines in the sand or gravel.

The boules and the cochonnet   The boules are made of metal or some synthetic material and must not be nailed or weighted with lead. They should be between 8.8. and 11 cm (3½ in and 4⅜ in) in diameter and weigh between 0.7 and 1.3 kg (1.5 and 2.8 lb). Boules are usually marked in some way for identification. The cochonnet is made

of wood and is 3.7 cm (1½ in) in diameter.

Duration and scoring   Rounds are divided into games that are played alternately in opposite directions. The round is won by the first team to score 13 or 15 points–the score being agreed upon in advance. A point is scored for each boule nearer to the cochonnet than the nearest opposing boule.

The types of game
a) Singles: between two players each having three or four boules.
b) Pairs: two against two, each player having two or three boules.
c) Triples: three against three, each

player having two boules.
d) Fours: four against four, each player having two boules.

The shots in boules   There are three basic shots in boules–the *boule pointée,* which is rolled along the playing surface; the *boule portée,* which is thrown through the air; and the *boule tirée,* which is thrown to hit a designated target. To be valid a boule pointée or portée must:
a) remain in play,
b) not run on more than 1 m (1.1 yd) after displacing a boule or the cochonnet,
c) not displace a boule or cochonnet by more than 1 m (1.1 yd),
d) approach to within at least 2 m (2.2 yd) of the front edge of the 5 m (5.5 yd) rectangle.
If these conditions are not fulfilled the shot is a foul and the advantage rule is applied. The opponents may accept the position or have disturbed objects re-positioned. The rules for a boule tirée are somewhat different. Before making a "tir" the player must designate the target. This can be an opposing boule or the cochonnet. A *baguette* is then used to trace arcs
a) 50 cm (20 in) in front of the designated target,
b) 50 cm (20 in) in front of any objects within 50 cm (20 in) of the designated target–providing the arc is also within 50 cm (20 in) of the target.
To be valid a tir must fulfil three conditions:
a) the landing point (the point where it

first hits the ground) must be within 50 cm (20 in) of the designated target,
b) the landing point must be within 50 cm (20 in) of the first object to be struck,
c) the object first struck must be within 50 cm (20 in) of the designated target–measurements are to the object's farthest circumference. If the tir is invalid, the advantage rules is applied.

Starting and playing the game   A coin is tossed to decide which team delivers the cochonnet for the first game. After that it belongs to the team that last scored. It must come to rest within the 5 m (5.5 yd) target area at the far end of the pitch. If it comes to rest within 50 cm (20 in) of an obstruction such as a rock or bush, it must be rethrown. Having thrown the cochonnet the same player then throws the first boule of the game. The feet must be kept together and the player may not step over the throwing line until the boule has come to rest.
The main rule regarding turn of play is that the team continues to throw as long as an opposing boule lies closest to the cochonnet. Therefore the team that begins throws only one boule in the first turn of play. It does not matter if it lands close to or far away from the cochonnet–it must be the "best boule." The second team then throws and continues to throw until it has "best boule" or knocks the cochonnet closer to one of its boules. The first team then plays, and so on. If a team throws all its boules without achieving "best boule,"

the other team throws whatever boules are left, trying to better the score. As in flat green bowls, the "jack'" or cochonnet is always the target, even if it has been knocked away from its original position. The game ends when all the players have thrown all their boules. The score is then tallied and noted down and the next game begins.

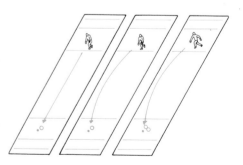

Above: *From left to right: the boule pointée, which is rolled along the ground; the boule portée, which is thrown through the air; and the boule tirée, which is aimed at a specific target. A baguette is used to draw arcs to measure the distance.*

Darts

"Game on" murmurs the referee and total silence falls over the hall. A short, stocky figure steps forward, takes aim and throws his first dart. There is an almost inaudible "thud" as it strikes the board within a wire rectangle only 8 mm ($5/16$ in) wide and 2 cm ($3/8$ in) long. This dart is followed by two more, both nestling inside the same rectangle. A roar goes up from the spectators. "One hundred and eighty" calls the referee–the best possible score which can be thrown with three darts.

There are two theories as to when and where darts originated. One school of thought has it that the game began in Scandinavia, where the Vikings amused themselves by practicing spear throwing during the long winter nights. The other school of thought maintains that the archers of medieval England were the first darts players. These yeomen carried short, heavy throwing arrows, which they used for self-defense in close quarter combat. They would practice their skills (and amuse themselves at the same time) by throwing these arrows at the butt end of a cut-down tree. In the winter, a sawn-off section of a tree trunk would be hung on the tavern wall to play the game indoors.

During the reign of the Tudor monarchs in England, darts became a refined pastime in court circles. It is recorded that Anne Boleyn, second wife of Henry VIII, presented her husband with a set of "dartes of Biscayan fashion, richly ornamented." Not that it did her much good, for she was beheaded shortly afterwards–but whether the two incidents were connected is unclear! The medieval form of darts, however, was quite unlike the modern game, which dates back to the end of the last century. Around that time, the folded paper flight was invented and the standard arrangement of numbers round the present-day board devised. Metal-shafted darts, which are now universally used, were invented in 1936, when a Hungarian who lived in Britain decided to improve on the wooden-shafted darts then in use. Nowadays players can choose from an enormous variety of commercially-made darts in several sizes and weights to suit any particular playing style. Most experts favor darts made from tungsten. This metal has a high density; darts can be made of it that are slim (which facilitates close grouping) and at the same time reasonably heavy. It is difficult to control the flight of a dart that weighs much less than 16 or 17 grams (.5 oz).

190

The basic object of all darts games is to aim and throw a series of darts from a certain distance so that they strike a certain target. The target (a dartboard), the distance and the darts vary widely from area to area.

The board

There are several traditional and regional dartboards and these vary in size, in the arrangement of the numbers, and in the width of the doubles and trebles rings–some, indeed, do not have a trebles ring. The materials from which these dartboards are made vary also. In the north of England, clay boards are common, while in other areas elm and cork boards are found. The standard international board, illustrated on this page, is the one which is most widely used. It is made of bristle and the fibers are tightly packed so that not only is the point of the dart held fast when it enters the board, but the hole it makes closes up after the dart has been removed. This means that the board is durable and lasts for months, even when it is in constant use.

The board is divided into 20 sectors each of which has a value between 1 and 20. The numbers are arranged so that the higher numbers lie between two lower numbers. This arrangement rewards accuracy and penalizes inaccuracy. A narrow band around the perimeter of the scoring area forms a doubles ring in which a dart scores double the value of the sector. This part of the board is very important as many games are "double out"–the final dart must fall in the required double (see The Various Darts Games). Closer to the center of the board is a narrow trebles ring, in which a dart scores treble the value of the sector. This is also an important area because in many games the object is to score a certain number of points before your opponent. At the center of the board is the inner bull, worth 50 points. Around it lies the outer bull, worth 25. The inner bull also counts as a double for finishing purposes.

The dimensions of the standard international boards are as follows:
Over-all board diameter (including the non-scoring area around the edge: 18 in (457 mm). Diameter of scoring area: 13.38 in (340 mm). Outside edge of treble wire to the center of the inner bull: 4.21 in (107 mm).
Inside diameter of double and treble

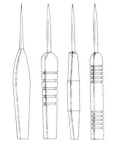

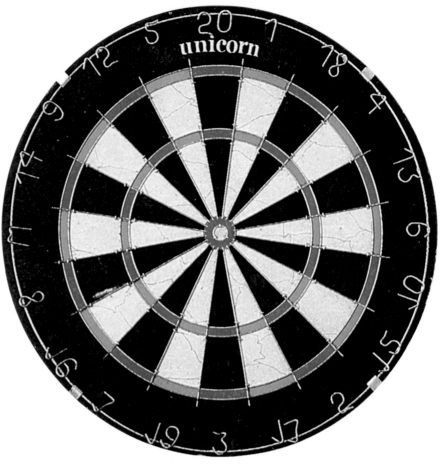

rings: 0.3125 in (8 mm). Inside diameter of bull: 0.5 in (12.7 mm).

Note: The arrangement of numbers on the standard board is arguably not the most logical. The sums of pairs of adjacent numbers range from 16 to 26 and there are four consecutive odd numbers (17, 3, 19 and 7) at the bottom of the board. On the much smaller Manchester board the numbers are arranged so that there are never more than two consecutive even or odd numbers, and the range of the sums of adjacent pairs is 17 to 25.

Setting up the board

In 1976, the Wold Darts Federation was set up to regulate the sport on an international basis. This body approved a minimum throwing distance of 7 ft 9¼ in (2.37 m) and this is the distance which is now commonly used, although others, notably 8 ft (2.44 m), are sometimes found. This throwing distance is marked by a line on the floor or by a raised *oche* (pronounced "ockey"),

a strip of wood or metal behind which the players stand. The board is set so that the center of the inner bull is at a height of 5 ft 8 in (1.73 m) from the ground. When the board is set up correctly, the distance from the center of the inner bull to the front of the oche is 9 ft 7½ in (2.93 m). The board is lit by spot lamps positioned above and in front of the board in such a way that the darts do not cast any shadows.

The darts

Every serious darts player owns his own set of darts and it is worthwhile testing several sizes and weights before buying. Specialized darts shops have practice boards and you can try out as many sets as you wish before selecting one that feels "right." The over-all maximum length has been fixed at 12 in (30 cm) and the maximum weight at 50 g (1.75 oz), but darts of this length and weight are rarely seen. Most are roughly the length of a ballpoint pen and weight between 16 and 28 grams (.5 and 1 oz).

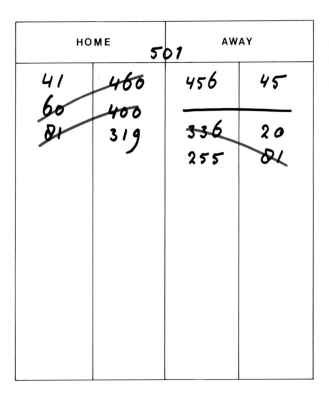

HOME		AWAY	
	501		
41	460	456	45
60	400		
81	319	336	20
		255	81

	A	B	C
	25	25	25
20	85	45	105
16	117	61	153
3DC	59	125	77
Tr.			
19			
3SC			
D			
15			
17			
⊙ 8			

Left: A typical start to a club game of 501. The line above the 20 in the away player's score represents 100 points and indicates that he has scored 120 (100 + the 20 written below the line) on his second throw.

Above right: A typical example of halve-it. 3DC stands for 3 different colors. This means that if any two darts land in an area of the same color, no score is made. If all three land in different colors, the value of whatever is scored is counted. In the same way, 3SC means three have to land in the same color to score. Tr means trebles and D means doubles. The target stands for the bull.

A dart consists of four elements–the point, the barrel, the shaft and the flight. Of these elements, the barrel is the most important because it is this that gives the dart its weight, balance and grip. Most expert players prefer barrels made of tungsten. This is a high density material, which means that a dart can be very slim and still heavy enough to throw accurately. Tungsten darts, however, are expensive, and many players use cheaper, brass-barrelled darts. Most barrels have ridges cut into them to improve the grip. A needle point is fixed in the barrel, but this can be removed and replaced if necessary. The shaft is usually made of fiberglass or plastic and screws into the barrel. Shafts are easily damaged and are replaced regularly. The flight, which gives the dart stability as it flies through the air, slots into a cross-shaped groove at the end of the shaft. Flights are usually made of paper or plastic, although some players use flights made from turkey feathers, but these are expensive. Flights are also replaced regularly. A fifth element, a flight protector, is also used by many players. This is a small metal cap that fits on the end of the flight and prevents damage occurring if the flight should be hit by another dart.

Technique and practice
Darts has become incredibly popular among British television viewers and the best players have become household names. When watching these players in action, it is immediately obvious that each has his own individual stance and grip. These two features are of basic importance to any aspiring player. First, stance. It is impossible for a darts player to throw well unless he is in balance and feels comfortable. Most players stand with their front foot against the oche, in line with the board, and their back foot about 30 cm (1 ft) behind it and at an angle of 45°. In this position, the body is leaning forward slightly so the weight is directly above the front foot. Try different stances until you find a position in which you feel comfortable.

Next, the grip. Most beginners grip a dart in the same way as they grip a pencil. This is not correct. The dart should be held so that the point is supported in some way. Try out different grips until you find one that feels right. The most important thing about the throwing action is that it should be smooth and free, the elbow being a pivot. The dart is released just before the arm is at its full extent, and the arm should then follow through. The follow-through action is necessary to prevent the dart dropping during its flight. When aiming the dart concentrate your attention and focus your eyes on that part of the board you wish to hit. These are the three most important elements in good play–stance, grip, concentration. The fourth element is practice. The top players practice several hours a day in order to maintain their standards. Practice half an hour on doubles, half an hour on trebles and half an hour on finishes–170, 167, 164, 161, 160, 158 and every number below this can be thrown out in three darts–remembering that the last dart must land in a double!

The Various Darts Games

The game of 501 is the basic darts game played in championship matches. It is a race between two players, each trying to reduce an opening score of 501 to zero exactly, the last dart being a double. If a player scores more than 501, the last throw does not count. For example, if 2 points are required, the player must throw double 1. If he throws a single 1 or any other scoring dart, his turn is over and he must try again in his next turn of play. A turn of play consists of three darts, and players throw alternately trying to score as many points as possible. The highest number of points that can be scored with a single dart is 60 (treble 20) and the highest number that can be scored in a turn of play is 180 (3 x treble 30)– in the words of a song: "the darter's favorite score!" It is possible, although extremely difficult, to complete 501 in nine darts. John Lowe, one of the world's great professionals, did exactly this in a televised championship in 1986. It was the first time it had ever been done in a televised match, and Lowe won a prize of £ 102,000. His perfect game was 3 x treble 20, 3 x treble 20, treble 17, treble 18, double 18. When interviewed later, the phlegmatic Lowe shrugged his shoulders and said simply: "A win is a win." A game of 501 consists of a number of "legs." "Best of 3" is played by less expert players, "best of 5" or "best of 7" by better ones. Professional matches consist of a number of "sets," each set consisting of several "legs." The right to throw first is decided by the toss of a coin before the first game and then players open alternately. The score is kept by an independent "chalker," responsible for adding up the points scored and deducting the total from the score remaining before the throw.

In British pubs it is customary for a person wanting a game to write his initials on the scoreboard. In his turn he "takes the chalks"–scores a game. He then has the right to play the winner of the game he has just scored. In other countries the "winner stays on" custom does not usually apply, and players simply take turns to play.

The game of 301 This is a variation of 501. As in 501, a player must reduce his opening score (301) to zero, ending with a double. The difference in 301 is that he must also open his score with a double. No dart thrown before a double is scored is counted.

Twice round and two tops This is a "round the clock" game that is popular in Lancashire, in the north of England. Players must first throw 1, then 2, and so on to 20. This sequence is repeated and finally two double 20s (tops) must be thrown. In this game doubles count, so that if double 1 is thrown, the player misses out 2 and passes straight on to 3, etc. A "perfect" game is: double 1, 3, double 4, 9, double 10, double 1, 3, double 4, 9, double 10, double 20, double 20 (12 darts). Should a player score single 10, he must then throw 11, 12 etc. Any doubles thrown above 10 allow the player to skip the following number. Thus, a throw of double 11 allows the player to move on to 13.

Round the clock This is a simpler form of the last game. Doubles do not count and each number must be thrown in sequence. Outer and inner bulls must be thrown after the 20.

Shanghai This is another round-the-board game. Players throw three darts for the 1, doubles and trebles counting. The score is noted and in the next round, they throw for 2s, adding any points scored to the total. The game continues to 20s. The player with the highest total is the winner. In some versions there are penalty numbers–usually alternate odd numbers. Players failing to score with at least one dart on

these numbers are eliminated from the game. Any player scoring a single, double and treble on any one number in any one throw has gone "Shanghai" and wins the game. In some versions, play continues in case another player goes "Shanghai." If this happens the one with the highest score is the winner.

Darts cricket This is a game for two players–a "bowler" and a "batsman," throwing three darts alternately. The batsman attempts to score as many points as possible, doubles and trebles counting. The bowler attempts to take "wickets" by scoring bulls. An inner bull is worth two wickets, an outer is worth one. The "innings" ends when the bowler has taken 10 wickets. If the batsman inadvertently throws an outer or inner bull the wicket(s) count against him. If the bowler throws a dart outside the trebles ring, the score is credited to the batsman as "extras."

Tac-tics (or Mickey Mouse) This game is popular in the United States, in Britain and in the Netherlands. Only the numbers from 10 to 20 and the inner and outer bulls are used. The basic tactic is to hit each number three times, doubles and trebles counting as two hits and three hits respectively (the inner bull is a double outer bull). When a player has done this, any further hits on that number are credited to his score–as long as that number remains in play. The number remains in play until the opponent has also hit it three times, at which point it is eliminated from the game and no further hits count.

Tac-tics is a game that becomes more fascinating the more you play it. It is a game in which a good player can put his opponent under psychological pressure and force him to do what he wants him to do.

Suppose, for example, Player A opens by throwing at 20 and with his first dart scores a treble. The number is now "his" number and he is immediately faced with a decision–to score points on 20 or to turn his attention to another number, perhaps 18 or 19, in an attempt to close it off to his opponent. Player B must also make a decision– does he try to eliminate the 20s to stop Player A scoring, or does he attempt to establish a number for himself? Players are constantly faced with this type of decision. As the game goes on there are

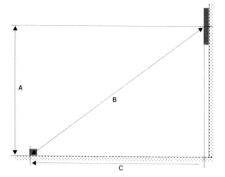

Above: *The board is set up to exact measurements. A = 5 ft 8 in (1.73 m) B = 9 ft 7 in (2.93 m) C = 7 ft 9 in (2.37)*

more and more decisions to make and they become more and more difficult to make. Tac-tics is a fascinating game and the only way to learn how to play it is to play it!

Halve-it This is a game in which a series of specific categories are chosen and written down on the scoreboard. Each player in turn then attempts to score points in these categories. If he fails to do so, his total score is halved (an odd-numbered score is rounded off–137 becomes 69, etc.). Each player starts with a certain number of points, usually 25. The winner is the player with the most points after the last category has been thrown.

Games of the American Indians

Games of various types played an important role in the culture of the Indians of the North American continent. Stewart Culin, the accepted authority on the history of Indian games, lists dice and guessing games, dexterity games and ball games as the most important. Examples of dice and guessing games–the bowl game and the moccasin game–have already been described. The dexterity games, such as snow snake and hoop and arrow, were tests of strength and hunting skills. Two groups of ball games were played universally. The first were lacrosse games played with a racket. The second were games in which a ball was struck with a club or bat. Although games in this group differed slightly from tribe to tribe–some being played only by women, some only by men, some by both, and in one tribe (the Crow) by men against women–they are generally regarded as being basically one game: the game of shinny. No one knows when or where this game originated, but according to a Wichita legend, it was introduced after the creation of mankind by Darkness, the first man.

Shinny

Some authorities believe that shinny is the precursor of hockey. There are, indeed, several similarities–in both games opposing teams, armed with sticks, attempt to hit a ball towards a fixed goal. But while hockey is played between teams of 11 players on a pitch of fixed dimensions and within a strict framework of rules, shinny was played by teams of unlimited numbers on pitches that varied enormously in length and area and to rules, which, if they existed at all, were extremely lax. Lax is perhaps the wrong word, for in his account of the origins of the *Arikara*, Dr George A. Dorsey records:

"They made games at this place. The first game they played was the shinny ball and four sticks. The land was marked out by four sticks which enclosed an oblong extending from east to west. Each side tried to force the ball through the other's goal. When one side was beaten it immediately began to kill those of the other side."

Such extreme behavior gives the phrase "bad losers" a new dimension. However, it seems to have been the exception rather than the rule, for although shinny was undoubtedly a rough and dangerous game, there is no mention of similar violence in the many other existing accounts, even though the shinny stick can be regarded as analogous to the club of the war gods.

Right: The balls used in shinny *were made of wood or of buffalo hair covered in buckskin. They varied in size but in general were between 8.5 cm (3⅜ in) and 10 cm (4 in) in diameter.*

Right: Shinny *was played on "pitches", which varied in length from about 200 m (220 yd) to 1,200 m (1,320 yd) or more. The goal was sometimes a line and sometimes a tree or upright stick. There were few rules and shinny was a rough and dangerous game.*

Opposite page: An old Indian man with stick and ball out on the road. The sticks were curved at one end and roughly 1 m (1.1 yd) in length.

Lacrosse

In his *Games of the North American Indians*, Culin quotes from a manuscript on the Winnebago Indians of Wisconsin: "The vigorous game of lacrosse was, in earlier days, much played by the Winnebagoes. It was usually played at La Crosse–Prairie La Crosse deriving its name from this fact–during the general rendezvous after the winter's hunt. The Winnebagoes having always clung to the watercourses and heavy timber, during their winter's trapping and hunting, would float down the rivers to La Crosse, and there have their feasts and lacrosse games, meet the traders and indulge in a big spree. Occasionally they played lacrosse in their villages, but this was not common. It was considered to be more especially a spring festival game. These games were always for heavy stakes in goods."

On January 1, 1859, lacrosse became the national game of Canada and it is still very popular. But the formalized game we know today bears little resemblance to the rough-and-tumble racket games played for centuries by Indian tribes all over the North American continent.

The origins of lacrosse

There is a theory that lacrosse is a modification of an old French game called *soule*, which was played by the mountaineers of the Ardennes. This game, according to the theory, was brought to North America by the first French settlers. This opinion, however, seems to have been largely discredited by modern scholarship, and there is little doubt that the game is derived from the ancient Indian games of ball and racket. These games were distinctly for men, as opposed to shinny and other ball games, which were commonly played by women. Ball-and-racket games varied widely from tribe to tribe

Above: Lacrosse *is one of Canada's most popular sports. This 5-cent stamp features modern players, with an Indian player in the background. The Indians played lacrosse before North America was colonized.*

Right: *This etching by Seth Eastman dates from 1850 and shows the Dahcota (Sioux) Indians engaged in a rough-and-tumble* lacrosse *game. This looks like a good way to keep warm in the depths of winter!*

and from region to region, although the general principles were much the same. The games were played between teams of varying numbers of players, sometimes as many as several hundred being involved. Each player carried a racket, which was basically a stick curved at one end and with bark or leather strings attached. The ball was probably originally made of wood but later balls of deerskin stuffed with hair were substituted. The word "ball" is perhaps a misnomer, for it was often flattened in the shape of a thick, round disc. Ball-and-racket games were played on fields that varied greatly in size, but in general they were remarkable for their length–in some the goals were several kilometers apart. The field was usually laid out from east to west or from north to south, which had a mystical significance. The goals were usually two sets of poles or posts driven into the ground at each end of the field, between which the ball had to be driven. Sometimes the goal was a single post or a square mat, and one tribe, the Choctaw, connected the tops of the posts with a pole–the first recorded instance of a crossbar. The playing season varied, too, some tribes playing in summer, others in winter or spring.

The game

There are dozens of contemporary eyewitness accounts of racket-and-ball games played among and between tribes in almost every part of the North American continent. The report chosen here was by Dr. Walter J. Hoffman who described a game played by the Ojibway Indians of Minnesota. This report first appeared in *The American Anthropologist* in 1890 and was reprinted in *Games of the North American Indians*, by Stewart Culin.

"If the condition of the ground permits, the two posts or goals are planted about one third of a mile apart... the best players of either side gather at the center of the ground. The poorer players arrange themselves around their respective goals, while the heaviest in weight scatter across the field between the starting point and the goals. The ball is tossed into the air in the center of the field. As soon as it descends it is caught with the ball stick by one of the players, when he immediately sets out at full speed towards the opposite goal. If too closely pursued, or if intercepted by an opponent, he throws the ball in the direction of one of his own side, who takes up the race.

The usual method of depriving the player of the ball is to strike the handle of the ball stick so as to dislodge the ball; but this is frequently a difficult matter on account of the peculiar horizontal motion of the ball stick maintained by the runner. Frequently the ball carrier is disabled by being struck across the arm or leg, thus compelling his retirement. Severe injuries occur only when playing for high stakes or when ill-feeling exists between some of the players.

Should the ball carrier of one side reach the opposite goal, it is necessary for him to throw the ball so it touches the post. This is always a difficult matter, because even if the ball be well directed, one of the numerous players surrounding the post as guards may intercept it and throw it back into the field. In this manner a single inning may be continued for an hour or more. The game may come to a close at the end of an inning by mutual agreement of the players, that side winning the greater number of scores being declared victor."

A report dating from almost a hundred years earlier describes the game in almost identical terms, adding:

"They are so exceeding dexterous in this manly exercise, that the ball is usually kept flying in different directions by the force of the rackets, without touching the ground–during the whole contention."

Rites connected with lacrosse
Success at racket-and-ball games was of great importance to the American Indians. There would appear to be two basic reasons for this–first, intertribal games were a kind of ritualized warfare and therefore a matter of honor and prestige; and secondly, large amounts of goods of various kinds were invariably wagered and so success was also a matter of economics.

In order to ensure success, various magical and mystical rites came into being–dances, sacrifices taboos, ritual pregame bleedings–and many more that varied from tribe to tribe.

Two writers–John Bartram, writing in 1791, and James Mooney, writing exactly 100 years later–described in great detail the various customs and rites of the Cherokee Indians, who lived in North Carolina. Bartram's account of the ball dance (reprinted in *Games of the North American Indians,* by Stewart Culin) describes how the musicians and members of the tribe assembled to listen to a long oration spoken by an aged chief. In this oration the chief mentioned the many brilliant victories gained by the town against other towns of the Cherokee nation, not forgetting, in Bartram's words, "to recite his own exploits, together with those of other aged men present, in the performance of these athletic games in their youthful days." This speech was meant to inspire and excite the young players

who would play on the following day. When the chief had finished speaking the musicians began to play, accompanied by a group of young girls, singing and dancing. After about 15 minutes, the players marched in, well-dressed, painted and ornamented, and carrying their rackets in one hand. The ritual dance that followed was complex in the extreme and Bartram devotes several paragraphs to it.

Below: *A typical racket and ball used in Indian* lacrosse *games. The racket is 33 in (80 cm) long. The disc-shaped ball is 2¾ in (6.8 cm) in diameter. Both were used by the Seminole Indians of Florida.*

Below: *Menomini Indians raise their rackets in the pre-match ceremony.*

The lower picture is an action shot of the game of la-crosse *in progress.*

Left and below left: Lacrosse *rackets* varied widely in length and design. The pair of rackets used by the Seminole Indians of Florida are only 31 cm (13 in) long, while that used by the Sauk and Fox

Indians of Oklahoma is more than a meter (42 in) in length. The crook-shaped racket is very like a modern lacrosse racket and was used by the Nishinam Indians of California.

Above: *Young Cherokee Indians enjoying an informal knockabout game with* lacrosse rackets.

Above left: *Three ball players selected by their chiefs as the most famous in their tribes.*
From left to right they represent the Choctaw, the Ojibbway and the Sioux.

Racket and ball was usually played in the fall after the harvest when the men had abundant leisure. Some time before the game—usually 28 days (4 x 7, which were sacred numbers)—the players were put under a strict taboo. They were forbidden to eat the flesh of certain animals and fish or to take salt. The strictest taboo was that no player was allowed to touch a woman and any player who violated this rule was most severely dealt with by his fellows.
The shamans, or medicine men, played an important role in the pre-match preparations. They performed special incantations to encompass the defeat of the opposing team or even bring about the disablement or death of a particularly feared rival. They were also in charge of the mystic rite of "going to water" which was conducted at regular intervals during training and several times during the night preceding the game.
Before the game each player underwent the ordeal of scratching. This was carried out by the shaman's assistant who used a seven-toothed comb made from sharpened splinters of bone from the leg of a turkey. This was drawn four times down both upper and lower arms and legs and down the back—almost

300 scratches. The players endured this willingly, believing that it was a necessary part of the ritual to ensure success in the forthcoming game. When this ceremony had been completed the players washed away the blood in the waters of the river and dressed for the game.
Judging by contemporary accounts, racket and ball must have been quite a spectacle–a spectacle that alas, can no longer be witnessed. Most of the ancient rituals have now died out, partly because so many Indians have integrated into North American society and no longer adhere to the customs and traditions of their ancestors. Those who remain on the tribal reservations do not seem to have the same enthusiasm for racket and ball as their forefathers.

How to Make a Lacrosse Racket

Materials
A willow branch about 1.50 m (approx. 5 ft) in length and 4 cm (1⅝ in) in diameter at its widest part, approx. 3 m (approx. 10 ft) of leather strip 4 to 5 mm (³⁄₁₆ in) thick.

Tools
Hobby knife, 5 mm (³⁄₁₆ in) drill.

Method
Mark a point about 50 cm (20 in) from the thinner end of the willow branch. From this point, pare one side of the branch so that it is a little less than half its original thickness and tapers slightly towards the end. This part of the branch should now be flexible enough to be bent to form an oval–rather like the head of a tennis racket. If it is not sufficiently flexible, pare a little more until the branch bends easily. The last 10 cm (4 in) of the pared branch should lie along the handle, to which it must be tightly bound with about 2 m (6 ft 6 in) of leather strip. This should be done from the handle end up, so that the remaining length of strip lies in the V formed where the racket head meets the handle. Now drill 5 mm (³⁄₁₆ in) holes through the head of the racket and through each side at opposite points (see illustration of the two rackets on the left). The remaining length of strip should now be woven through the top hole, taken around the outside and woven through the side holes. Make sure that the strip is well tensioned and then tie it off.

Hoop and Arrow

The game of Hoop and Arrow was played in one form or another by Indian tribes throughout the North American continent. It was a target game and consisted essentially of throwing a pole, or shooting or throwing an arrow at a hoop or ring, the score being determined by the way the pole or arrow fell with reference to the target. There were two basic forms of the game. In one, a small beaded hoop was rolled along the ground towards a log. Just before the hoop hit the log, the contestants hurled their poles at the hoop, points being scored according to which part of the hoop was in contact with the pole when it fell. In the other form of the game, a netted hoop was rolled along the ground between the contestants, who attempted to throw the arrows so that they passed between the strings as near to the center of the hoop as possible. Hoop-and-arrow games demanded a high degree of skill and large wagers were laid on the outcome of contests.

Right: *A Cheyenne youth playing* hoop and arrow *on a reservation in Oklahoma. This photograph was taken more than 75 years ago.*

Below: *The simplest possible materials are needed to make this authentic game.*

How to Make Hoop and Arrow

Materials
A flexible reed 1.50 m (5 ft) in length, a thin branched twig 75 cm (30 in) in length (see photograph), glue, feathers, acrylic paint, soft leather thong.

Tools
Hobby knife, paintbrush.

Method
Pare opposite sides of opposite ends of the reed so that they are about half their original width. Bend the reed into a circle and glue and pin the flattened ends together. Bind leather thong around the hoop, weaving it into an open mesh. Trim the twig, sharpen one end and paint to choice. Bind feathers to the two end branches with leather thong.

How to Play Hoop and Arrow

This is a game for two players. One rolls the hoop along the ground and the other tries to throw the arrow through it. Points are won according to how close the arrow is to the center of the hoop. As you become more skilful, increase the throwing distance. A variation of the game is to mark the hoop at each quadrant with four differently-colored wools, each color representing a certain number of points. Try to throw the arrow so that it knocks the hoop over and comes to rest on it or near it. The color nearest to the tip of the arrow counts for points. Again, increase the throwing distance as you become more skilful.

Snow Snake

Snow-snake games were games in which darts were hurled along snow on ice or through the air in competition to see which went farthest. They were only played by those Indian tribes who lived in the north where snow and ice were common in winter. There were three principal varieties of this game: the snow snake proper, in which a long, polished rod was made to glide along the snow or ice; the bone slider, in which a piece of bone or horn, decorated with feathers, was made to slide along the ice; and a game in which a javelin was made to slide or fly through the air. The original game is reputed to have been invented by the Ojibwa Indians. The "snake" was a piece of polished hardwood, about two meters in length and two centimeters in diameter. The head was bulb-shaped and had eyes and a cross cut to represent the mouth. This rounded end allowed the snake to pass over irregularities in the ice or snow. Sometimes a ridge of snow was built so that when the snake was skimmed along the ice, it took off like an airplane and flew through the air. It is recorded that distances of well over a kilometer (no, we don't believe it either!) were achieved. A variation of snow snake was played by the Iroquois, who raced small wooden canoes down trenches that had been trodden into the snow of a hillside and then watered. According to eyewitness accounts, these competitions were the occasion of much excitement and a great deal of betting.

According to a contemporary report:
"The thumb is placed on one side of the bone, the forefinger between the sticks, with the end against the end of the bone, and the other three fingers opposed to the thumb against the other side of the rib, the convex side of which is down. It is then thrown down and forward against a smooth surface, preferably ice, so that it glances forward as throwing sticks and snow-snakes do."

The report goes on to describe the markings on the bone:
"The marks etched on the bone represent a horned toad, a tarantula, the milky way and the moon. The four marks invoke the four winds and the six legs of the tarantula represent up and down and the cardinal points."

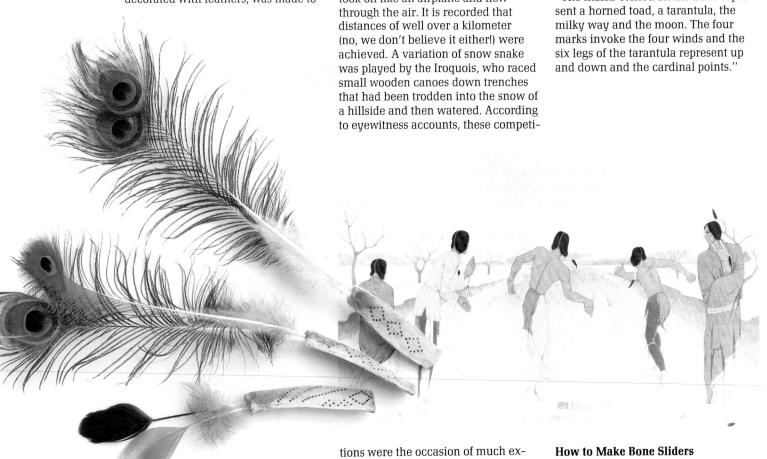

Above: *Peacock feathers have been used to give the bone sliders a most attractive appearance. Indians often used short thin twigs with feathers attached to the ends.*

Above right: *This stylized drawing shows young men playing* woskate hutanacute *(winged bone game) on a frozen stream in South Dakota.*

How to Play Snow Snake

Most of the northern tribes played the game with the long sticklike snakes and these may have represented the clubs of the twin war gods. A few tribes, however–Algonquian, Kiowan and Siouan–played the game exclusively with bone sliders. The origin of these is unknown, but the form suggests that they represented birds of some kind. Made from bone and feathers, they were extremely light and it must have been difficult to throw them any distance.

How to Make Bone Sliders

Materials
Beef or pork rib bones, feathers, glue, varnish.

Tools
Set of drills, paintbrush.

Method
Clean the bones. Drill two holes in one end of each bone and glue the feathers in them. The bone patterns (see photograph) are made with a fine drill. Finally the sliders are varnished to give them a glossy surface. This helps them to slide along the ice better.

Disc and Cross

Disc and cross originated in France. According to contemporary writings, it was very popular at the court of Louis-Philippe of Orleans, who reigned between 1830 and 1848. But long before that the game had been introduced into North America by the early colonists. It was adapted by the Native Americans who used it as a target game.

In its original form the game was played on cross-shaped courts marked out on a grass lawn.

Brightly-colored posts were planted to show the center square, which was the target area. The discs were sometimes hoops and sometimes solid wood. The game was for two competing couples, who occupied opposite arms of the cross. One couple rolled the disc back and forth between them, while the other couple attempted to roll their disc so that it struck the first disc within the center square. A point was scored for each successful "run." When the disc was struck within the target area, the turn of play passed to the striking couple. Play continued in this way until one couple had scored an agreed number of points, at which point the area of the target square was reduced by moving the posts.

How to Make Disc and Cross

Materials

a) For the discs: 2 plywood sheets 30 cm x 30 cm x 16 mm (12 in x 12 in x ⅝ in), blue and green acrylic paint;

b) For the posts: 2 broom handles, 4 wooden balls 6 cm (2⅜ in) in diameter, glue, double-ended nails, white, blue and green acrylic paint, a roll of 3 cm (1³⁄₁₆ in) red adhesive tape.

Tools

Steel ruler, pencil, large drawing compasses, scroll saw, rasp, sandpaper, hobby knife, paintbrushes.

Method

A) To make the discs: draw the two diagonals on one sheet of plywood. The point where they cross is the center of the sheet. Place the point of the compasses at this mark and describe a circle of radius 30 cm (12 in). Cut out the disc using a scroll saw. Round off the edges with a rasp and sand smooth. Make the other disc in the same way. Paint one in blue and one in green acrylic.

b) To make the posts: cut the broom handles in half and sharpen one end of each piece to a point. Flatten one side of each wooden ball with a rasp, then glue and pin to the posts using double-ended nails. Paint the posts white and two balls in blue and two in green acrylic. Decorate the painted posts by winding the red adhesive tape spirally around them to give a barber's pole effect.

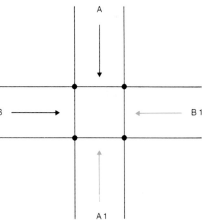

Left: *The equipment needed to play this old French game is not difficult to make.*

Above: *The course for disc and cross. This can be roughly drawn with chalk or marked with colored string. The black dots show the positions of the corner pegs.*

Cat's Cradle

The game we know as cat's cradle–string figures woven between the hands–is called *na-ash-klo* (continuous weaving) by the Navaho Indians, *aya-ito-tori* (woof-pattern string-taking) by the Japanese, *hei* (net) by the Hawaians, *toêka-toêka* (ladder, ladder) by the inhabitants of Celebes, and is known under many other names. Cat's cradle, reputed to have originated in one of the Far East countries hundreds of years ago, is probably one of the most widely played games in all the world.

Most of us, of course, know how to play cat's cradle and to most of us it is essentially a children's game. But how many of us are aware that the making of string figures is one of the oldest of the arts and the most universal of games among the primitive peoples of the world?

In the Canadian Arctic, Inuit make pictures of caribou, bears, sledges. (Many Inuit believe that there is a "Spirit of Cat's Cradles," which can get into its power anyone who spends too much time playing this game. In certain Inuit tribes, string figures are only made by girls, because it is believed that if young men make the figures, they will entangle their fingers in their harpoon lines during the hunt. The girls play it particularly in the autumn, believing that it can delay the onset of the dark winter days by entangling the legs of the departing sun. Some tribes forbid the playing of the game except in the winter months, while others place no restrictions whatsoever on the playing of string games.

In the southwestern United States the Navaho and Apache make stars of many sorts, storms, teepees and animals like coyotes and rabbits. In New Guinea you will find string pictures of headhunters, spears, drums, canoes, fishes and crabs.

Each people has its own string figures, but at the same time there are people from widely divergent cultures who make certain string figures that are exactly the same. Often special songs are sung during the making of a string figure, relating an accompanying story. A player may extend a single figure into a long series of linked figures, altering each one by moving his hands, using his teeth, or even his toes as a third hand, or passing the string to the fingers of another player.

The tales and legends recounted while making the string figures often are complex and are handed down in the same way from generation to generation.

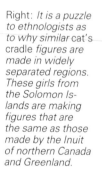

Right: *It is a puzzle to ethnologists as to why similar* cat's cradle *figures are made in widely separated regions. These girls from the Solomon Islands are making figures that are the same as those made by the Inuit of northern Canada and Greenland.*

How to Play Cat's Cradle

The only equipment needed to make any kind of cat's cradle figure is two yards or so of string or cord, the ends of which are tied together with a reef knot (left over right and under, right over left and under, for those readers who are not sailors!). For most figures the string should be soft and pliable, for others it should be a little stiffer.

In the directions overleaf for making individual string figures, the fingers are referred to as the thumb, the index, middle, ring and little finger.

In constructing figures the strands or loops of string near the body are called the "near strings" and the strands or loops further from the body are called the "far strings." Strings lying in front of the palm are called "palmar strings."

The instructions may seem a little difficult to follow at first, but as you construct the figures with the help of the illustrations, everything should become clearer and eventually fall into place. As with any game involving manual dexterity, the old adage of "practice makes perfect" is the name of the game!

To make the basic cat's cradle, put the string behind your thumbs and little fingers, so that it crosses the palms of your hands, as in the position in the illustration below left. Now put your right index finger under the left palmar string, and the left index finger under the right palmar string. Draw both hands apart to arrive at the position shown in the illustration below right. This is the basic cat's cradle. You will notice that the palms on your hands are facing each other, which is generally the case in most string figures. This position is usually repeated after each individual movement.

The simplest form of this dexterity game is the one after which it was called—cat's cradle. It is the basis for all the string figures made by Eskimos, Indians, Papuans, Maoris and many other tribes.

Many of the different figures—wood carrier, breastbone with ribcage, two fighting men, apache door, man in bed and howling monkey, to name a few—were created while people were just "playing around" with the weaving of string between their fingers.

The string figures on the following pages were chosen for you to practice on and thus become as light-fingered as possible. Don't be discouraged if at times the string slips from your fingers.

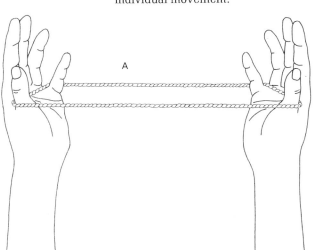

A

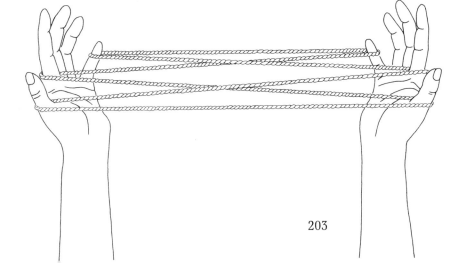

Wood Carrier

Start with opening A. Pass both *thumbs* and *index* fingers over the *index* loops and up into the *little* finger loops from below. Then up the *near little* finger strings and return releasing the *little* fingers as you go. The lower loops in the *thumbs* and *index* fingers are now lifted off over the loops you have just picked up. Do not pull the figure tight at this stage. Now the loop just lifted off will be lying across the *thumb* loops. Move both *thumbs* away from you over the upper string of this loop and let the original *thumb* loop slip off. Make sure the *thumbs* are still pointing away from

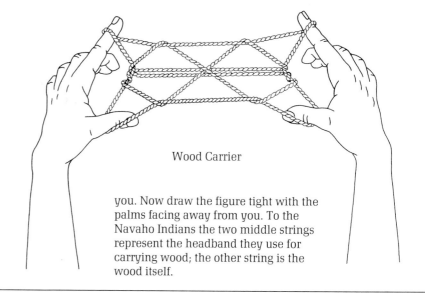

Wood Carrier

you. Now draw the figure tight with the palms facing away from you. To the Navaho Indians the two middle strings represent the headband they use for carrying wood; the other string is the wood itself.

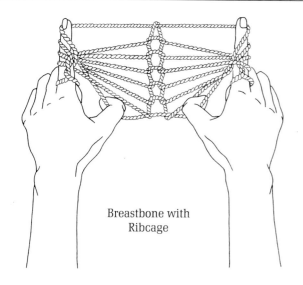

Breastbone with Ribcage

Breastbone with Ribcage

This figure from the Navaho Indians has its own opening. Loosely wind the string four times round the *left index* finger in a clockwise direction, starting at the base, towards the tip. Keep the strings in place by pressing the *middle* finger against them. Now move the *right index* finger without disturbing the order of strings. Draw the hands apart with the index fingers pointing upwards. This should produce a figure with four parallel strings on the near strings, while on the far side the top left string slants downwards to become the bottom right string. Pass the *right middle* and *ring* fingers towards you over the top of the slanting string and pull it downwards. The *left middle* and *ring* fingers are moved under the lowest of the straight far strings. This is drawn back and with the *left middle* and *ring* fingers catch down the string held by the right middle and ring fingers. You will find that the middle and ring fingers, left and right, now make two triangles, pointing towards you. Move them forward and between them catch the lowest near string and draw it back through the triangles.

Two Fighting Men

You need quite a stiff string for this figure, which tells its own story. Start with opening A. Move the *little* fingers over the *index* loops and over into the *thumb* loops from above. With the backs of the *little* fingers take up the *near thumb* strings and return, releasing the thumbs. Move the *thumbs* under the *index* loops and up to the *little* finger loops. With the backs of the *thumbs* take up both the *near little* finger strings and return, releasing the little fingers. Pass the *little* fingers over the *index* loops and up into the *thumb* loops from below.

Take up both far thumb strings on the backs of the thumbs and return. You now have a triangle in the center of the figure. Into it insert both index fingers from underneath and take up the sides of the triangle onto the backs of the index fingers. Using your teeth, lift off the lower loops from the index fingers and pass them over the upper double loops. Release the thumbs, draw the figure tight and twist the index loops several times away from you, releasing them. Finally insert the four fingers of both hands into the little finger loops and you have two fighting men from Torres Straits—one from Murray Island and one from Dauar Island. As you slowly draw the strings apart, the men go on fighting each other. Pulling only the left strings they will fall free and the Dauar man falls dead.

Continue pulling the left strings and the Murray man cuts off his adversary's head and goes home with it in triumph.

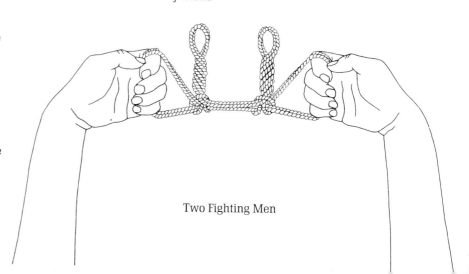

Two Fighting Men

Apache Door

Start with opening A. First pass the *middle, index* and *ring* fingers, followed by the *thumbs,* into the *index* loop from below. Keep this loop loose and let it slide down the wrist. Move the *little* fingers from below into the *thumb* loops. Pick up the *far thumb* strings from below into the *little* finger loops. Pick up the *near little* finger strings and return. With the right hand bending downwards, grasp all the strings and pass them from right to left between the left *thumb* and *index* finger as far as

Howling Monkey

This figure has its own opening. Place both hands in the string to make a wrist loop. Take the strings near the center with the right hand and pass them over the left fingers so that the *near* string passes between the thumb and *index* finger, and the *far* string to the front of the left hand by passing both between the *index* and *middle* finger. Pass the nearest string, which is the *far index* string, between *thumb* and *index* finger and around the *thumb* to the front of the hand. Now pass the furthest string,

which is the *near middle* string, between the *ring* and *middle* finger and around the *little* finger to the front of the hand. Release the strings you are holding in the right hand, except for the wrist string. Move the right *index* and *middle* fingers from underneath up into the left *index* and *middle* finger loops respectively and draw tight. Slip the wrist string off the left hand. Finally, place the tips of the *middle* and *index* fingers of both hand together and slip the loops on the right fingers over onto the left fingers. Take hold of the original left *index* and *middle* finger

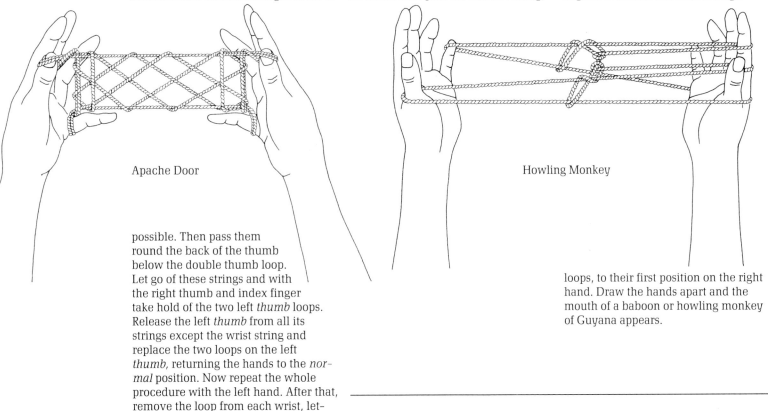

Apache Door

Howling Monkey

possible. Then pass them round the back of the thumb below the double thumb loop. Let go of these strings and with the right thumb and index finger take hold of the two left *thumb* loops. Release the left *thumb* from all its strings except the wrist string and replace the two loops on the left *thumb,* returning the hands to the *normal* position. Now repeat the whole procedure with the left hand. After that, remove the loop from each wrist, letting it lie on the strings between the hands. Put the hands together and draw apart. The figure representing the ornamented flap of an Apache teepee will appear.

loops, to their first position on the right hand. Draw the hands apart and the mouth of a baboon or howling monkey of Guyana appears.

Man in Bed

Start with opening A. Now move the thumbs away from under the *index*

loops and up into the *little finger* loops below. Take up the near little finger strings and return them under the index loops. The next move is to pass the little fingers towards you over the top of the far index strings. Then pick up the *far thumb* strings from below and return. Finally release the *index* fingers and draw the figure tight. To the people of Torre Straits (to the east of Australia) this represents a man lying on a bed. Traditionally, a chant is sung: "Man in bed, falls asleep, bed breaks." At which point the little fingers are suddenly released!

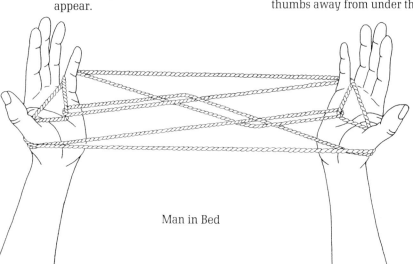

Man in Bed

Ball Games

Ball games are universally popular and have been for centuries. Many of our organized sports and games, both amateur and professional, involve the use of a ball. In many parts of the world balls are among the very first toys that children play with–and a great number of people continue to play ball games well into middle age and sometimes beyond. Formalized ball games–games for which a body of rules has been laid down–can be roughly divided into two groups. First, there are those games in which a ball is propelled by a part (or parts) of the body towards some fixed goal or target. Games in this group include the various football games; the various bowls games; basketball, netball and korfball; volleyball and handball.

The second group comprises games in which some kind of instrument is used to strike a ball towards a fixed goal or target. Games in this group include the various hockey games; baseball and cricket; tennis and squash; and golf.

These games are essentially modern and western in nature. The games described here, however, are quite a bit older, and also less regulated.

Hakozaki

Right: The young spectators at this Malaysian foot tennis *game seem to be more interested in the photographer than they are in the game!*

Hakozaki-gu no tama-seseri, "the ball struggle of Hakozaki Shrine," takes place in Fukuoka City, Japan, each year on January 3. It is said to have originated when two balls–one "male" and the other 'female'–were found floating in a nearby river and presented to the shrine. Each year the public were allowed to view them and they were said to give happiness to all who touched them. As more and more people attended the festival, the struggle to touch the balls took on a competitive aspect.

The male ball undergoes a series of purification ceremonies and is then delivered to the players, who themselves have also taken ritual baths. Dressed only in scanty loincloths, the players struggle to obtain possession of the ball and return it to the shrine. Tamotsu Yato, in *Naked Festivals of Japan,* writes: "The ensuing scene of fighting and pushing and shoving to get possession of the ball, with younger, lighter-weight boys sitting astride their elders' shoulders to get the advantage of height, is truly as wild as the nature of the men of Kyushu is reputed to be."

Below: The ball used in foot tennis *is woven from rattan and is a little smaller than a soccer ball.*

Right: It's easy when you know how! This Malaysian foot tennis *player demonstrates exactly how it should be done.*

Earthball

This is a modern American version, played in California, of an ancient tribal game in which two teams fight for possession of a huge ball–almost two meters in diameter (6.6 ft)–attempting to force it in the direction of the opposing goal line. It is essentially a high-spirited, energetic game in which the dominant element is the sense of "tribe" it communicates to the players. In many cultures this type of game was ceremonial and expresses a belief in the regenerative forces of nature. Similar games are sometimes played between villages in parts of Britain, albeit with smaller balls!

Indian Kickball

The Tarahumara Indians of Mexico derive their name from a word meaning 'foot-runners'–an indication of the importance of kickball racing in their culture. These races, which usually take place in the growing season, are run over a course of between 35 and 65 km (21 and 39 mi) set in the most rugged and rocky terrain. The teams of three to six runners, representing their village or region, kick a wooden ball–carved from the root of an oak tree and about 8 cm ($3^3/_{16}$ in) in diameter–before them as they run. The races have a spiritual significance but also give way to much excitement and betting.

Foot Tennis

This game is popular in Malaysia and other countries of the Far East and is played between two teams of two players each. The ball is the size of a soccer ball and is wickerwork–strips of rattan interwoven in bands. A net is stretched tightly between two posts and the boundary lines scratched into the ground. The object of the game is to keep the ball in the air, using only the feet, knees or thighs, passing it back and forth over the net. A point is scored each time it touches the ground inside the opposing half of the court or the opponent's kick it into the net.

Right: All children love chasing a ball. These youngsters, who live on Irian Jaya, in Indonesia, are no exception.

Below: Basketball stars in the making? Perhaps not, but these children in the southern highlands of Papua New Guinea are nevertheless enjoying their game.

Tlachtli

The exact origins of tlachtli are unknown, but figures of ball players have been discovered in Tlaltilco, in Mexico, which was inhabited as early as 1500 B.C. In its heyday this ancient game was played from El Salvador to northern Arizona and throughout the Antilles, but today it is confined to the Sinaloa and Nayarit natives who live on the northwest coast of Mexico.

Cortez and his conquistadores were the first Europeans to witness the game and the magnificent ceremonial that accompanied it, and in 1528 Cortez took a team of Aztec tlachtli players to Spain and presented them at the court of Charles V. Played on a walled I-shaped court, about 40 m (132 ft) long and 15 meters (49½ ft) wide, with a rubber ball weighing about 2 kg (4.4 lb),

tlachtli was a ruthless and dangerous game. The ball was played between two teams and was not allowed to touch the ground or to come to rest. Only the hips, knees and elbows could be used and the players wore pads to protect themselves. Even so, it was not unknown for players to be seriously injured or even killed. Points were scored when a team failed to return the ball, but the highlight of the game came when a player managed to ricochet the ball from his body through one of the vertical stone rings set in the center of the court walls. When this occurred, the star player could claim jewels, gold or almost anything he wanted from the opposing team and the audience. In victory, the captains were showered with the highest honors, in defeat they were often sacrificed to appease Xolotl, the god of the ball game.

Children's Games

Play is an essential part of the learning process and most children begin to play simple, informal games at an early age. As they grow older, their games become more formalized and rules are introduced. It is a well-known, but nonetheless astonishing, fact that many of these games are international and have been played for centuries by children from differing cultures. Most of the games included in this section–rope jumping, marbles, soap bubbles and spinning tops– are games of this type. So, too, is hopscotch, which has been played since Roman times.

The oldest known hopscotch diagram is inscribed into the floor of the Forum in Rome. As the Roman empire expanded, the legions built cobbled roads connecting major settlements. These paved surfaces proved ideal for hopscotch and the Roman soldiers taught it to the children of France, Germany and Britain. The game has remained popular with European children ever since. It is also very popular in the United States and in countries as diverse as Russia, India and China. The games on these pages are described following the rules generally used in the Netherlands.

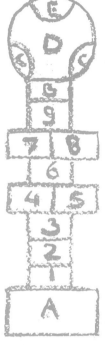

Heaven and Earth
Hopscotch

Send-a-Letter
Hopscotch

Hopscotch

Heaven and Earth Hopscotch

The diagram for heaven and earth hopscotch is the upper one in the left margin. The rules, with only slight variations, will apply to almost any hopscotch game.

General Rules
1. Stand on earth (a) and throw the marker (a beanbag or a bag filled with sand is ideal) into block 1. Hop on one foot from A to 1, pick up the marker and hop back to A. Now throw the marker into block 2, hop to 2 via 1, pick up the marker and throw it back to A. Hop 2, 1, A.
Begin again, tossing the marker into block 3 and continue in the same way

until you reach block 9, hopping back to A each time. If the marker lands in the wrong block or lands on a line, the turn ends and the next player begins. The player whose turn is over may begin again where he made his mistake, but only after the other players have their turns.
2. After hopscotching from 1 to 9, the marker is thrown into heaven (D). If it lands cleanly in one of the areas marked C, the player may skip any one of the steps 3 to 11. If the marker lands in D, hop there, block by block, pick up the marker and throw it into 9. Follow the same procedure as in step 1, but in reverse, hopping back to A.
3. The whole game is played again but instead of throwing the marker, push it with your foot.
4. Balancing the marker on one foot,

hop through all the blocks from A to D and back again. If the marker falls the turn is over.
5. Do the same, balancing the marker on your head.
6. Do the same, balancing the marker on your index finger.
7. Do the same, balancing the marker on your forearm.
8. Do the same, balancing the marker on your right knee.
9. Do the same, balancing the marker on your left knee.
10. With eyes closed and head erect, hop through all the blocks from A to D and back again. Players call "hot" if you hop correctly, "cold" if you miss.
11. Standing in A, with your back to the diagram, throw the marker over your shoulder. If the marker falls cleanly into one of the blocks, write your name

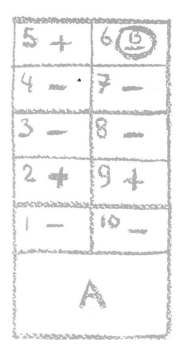

Moon Hopscotch

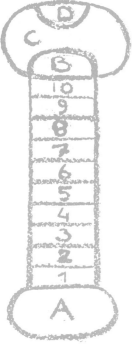

English Hopscotch

in that block. This is now "house" and in subsequent games you may rest there with both feet on the ground. The other players must skip this block next time around.

Send-a-Letter Hopscotch

The diagram is the lower one in the far left margin. In this game no marker is used. First hop on both feet through to block 9 and back again. Then hop on your right foot from 1 to 4, hop on to 5 with your left foot and 6 with your right. Then hop on both feet to 8 and 9. Jump around so that your right foot is in 9 and your left in 8. Hop once so that your legs are crossed, left foot in 9, right foot in 8. Then hop on one foot through 7 and 6, hop on both feet through 5 and 4 and hop on one foot back to 1.

English Hopscotch

The diagram is the one in the left margin. English hopscotch is almost identical to heaven and earth hopscotch. The main difference is that you hop over the block containing the marker and pick it up on the way back. Otherwise the general rules for heaven and earth hopscotch apply.

Water Hopscotch

The diagram for this game is the one in the middle column. The area marked A–the water–is forbidden territory. If a player or his marker trespasses into the water, he is out of the game. Areas 3, 6, and 9 (marked B) are rest areas. In addition to these rules, there is a last step, which is played without a marker. The

Water Hopscotch

player must hop on one leg three times around the diagram without pausing.

Moon Hopscotch

The diagram is the one at top right. The blocks marked with a minus sign (−) must be hopped on one foot; those with a plus sign (+) are hopped on both feet. Neither the player nor his marker may enter the moon circle (B) in block 6. From Earth (A) the marker is thrown into block 1. The player hops to 1, kicks the marker to 2, hops there, and so on. The game then continues, following the general rules 4 to 11. If the marker lands in A, the game is lost.

Alphabet Hopscotch

The diagram for alphabet hopscotch is below. The general rules apply to this game with the following exceptions. The rest block is H. Step 1 differs in that the player throws the marker from A to B, hops over B and on to H, where he rests, then back to C. Here he picks up the marker and hops over this block again back to A.

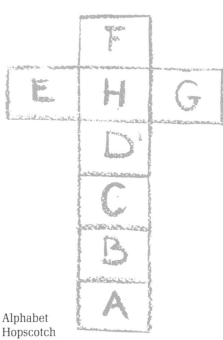

Alphabet Hopscotch

Rope Jumping

Rope jumping, nowadays played mainly by young girls, is one of the many games that have their origins far back in the mists of time. Nobody knows for certain at what point in history our earliest ancestors began to make games out of the skills that were so essential to their survival, but it was certainly thousands of years ago. Running, leaping and throwing were of vital importance to these primitive hunters and we can surmise that young children watched and imitated the actions of their elders. These skills slowly became formalized and by the time of the ancient Greeks athletic sports had come to play a most important role in everyday life.

The first jumping games were perhaps contests in leaping across a stream or over a rock, and children all over the world still enjoy games of this sort. Later, perhaps thousands of year later, some fibrous material, perhaps a vine-like creeper such as liana, was used as a "bar" to leap over. In some countries, this type of material is still used to make "ropes" for jumping games.

This, however, is conjecture. What we do know for certain is that rope-jumping games are played by children in almost every country of the world and that the games they play bear remarkable similarities.

Rope jumping is a very rhythmical game, and therefore it is not so surprising that children in many different countries chant traditional rhymes in time to the beat of the rope on the ground. Along the border between Texas and Mexico, for example, the children jump rope to the chant of:

"Brown as a coffee-berry, red as a bean, that's the prettiest color I've ever seen. Yellow as a daisy, black as ink, that's the prettiest color I do think. Orange as a pumpkin, green as grass, keep on jumping as long as you last."

In Britain, one very common rhyme, with many regional variations, is:

"One, two, buckle my shoe. Three, four, knock at the door. Five, six, pick up sticks. Seven, eight, don't be late. Nine, ten, start again."

Above: *These Tanzanian girls are using a "rope" made of short lengths of twisted fibers knotted together.*

How to Play Rope Jumping

This is a game for one, two or several players. If alone, the player holds one end of the rope in either hand, lets the rope hang behind him to touch his ankles, then swings it in an arc over his head. As the rope reaches his feet he jumps or hops over it. This movement is continued rhytmically until the feet finally catch in the rope. This basic form of rope jumping is a favorite form of training for some athletes, particularly boxers. They build up such a fast rhythm that it is impossible to see the rope as it is moving so quickly.

If two are playing, they stand side by side, each holding one end of the rope and jumping together. Another way of playing with two is to tie one end of the

rope to a post. One player swings the rope and the other jumps. When the jumper misses his footing, the players change places. When a group play, two hold the ends of the rope and swing it as quickly as they can while the others take turns jumping in and out of the arc without breaking the rhythm. Anyone touching the rope exchanges places with one of the "turners." A few of the more popular rope jumping games are described here.

Follow the Leader

Two players swing the rope. The others stand in file behind a leader. The lea-der jumps into the rope arc, chants a rhyme and jumps out. The following person now jumps in, without breaking the rhythm, chants the same rhyme and jumps out. This process continues until someone fails to clear the rope. This person takes the place of one of the turners.

Running Through

Two players swing the rope. The other players take turns in running in, jump-ing the rope once, and running out again. The second time around, each player must jump the rope twice, and so on. Players who fail drop out of the game and take the place of the rope turners.

Rocking the Boat

Instead of swinging the rope in a com-plete circle, the turners let it swing back and forth in a low arc. Each player must enter, jump twice and exit. If all the players do this successfully, the rope is raised an the game repeated. The height of the rope is increased each time until all the players except one–the winner–have dropped out.

The Clock

One player holds one end of a long rope. The other players space them-selves around him in a circle whose radius is just less than the length of the rope. The central player swings the rope around as fast as he can, just above the ground, while the surround-ing players jump over it. Any player touching the rope is out. The game continues until only one player is left.

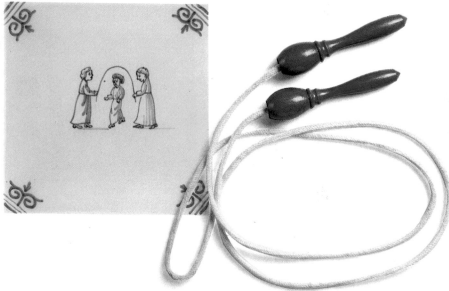

Above: *This very old, hand-painted Dutch tile pictures three children jumping rope.*

Above: *An example of a modern skip-ping rope made of finely woven, strong material. The* carved wooden handles fit snugly into the palm of the hand.

Chinese Rope Kicking

This is very popular in China and is a version of an old English rope jumping game called "high water-low water." Two players hold a long rope taut between them at about waist height. The other players take turns in kicking the rope, first forwards, then back-wards. If both kicks are successful, the rope is raised a few inches and the players try again. Players failing with either kick drop out of the game. Play continues until only one player is left.

Marbles

A steady hand, accurate aim and lots of practice–these are the attributes of a skilful marbles player and many a childhood reputation has been made or broken by the flick of a thumb against a small glass sphere. How many of us still hold nostalgic memories of the delight of "bombing" a despised rival or the agony of losing a favorite "shooter"? Like so many children's games, marbles is played all over the world and has been for centuries. The ancient Egyptians knew the game and versions of it were played in pre-Christian Rome. In the Middle Ages, schoolboys used the game as an escape from the rigors of the classroom. An anonymous English poem from the 1600s describes a boy as "a dunce at syntax, but a dab at taw"; "taw" being an old word for "marbles."

But marbles has never been exclusively a game for children. As can be seen in the engraving on the opposite page, the upper classes in 17th-century France amused themselves by playing "bridge," a game in which marbles are flicked through gates to score points. It is said that Abraham Lincoln was an expert at old bowler, a marbles game that involves precision shooting. Nowadays, there is a world championship, held annually, in which dedicated marbles players from all over the world compete. On a less esoteric level, the child in all of us can rediscover one of the lost joys of yesteryear. All we need are a handful of little glass spheres and a patch of vacant ground.

How to Play Marbles Games

There are dozens of marbles games, most of them having no limit on the number of players. The basic idea in all of them is to flick a marble so that it strikes an opponent's marble, according to the particular rules of the game being played. A successful player generally takes possession of any marble he hits, and the common expression "to play for keeps" very probably derives from this practice.

To propel a marble (called a *shooter*) it is balanced in the curled forefinger and flicked with the thumb. A player may squat or kneel on one or both knees to obtain the best aiming position, but in serious play–i.e., for keeps–any forward movement of the hand is forbidden.

The Game of Potty

A hole is dug in the ground with the heel. A line is drawn two meters from the hole and players toss a marble in

Right: *These children in Katmandu, the capital city of Nepal, are playing a form of potty–a game in which the players attempt to flick their marbles into a bowl-shaped hole in the ground.*

turn at the "pot." The player whose marble is closest goes first. He then shoots for the pot and, once in, can use "spannies" to win other marbles; that is, any marble close enought to the pot to fall within the span created by stretching the forefinger and thumb becomes his property. If two players get marbles into the pot on the first throw, they each have three chances to shoot the other out, so winning the marble.

The Game of Ringer

a circle of about 30 cm (12 in) in diameter is drawn or scratched in the ground and each player puts three marbles inside it. An outer shooting circle of about 2 meters (6½ ft) in diameter is drawn round the smaller circle. Players shoot in turn, trying to knock the marbles out of the circle. Players con inue to shoot as long as they are successful. In one version of ringer, players arrange their marbles in a circle, equally spaced a few centimeters (inches) apart. A target marble is placed in the center of this circle, and each players aims for this target from a line drawn 2 meters (6½ ft) away. When he has hit the target marble he can aim for any marble in the circle. If he hits it, he can aim for another with the same shooter from the position in which it comes to rest. When he misses, his turn is over and his shooter remains as a target.

The Game of Old Bowler

A square 1 meter (approx. 3 ft) in diameter is scratched or drawn, together with its diagonals. Marbles are placed at the four corners and at the center. Players shoot out the marbles one by one in the counterclockwise order, ending with the center marble. If all five are not hit, they are replaced and the next player tries.

The Game of Dirty Pool

This is a shooter's game and the diagram is a series of five concentric circles about 10 centimeters (4 in) apart. The bull counts 50 points and the rings respectively 40, 30, 20 and 10 points. Players shoot an agreed number of marbles, or to an agreed score. The winner takes his opponent's marbles.

The Game of Bombadier

This is a cutthroat game designed to win enemies rather than friends. Each player places a number of prized marbles in a circle. In turn each player holds a marble at arm's length above the pile and "bombs" it. Marbles knocked out of the circle become the property of the bombadier, who also retrieves his "bomb." The game ends when the circle is empty.

Above: Le jeu de troumadame, *an engraving from the 17th century by the French artist Ménian. The object of the game was to score points by flicking the marbles through a series of differently sized bridges. Nowadays this game is known as bridge; the "bridge" can be made by cutting holes in an old shoebox.*

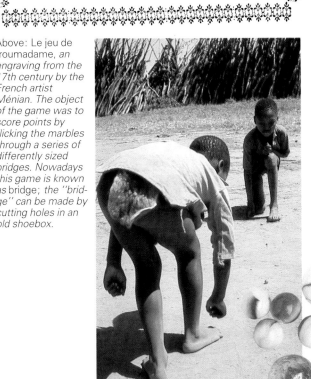

Left: *Children all over the world play marbles games that are remarkably similar.*

Below: *Marbles come in many different sizes and are made of many different materials:* alabaster, glass, metal and clay being the most common.

Right: *This portrait of an unknown boy blowing soap bubbles is dated 1663 and was painted by the artist Frans van Mieris (1635-1681), who lived and worked in the Dutch university city of Leiden.*

Soap Bubbles

"I'm forever blowing bubbles,
Pretty bubbles in the air..."

These are the opening line of a song that was popular in the music halls of Britain many years ago. In fact, it is still the theme song of one of England's best-known soccer clubs–West Ham United, of London. Children have amused themselves for centuries by blowing soap bubbles. Jean-Baptiste Chardin (1699-1779), a French artist who was well-known for portraying children at play, painted a picture of a young boy happily engaged in the pastime; while Frans van Mieris (1635-1681), the Dutch artist, painted the picture shown on the opposite page.

The equipment required for blowing soap bubbles is basically simple. All you need is a loop of wire and some soap mixture. The wire loop is dipped into the soap mixture so that a thin film adheres to it. If you blow gently on this film, a bubble will form, detach itself from the loop and float into the air. Similar bubbles can be formed by dipping one end of a drinking straw in the mixture and blowing gently through the other end.

More complex "crystal" bubbles can be made by twisting thin wire into variously shaped frameworks, dipping them in the soap mixture and placing them in the freezing compartment of your refrigerator until they freeze solid. Other shapes can be made by using two wire loops. Soap mixture adheres between the loops, and when they are gently pulled apart barrel-shaped and hourglass bubbles can be made.

How to Make Soap Mixture

Materials
Four tablespoons of glycerine, four tablespoons of soap powder, a quart of water.

Tools
A spoon, a deep mixing bowl.

Method
Mix the ingredients together. Heat gently until warm, stirring from time to time. Allow to cool.

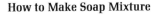

Below: *Making rings for bubble blowing is simply a matter of twisting thin wire into the required form. Squares, ellipses and many other shapes can also be used for bubble blowing.*

Right: *"The bigger the better" is the motto of this entertainer.*

Spinning Tops

The curious and puzzling phenomenon of similar or identical games being played by people of widely differing cultures in widely differing parts of the world has been mentioned before in this book. Some children's games, such as hopscotch, marbles and rope jumping, have been played almost universally for centuries; while others, such as cat's cradle, play an important part in the folklore of peoples as diverse as the Maoris of New Zealand and the Inuit of northern Canada and Greenland. Spinning tops is yet another game that falls into this category. It has certainly been played for more than 2,000 years, for it is recorded that Cato, the Roman statesman, recommended the game to parents as a more suitable pastime for children than dice.

Tops were very common in 14th-century Europe, especially in England, and they may have been connected with some early Christian church ceremony. Each parish had its own top, and on Shrove Tuesday (the day before Lent–a time of fasting in medieval times) top races were held on the roads between parishes. A top that had stopped spinning, or which had been put away until the following year, was said to be "sleeping," from which we derive the expression "to sleep like a top." The game was also popular among the Indians of both North and South America, and was played long before the first white settlers arrived on their shores. In North America it was commonly a winter game and was played on ice. The Inuit spun their tops and attempted to run around the house before they stopped spinning. In Africa, grooves were often cut into the tops so that they would hum as they spun. Tops of vary-

ing shapes and sizes are also found throughout the Far East. In Japan, for example top making is a traditional skill. The craftsmen are noted for their originality and among the many novel tops they make is the "childbearing top," which releases smaller tops as it spins.

In New Guinea and Borneo, tribesmen spin tops after the seasonal planting of their staple crops. This ritual is intended to encourage the young shoots to thrive. In some areas of Australasia, big spindle tops are turned against each other in "the battle of the giant tops." During the last decades of the 19th century the game of whip tops was very popular among schoolboys in New Zealand. In his scholarly work *The Folkgames of Children*, Brian Sutton-Smith describes how they would race their tops along the rural road to school, sometimes for a mile or more. They made whips from strands of flax

and a skilled player could whip his top for a distance of 15 yards or more. One of the great dangers was "undercutting," which sent the top flying through the air, sometimes through a nearby window! As it was the custom for a top to bear the name of its owner, there was little point in fleeing from the scene of the crime!

How to Play Spinning Top Games

The top is set in motion either by twisting the spindle quickly between the palms of the hands or by winding a string around the upper part and jerking it free. With practice most players can make the top spin for a remarkable length of time before it slows and falls over. Traditionally, once a top has been spun it is kept in motion by striking it with a whip of some sort. The end curls around the top and imparts extra spin to it. Once a player has mastered the techniques of spinning and whipping

Below: *This very old wooden spinning top is in the collection of the Musée de l'Homme in Paris. The top suggested in the "How to Make" section is based on the same idea as this one.*

Right: *Indian boys spinning their tops in the shadow of the Temple of Madurai.*

the top, there are a number of games that can be played. The Romans had a game called *turbo* in which a large circle was drawn on the ground and divided into 10 numbered segments. The players scored points according to the segment in which the top came to rest. Obstacle races, in which the top must be whipped around tin cans, trees etc. are also great fun.

How to Make a Spinning Top

Materials
A sheet of plywood measuring 5 cm x 15 cm x 12 mm (2 in x 6 in x ½ in), a half-sphere of softwood approximately 7 cm (2¾ in) in diameter, approximately 15 cm (6 in) of 5 mm (³⁄₁₆ in) dowel, a short length of hollow wooden tube with a internal diameter of 5 mm (³⁄₁₆), a rubber grommet whose internal diameter is equal to the external diameter of the hollow wooden tube, glue, varnish, 1 m (3.3 ft) of string.

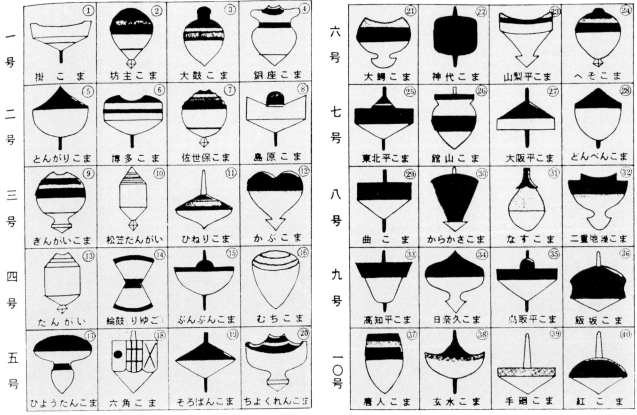

Tools
Steel ruler, pencil, scroll saw, sandpaper, 5 mm (³⁄₁₆ in) drill, vise.

Method
a) To make the handle:
Draw a grid of 2½ cm x 2½ cm (1 in x 1 in) squares on the plywood sheet. Draw the handle using the gridded diagram on page 218 as a guide. Cut the handle out using a scroll saw and sand the edges smooth. The large hole is cut by first drilling a series of holes around the inner edge of the circle and then using a scroll saw to cut out the waste wood. Sand the inside of this hole smooth. Fix the handle in a vise so that the curved part faces downwards. Drill a hole, using a 5 mm (³⁄₁₆ in) drill, downwards through the center of the cut-out circle.

b) To make the top itself:
Drill a 5 mm (³⁄₁₆ in) hole through the

217

center of the half-sphere. Sand one end of the 5 mm (³/₁₆ in) dowel to a blunt point–a fine rasp or file can be used to do this. Coat the pointed end with glue to about halfway along the rod. Tap the rod through the half-sphere (from the flat side) until about 4 cm (1⅝ in) protrudes from the rounded side. Slide on the wooden sheath. Wipe off any surplus glue and allow to dry. Slide the rubber grommet over the sheath. If it fits only loosely add a dab of glue to the inside. Finish with varnish!

To Spin the Top

Slide the handle over the dowel. Lay one end of a length of string along the dowel within the hole in the handle. Turn the top slowly so that the string winds itself round the dowel. When this has been done, hold the top in one hand so that the point is at an angle to the ground. Take the string in the other hand and pull it firmly and quickly so that it unwinds, causing the top to spin. As the inside end of the string comes free, turn the point of the top to the ground, so causing it to fall away from the handle, strike the ground point first and spin.

Above right: *This top is very easy to make.*
Use the grid shown to draw the shape of the handle.
The unit square is 2½ x 2½ cm (1 in x 1 in).

Right:
L'enfant au toton *(Child with top) by Jean-Baptiste Simeon Chardin (1699-1779). This painting hangs in the Louvre, in Paris.*

Yo-yo

The yo-yo is said to have originated in ancient China. It was played in ancient Greece–evidence of this exists in the form of pictures on classical Greek pottery. During the 18th century, both the French and British aristocracy were very much taken with the device. It was then known variously as the quiz, the bandalore or the Prince of Wales' toy. In France, in the late 18th century, the yo-yo became known as *l'émigrette*, because it had become a favorite pastime of the *émigré* nobles driven into exile during the French Revolution. A few years later the famous Duke of Wellington was an addict of the toy. The yo-yo has never lost its popularity and today there are clubs all over the world.

How to Play Yo-yo Games

Wind the string round the spool of the yo-yo and insert your index finger into the loop at the end of the string. Hold the yo-yo with the other fingers and let it ride down the string. When it is almost at its fullest extent, jerk the string to bring it back up to your hand. This movement is like bouncing a ball and can be continued indefinitely. If you flick the yo-yo down hard and do not jerk your finger, it should stay spinning at the end of the string until you recall it by jerking your finger. Once you have mastered this trick, you can make a number of figures by folding the string around your hands in the manner of making cat's cradle figures.

Center: *A collection of yo-yo's.*

Bottom right: *A cartoon of a French officer playing* le jeu de l'emigrette.

Below: *An expert demontrates one of the many figures that can be made with a long-stringed yo-yo.*

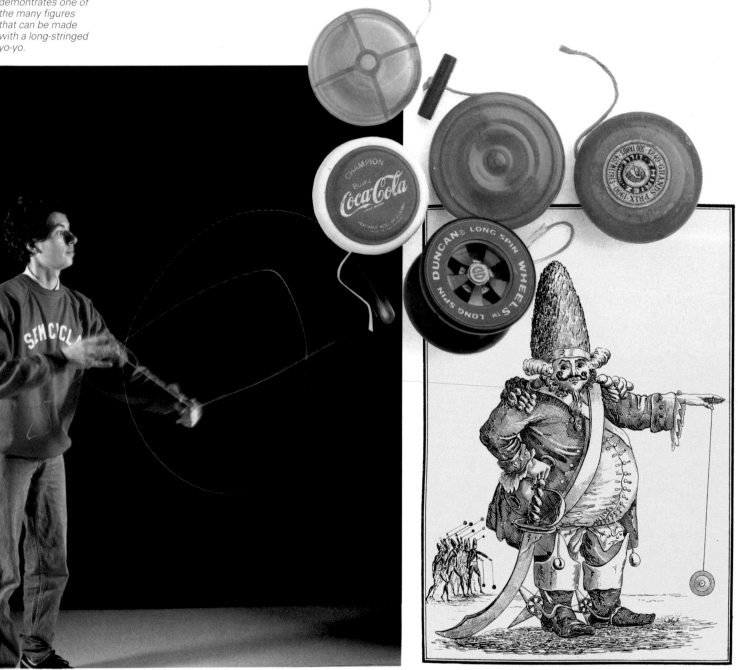

220

A diabolo.

Diabolo

Diabolo is probably best known today in the West through the breathtaking exploits of troupes of jugglers in Chinese circuses. They know diabolo as *tjouk-pag-oul* and are capable of making this spinning double cone perform the most amazing feats. The diabolo is set revolving back and forth along a string by alternately raising and lowering the two sticks between which it is attached. As it picks up speed, the diabolo begins to hum loudly. The juggler then flicks it high into the air and catches it, still spinning, on the string as it falls. As a variation, the juggler might flick the diabolo high into the air towards another member of the troupe, who catches it and in his turn flicks it to a third member. This trick, however, is only the beginning of the routine! Among other feats, the juggler catches the diabolo on a stick and makes it run up it–in apparent defiance of the laws of gravity.

The game was introduced into Europe in the late 18th century by the then British ambassador to China, Lord Macartney. Known as the "flying cone" or the "devil on two sticks," it became immediately popular. In France, *le diable* was played as widely and as fanatically as bilbouquet had been almost 250 years previously. Models were made in the rarest and most expensive woods and even in glass, which was popular because of the singing sound it made. Although the game fell out of fashion during the later years of the 19th century, it was revived in the 1900s when a French engineer, Gustave Phillipart, improved its design and christened it "diabolo," a name it still bears.

How to Play Diabolo Games

Place the diabolo on a flat surface. Take the sticks, one in each hand, and position the string under the diabolo at the narrowest point between the cones. The diabolo should be close to the right-hand stick and the string should be fairly taut. Raise the right-hand stick so that the diabolo rolls along the string towards the left-hand stick. Just before it reaches this stick, raise it, and at the same time lower the other, so that the diabolo rolls back along the string. This action is repeated over and over until the diabolo picks up speed and begins to hum. To achieve this takes a little practice, but soon you will be able to control the diabolo fairly well. At this point, flick the diabolo gently into the air, so that it only just leaves the string, and catch it as it falls. Continue practicing this, each time flicking the diabolo a little higher. In time, you may become as expert as the jugglers of the Chinese circus!

Below: A 1916 poster picturing the skills of one Mac Sovereign, a noted diabolo player.

Kites

Left: *Huge kites of ancient Mayan design are launched at the Guatemalan village of Santiago de Sacatepequez to celebrate the dry season. The local cemetery doubles as an arena for the kites, which symbolize the spirits of the dead.*

As is the case with so many other games described in this book, kite flying originated in Asia, where kites have been flying since time immemorial. In the West, kites are very occasionally used for practical purposes but in nine cases out of ten, kites go up in the air because the owners holding the strings enjoy flying them. In Asia, however, kites are still used for a variety of practical–or impractical, depending on the way you look at it–purposes that have little do with "just fun." For example, in Korea and Malaysia, flying kites is considered to be a way of getting rid of all sorts of ailments and problems, for driving out evil spirits and for securing a prosperous future for a new-born child. In Far East countries, kites have also always been a tactical weapon in warfare. History books mention a Chinese general named Han Hsin, who in 200 B.C. used a kite as a surveying instrument, to measure the distance between his army and the heavily defended city he wanted to conquer. As a result, his soldiers managed to dig the correct length of tunnel and took the city by surprise. The Venetian merchant Marco Polo was probably the first European to see a kite. He did not fail to notice that in some cases a human being was tied onto the kite, but from the reports he wrote to Venice it is clear that he assumed that the person must be a criminal condemned to "flying," a drunk or an idiot, as no one in his right mind would take such a risk. Marco Polo was a genius, but he could not see into the future. For the people who tried flying themselves, carried by a kite–an idea that was popular in various places in the 19th century–were by no means mad. The first manned flight supposedly took place in 1853, when the British kite flyer, Sir George Caley, asked his coachman to fly the double kite Caley had constructed (apparently Sir George did not want to take the risk himself!).

The idea of using a double kite emerged again at the end of the 19th century, when the inventor of the telephone, the Scotsman Alexander Graham Bell, began experimenting with kites in a bay in Canada. Bell's greatest triumph was a flight of seven minutes made by the American Selfridge, in a kite built by Bell. Selfridge went up 50 meters (165 ft) in the kite, which was pulled by a steamer. In 1907 this caused an immediate sensation. Another famous scientist who experimented with kites was Benjamin Franklin who in 1752 used a kite to prove that electricity in lightning was the same as electricity on earth.

In conclusion, kites have been and still are used for a variety of purposes, useful, not so useful, noble and less noble. But the most important thing is that they can provide hours and hours of great fun. Many people become quite passionate about kite building and kite flying–some even become fanatic. Think of the unhappy character in one of Somerset Maugham's stories, *The Kite*. This man ended up rotting in a damp, dark dungeon because he refused to pay alimony to his wife, who had cut his favorite kite in two!

Below: *A diamond-shaped kite from Nagasaki. It is a Hata, which means "flag," but some Japanese say the word derives from bata (horsefly), referring to the buzzing sound made by the streamers when the kite flies.*

Below right: *Japanese kites are often square and colorfully decorated.*

Indian Fighter Kite

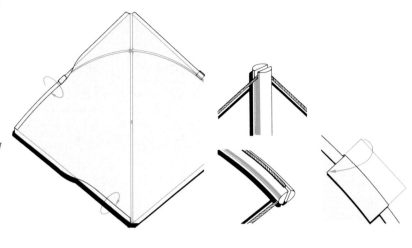

The Indian fighter kite has been called the Porsche of kites, and with good reason. It is probably one of the most popular kites around and it looks very simple, but it has a mind of its own. It requires a sensitive touch, both for its construction and when you are actually flying it. The Indian fighter kite is not found just anywhere. It is often a bully and has been described as a very self-willed object.

It may look rather plain: flat, no tail, an uninspiring square shape. If you don't keep the string taut, it flutters all over the place, and goes anywhere except where you want it to. But when the wind suddenly tugs at it, the Indian fighter kite once again reveals itself to be a rogue, racing through the atmosphere like a rocket. It can be used to conduct an entire air battle, and these have been held in India for centuries. The Indian fighter kite is considered to be the mother of all the other notorious fighter kites that battle for supremacy over countries such as Korea, Thailand and Japan. The hata is one of these descendants–a famous Japanese robber from Nagasaki. The Korean fighter kite with its strange fins is another kite that

is descended from its Indian ancestor. It is therefore a classic kite, and its purpose is purely to lord it over the heavens. It can move as fast as lightning and turn like a slalom skier. A great deal of patience is needed to learn to control it properly, before it will do exactly what you want it to do. But this is the charming side of the rascal. Once you've learned to control it, you couldn't wish for a better kite.

How to Make an Indian Fighter Kite

Although other materials can be used, it is best to make the Indian fighter kite in the traditonal way from paper and split bamboo. The two bamboo sticks should be respectively 60 and 40 cm (24 and 16 in) long. The 60 cm (24 in) stick should taper to a point at both ends, and be attached to the 40 cm (16 in) stick about 7 cm (2.8 in) from the top. Stretch thin string around this frame so that the cross-spar is curved

(see illustration) and then line the frame on the sheet of paper. Cut out the patterns allowing 1½ cm (⅝ in) for the hem. It's a good idea to reinforce the construction using some extra paper at the point were the string and the bent cross-paper come together. The tail should be made of two pieces of paper. Stick these pieces on the front and back of the kite with two sticks between them to reinforce it. Attach the bridle as shown in the illustration, and if necessary, reinforce the bridle points with paper. This kite is an excellent one to decorate with your initials (or even with a coat of arms, if your family has one!). As the Indian fighter kite is meant to be quite small, beware of making it too large. Think of the saying "Small is beautiful!"

224

Tetra (Nick Morse)

The modern tetra kite is based on the kites of Dr. Alexander Graham Bell, the inventor of the telephone. However, Dr. Bell's kites had one disadvantage: the frame consisted of innumerable sticks and rods so that the *tetrahedron* (structure) was often heavy, although certainly stable and quite strong. (Once, one of these tetrahedrons took one of Bell's assistants almost 10 meters (33 ft) up into the air!)

Bell achieved startling results with his kites, but his successes were rather eclipsed with the development of aviation. Also, Bell's kites were difficult to build for most people and ungainly. However, that problem was solved when, not all that long ago, an Englishman named Nick Morse invented a type of umbrella construction that meant that Bell's "tetra" could be folded open. Moreover, he used four instead of six cells and made them of the lightest possible material.

Even Alexander Graham Bell would have been delighted with the result, if he had lived to see the tetra with its infinite possibilities. By using special fabrics and fixing the strings in a particular way, the kite has a unique shape and in its modern version it has retained its prewar strength and durability.

How to Make a Tetra

As was mentioned before, the Tetra kite has a unique shape. Its construction is based on the same principles as that of an umbrella. Its dimensions can vary, of course, but for the one pictured on this page, which has 40 cm x 40 cm (16 in x 16 in) cells, you need a stick 5 m (5.5 yd) long with a diameter of 4 mm (¹⁄₁₆ in). You also need over 80 cm² (1 yd²) of cloth which is cut into eight triangles with two sided of 40 cm (16 in) each. These triangles are necessary because the grain of the fabric is important when the cloth is pulled taut. Every cell is held by four sticks that meet at a crosspiece made of two pieces of PVC tubing tacked together. One side has a hole so it is easier to mount the cloth (see example). The corners are joined together with rubber tubing and rings. The strings in the cell keep the whole thing in shape. The inventor of the tetra kite, the Englishman Nick Morse, constructed this unique contraption in such a way that the possibilities of it are indeed infinite. You can see yourself how easy this kite is to fly, using a three-point bridle.

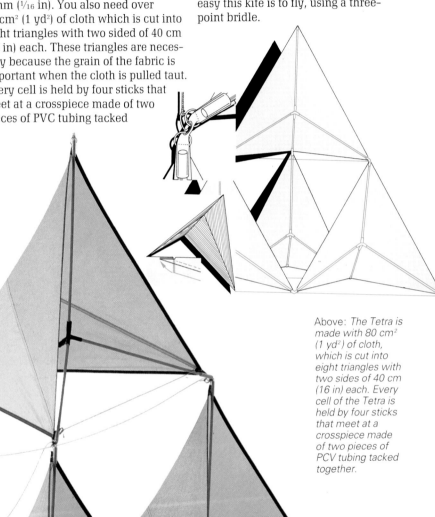

Above: *The Tetra is made with 80 cm² (1 yd²) of cloth, which is cut into eight triangles with two sides of 40 cm (16 in) each. Every cell of the Tetra is held by four sticks that meet at a crosspiece made of two pieces of PCV tubing tacked together.*

Above: *Fixing the bridle.*

Below: *One side of the crosspiece—made of two pieces of PCV tubing—has a hole so that it is easier to mount the cloth.*

Above: *The Tetra kite: a modern version of a solid pre-war model.*

Cody Kite

Above: *Samuel Franklin Cody in his ordinary clothes.*

Top right: *The King of the Cowboys, Samuel Cody, as he liked to be portrayed–rather like the legendary Buffalo Bill, whom he resembled.*

Bottom right: *One of the first Cody kites, held by the grand master himself (right) and an assistant. Cody had attached wings to the box kite originally designed by Hargrave.*

At the beginning of this century, Samuel Franklin Cody (born in Birdville, Texas, in 1861) was a famous kite flyer and kite builder but his name will no longer be familiar to the general public and even most kite enthusiasts will be at a loss if asked who he was. Cody was already famous before kites entered his life. He traveled around America with a circus and was billed the King of Cowboys. Apparently–if his biography, *Pioneer of the air*, by G.A. Broomfield is to believed–there was no one in the still very wild Wild West of the United States who was quite as handy or as fast with a Winchester or a lasso. Following the example of his contemporary, the legendary Buffalo Bill, Cody organized a Wild West show and took it to England, where he became a great success.

The "cowboy" on his white stallion, with his long hair, pointed beard, enormous moustache, Stetson, wide leather belt, very pointed cowboy boots and the ever-ready lasso in his right hand, was a sensation.

Fortunately, at least for kite enthusiasts, Cody soon tired of the daily routine of the show and began to look for other challenges. He discovered the hobby of his son, Leon, who had become addicted to flying kites. Cody felt it should be possible to get a man in the air using this method and started work on this project straightaway. He turned out to be a born kite builder and his experiments soon produced results. By 1901 he had successfully managed to go up in the air with a kite. He continued making improved versions of his kite and built increasingly large contraptions. Then he began to do stunts. In November 1903 he even dared to attempt to cross the English Channel from Calais to Dover. Needless to say, he did not cross it flying a kite. He made his attempt in a sloop, but the sloop was pulled along by a Cody kite. He succeeded and the publicity he gained from this enterprise earned him the attention and admiration of the military authorities, whom he had unsuccessfully tried to impress with his kites in the past. Then a courageous soldier name Moreton went up a good 800 meters (2,640 ft) with one of the Cody kites. This clinched the matter. Cody was immediately promoted to the rank of an officer in the British Army and was appointed chief kite instructor. His task was designing and building

even better kites, as well as supervising the training of up-and-coming kite fliers. "Cody's kite" became almost a household word. His kites always made a big impression, not only because of their tremendous lift, but possibly even more because of their extraordinary construction. For Cody did not simply launch one kite at a time but would send up a whole fleet into the sky at once. After all, once a showman, always a showman.

Cody went on to building motorized aircraft, instead of kites and flying them himself. There is a famous photograph in which he can be seen at the wheel of a warplane he constructed in 1909 in Aldershot. The former cowboy had become a real aviator. And it was as an aviator that he was killed, in 1913, in the sky above Aldershot. A sudden gust of wind ripped apart the "Waterplane" that he had built himself.

Top left: *This picture gives a fairly accurate idea of the size of the giant Cody kite.*

Most of the illustrations in this section are reprinted from Kite Flights *(Henry Holt and Company, New York, 1986), by Alice Weve and Jack Botermans.*

Left and above: *A giant Cody kite at a kite festival in 1986 at Scheveningen, the Netherlands.*

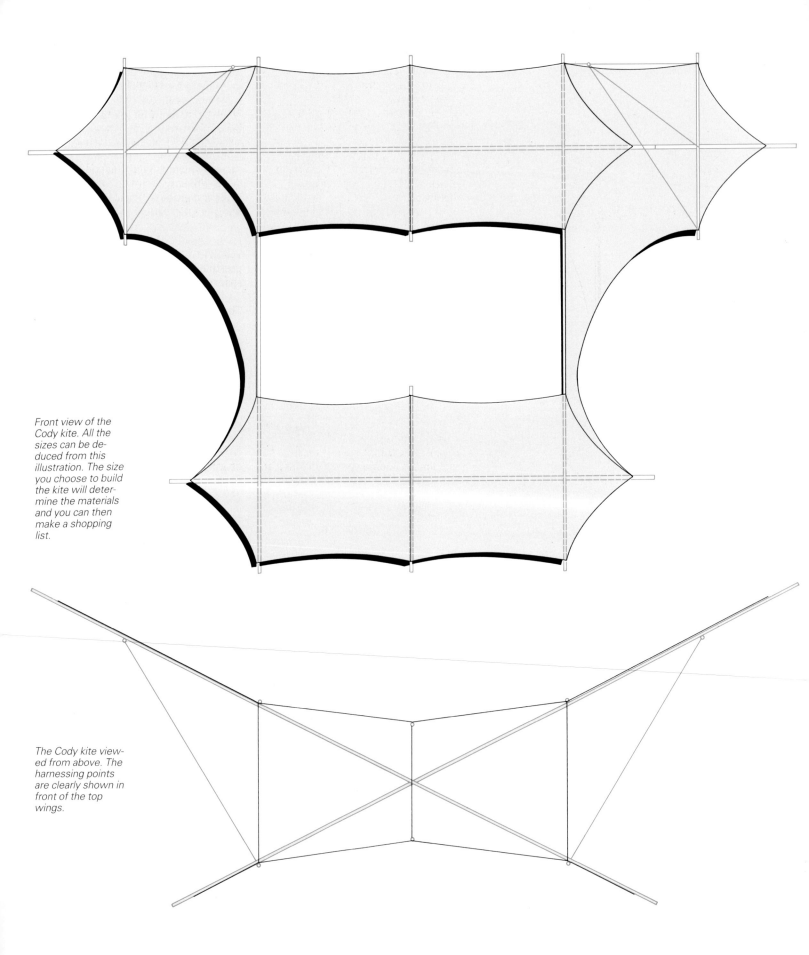

Front view of the Cody kite. All the sizes can be deduced from this illustration. The size you choose to build the kite will determine the materials and you can then make a shopping list.

The Cody kite viewed from above. The harnessing points are clearly shown in front of the top wings.

228

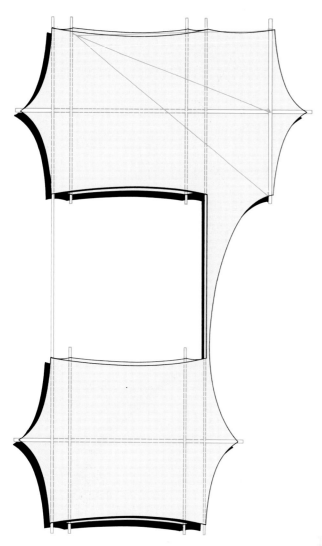

Side view.

Fixing the bridle.

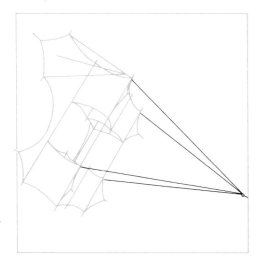

How to Make a Cody Kite

The amount of material bought for this kite depends entirely on the size you wish to build.

To build a kite 2.1 m (7 ft) tall with a span of 3.5 m (11½ ft) you will need over 2.7 m² (30 ft²) of spinnaker cloth and 19 m (21 yd) of stick with a diameter of 1 cm, 2 cm and 6 cm (⅜ in, ¹³⁄₁₆ in and 2⅜ in) respectively.

Before starting it's a good idea to make up a shopping list after studying the illustrations on these pages. If you decide to construct the cells 40 cm (16 in) high, you can work out the other sizes in relation to the sizes given in the example. Te cross-spars should be thicker than the vertical sticks.

Start by copying the patterns of the cells, wings, reinforcing struts and tunnels exactly onto paper, except for the curved parts of the wings, which should be copied onto thicker pieces of card. This can then be used for cutting the cloth when all the pattern pieces have been cut out. Then use a stapler to staple all the pieces together, checking that all the sizes are correct. Now you're ready to stitch the pieces together. Do double rows of stitching and use a tape of synthetic material to hem the cloth. This should be stitched on when the fabric is stretched over the frame, to prevent any folds or creases in the covering. The cells are attached to the covering by means of loops, and to the vertical sticks with cord. The lower wings have loops that fit into the grooves notched into the ends of the sticks. The upper wings should also be fitted with cords through the same loops and grooves. Try to keep everything as symmetrical as possible. The sticks can be collapsible if aluminium tubes are used. The cylinders of the vertical spars should be as compact as possible, while the tunnels of the cross-spars can be rather larger.

The illustrations indicate how and where the reinforcement struts should be filled. The bridle on the upper wings is filled on the side. When the bridle is pulled tighter or relaxed, the kite will respond by moving smoothly or jerkily. Cody designed a number of different wings. The curved lines do not necessarily mean that there will be a better lift, but they do give this special, as well as historic, kite its own particular charm.

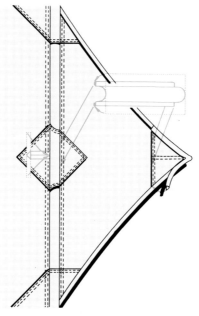

The position of the tunnels for the cross-spars.

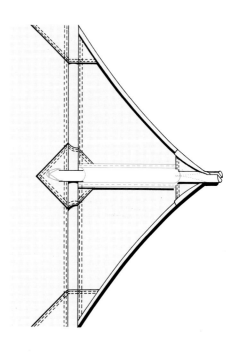

The points of the wings in the bottom of the cross-spar.

229

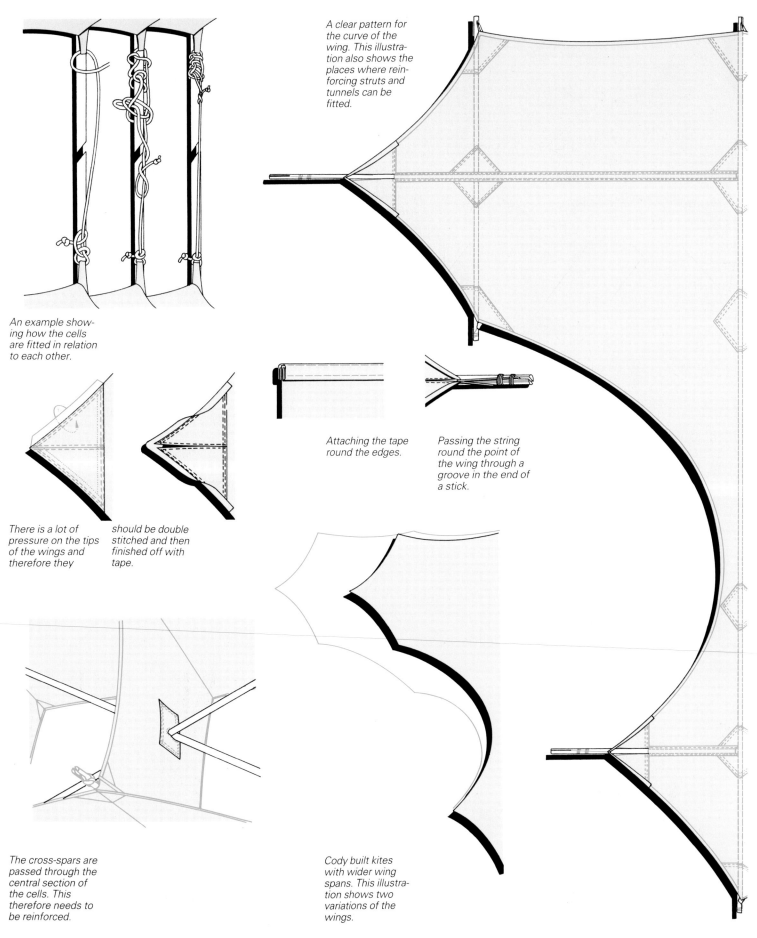

An example show-
ing how the cells
are fitted in relation
to each other.

A clear pattern for
the curve of the
wing. This illustra-
tion also shows the
places where rein-
forcing struts and
tunnels can be
fitted.

There is a lot of
pressure on the tips
of the wings and
therefore they

should be double
stitched and then
finished off with
tape.

Attaching the tape
round the edges.

Passing the string
round the point of
the wing through a
groove in the end of
a stick.

The cross-spars are
passed through the
central section of
the cells. This
therefore needs to
be reinforced.

Cody built kites
with wider wing
spans. This illustra-
tion shows two
variations of the
wings.

One of the less
well-known, but by
no means less inter-
esting, kites built by
the grand master of
kite building,
Samuel Franklin
Cody: the Cody
Compound.

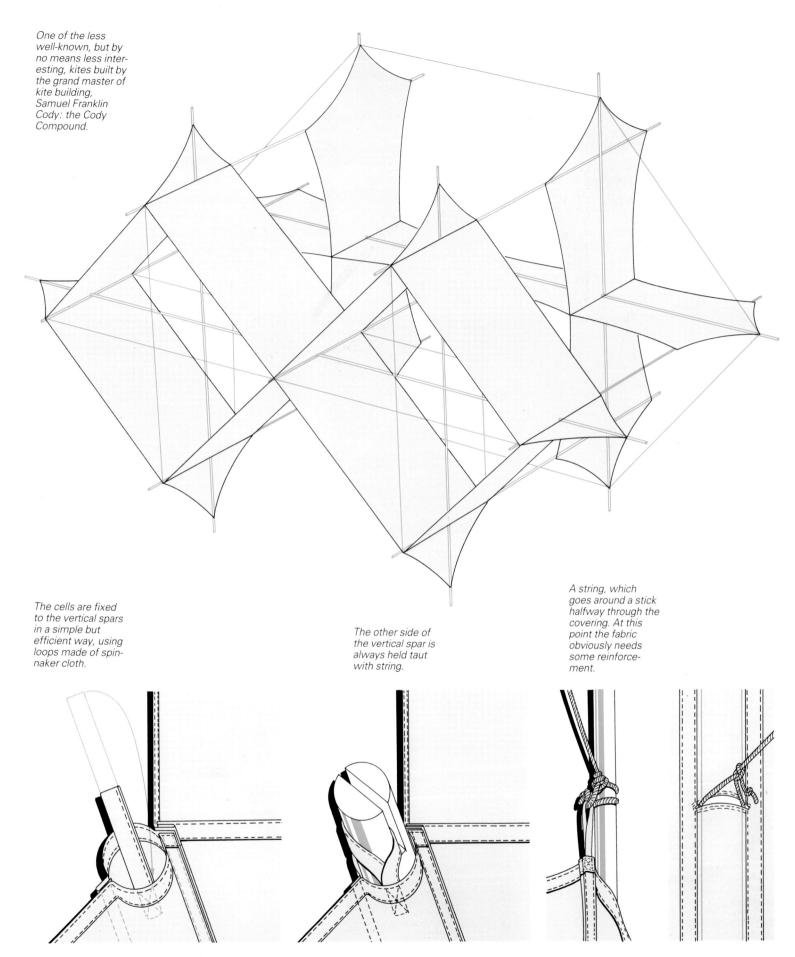

The cells are fixed
to the vertical spars
in a simple but
efficient way, using
loops made of spin-
naker cloth.

The other side of
the vertical spar is
always held taut
with string.

A string, which
goes around a stick
halfway through the
covering. At this
point the fabric
obviously needs
some reinforce-
ment.

Puzzles

Below center:
Three examples of ajagag, *the Inuit form of bilbouquet. The one of the left is a rabbit's skull. The middle one is made from a tooth. The one on the right is carved in the shape of a polar bear. Each hole has its own value.*

Although puzzles are not games in the strictest sense –games are generally played between two or more people in competition, while puzzles are more of a solitary occupation–the two have much in common. Both require a degree of skill, both are played primarily for amusement and both have been played by people all over the world since time immemorial. Puzzles can be divided into a number of subgroups, according to the specific character of the puzzle and the particular skill required to solve it.

Bilbouquet is both a game and a dexterity puzzle and is popular with the Inuit of northern Canada. The sliding tangram puzzle is a two-dimensional assembly puzzle, but has been adapted here into a dexterity puzzle. Both the sphinx puzzle (in which the positions of the pieces are exchanged) and the shunting puzzle (in which the positions of railroad cars are reversed) are sequential movement puzzles. The double star puzzle is a disentanglement puzzle in which the object is to separate one star from the other.

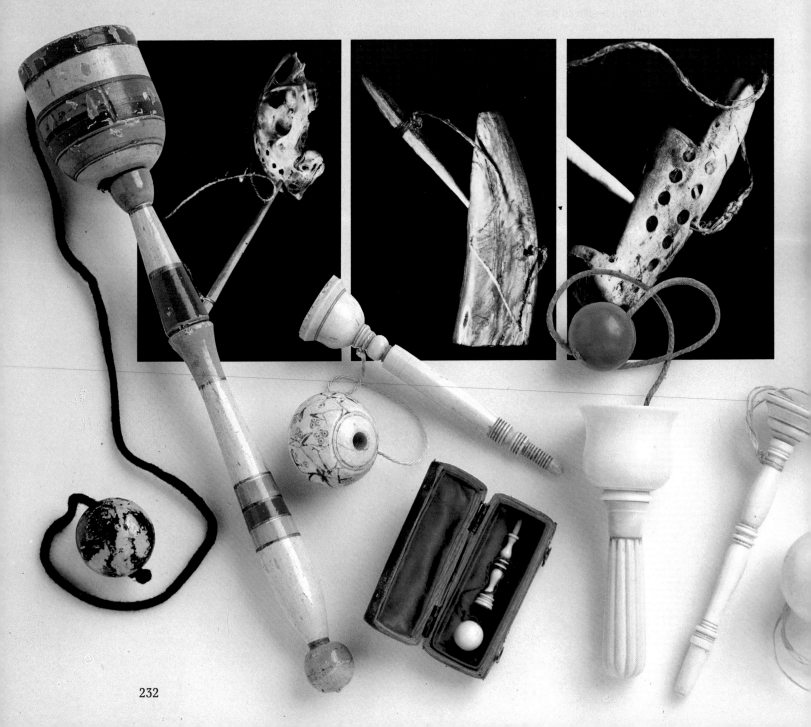

Bilbouquet

Below: *This diagram shows how to make your own bilbouquet.*

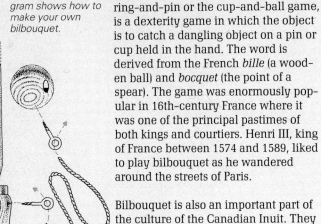

Bilbouquet, sometimes known as the ring-and-pin or the cup-and-ball game, is a dexterity game in which the object is to catch a dangling object on a pin or cup held in the hand. The word is derived from the French *bille* (a wooden ball) and *bocquet* (the point of a spear). The game was enormously popular in 16th-century France where it was one of the principal pastimes of both kings and courtiers. Henri III, king of France between 1574 and 1589, liked to play bilbouquet as he wandered around the streets of Paris.

Bilbouquet is also an important part of the culture of the Canadian Inuit. They know the game as *ajaqaq*, and instead of using a wooden ball, they carve the components from the bones of the animals they hunt. The Inuit endow the game with great magic. It is played in the dark months of the Arctic winter and in early spring and is supposed to hasten the return of the sun.

The Indians who lived on the northwest coast of Canada, the Kwakiutl, knew bilbouquet as *dzagzegala*. American Indians were notorious gamblers, and heavy wagers were staked on the outcome of the game. It was not unusual for a chief to wager canoes, slaves, women and even the highly valued "coppers"-heavy copper plates inscribed with totemic designs-on the outcome of a dzagzegala contest.

The design of the game varies from place to place. The French version consisted of a ball and cup. In a Japanese version of the game there are three cups instead of one, each cup being a different size. The Inuit use a bone or skull drilled with holes of different sizes, some of which are easier to pierce than others and consequently score higher.

The model offered here is one of the basic versions–the spear and ball.

How to Make Bilbouquet

Materials
A wooden handle approx. 12 cm (5 in) in length, approx. 20 cm (8 in) of 3 mm (1/8 in) welding wire, two eye screws, approx. 30 cm (1 ft) of cord, a wooden ball, approx. 8 cm (3 1/4 in) in diameter.

Tools
1 mm (1/16 in) drill, 5 mm (3/16 in) drill, file, hammer, vise.

Method
File one end of the welding wire to a point and tap it firmly into the handle. Clamp the wire in a vise at a distance of about 3 cm (1 3/16 in) from the end and bend at right-angles. Drill 1 mm (1/16 in) "starter" holes in the handle and the wooden ball. Fix the eye screws. Drill a 5 mm (3/16 in) hole in the ball. Knot the cord to both eyes to join the assembled handle to the ball.

The photographs on this page show a wide variety of bilbouquet games— mostly the cup-and-ball variety. These are much easier than the pin and hole bilbouquet-type games.

The Sliding Tangram

Dissection puzzles are among the oldest and most popular forms of mathematical recreation. They are plane or solid figures cut into a number of pieces. The problem is to fit the pieces together to form the original figure, or to form other interesting figures. Of all the dissection puzzles, the tangram is probably the most outstanding. This puzzle is a variation on the tangram theme, the aim being to reassemble the original square by sliding the pieces into place.

How to Make the Sliding Tangram

Materials

A 14 cm x 14 cm (5⅝ in x 5⅝ in) square of plywood 8 mm (5/16 in) in thickness, a similar square 16 mm (⅝ in) in thickness, a 14 cm x 14 cm (5⅝ in x 5⅝ in) square of yellow formica (or similar plasticized material), a 8 cm x 8 cm (3¼ in x 3¼ in) square of plywood 4 mm (⅛ in) in thickness, a 14.4 cm x 14.4 cm (5¾ in x 5¾ in) square of 2 mm (1/16 in) transparent plastic, 60 cm (24 in) of planed softwood measuring 3.5 cm x 8 mm (1½ x 5/16 in), glue, panel pins, black acrylic paint.

Tools

Electric saw, handsaw, sandpaper, drawing pen, steel ruler, hammer, paintbrush.

Method

Set the electric saw to a depth of 2 mm (1/16 in) and a width of 3 mm (⅛ in) and cut a groove along the length of the softwood strip. A normal electric saw should cut a groove a fraction over 2 mm (1/16 in) in width, which will allow the plastic sheet to slide into it. From the grooved strip, cut two lengths of 14 cm (5⅝ in) and two lengths of 14 cm (5⅝ in) plus twice the thickness of the strip (if the wood is exactly 8 mm (5/16 in) in thickness these lengths will be 15.6 cm (6¼ in), but the width of planed softwood may vary fractionally from shop to shop). Sand and varnish the four pieces. Glue and pin the two longer pieces to each end of one 14 cm (5⅝ in) length to make three sides of the box. Slide in the transparent plastic and glue and pin the fourth side in place. Glue and pin the 8 mm (5/16 in) and 16 mm (⅝ in) plywood squares together. Glue the formica to the assembled block. Draw the tangram pattern as shown in the diagram using a drawing pen, a steel ruler and black acrylic. This square measures 8 cm x 8 cm (3¼ in x 3¼ in) and it is at a distance of 3 cm (1 3/16 in) from the edges of the formica. Draw the same pattern on the 8 cm x 8 cm x 4 mm (3¼ in x 3¼ in x ⅛ in) plywood square and cut along the marked lines to make seven pieces. Paint one side and all the edges of the pieces in black acrylic. Glue the rhombus (lozenge-shaped) and the small triangle at bottom left (see photograph) in position on the tangram pattern on the formica. Lay the other pieces in position but do not glue them. Slide the assembled block into the box. Make sure that there is a small space between the pieces of the puzzle and the plastic lid, then glue and pin the block and the box together. Now shake the puzzle thoroughly to dislodge the pieces. The object is to shake and tap the box to return the five loose pieces into their original positions.

Right: *This most attractive sliding tangram puzzle is not difficult to make. It is, however, rather difficult to get the pieces in position by shaking and tapping the box!*

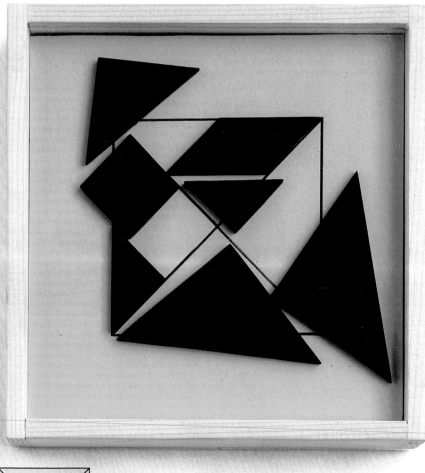

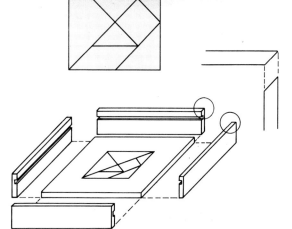

Left: *The tangram pieces can be made from a larger sheet of plywood to give an additional puzzle. The exploded diagram shows how the box should be assembled.*

The Sphinx Puzzle

The Sphinx Puzzle is one of a group of puzzles known as hop-over puzzles. The object of all these puzzles is the same—namely to exchange the positions of the pieces on the right with those of the pieces on the left, in as few moves as possible, by moving one piece at a time one step in a forward direction. A piece may hop over any adjacent piece into a vacant position immediately beyond that piece. The pieces in hop-over puzzles are differentiated in some way, usually by color. This type of puzzle was very popular around the turn of the century, particularly in the United States and France. The photograph shows a puzzle from this period. As it says on the box lid:– "Not too difficult, yet sufficiently perplexing to make it fascinating."

How to Make the Sphinx Puzzle

Materials
a) For the pyramid: a block of good quality hardwood such as mahogany measuring 2 cm x 12 cm x 22 cm (1 in x 6 in x 11 in), teak oil or varnish;
b) For the sphinxes: 10 wood balls approx. 1.5 cm (⅝ in) in diameter, 5 in a dark hardwood such as mahogany and 5 in a light hardwood such as oak; varnish.

Tools
Steel ruler, pencil, hand saw, vise, sandpaper, rasp, paintbrush.

Method
a) To make the pyramid:
Draw a grid of 2 cm x 2 cm (1 in x 1 in) squares on each side of the hardwood block, using a hard pencil. Each step of the pyramid is 2 cm (1 in) in length and 2 cm (1 in) in height. Using the illustration on this page as a guide, draw these steps, again on both sides of the hardwood block, using a soft pencil. These lines should be thicker than the lines of the grid so that the step pattern is clearly visible. Draw a line from the edge of the first step on the right-hand side (i.e., 2 cm (1 in) from the base of the wood) to the edge of the "summit" step (i.e., a point 10 cm (5 in) in from the right hand side of the wood). Draw similar lines on the left-hand side and on the other face of the block. Clamp the block in a vise and using these lines as a guide cut away the waste wood with a sharp hand saw. Now cut out each step, again following the pencil lines carefully. If necessary use a square-section file to clean out the corners. Sand the pyramid smooth and give it a coat of varnish. Rub it well with teak oil.
b) To make the sphinxes:
Clamp each wooden ball in turn in the vise and flatten the top using a rasp. Varnish.
Note: It may prove difficult to buy small wooden balls in differently colored hardwoods. If they cannot be obtained, use 10 wooden balls of white softwood. Paint five of them in blue acrylic and five in red, or in any other contrasting colors. Finish the pieces off with a coat of clear varnish.

Right: *Draw the steps on each side of the block using a grid of 2 cm x 2 cm (1 in x 1 in) squares.*

Left: *The sphinx and pyramid puzzle is a hop-over type puzzle, in which the object is to exchange the pieces on the right with those on the left in as few moves as possible.*

The Double Star Puzzle

The double star is an example of a disentanglement puzzle, a group of puzzles that involve detaching (or attaching) one part of the puzzle. They range from simple interlocking bent nail puzzles to beautiful and intricate Chinese wire puzzles.

How to Make the Double Star Puzzle

Materials
Two 11 cm x 11 cm (5½ in x 5½ in) squares of 4 mm (⅛ in) plywood, an 8 cm x 17 cm (4 in x 8½ in) rectangle of 4 mm (⅛ in) plywood, a 6 cm x 4.5 cm (3 in x 2½ in) rectangle of 4 mm (⅛ in) plywood, two thin wire key rings, red, blue and yellow acrylic paint.

Tools
Steel ruler, pencil, protractor, scroll saw, sandpaper, rasp, 4 mm (⅛ in) drill, paintbrush, ½ in grids (see diagram.)

Method
a) To make the stars:
The stars are drawn by joining each point of a regular pentagon to the two opposite points. To draw a pentagon: mark points on the base of one plywood square at distances of 2 cm (1 in) from each end. Using a protractor and ruler, draw lines 7 cm (3 in) in length from each point at an angle of 108⁰ to it. Draw similar lines at the same angle from each of these new points. Join each point of the pentagon to the two points opposite it to make a five pointed star. Draw another star, 5 mm (³/₁₆ in) inside the first. Use a scroll saw to cut the star out. Round off the points with a rasp and sandpaper. Cut out the center of the star and sand smooth.
b) To make the crescent:
Draw the crescent on the 8 cm x 17 cm (4 in x 8½ in) piece of 4 mm (⅛ in) plywood using the grid as a guide. Cut it out with a scroll saw and sand the edges smooth. Drill 4 mm (⅛ in) holes in the arms of the crescent as indicated in the diagram. Make the U-shaped piece using the grid as a guide. Drill holes in the arms. Paint the crescent and the U-shaped piece in blue acrylic. Paint one star in red acrylic and the other in yellow. Interlock the stars as shown in the photograph and slide them on the U-shaped piece. Join the crescent and the U-shaped piece with the thin wire key rings.

Right: *The solution to the double star puzzle: Fold the U-shaped piece down so that the stars are in the position shown in the second diagram. Place one of the points of the star to be removed over the end of the crescent, as shown in the third diagram. The star is removed by guiding it around the crescent in the direction of the arrows.*

Below: *This photograph shows the position of the stars in the assembled puzzle.*

Right: *The completed puzzle must now be solved. The solution is written down but don't spoil your fun by looking at it before you have tried to solve the puzzle.*

Shunting Puzzles

This type of puzzle dates back to the golden age of railroading, when the business of marshaling cars and locomotives to assemble a train was a far more complex business than it is today. The basic idea behind a shunting puzzle is to reverse the order of the "cars" in as few moves as possible.

How to Make the Shunting Puzzle

Materials   A 32 cm x 52 cm (13 in x 21 in) sheet of 14 mm ($^9/_{16}$ in) plywood, 102 cm (45 in) of softwood 8 mm ($^5/_{16}$ in) in thickness, 2 cm ($^{13}/_{16}$ in) wide on one side and 1 cm ($^3/_8$ in) on the other (see diagram in margin), 6 cm ($2^3/_8$ in) of softwood 2 cm x 8 mm ($^{13}/_{16}$ in x $^5/_{16}$ in), 30 cm (1 ft 2 in) of softwood 3.5 cm x 16 mm ($1^3/_8$ in x $^5/_8$ in), a half-spherical stud 2 cm ($^{13}/_{16}$ in) in diameter, round-headed brass panel pins, glue.

Tools   Handsaw, rasp, sandpaper, hammer, paintbrush.

Below: *The cars are made by glueing the half-widths of tapered softwood to the 5 cm (2¼ in) blocks. They must slide freely along the tracks.*

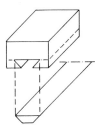

Method   a) To make the track: Find the center point of the top edge of the plywood sheet. Connect this point to the opposite corners to form an isosceles triangle. Cut away the surplus wood and sand the edges smooth. Varnish. Cut two lengths of 20 cm (9 in), two of 12 cm (5 in), one of 8 cm (3½ in) plus one of 30 cm (1 ft 2 in) from the

Right: *This diagram shows how the tracks must be laid down. A = 34 cm (15½ in); B = 39 cm (17 in); C = 14 cm (6 in). These are the distances between the pivot points.*

Far right: *A block must be fixed to each of the pivoting pieces so the cars cannot slide off the track.*

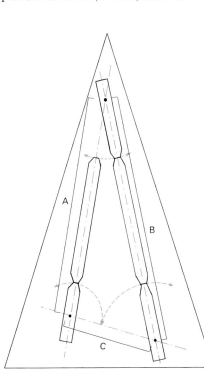

The solution to the shunting puzzle:
To begin: locomotive and cars 1 to 5 (from top to bottom) are on the right-hand track.
a) Move car 1 to the left via the top switch with the locomotive. Then do the same with cars 2 to 4. Car 5 is pushed back on the bottom right switch.
b) Via the right bottom switch, move the locomotive to bottom left and then push cars 4 and 3 to the top switch. Return the locomotive via the two bottom switches (car 5 remains on the bottom right switch) so that it can pull cars 4 and 3 to the right hand track. Do the same with cars 2 and 1.

tapered softwood. Cut three 2 cm ($^{13}/_{16}$ in) lengths from the 2 cm x 8 mm ($^3/_{16}$ in x $^5/_{16}$ in) softwood and glue and pin them to one end of the 8 cm (3½ in) length and both 12 cm (5 in) lengths. These are the "buffers" to block the "cars" (see diagram at the foot of the center column). Round off the other seven ends with a rasp. Lay the pieces on the plywood sheet as shown in the diagram. The 20 cm (9 in) lengths are glued and pinned in place. The other lengths are pinned in the positions shown by the dots and should rotate freely. Varnish.

c) Via the top switch, the locomotive now pulls car 2, followed by, respectively, 1, 4, 3 and 5, to the left hand track.
d) Move the locomotive to the bottom right switch. Now pull car 2 via the bottom left switch and push it up to the right hand track. Repeat with 1, 4 and 3. Car 5 stays on the left hand track and is pushed onto the top switch.
e) Repeat this procedure but in reverse, from d) to a), starting by pushing car 3 to the left-hand track.
Note: If you manage to find a shorter solution, please let the authors know!

b) To make the cars: Cut a 30 cm (1 ft 2 in) length of the tapered softwood in half lengthways. Cut both halves into 5 cm (2¼ in) lengths. Cut the 3.5 cm x 16 mm ($1^3/_8$ in x $^5/_8$ in) softwood into six 5 cm (2¼ in) lenghts. To assemble the cars, glue two tapered lengths to each flat length as indicated in the diagram in the margin. Pin the stud to one of the cars to make the locomotive. Number the cars from 1 to 5 and varnish. Slide them onto the track in order. They should slide freely without sticking.

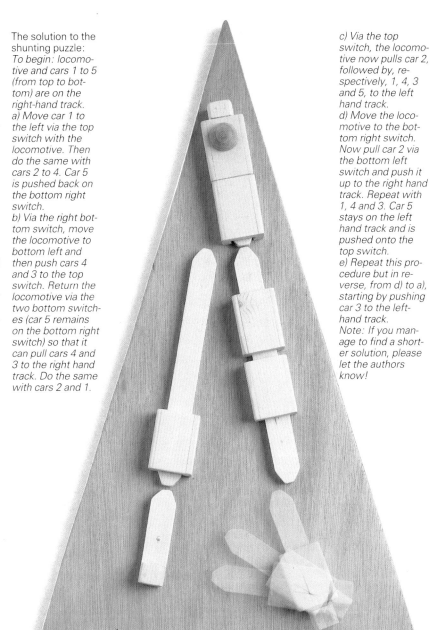

BIBLIOGRAPHY

Ainslie, Tom. AINSLIE'S COMPLETE HOYLE. Simon and Schuster, N.Y., 1975, 526 pp., hb.

d'Allemagne, Henri René. RECREATIONS ET PASSE-TEMPS. Librairie Hachette, Paris, 1906, 380 pp., hb., (French).

Andersen, Ian. TURNING THE TABLES ON LAS VEGAS. Vanguard Press, N.Y., 1976, 210 pp., hb.

Appell, Claude. JEUX DE PLEIN AIR. Gautier-Languereau, Paris, 1973, 252 pp., hb., (French).

Armanino, Dominic C. DOMINOES. Cornerstone Library, N.Y., 1977, 192 pp., pb.

Arnold Peter (ed.). THE BOOK OF GAMES. Viscount Books, 1985, 256 pp., hb.

Autenboer, Dr. Eugeen Van. DE SPEELKAARTEN VAN NEDERLAND III. Aurelia Books, Brussels, 1976, 156 pp., hb., (Dutch).

Beaver, Patrick. VICTORIAN PARLOUR GAMES FOR TODAY. Peter Davies, 1974, London, 140 pp., hb.

Bell, R.C. BOARD & TABLEGAMES I. Oxford University Press, London, 1969, 210 pp., pb.

Bell, R.C. BOARD & TABLEGAMES II. Oxford University Press, London, 1969, 156 pp., hb.

Bell, R.C. THE BOARDGAME BOOK. Exeter Books, N.Y., 1983, 160 pp., hb.

Bell, R.C. DISCOVERING OLD BOARDGAMES. Shire Publications, 1973, 80 pp., pb.

Benarde, Anita. GAMES FROM MANY LANDS. The Lion Press, N.Y., 1970, 64 pp., hb.

Berndt, Fredrik. THE DOMINO BOOK. Bantam Books, N.Y., 1975, 196 pp., pb.

Botermans, Jack; Delft, van, Pieter; Dobbelsteen, van den, Rob. DENKSPIELE MIT DOMINO, WURFEL UND STREICHHOLZ. Deutsche Taschenbuch Verlag, 1982, 144 pp., pb., (German).

Botermans, Jack; Delft, van, Pieter; Dobbelsteen, van den, Rob. SPELLETJES EN PUZZELS ALS TIJDVERDRIJF. H.J.W. Becht, Amsterdam, 1981, 96 pp., pb., (Dutch).

Botermans, Jack; Delft, van, Pieter; Dobbelsteen, van den, Rob. SPELLETJES EN PUZZELS MET LUCIFERS, POTLOOD EN PAPIER. H.J.W. Becht, Amsterdam, 1980, 96 pp., pb., (Dutch).

Botermans, Jack; Delft, van, Pieter; Dobbelsteen, van den, Rob. SPELLETJES EN TRUCS MET SPEELKAARTEN. H.J.W. Becht, Amsterdam, 1982, 96 pp., pb., (Dutch).

Botermans, Jack, and Weve, Alice. KITE FLIGHTS. Henry Holt and Company, N.Y., 1986, 120 pp., pb.

Brandreth, Gyles. DOMINO GAMES AND PUZZLES. Transworld Publishers, 1975, 128 pp., pb.

Butselaar, A.C. DUBBEL-PATIENCE EN KIBBEL-PATIENCE. G.B. van Goor Zonen's Uitgeversmaatschappij, The Hague & Batavia, 1946, 64 pp., pb., (Dutch).

Cadogan, Lady Adelaide. ILLUSTRATED GAMES OF PATIENCE. Leslie Frewin, London, 1968, 48 pp., hb. (Facsimile of the edition published in 1875 by Sampson Low, Marston, Low and Searle, London.)

Carter, W.H. NORTH AMERICAN INDIAN GAMES. Namind Printers & Publishers, London, Ont., 1974, 94 pp., pb.

Chicandard, C.; Cantineau, S.; Pichard, G. JEU D'INTERIEUR. Gautier-Languereau, Paris, 1974, 240 pp., hb., (French).

Clidière, Martine. SPELLEN EN SPELEN. Elsevier, Amsterdam/Brussels, 1971, 176 pp., pb., (Dutch).

Cordier, M. MAH-JONG ALS GEZELSCHAPSSPEL. C.A. Langerveld & Zn, The Hague, 40 pp., pb., (Dutch).

Culin, Stewart. CHESS AND PLAYING CARDS. Government Printing Office; Washington, 1898.

Culin Stewart. GAMES OF THE NORTH AMERICAN INDIANS. Dover Publications, N.Y., 1975, 846 pp., pb. (Originally published by the Government Printing Office, Washington, 1907.)

Culin, Stewart. KOREAN GAMES. University of Pennsylvania, 1895, 178 pp.

David, F.N. GAMES, GODS AND GAMBLING. Charles Griffin, London, 1962, 276 pp., pb.

Deledicq, A. and Popova, A. WARI ET SOLO. Cedic, Paris, 1977, 206 pp., pb., (French).

Falkener, Edward. GAMES ANCIENT AND ORIENTAL AND HOW TO PLAY THEM. Dover Publications, N.Y., 1961, 366 pp., pb. (First published by Longmans, Green and Company, 1892.)

Ferretti, Fred. THE GREAT AMERICAN BOOK OF SIDEWALK, STOOP, DIRT, CURB AND ALLEY GAMES. Workman Publishing Company, N.Y., 1975, 240 pp., pb.

Fiske, Willard. CHESS IN ICELAND AND IN ICELANDIC LITERATURE. The Florentine Typographical Society, Florence, 1905, 400 pp.

Gould, D.W. THE TOP. Clarkson N. Potter, N.Y., 1973, 276 pp.

Griaule, M. JEUX DOGONS. University of Paris, 1938, 296 pp., (French).

Grimberg, M.L. SOME GAMES OF ASIA. Asia Pacific Press, Singapore, 1974, 98 pp., pb.

Groningen, van, S.H. HET KAARTSPEL. Bigot & v. Rossum, Blaricum, 138 pp., pb., (Dutch).

DAS GROSSE BUCH DER SPIELE. Editions des Connaissances Modernes, Freiburg, Switzerland, 1974, 192 pp., hb., (German).

Grunfeld, Frederic V. (ed.). GAMES OF THE WORLD. Holt, Rinehart and Winston, N.Y., 1975, 280 pp., hb.

Hagenaar, J. DE VOLMAAKTE KAARTSPELER. G.B. van Goor Zonen, Gouda, 120 pp., pb., (Dutch).

Harbin, E.O. GAMES OF MANY NATIONS. Abingdon Press,